London's Urban Landscape

London's Urban Landscape
Another Way of Telling

Edited by

Christopher Tilley

First published in 2019 by
UCL Press
University College London
Gower Street
London WC1E 6BT
Available to download free: www.ucl.ac.uk/ucl-press

Text © Contributors, 2019
Images © Contributors and copyright holders named in captions, 2019

The authors have asserted their rights under the Copyright, Designs and Patents Act 1988 to be identified as authors of this work.

A CIP catalogue record for this book is available from The British Library.

This book is published under a Creative Commons 4.0 International license (CC BY 4.0). This license allows you to share, copy, distribute and transmit the work; to adapt the work and to make commercial use of the work providing attribution is made to the authors (but not in any way that suggests that they endorse you or your use of the work). Attribution should include the following information:

Tilley, C. (ed.). 2019. *London's Urban Landscape: Another Way of Telling*. London, UCL Press. https://doi.org/10.14324/111.9781787355583

Further details about Creative Commons licenses are available at http://creativecommons.org/licenses/

Any third-party material in this book is published under the book's Creative Commons license unless indicated otherwise in the credit line to the material. If you would like to re-use any third-party material not covered by the book's Creative Commons license, you will need to obtain permission directly from the copyright holder.

ISBN: 978-1-78735-560-6 (Hbk.)
ISBN: 978-1-78735-559-0 (Pbk.)
ISBN: 978-1-78735-558-3 (PDF)
ISBN: 978-1-78735-561-3 (epub)
ISBN: 978-1-78735-562-0 (mobi)
ISBN: 978-1-78735-563-7 (html)
DOI: https://doi.org/10.14324/111. 9781787355583

Contents

List of figures	vii
List of tables	xv
Notes on contributors	xvii
Preface	xxi

    Introduction: Materialising the urban landscape   1
    Christopher Tilley

Part I: The domestic and residential sphere

1 Change and continuity in a central London street   67
   Ilaria Pulini

2 Towards a phenomenology of the concrete megastructure: Space and perception at the Brunswick Centre, London   117
   Clare Melhuish

3 Isolation: A walk through a London estate   149
   Dave Yates

4 The making of a suburb   178
   David Jeevendrampillai

5 The linear village: Experience of continuous cruising on the London waterways   204
   Titika Malkogeorgou

Part II: The public sphere

6 'We're all mad down here.' Liminality and the carnivalesque in Smithfield Meat Market   263
   Caroline Wilson

7 Observation and selection: Objects and meaning in the Bermondsey Antiques Market   301
   Dave Yates

8	Rank and file on Harrington Road. Rhythmanalysis: Stories of place and the place of stories *Alex Young*	325
9	*Holland Park:* An elite London landscape *Christopher Tilley*	353
10	From pollution to purity: The transformation of graffiti and street art in London (2005–17) *Rafael Schacter*	403

Index 426

List of figures

0.1	Map showing the places in London discussed in the text. Source: author	46
1.1	Cheniston Gardens (encircled in red) and the surrounding area of Kensington. Source: Ordnance Survey open data, 2017	68
1.2	The Muffin Man at the corner between Cheniston Gardens and Wrights Lane. Source: author	69
1.3	View of Wrights Lane from north, before 1881. The brick wall enclosed the rear gardens of houses facing High Street Kensington. The small cottage at the bottom, used as a stable or a warehouse, was later incorporated into the northern sector of the Cheniston Gardens development. © RBKC Local Studies & Archives department	70
1.4	Nos 7–11 Cheniston Gardens – contrasting facades. Source: author	70
1.5	Examples of doorbells in Cheniston Gardens. Source: author	71
1.6	Bedrooms at no. 17 before the auction of the building (2014) and after renovation (2016). Source: author	77
1.7	Kitchens at no. 17 before and after renovation. Source: author	78
1.8	Diagram showing the variation in occupation density of Cheniston Gardens houses from 1881 to 2015. Source: author	83
1.9	Map of the area before Cheniston Gardens was developed. Source: Ordnance Survey Map 1871, Sheet 74 Kensington	84
1.10	Entrance to Cheniston Gardens studios nested among two rows of townhouses. Source: author	84

1.11	Cheniston Gardens, view from south. To the left Cheniston Lodge and the apartment house that were added to the row of townhouses in 1885 and 1895. Source: author	85
1.12	Charles Booth's map of London poverty (1891). The CG houses are highlighted in yellow, the colour of the upper-middle and upper classes. © The British Library Board, Maps C.21.a.18 det.	87
1.13	Maid on the front door of a Cheniston Gardens townhouse. Photo by Edward Linley Sambourne, 29 July 1906. © The Royal Borough of Kensington and Chelsea, 18 Stafford Terrace	88
1.14	Aerial view of the rear extensions of the central group of Cheniston Gardens townhouses. © Google Earth	91
1.15	Place of birth of Cheniston Gardens' residents in 2011 Census. Source: author	96
1.16	Cheniston Gardens – view towards the central corner of the street with the birch trees from a top-floor flat. Source: author	102
1.17	Emma's neighbourhood map. Source: author	103
2.1	View from east through Brunswick Square's porticoed entrance, O'Donnell Court © S. Stone	119
2.2	View of winter gardens, O'Donnell Court, prior to 2006 refurbishment. Source: author	120
2.3	View through A-frame structure, Foundling Court, first floor level. © S. Stone	121
2.4	Front door, Foundling Court. Source: author	122
2.5	Brunswick Centre shopping precinct, view from south, prior to 2006 refurbishment. Source: author	123
2.6	'A high street for Bloomsbury': view through shopping precinct after refurbishment, showing new supermarket at northern end. Source: author	123
2.7	Interior view looking across the precinct from O'Donnell Court, 2006. © S. Stone	132
2.8	View of internal circulation spaces, Foundling Court, 2001. Source: author	138
2.9	View through second floor access gallery to flats (perimeter block, Foundling Court) 2001. Source: author	139
3.1	Rosemary Avenue looking west. Source: author	150
3.2	Hounslow West – station to the far right, with the Beavers (the Meadows) Estate to the left visible by the trees (Google Maps, 2016 – accessed 14 December 2016)	152

3.3	Entrance to the Beavers Estate from Vincent Road. Source: author	153
3.4	Beavers Estate C1971–3. © London Metropolitan Archives 2016 (GLC/AR/PL/17)	154
3.5	The 'bison frame' blocks today. Source: author	155
3.6	The Beavers Estate tunnel. Source: author	158
3.7	The play park in the centre of the estate. Source: author	161
3.8	Shopping area at 'the bottom'. Source: author	168
3.9	The Hub. Source: author	169
3.10	'The stones'. Source: author	172
4.1	A map of Surbiton, South West London and its relation to Kingston (map made by author using OS data copyright 2014).	182
4.2	Walking by the river promenade. Photograph by Tangle Photography, reproduced with permission.	183
4.3	The filter beds and the busy Portsmouth Road. Source: author	184
4.4	The high street (main shopping area) of Surbiton, Victoria Road. Source: author	184
4.5	The town houses of Surbiton, designed by Thomas Pooley. Source: author	185
4.6	A Pooley town house. Source: author	186
4.7	The workers' cottages on a 'river road'. Source: author	187
4.8	Classic Tudor-style 'Jones' houses, typical of inter-war housing. Source: author	187
4.9	A Seething parade along a Pooley-designed street. Source: author	191
4.10	The Lefi parade on Surbiton high street (Victoria Road). Source: author	191
4.11	The Legends of Seething. Made by Hutchinson 2014. Reproduced with permission	193
4.12	The Seething freshwater sardine procession. Source: author	194
5.1	West Ham Stadium, Olympic Park, Stratford, east London. Source: author	205
5.2	White building, art and technology called 'Space', and Sweet Toof street art, east London. Source: author	206
5.3	Political satire on display in the linear village, Lee Navigation, Stratford, east London. Source: author	207
5.4	Entering the cut from the River Lee, Hertford Union Canal, Hackney, east London. Source: author	207

5.5	A quiet afternoon, leisure time and sports in Bow, Old Ford Lock No 19, east London. Source: author	208
5.6	Cafes, bars, restaurants and artists' studios line the river bank, boat traffic unabated. Bow, east London. Source: author	209
5.7	'Considerate constructors' panelling is all pervasive around Fish Island and the Olympic Park, east London. Source: author	210
5.8	In Victoria Park, mooring is regularly two deep. Hertford Union Canal, Tower Hamlets, east London. Source: author	220
5.9	Mixed mooring in Tottenham Hale, a popular destination, Lee Navigation, north London. Source: author	221
5.10	Part of the Hertford Union canal is overlooked by private town houses and their gardens. Victoria Park, Tower Hamlets, east London. Source: author	222
5.11	Cruising and looking for space to moor can be daunting in busy areas. Hertford Union Canal, east London. Source: author	223
5.12	Anchor and Hope pub opposite Walthamstow Marshes, Lee Navigation, north London. Source: author	226
5.13	Map of Regent's Canal, Hertford Union Canal, Lee Navigation, and the River Stort. Design by Simon Harold. Source: author	231
5.14	Lee Valley Marina, Springfield, north London. Source: author	233
5.15	Anything can be a boat, this one is on sale for £950, down from £1,000. Stonebridge Lock No 16, Lee Navigation, Tottenham, north London. Source: author	236
5.16	Dutch barge on the River Lee, Hackney Marshes, north-east London. Source: author	238
5.17	The River Stort is much loved by boaters, but only gets busy in the summer, River Stort, Roydon, Essex. Source: author	248
5.18	My neighbour's early breakfast on the water. Lee Navigation, Clapton, north-east London. Source: author	249
5.19	In January 2017 the Lee had frozen in certain parts, and continuous cruising was suspended. Stanstead Abbotts, east Hertfordshire. Source: author	249
6.1	Smithfield and its surroundings. Source: adapted from Forshaw (1990)	264

6.2	The entire market as seen from west Charterhouse Street. General Market (GM) is in the foreground, followed by Poultry Market (PM), then Main Market (MM) in the background. Source: author	265
6.3	Main market building, daytime, from Charterhouse Street. Source: author	265
6.4	Smithfield Market floor plan (adapted from SMTA 2018)	268
6.5	Loading machinery in the loading bays. Source: author	269
6.6	Service corridor. Source: author	269
6.7	A cutting room. Source: author	270
6.8	Shop fronts. The purple pillars of the original building are still visible on the right. Source: author	270
6.9	The gate at the entrance to Buyer's Walk, seen from Grand Avenue. Source: author	272
6.10	The top part of the building, seen from East Market looking downwards towards West Market. Plaque is visible in the centre at the bottom. Source: author	273
6.11	'Where's Danny?' 'Round ya mum's.' Banter via graffiti on the walls of PM. Source: author	280
6.12	Graffitied signs. Source: author	283
6.13	A ghost town: inside Poultry Market. Source: author	290
6.14	General market against the office block, seen from West Smithfield. Source: author	294
6.15	An image from the collection *Bummaree* in the reception area of offices along East Poultry Avenue. The bummaree can be seen pulling his barrow behind him; bummarees no longer work like this. Source: author	295
7.1	Bermondsey Antiques Market around 2a.m. Source: author	302
7.2	'Edna' stalling out at Bermondsey Antiques Market: each item touched, each history remembered. Source: author	304
7.3	Bermondsey Antiques Market shown in relation to London Bridge Station. Satellite image with shaded area showing the market space. Source: author	307
7.4	A very quiet early start for the traders at Bermondsey Antiques Market, around 4a.m. Source: author	308
7.5	The timeline of an object – 'from rubbish to antique in a week'. Source: author	321
8.1	Two women exchanging goodbyes as they leave Cafe Floris. Source: author	326

8.2	The Ampersand Hotel at dusk, towering over a full rank on Harrington Road. An Uber driver is waiting for their passenger on the double yellow lines opposite. Source: author	327
8.3	A potential passenger shows a cab driver a piece of paper with the address of his destination written on it before getting into the back of the taxi. Source: author	331
8.4	A driver breaks away mid-rank. Mostly this happens when the driver has accepted a fare on one of the ride-hailing apps that the profession uses, such as Hailo or Gett. Source: author	333
8.5	A cab driver sits on the bonnet of his cab while smoking a cigarette between jobs. Source: author	334
8.6	Besides the rank on Harrington Road, waiting for the traffic lights to turn green, two drivers express different views on the author. Source: author	336
8.7	A cab driver reading a book on her Kindle between jobs. Source: author	336
8.8	A cab driver resting their head on their hand and looking at a photograph of a woman while inching towards the front of the rank. Source: author	337
8.9	People wait as the digital timetable counts down to the arrival of the next buses. Source: author	339
8.10	A woman staying at one of the luxury serviced apartments opposite The Ampersand Hotel stands and watches as her luggage is loaded into the Middle East Cargo Services freight van. Source: author	340
8.11	The doorman of The Ampersand Hotel holds the door open for a guest. Source: author	341
8.12	An Uber driver in a Toyota Prius waits at the side of the road with their hazard lights flashing, the rank can be seen in the distance. Source: author	342
8.13	A black cab driver smiles as he drops off a family arriving at The Ampersand Hotel. Source: author	343
8.14	The doorman stands alone waiting in the lobby of The Ampersand Hotel. Source: author	344
8.15	Harrington Road seen through the rear windscreen of a hackney carriage. Source: author	345
9.1	Looking west down Chestnut Walk. Source: author	354
9.2	Map of Holland Park (Courtesy of the Friends of Holland Park)	355

9.3	A pigeon on Lord Holland's head. Source: author	356
9.4	The entrance to the Japanese Garden. Source: author	356
9.5	Inside the Kyoto Garden. Source: author	357
9.6	The crack under the bench in the Kyoto Garden. Source: author	358
9.7	Walking man. Sculpture by Sean Henry. Source: author	358
9.8	View of the Dutch Garden, opera tents beyond. Source: author	359
9.9	*Meridiana* by Helaine Blumenfeld. Source: author	359
9.10	The chess set. Source: author	360
9.11	Outside the Belvedere restaurant. Source: author	361
9.12	Mural in the arcade leading to the Orangery by Mao Wen Biao. Source: author	362
9.13	The opera pavilion. Source: author	363
9.14	View south across the sports field to the high-rise flats on Kensington High Street. Source: author	364
9.15	Defaced anti-climb paint sign. Source: author	365
10.1	A Shoreditch canvas: a plethora of tags, posters, stickers and paste-ups. Source: author	404
10.2	Shoreditch beach: artificial turf, deckchairs and wide-screen TV. Source: author	405
10.3	The images everywhere: tags, stickers, and admissible dissidence. Note the small red sticker placed over the nose of the pasted-up 'one love' kid. Kitsch resistance. Source: author	406
10.4	Graffiti as archetype/street art as stereotype: a street art mural 'dogged' by a series of silver and black 'throw-ups'. Source: author	408
10.5	From avant-garde to passé: street art as the ultimate in kitsch. Source: author	409
10.6	*Passé* by OX, Paris, 2017: street art through the looking glass and back (to a space of actual innovation). Image courtesy of OX	410
10.7	Still antagonistic: standing out amidst a wealth of other tags, OKER and OFSKE remain proudly antagonistic. Source: author	422
10.8	Still other: again, OKER and OFSKE make their presence felt. Source: author	423

List of tables

1.1	List of people interviewed in Cheniston Gardens	99
6.1	Smithfield market workers	275
6.2	Oppositions between meat eating and vegetarianism	287
9.1	The ages of 75 park users interviewed	367
9.2	The nationality/ethnic heritage of the park users interviewed	367
9.3	Places where the 75 park users interviewed came from	368
9.4	Time spent in and frequency of visits to Holland Park by the 75 park users interviewed	368
9.5	The occupations of the 75 park users interviewed	369
9.6	Principal reasons why the interviewees visited the park	369
9.7	Use of park facilities by 75 park users	370
9.8	Some generalised contrasts between park workers and regular park users	377
9.9	The likes and dislikes of 75 park users	379
9.10	Named favourite areas given by 75 park users	380
9.11	Analysis of the words and phrases used by 75 park users to describe Holland Park	380
9.12	The responses of 69 park users in relation to the hypothetical question: 'If you should decide the park budget what would you spend the most and least money on?'	386

Notes on contributors

David Jeevendrampillai is Research Fellow in the Department of Social Anthropology, University of Trondheim, Norway. His research explores the relationship between people and place, particularly in social arenas marked with political/cultural difference. His doctoral thesis examined practices of knowing and representing place, including mapping, walking, parading and 'local' carnivals, and how indigenous or 'local' claims are incommensurate with planning policy, academic research and systems analysis. He is co-editor of *The Material Culture of Failure: When Things Do Wrong* (2017).

Titika Malkogeorgou is an anthropologist currently working with houseboat dwellers in north-east London. Her PhD thesis investigated the ethics of conservation practice when based at the Victoria and Albert Museum as a visiting researcher. She has studied art and she is a trained conservator in wall painting and the built environment. Her research interests include anthropological and phenomenological approaches to heritage and object conservation, cultural knowledge, identity, materiality and social transformation. In *Re-conceptualising Shapes and Bodies* (2014) she explores the woman's bodily transformation and sense of self through a series of museum interventions in the conservation of an eighteenth-century English court dress.

Clare Melhuish is Director of the UCL Urban Laboratory and Senior Research Associate in the Bartlett Faculty of the Built Environment at UCL, where she has been working on the role of university spatial development projects in urban regeneration and the production of cosmopolitan urbanism and imaginaries in the UK and abroad. Her background lies in architectural history and criticism, anthropology and cultural geography. She draws on ethnographic and visual research methods to interpret and understand architecture and the built environment as a social and cultural setting. Her particular areas of interest and expertise include the Modern Movement and contemporary architecture, post-colonial urban aesthetics and heritage, and urban regeneration processes and practice, with specific area specialisations in the architecture and planning of the UK, France, Gulf and Caribbean. She works both within and beyond the academic context, drawing on many years' experience as a journalist, author and curator in architecture and design.

Ilaria Pulini is currently researching her PhD thesis in the Department of Sociology, Goldsmiths, London – a place-bound study of the west London social elite, focusing on Kensington. For over 20 years she was Director of the Civic Museum of Archaeology and Anthropology in Modena. She has published widely about the history of ethnographic collections and museums and material culture, and has curated numerous exhibitions. Her publications include *Tessuti precolombiani. Museo Civico Archeologico Etnologico di Modena*, (with Sophie Desrosiers) and *People, Il catalogo degli umani tra 800 e 900* (with Maria Giovanna Battistini).

Rafael Schacter is an anthropologist and curator based in the Department of Anthropology, UCL, working on issues related to public and global art and socially engaged art practice. He has published three books, the recently published *Street to Studio* (2018), the award-winning *World Atlas of Street Art and Graffiti* (2013) and *Ornament and Order: Graffiti, Street Art and the Parergon* (2014). He has also participated in numerous exhibitions, curating the *Walking Tour* element of the exhibition *Street Art* at the Tate Modern in 2008, and sole-curating *Venturing Beyond* at Somerset House in 2016. He is currently working on *Motions of this Kind*, an exhibition featuring nine artists from the Philippines, which will take place at London's Brunei Gallery in April 2019.

Christopher Tilley is Professor of Anthropology at UCL. Recent publications include *An Anthropology of Landscape* (with Kate Cameron-Daum, 2017) and *Landscape in the Longue Durée* (2017). He combines anthropological and archaeological approaches to landscape and place. His current research interests are urban parks, the everyday life of London streets, the relationship between islands and social identities, and southern Scandinavian Bronze Age rock art.

Caroline Wilson is a PhD student in the Department of Anthropology, UCL. She is currently researching the relationship between parks and local communities in east and south London.

Dave Yates is an independent ethnographer. His PhD thesis was entitled *Continuity Through Change: Urban Ecology in a South London Market* and looked at urban landscapes and identity across two markets: Bermondsey Antiques Market and Spitalfields. Dave's specialism is in place-based research in complex urban settings. Currently, he works freelance for small and large companies, developing research strategies, conducting ethnographic studies on old and new developments, and providing reports for master plans.

Alex Young studied digital anthropology and material culture at UCL. He is an independent ethnographic researcher currently working on a film with the contemporary artist Camille Henrot on Seventh Day Adventists in the South Pacific and the USA. Other research interests include the sharing economy and the rise of the alt-right.

Preface

This book arises as a result of the general frustration I have found with a great deal of the literature on urban studies. For many years, I have been teaching a course to undergraduate and postgraduate students in the Anthropology Department at UCL, entitled 'Social Construction of Landscapes'. Part of this course considers the urban as a landscape and the manner in which an anthropological understanding of the urban can be developed through a broadly phenomenological understanding of place and space. The coursework assessment for students involves them undertaking a small research project in which they attempt to write a 'thick description' of a particular place, observe and analyse the manner in which it is used by people in their everyday lives, and interview individuals about what this place means to them, why they go there or inhabit it, their likes, dislikes and preferences. UCL's location in the heart of London, and the fact that the vast majority of the students are resident in London, has meant that many of them over the years have consistently chosen to study particular aspects of London's urban landscape. Examples, in no particular order, include the Regent's Canal, Kew Gardens, Chelsea Football Club, Golders Green, Columbia Road flower market, Portobello Road, Hyde Park Corner, following in the footsteps of Woolf's Mrs Dalloway walking the streets, St Pancras railway station, the London Eye, the Millennium Bridge and the Tate Modern, a Soviet-built battle tank on Mandela Way, Bermondsey, Highgate Cemetery, Brick Lane, shopping in Selfridges, skateboarding on the South Bank, Canary Wharf, London Zoo, Notting Hill Carnival and following the course of the London Marathon. The extraordinary variety and diversity of the places to study is immediately apparent from the list, and students were spoilt for choice.

Nevertheless, I was always faced with two challenging questions and lacked satisfactory answers. The first question concerned examples of high-quality phenomenological writing about place and landscape: where were the 'thick' evocative anthropological descriptions to be found and how were they written? The ones that came to mind were to be found in ethnographic work conducted in very different landscapes and social worlds. In relation to London, they seemed to be a bit 'off message' in this respect. The second related question concerned what anthropological books or articles there were discussing particular places in London that might provide inspiration for a substantive study of the relationship between material culture and the practices of everyday life in the city. Again I struggled to think of examples. Those that I could think of were not written by anthropologists, but by social historians or human geographers or sociologists. But none of these were particularly concerned with discussing the materiality of these places from a phenomenological perspective in relation to everyday life. The places were usually discussed simply in terms of providing a rather generalised setting or backdrop for a discussion of people's lives. In this sense, place hardly seemed to matter. All the stress was on social and political relations, social class, ethnicity and multiculture. There was little sense in these writings of a dialectic between the built environment and the people inhabiting it, the sensuous agency of places as material things, in relation to the people who moved through or inhabited them. The places, in this respect, were all strangely dematerialised, their material specificity neglected and overlooked.

So this book aims to at least partially, and in an exploratory way, fill these two gaps in the literature: a) the paucity of thick ethnographic descriptions of places in London, and b) discussion of the material significance of the places forming London's urban landscape in relation to everyday life. Filling them amounts to 'another way of telling' about the city, the subtitle to this book. It aims to provide an original perspective from the standpoint of anthropological studies of material culture. The subtitle, of course, alludes to John Berger and Jean Mohr's discussions of the power of visual imagery to tell another kind of story in their book *Another Way of Telling: A Possible Theory of Photography* (London: Bloomsbury, 1995). The lack of visual imagery in most academic writing about cities is quite striking. This book, by contrast, contains many images in the various accounts of place. They both help to tell the narratives of place and are part of the attempt made to materialise the social construction of place.

All the contributors to this book have, at some stage in their academic biographies, studied for the Master's Degree in Material and Visual Culture at UCL (which I coordinate), or have participated in or taught on it, and/or my Social Construction of Landscape course. So there is a shared communality of perspectives and interest between the contributors in the manner in which they write about place from the particular theoretical and conceptual perspective of the anthropology of material and visual culture.

Each chapter discusses and analyses a particular place in the city. The places discussed in the book were chosen to represent as wide a range of different places as was possible in the scope of a short book. Both the residential and public spheres are considered. The individual discussions range from streets to housing estates to markets and parks, from living on a houseboat to the rhythms of a taxi rank, to the material politics of graffiti and street art.

The particular research methodologies employed in these studies of place, and the manner in which the research was actually undertaken in the individual studies, are discussed at the end of each chapter in the form of methodological notes.

Introduction
Materialising the urban landscape
Christopher Tilley

Simone de Beauvoir tells the following story about a meeting between herself, Jean-Paul Sartre and Raymond Aron in the Bec-de-Gaz bar on the rue du Montparnasse in Paris. They were drinking apricot cocktails, the speciality of the house.

> Aron said, pointing to his glass: 'you see, my dear fellow, if you are a phenomenologist, you can talk about this and make philosophy out of it!' Sartre turned pale with emotion at this. Here was just the thing he had been longing to achieve for years – to describe objects just as he saw and touched them, and extract philosophy from the process. Aron convinced him that phenomenology exactly fitted in with his special preoccupations: bypassing the antithesis of idealism and realism, affirming simultaneously both the supremacy of reason and the reality of the physical world as it appears to our senses. (de Beauvoir 1965:135)

Substitute the term 'place' for the apricot-cocktail glass, and you have the overall theme of this book. It puts forward an account of London's urban landscape by considering it as a constellation of places linked by paths of movement between them.

The aim of this book is to describe these places as faithfully as possible through phenomenological description grounded in participant observation. It is claimed that it is only through ethnographic research that we can understand the reality of contemporary urban experience and the meanings that people give to their lives. We achieve this by a thick description of the deeply sensuous character of the places in which people work and dwell and think and move between. This is a return from the abstracted character of most discussions of cities to the things themselves, the people themselves and the materiality of the built environment that the people inhabit.

One of the aims of this introduction is to justify this view of London as a collection of places that holistically constitute its urban landscape and make the city what it is and distinct from others. Through the buildings *in place*, we can understand the people, and through the people the buildings. Through an entangled dialectic, they form part of each other and mediate each other's existence and significance in the practices of everyday life.

I also attempt to situate the book and the individual studies in it in relation to some of the relevant themes and perspectives in the vast and burgeoning literature on urban studies by social and cultural geographers, sociologists and ethnographers, and, more specifically, from the standpoint of material culture studies in anthropology.

Big data and the problems of abstraction in urban studies

In this section I provide a brief critique of the dominant trend in recent urban studies in human and cultural geography and sociology, underlining their shortcomings, to provide a counterpoint to the alternative perspective put forward in this book.

Danny Dorling's book *The 32 Stops* is an account of the Central Line on the London Underground. The subtitle is *Lives on London's Central Line* (Dorling 2013). It is one of a series of 13 books in which individual authors write about different London Underground lines through their personal experience of using them, thus conveying a sense of the urban through use of the city's transport network and the places along it. Dorling's book is undoubtedly the most accomplished of the series in terms of the manner in which we can understand a succession of different places across the centre of the city, from West Ruislip at the western end to Woodford in the east.

Dorling's account, written for a popular audience, is in many respects quite typical of mainstream geographical approaches to urban analysis. The 32 Central Line stops simply become names in the account. They are not considered as distinctive places or locales along the line. There is no description of any of them. In this sense, the names are just empty signifiers of place.

Moreover, Dorling has not gained any information about the people living around the underground stations by observing or talking to them, or by walking around in their vicinity. His work is entirely a desk-based analysis dependent on official and other statistics: GCSE educational scores, numbers of children classified as living in poverty, average household income, life expectancy, percentages of children under 16, voting patterns in relation to political parties, percentages of residents working in banking or the service sector of the economy, and so on. These are graphically represented by bar charts and snippets of information to explain them. For example:

> To travel from Bond Street to Holborn is to move towards a swiftly rising rock face. As you journey east, more and more of your neighbours are childless, young and pay high rents, rents that use up most of their incomes. Those few who are elderly have less and less in common with the young. The loneliness may be harming their health. (Dorling 2013:63)
>
> What does stand out about this part of the line [Bethnal Green to Leyton] is how along the course of four widely spaced stops, between 40 per cent and almost half the children are living in poverty. (Dorling 2013:118)

To add 'colour' to this story of human geography, a few local facts are added from government and local authority press releases, newspaper articles and gossip columns, and information from the electoral ward, or wards, closest to the stops. All this supposedly represents nearly half a million people who live in the vicinity of the Central Line (Dorling 2013:134). Further 'colour', in an attempt to humanise the account, is provided by fictional individual caricatures of the people Dorling imagines to live around the stops. For example, the Harley Street doctor living in the vicinity of Bond Street, with a lucrative consultancy, pleading poverty and exploiting junior staff (Dorling 2013:65–71), or the mother dependent on benefits living in Northolt struggling to support herself and her son (Dorling 2013:12–14), or the black great grandfather living in Leytonstone, a stowaway on a troop ship from Jamaica in the 1940s (Dorling 2013:118–20).

Dorling provides us with many interesting and, indeed, some quite striking statistics, but the people, the places, the architectural forms of the stations and their histories are strikingly absent. He makes up 'representative' cardboard characters inhabiting the vicinity of the stops in an attempt, necessary perhaps in a popular work, to compensate for an obvious absence.

A substantial number of human and cultural geographers share with most sociological accounts of cities a similar perspective on the city.

Rather than leaving their desks and engaging with people's lives, they usually prefer the comfort of an abstracted view of the city. Removing themselves from the streets and the people, they typically like to look down on urban life from above. Cities, such as London, are to be understood not on the basis of how people actually dwell in them and make sense of their lives and identities within particular urban contexts, but in terms of a consideration of abstracted spatial global flows. The actors in this framework are not people relating to each other, but cities themselves personified and anthropomorphised as if they were people.

Viewing the city like gods, some urban geographers dream of producing disembodied macro-spatial maps from which the organising principles of contemporary cities can apparently be deduced without reference to people (e.g. Soja 1996). These are concerned with generalised spatial geographies of resource impacts, capital accumulation and environmental impacts far removed from the day-to-day life of city dwellers and their urban experiences (Davis 2007; Hamnett 2003a; Harvey 1973, 1989, 2001; Soja 1989, 1996).

In a book somewhat curiously entitled *The Urban Experience*, Harvey tells us that:

> I am looking to understand the forces that frame the urban process and the urban experience under capitalism. I focus on the themes of money, space and time because thinking about them helps clear away some of the clutter of detail and lay bare the frames of reference within which urbanism proceeds. (Harvey 1989:164)

We might rhetorically ask: whose experience is that? Apparently theoretical abstraction produces its own kind of profound super- or *supra*-experience entirely removed from people and their doings, framed by the 'concrete [sic] abstractions of space and time' and 'nourished out of the metabolism of capitalist production for exchange on the world market and supported out of a highly sophisticated system of production and distribution organised within its confines' (Harvey 1989:229). Even Harvey's recent book *Rebel Cities*, which we might imagine could involve a discussion of people and their values, framed as it is in terms of recent anti-capitalist protests in urban contexts, remains at a resolutely abstract and theoretical level of analysis and discussion (Harvey 2011).

Massey, in her *World City* (2007), has London, rather than an entirely abstracted global urban space in general, as the specific focus of her discussion. The book puts forward a cogent critique, as do Harvey's theoretical works on urbanism, of a hegemonic neoliberal world based on deregulation, privatisation and marketisation. This is laudable, but the lack of a more grounded analysis considering the way people actually live and feel seems to detract from the power and veracity of this critique.

The main difference in Massey's approach is her insistence that globalisation is made in places and needs to be understood in terms of those places. Although the book is about London, with a stress on the specificity of London as a particular kind of place in terms of, for example, its history as an imperial capital, the overwhelming economic dominance of the finance sector, its multicultural kaleidoscopic ethnic character, its cultural diversity, complex political structure, huge wealth and abject poverty, the main focus of this book remains highly abstract. The centre of attention is how the local (London) is a product of the global, and vice versa. She confesses that although the book is 'centered on London it is not really only about London. It is an essay, rather, that arises *from* London' (Massey 2007:12). So, London is both centred and simultaneously decentred from the discussions, entangled in a web of intermediated global and abstracted spatialities.

There is a striking contrast here between this book and some of Massey's other humanist writings which are grounded in a much more nuanced and sensitive approach to the materiality of place in relation to social identity and people's lives. See Massey's discussion of Wythenshawe, Manchester (Massey 2000) and of Kilburn High Street, discussed below.

Amin and Thrift (2002) similarly valuably discuss a much more grounded approach to the everyday life of the city in a general way, yet a so-called 'relational ontological turn' (Amin and Thrift 2017) in urban studies unfortunately takes us straight back to abstractions. It now invites us to consider cities as 'a combinatorial force field' and as a 'complex adaptive assemblage'. According to Amin and Thrift (2017), a fresh and novel understanding of 'urbanicity' now requires 'an ontology of many kinds of gravitational force juxtaposed: metabolic networks, infrastructures and built forms, technical systems and institutions, diverse structures of authority, power and intelligence' (Amin and Thrift 2017:15). Knowing the contemporary city, we are told, requires 'likening cities to adaptive systems regulated by their combined pluralities and interactions' (Amin and Thrift 2017:22). This perspective appears to be strikingly akin to old systems theory perspectives, a revamped but veiled style of old functionalist analysis. Furthermore:

> This alternative science of the city learns how to scan the knowledge horizon in order to seek out and enjoin expert artefacts, people and

institutions and to harness machine intelligence for the common good. It concerns itself with making visible, rather than taking for granted, the hidden work of algorithms, machines and codes behind the city's many sociotechnical systems and their effects, so as to make the city fabric a heuristic space in which publics can engage with machine intelligence. (Amin and Thrift 2017:27)

The city apparently 'sees'. It is both 'person' and 'machine', but what really matters in this are not the people who actually see in it, but rather a better understanding of its 'aggregate urban dynamics' and anonymous networks.

A rather different approach to the urban is taken by Butler and Robson in their book *London Calling* (2003). The principal aim of this piece of sociological research, inspired by the work of Bourdieu (1977, 1984) was to investigate the consequences of the manner in which the aspirational middle classes appear to be remaking inner London, displacing in the process traditional working class communities, and whether there might be such a thing as a 'metropolitan habitus' in which significant differences emerge between London and provincial British cities, towns and suburbs in terms of the aspirations and lifestyles of the middle classes inhabiting them (Butler and Robson 2003:1).

Following Bourdieu, Butler and Robson conceive of different social groups in terms of the manner in which they deploy stocks of cultural capital (knowledges, skills, tastes, mannerisms, objectified in material form by possessions such as cars, clothing, books, and consumption practices such as food and drink and interests such as going to see particular types of films, engaging in particular sports etc.), economic capital (money and assets) and social capital (networks of friends and acquaintances) in different ways according both to their personal resources and their social aspirations for the kind of neighbourhood they wish to live in: 'perceptions of space and place are crucial in explaining how capital is deployed in building neighbourhoods' (Butler and Robson 2003:11).

Bourdieu's concept of the 'habitus' was intended to link the individual decisions people take about their lives and deep underlying structuring principles that constitute societies as a whole. Thus the intention was to avoid the opposition between the individual and individual differences and underlying ordering collective structural principles governing the social world. Bourdieu emphasised that the habitus has an endless generative capacity to produce thoughts, actions, ideas, perceptions and emotions, giving social life both its relative predictability and freedom. However, as many commentators have pointed out, the overwhelming emphasis in Bourdieu's account is on social reproduction rather than change. The weight of historical tradition and the material environment both constrain and condition people's access to material and non-material resources alike. There is a continuous dialectic between the generative structures of the habitus, agency and meaning.

Bourdieu's *Distinction* (1984) analyses the cultural basis of 'taste' in French society in the 1960s. The fundamental structural opposition here became social class – France as a class-divided society. Different social classes are argued to possess distinct dispositions to purchase various kinds of food and other consumer goods, read particular kinds of newspapers and books, engage in different kinds of sport, visit art galleries, museums and exhibitions or not, listen to different kinds of music and so on. Bourdieu regards them as being involved in a never-ending struggle to acquire, maintain and reproduce different forms of capital: economic (money, access to material resources), social (networks, relations with other people), cultural (legitimate and legitimated knowledges), symbolic (prestige, fame and social honour). These forms of capital can be converted into each other. So, money can buy private education and access to different social networks and prestige. People's tastes and preferences, lifestyles and patterns of consumption, become objectified through the clothes they buy and wear, the foods they eat, their table manners, the kinds of cars they drive, the kinds of social events and performances with which they engage, and so on in a systematic and predictable manner.

This is the underlying conceptual framework on which Butler and Robson (2003) draw. However, in their actual research practice they use ACORN (consumer survey) clusters to systematically investigate links between housing, employment, education and consumption and the way people 'realise' different forms of habitus in seven different study areas in London. ACORN clusters are a popular marketing analysis tool, grouping together what is known of the inhabitants of different types of areas by their consumption patterns. These profiles are accessible via postcode data. Overall, ACORN produces 54 'ideal type' profiles of postcode areas of the UK as a whole.

The neigbourhoods analysed in Butler and Robson's 2003 study – Barnsbury, Telegraph Hill, Brixton, Battersea, Docklands, with sub-divisions in a couple of cases – are characterised in terms of the ACORN cluster typology, so Telegraph Hill is a 'type 24 area – partially gentrified multiethnic' (Butler and Robson 2003:57) and Barnsbury 'type 21, prosperous enclaves, highly qualified executives... very affluent neighbourhoods containing well-educated, mobile, younger professionals living in flats' (Butler and Robson 2003:53).

The types of houses people live in and the material possessions they have do not form part of the analysis. Similarly, the built environment and the character and texture of these places/study areas is scarcely described. The residential neighbourhoods are represented solely as a series of framed street maps, and nothing more. In terms of conveying a sense of the nature and character of these places, the names, as in Dorling's 2013 study, are empty of any content. The character of the streets and the materiality of the built environment, the houses people live in and their material possessions are all apparently insignificant in relation to the social construction of the habitus of their inhabitants or, at the very least, remain taken for granted and not worth describing or discussing.

Socially, Barnsbury is characterised, by Butler and Robson's analysis, as having the following characteristics: high numbers of graduates and professionals; a high propensity towards vegetarianism and taking exercise; below-average car ownership, but a tendency for those with cars to buy new and expensive models; buying CDs and hardback books in greater than average numbers; double the average proportion of those earning over £40,000 per annum; being well provided with pensions; by far the most popular daily paper being the *Guardian*. People from Barnsbury take holidays in far-flung destinations, tend to drink and eat out, and shun traditional British food. Playing sport, and visiting museums and galleries, theatre and cinema are 'enormously popular', and by a long margin the people are gin drinkers (Butler and Robson 2003:53). In a concluding note, Butler and Robson state, 'It is only necessary to spend a short time in Islington to confirm that this judgement is likely to be accurate for the most part' (Butler and Robson 2003:53). People are reduced to a stereotype of the statistics, and it is apparently only necessary to spend a short time in the neighbourhood being studied to know everything that is significant about it.

Highly valuable but all too brief and highly selected personal interview data is presented from respondents in each area in chapters 5 and 8 of Butler and Robson's 2003 book. These interviews provide some useful personal insights into aspects of the lives of the gentrifiers. But in the text, the interviews seem instead to ultimately play a similar rhetorical role to Dorling's fictional characters (in Dorling 2013) – to humanise an abstracted statistical account. Dorling makes up the lives of his characters; Butler and Robson select some of their words instead, but the overwhelming emphasis of their study is based on an analysis of age, occupation, household income and composition. This facilitates the residents to be assigned to eight social classes and socio-economic groups. The real people talking thus become little more than a mirror of the statistics and the social categories derived from them. In the case of Barnsbury, an upmarket 'super-gentrified' area of Islington in north London, the people are drinking their gin, going to ethnically themed restaurants and reading, of course, the *Guardian*.

The inner-London middle-class gentrifiers, Butler and Robson's 2003 book concludes, are cosmopolitan in their outlook in contrast to the non-middle class in London and also those in other UK cities Here they include their middle classes, although this remains an assertion without evidential basis. Butler and Robson assert that the 'middle classes living in London at the beginning of the twenty-first century are living in the "great society" which has now moved beyond urban and national boundaries into the global stage' (Butler and Robson 2003:165). The diversity of London enables an extraordinary flexible form of the urban habitus to emerge in different areas (Butler and Robson 2003:192–3). This conclusion does not make any reference to the different places studied, so we get the impression that gentrification is pretty much the same everywhere in London, as are the gentrifiers. While there may be differences among them, their commonalities of a shared habitus result in similar attitudes and beliefs, strategies and perspectives in their lives.

But it is apparent from Butler and Robson's highly mobile and relatively affluent informants, who could live somewhere else, that the actual place where they chose to live mattered to them. Place mattered over price: 'people decided roughly where to live and then found a house or flat they could afford' (Butler and Robson 2003:75). Some of Butler and Robson's informants stated that they could not imagine living anywhere else: 'It's very friendly and very mixed – it's got diversity and a nice community feel about it. This is one of the nicest places in London – I have strong feelings about it' (Butler and Robson: 2003:82; informant speaking about Barnsbury); 'It's very pleasant and incredibly popular. Everything is here, you haven't got to go over the river for everything you want – we have our own department stores. It's very safe, very middle class' (Butler and Robson: 2003:85; informant speaking about Battersea). These sentiments are quite obviously place bound, and, if they had been explored further in the interviews and through walking with the informants around their neighbourhoods and spending more time with them, might have shown a far greater depth and variety in attachments to place in terms of the construction of individual and group identities than is evident from the book.

This general style of analysis has become de rigueur in urban sociology, adopted by many to characterise not only gentrifying neighbourhoods, but extending beyond this to consider nations and class structure in general (e.g. Bennett et al. 2009; Savage et al. 2015). In such work, it is Bourdieu's concept of social field rather than the more inclusive notion of habitus that has dominated. This is the manner in which struggles take place in relation to specific resources – cultural goods, housing, education, employment, political power, prestige, and so on – and access to them. It is a structured system of social positions occupied by individuals or institutions.

Butler and Robson (2003) examine four fields in their study – employment, housing, consumption and education – based on a statistical analysis, but the problem with this is that it only provides a shallow aggregate view of collective behaviour. The individual people discussed are only considered important insofar as they become token, or totemic, representations of wider generalised occupational and social categories: higher managerial and professional, old male, Somali woman, white working-class unmarried mother, and so on.

Read today, Bourdieu's own account of French society seems peculiarly stereotyped, if it was indeed ever really like this. One of the primary problems with Bourdieu's original research in *Distinction*, inspiring *London Calling*, was that it was carried out in the form of a large-scale statistical analysis based on brief interviews and a questionnaire survey, a methodological strategy more or less repeated in the more recent British sociological studies. Again, these scholars rarely feel the need to move from their desks, engage with and meet with people, participate (in the classical anthropological sense of participant observation) and engage in their lives for more than the brief period of conducting a questionnaire or a personal household interview, or listening to a focus group discussion. They do not usually observe houses or study their interiors in detail, analyse the contents of the home and the manner in which material culture is ordered (or disordered), attend football matches with their informants, go to pubs or restaurants in a neighbourhood, spend time in markets or parks, or walk repeatedly up and down streets (once is normally enough) to conduct their research.

A common feature of all these conceptualisations of the urban is that abstracted general theoretical frameworks are applied to the urban from the top down, and the city is understood and 'experienced' in terms of them. The city becomes dematerialised in the process. An obvious counterpoint is an attempt to do the reverse – to understand the urban from the bottom up, from the people themselves, in which the generalisations about city life arise from the lives of city dwellers, the streets, the neighbourhoods, the squares, the parks, the markets, the housing estates, the buildings themselves – a stress on the materiality of the city as being constituted in terms of persons and places and relations between them. This is the project of this book.

Bourdieu himself was interested in not just documenting differences in taste and lifestyles, but how these are mobilised in struggles for status and prestige and naturalised in various ways, made to appear self-evident and non-arbitrary. 'Cultured' individuals regard their own cultural distinction as taken for granted, normal and beyond dispute, natural, an inherent marker of their social value and status. It is taken for granted, rarely discussed, part of their everyday world, and materialised or made visible in their everyday practices.

In Bourdieu's ethnography of the Kabyle, a Berber community, the house itself was understood as the principal locus for the material objectification of the generative schemes, or underlying structures, from which the habitus arises; here, the actions of individuals are conceived in terms of structured binary oppositions that make up the habitus (inside/outside, dry/wet, male/female, east/west and so on) (Bourdieu 1977:89ff.; 1992, appendix). The process of socialisation into becoming a member of society is mediated through the house 'through the intermediary of the divisions and hierarchies it sets up between things, persons and practices, this tangible classifying system, continuously inculcates and reinforces the taxonomic principles underlying all the arbitrary provisions of the culture' (Bourdieu 1977:89).

Thus the house for Bourdieu was, in the context of Kabyle society, a material objectification of the habitus that is simultaneously embodied in the practices of those who dwell there. The material manifestation of the habitus becomes inculcated in the socialisation of children, the way they think and feel and understand themselves. Furthermore, the material manifestation of the habitus finds tangible material expression in the spatial divisions of the house and the practical taxonomies of the arrangements of material culture within it. Put another way, people think through the house and the structured assemblage of things within it. Thus, through living in a particular material environment, people come to know themselves and how to act, how to go on in the world, and this is a largely unconscious process of living and doing. In this analytical framework, social practices that incorporate things thus arise from the habitus or generative schemes and dispositions on which people draw. But through their practice, and through the practical outcomes and unintended consequences of their actions, this is also, in principle at least, open to continuous improvisation and change. In this theoretical framework, we do not move from mind to material objectifications of that mind, because the mind that is predisposed to think in a certain way is itself a product of material objectifications; a dialectic exists.

The importance of all this resides in the claims made by Bourdieu that there are systematic homologies in people's lifestyle choices that are objectified through a whole gamut of material forms and activities without which social status could neither be marked out or recognised. The *things themselves* objectify who people *are*. The qualities and forms of these things consumed, used and displayed become embodied – that is, they form part of the manner in which people think and feel about themselves and their relations to others. Things and their significance, the house, the built environment, are all conspicuously absent in Butler and Robson's and most sociological urban studies.

Emphasising the role and significance of material forms in constituting social lives is thus an alternative perspective that arises directly from Bourdieu's work and is emphasised in this book. Such a perspective has provided inspiration for many material culture studies in anthropology; we study the intimate details of people's lives, the wider landscapes that they inhabit, the manner in which they appropriate, in a consumer society, an alienated system of commodities, select and personalise them and make them their own in their dress, the furnishing and provisioning of the home, or in terms of the contents of their fridges, the way they cook, what they store in the attic or throw away, how they tend their gardens, and so on. The power and significance of the material world in constructing people's lives is persistently overlooked and remains unacknowledged in most urban studies. This book is intended to provide a kind of antidote to that perspective.

More specifically, this book provides a broadly phenomenologically inspired anthropological alternative to the abstractions of many urban studies, from the perspective of a substantial body of research in anthropological material culture studies focusing on the manner in which people make things and places their own through their practices, and vice versa the manner in which things and people co-construct their identities and social relations (see, e.g., Appadurai 1986; Buchli 2002, 2013; Gell 1998; Henare, Holbraad and Wastell 2007; Hoskins 1998, 2006; Miller 1998a, 2009, 2010; Tilley 2007; Tilley et al. 2006; Tilley 2017; Tilley and Cameron-Daum 2017; Weiner 1992).

Phenomenological perspectives

Phenomenology is, above all, a philosophical position emphasising the basis of all our experience and knowledge of the world in situated small embodied acts (Abram 1997; Csordas 1990; Desjarlais and Throop 2011; Merleau-Ponty 1962, 1968; Tilley 1994, 2004, 2008, 2010; Tilley and Cameron Daum 2017). That is to say that we engage with material and social worlds through our immersion within them. We are part of them, and they are part of us; we feel the world of which we are a part, and that world feels us, our presence, our carnal being. Direct sensory experience of this world is a fundamental and primary part of our social being-in-the-world. We perceive and understand how and why to act and go on through the fleshy medium of our embodied selves; through participating in the social and material worlds, we seek to understand and reflecting on them.

The concept of embodiment provides the fundamental starting point to discuss, phenomenologically, the constitution of social identities in place. The immediacy of our embodied experiences of the world has a profound effect on the manner in which we relate to both persons and things, and the things themselves and the places in which they are found are extensions of the self. So social identity is about the body in the mind. The manner in which identity gets thought through relates to the manner in which agency is experienced through the body in place and in relation to things that extend it, such as the walker and her stick.

The description of materiality for the phenomenologist is the process of revealing the world that she or he encounters. It is not a low-level activity to be superseded by subsequent so-called abstract analysis of sensorial 'data'. To describe the world as fully and faithfully as we possibly can is always potentially to re-describe it and make that world anew, to see and feel and understand it in a different and revelatory manner. Thus, through the process of such research, we come to a more profound understanding of our own lives and those of others. Such description is inevitably selective; we cannot describe the entire world in which we and others are immersed, but we can highlight in our research what appears to be most significant. This is, if you like, the analysis that takes place within a phenomenological descriptive account.

Our descriptions are inevitably personal insofar as we cannot escape our own embodied engagement with the world from which they all flow. However, through observing and reflecting and talking to others and experiencing, through our participation, the material sensorious worlds with which they and we engage, we go beyond the self to reach an understanding that is broader and sensitive to cultural and political contexts, gender and identities, power and dominance, resistance and difference.

It is unfortunate that most negative commentaries on a phenomenological approach consistently and fatally conflate two very different aspects of experience: the personal and the subjective. They are not the same thing. Social research is inevitably subjective, since claims to a disembodied objectivity are simply myths inherited from the Enlightenment. We cannot escape our own bodies and sensory experiences. They are who we are and how we live. But the aim is to understand others and their worlds by reaching out, feeling, understanding, describing – beyond the petty limits of our own personal experiences – to engage with those of others and their sensorious engagement in the world.

Place

One very significant foundational philosophical tradition for understanding place comes from Heidegger's later thought. He stresses an intimate link between building, thinking and dwelling (Heidegger 2003). Dwelling is the essence of being-in-the-world. Building and thinking are intimately related as modes of dwelling. One form of philosophy going back to Descartes and 'I think therefore I am' is one that separates mind from body and the rational free-thinking subject from the world. By contrast, Heidegger's philosophy emphasises embeddedness. People think and act through dwelling, and this is a fundamental part of being human. Being rooted in one place is for Heidegger the proper condition for social being. Place provides ontological security. Places, like buildings or trees, are rooted in their very materiality. People dwell and think through places that have their own singular material characteristics. Places take on their significance through the manner in which we interact with them. Therefore, human consciousness is place bound. We have different intentional relationships to places in accordance with whether we live there, work there, or visit them briefly.

Knowledge of the world that is emplaced results in attitudes of care and concern for that place. We make sense of the world through the materiality of the things around us, not through abstract conceptual schemes. They are a matter of body rather than of mind. Places in all their concrete particularity create a sense of belonging, a centre from which to understand ourselves and our relation to the world. Dwelling is about the spiritual unity of people in relation to the earth and the sky. The earth is the ground on which people dwell, the source of all fruitfulness and growth. People dwell on the earth and under the sky. They are between earth and sky. The sky is the domain of the movements of the sun and the moon, the stars, the light of the day, dusk and dawn, of the weather of cloud formations, source of water, and so on. People live in relation to the earth and the sky (a vertical axis) and in relation to near and far, insides and outsides (a horizontal axis).

All places are thus constituted by a figure/ground relationship. Places are figures against grounds, a square or street or park in a city. One cannot be understood except in relation to another. Above all, places are foci that *gather*. They gather people, events, emotions, memories, stories, histories, meanings and associations. As such, they provide both the medium and outcome of dwelling.

Everyday life

A primary source complementing Heidegger's understanding of place as the centre of social being is the work of de Certeau and his collaborators on the practices of everyday life (de Certeau 1984; de Certeau, Giard and Mayol 1998). They too underline the significance of place, examining both its 'poetic' and its expressive elements and its inevitable pluralist characteristics. Life is lived from a point of view, a situation, being *in place*, resulting in an inclination, a tendency and disposition to behave and think and act in different ways.

The discussion by Mayol of the neighbourhood and the street (in de Certeau, Giard and Mayol 1998) is particularly relevant here to the theme of this book. The organisation of life is articulated in two main ways. First there is the manner in which people behave in the street, translated in dress, politeness codes (greetings etc.), the rhythm of walking and the avoidance of or the frequency of trips to particular places. Second is the expected symbolic benefits of behaving in particular ways. This is largely non-discursive, rooted in cultural tradition and appearing in a partial or fragmented way in the walk and the manner in which the walker uses or 'consumes' public space. The neighbourhood exists as a kind of social commitment, an act of coexisting with others, be they neighbours or shopkeepers or joggers, who are all linked by both proximity of encounters and repetition (de Certeau, Giard and Mayol 1998:8). 'A "practice" is what is decisive for the *identity* of the dweller or a group insofar as this identity allows him or her to take up a position in the network of relations inscribed in the environment' (de Certeau, Giard and Mayol 1998:9).

The lived-in neighbourhood allows one to acquire a certain mastery of it because of its familiarity, a known place in which persons know both themselves and that they are recognised by others. The public space of the city as a whole remains anonymous in contrast with the neighbourhood in which, little by little, people come to know themselves in relation to others. The neighbourhood is primarily known through the feet. It is a place in between the private interior place of the dwelling and the mostly unknown totality of the city. It mediates an interior inside place and an exterior outside space: 'It is less an urban surface transparent for everyone or statistically measurable, than the possibility offered everyone to inscribe in the city a multitude of trajectories whose hard core permanently remains the private sphere' (de Certeau, Giard and Mayol 1998:11).

Analogies may be drawn here between arranging one's own interior place in a house or a flat and arranging one's trajectories through urban space. Within the house, we find the 'comfort' of the things that surround us, an intimate phenomenology of space from the basement to the attic (Bachelard 1969); in the neighbourhood, we find the 'comfort' of the familiarity of a built environment through which we can move at ease, because it is a known configuration of streets and buildings and places. From childhood, one becomes socialised not only in the home but in the neighbourhood, or in multiple neighbourhoods, as one grows up and moves. The house and neighbourhood become part of the habitus of the urban dweller, and now they are usually separated from the place of work to which one commutes, rather than strolls directionally, covering the most ground in the least amount of time.

The subject living in a neighourhood effectively both poeticises part of the city and individualises it, makes it his or her own. Socially it can be characterised as a collective organisation of individual trajectories (de Certeau, Giard and Mayol 1998:15) in which the neighbours who surround you and live next to you are neither too close to bother you but never too far away to avoid. A good relationship with neighbours requires the practical mastery of social skills, adhering to a system of values and embodied relationships allowing people to get on and feel at ease or not, smiling or not smiling, being friendly or otherwise, the everyday symbolic capital of bodily gestures, words and phrases intimately related to gender, age, ethnicity and class.

A wonderful characterisation of the everyday life of a particular neighbourhood is found in Mayol's discussion of the Croix-Rousse neighbourhood of Lyons (de Certeau, Giard and Mayol 1998:62ff.). This starts from the R family's double apartment and a discussion of the intimacy of family relations. From there, the narrative proceeds into the rue Rivet, in which we meet Robert the greengrocer at one end of the street and La Germaine's grocery at the other. The account provides, among other things, a discussion of the everyday practice of shopping for groceries, the significance of bread and wine, the passage from the market to the cafe, and the contrasting forms of embodied socialities in these different settings.

The sheer complexity of even the simplest and most ordinary of social acts is underlined in the narrative. In the light of such an approach, the urban theorist's dream of capturing the essence of a city in terms of its monstrous abstracted and reticulated spatialities and networks collapses like a house of cards. All that they regard as somehow solid knowledge melts into air. The materiality and sociality of the city itself resists any attempt at an all-encompassing panoptic approach. We rediscover once more people and place and how people actually dwell.

This book builds on the perspectives of Heidegger and de Certeau in a general way, but more specifically on a considerable alternative body of literature, impossible to discuss in a short introduction, by humanistic geographers, environmental psychologists, anthropologists and others who have explored in a great diversity of ways the platial characteristics of dwelling and various forms of place attachment involving the bonding of people to place and the manner in which these may take multiple forms, bringing forth a range of different emotions and experiences (see, e.g., Adams, Hoelscher and Till 2001; Appadurai 1986; Atkinson, Fuller and Painter 2016; Buttimer and Seamon 1980; Cresswell 2004; Feld and Basso 1996; Lovell 1998; Low and Lawrence-Zúñiga 2003; Manzo and Devin-Wright 2014; Relph 1976; Seamon 1993; Taun 1974, 1977).

The most general points to be made here are that understanding the urban landscape from a phenomenological perspective involves considering the city in terms of the concrete specificity of its places and in terms of mobility and flows between them, in relation to other places outside the city, and in terms of rhythms and practices of everyday life. Places are integral to the setting and staging of everyday life as opposed to space that is merely an abstract container for it. They form the arena for a grounded phenomenology of the city. A place within a city may be a tree or a monument, a street corner, a cafe or pub, a meeting place, an underground or railway station, a street, a market, a park, a neighbourhood, a housing estate or a suburb. Places thus contain other places on a sliding scale or like a series of Russian dolls, one inside the other. They may have relatively clear or demarcated boundaries, beginnings or ends, passages into and out of them. The term is thus ambiguous and slippery.

This does not matter except when one wants to compare one kind of place with another, in which case they need to be of the same scale or material character. Thus one might compare different streets, but not a street and a suburb.

Place, biography, memory

While space remains an abstract, 'empty' analytical concept, places are always tangible and physical, their meanings built up by the people who inhabit, use or move through them (Tilley 1994). Places in the urban landscape forge individual and collective biographies, shared histories and memories, creating various forms of affective associations. Places, like people, have individual names, and these names form their identities as places, how they are understood, and how they may come to be represented in words and images. Thinking through places is a primary way in which people understand their world.

A striking counterpoint to Dorling's statistical analysis of London's Central Line, discussed above, is found in Augé's (2002) anthropological account of the Paris Metro. The subway map is one that brings forth personal memories. The names of the stations relate strongly to the biographies of people who live near them and use them from childhood onwards. The names are indelibly linked to the names of friends, families, colleagues, events, meetings and a host of other associations. Some, not visited, remain just names on the map; others are replete with associative memories of place. The personal sequencing and itineraries fostered by the Metro are shared with others in rhythms of movement and daily passage. The subway lines 'like lifelines on the hand, meet and cross – not only on the map where the interlacing of their multicolour routes unwinds and is set in place, but in everyone's lives and minds' (Augé 2002:6). A regular traveller on a line has a certain economy of using it, knowing exactly where to board a train in order to be closest to the exit when they get off, and how to move through individual stations, and, through a keen attention to sound, when to walk slowly or to rush. They know how to adapt themselves to the throng of bodies at rush hour, how long it will take between individual stops, where the journey becomes noisy and where it is quieter on the line. These are the daily routinised and embodied habitual skills of using the Metro. The names of certain stations recall a wider history and monuments and streets and events, memories of the past in the present. Names connect people and the past in the present. This is the Metro of everyday life.

Both discursive consciousness, thoughts that are verbalised and can be discussed, and practical habitual routinised activities that are lived rather than thought through are always related to places. They take place *in place*. Place is thus an elemental existential fact, and the social construction of a sense of place is a universal experiential medium. Places, rather than spaces, are the manner in which people understand their urban landscapes. Every narrative about the city and city life invariably traces its course in an arrangement of dwellings and streets and squares that are joined by paths of movement. The sum of the life of a city dweller can, therefore, be conceptualised in terms of the places in which he or she has been through and between which he or she moves.

The urban landscape is thus a set of platial rather than abstracted spatial relationships, in which the existence of one place depends on its relationship with another and its mode of directional encounter. According to how and from where and when one approaches a place, it may appear to be entirely different, and in relation to how one moves, what one experiences as one moves to the left or right, or whether one continues moving straight ahead, or in terms of looking up or down or towards something or whether one encounters it suddenly or from a long distance away.

Contestation

Because places are always plural, they are as often as not contested, because different individuals and groups are likely to think about them and value or not value them in different ways (Bender 1993, 2006; Bender and Winer 2001; Tilley and Cameron-Daum 2017). In this sense, places are never static. Places themselves are in a continual process of being and becoming places. De Certeau (1984) strongly emphasised places as sites of resistance in the city, and practices of walking as both appropriation of the topographical system of streets and places, a spatial acting out of the place and an act of resistance to the city planners: 'walking affirms, suspects, tries out, transgresses, respects etc. the trajectories it "speaks"' (de Certeau 1984:99).

The contested character of place is one of the major themes informing the discussions in the individual chapters of this book. Melhuish (chapter 2) relates this to people's age and their length of occupancy, where people dwell within the Brunswick Centre, and whether they are regarded as insiders or outsiders in terms of family ties and commitments. These are also key factors in Yates's discussion of the Beavers/Meadows west London housing estate (chapter 3). Differences are highlighted here between a group of old ladies who moved into the estate immediately after it was built and people who were housed there later, between those with strong family ties and those without, and between the group of 'boys' who hang out at the betting shop and around the 'stones' – an outdoor meeting place on the eastern periphery of the state. The material isolation and insulation of the estate from its surroundings means that social and ethnic tensions within it become accentuated, while at the same time strong community ties exist between some of its residents. The estate is both refuge and prison in relation to the outside world. The young and not so young men taking drugs, smoking, drinking, visiting the betting shop and urinating in a nearby alley are both feared for their antisocial behaviour but also appreciated by different groups of residents, as they are like an unofficial police force. They are acutely attuned to the presence of unwelcome strangers, faces they do not recognise, and act as a deterrent to them entering the estate.

Young's account of a taxi rank (chapter 8) examines the direct manner in which contest takes place between black-cab drivers and Uber drivers and the perceived threat to the living of former by the latter. Both Yates (chapter 3) and Wilson (chapter 6) show how contestation is linked to feelings of threat and uncertainty and resistance to an outside world. It becomes part and parcel of the fabric of the place itself.

The routes of places and non-places

An increasingly prominent thread in considerations of the city is that the significance of place has been eroded in our 'post-modernity'. If places were significant in the past, they are now less so, lacking clear boundaries and any sense of community or ethnic coherence. We are in an entirely different world from Heidegger's idealised and essentially conservative vision of the Black Forest rural white German community forming the basis for his reflections on identity, dwelling and belonging to place (Heidegger 2003), or Mayol's discussion of the everyday life of French-speaking kith and kin in Lyons in the mid 1970s (de Certeau, Giard and Mayol 1998). It is perhaps then an inherently unsatisfactory way to characterise place in London or any other contemporary town or city after all. Rather than talking about the rootedness of place in an essentially conservative manner in relation to the lives and identities of its inhabitants, we need to think instead about the routes of place, how places have been completely transformed through movement and an increasingly cosmopolitan culture of the city (Blokland 2017; Clifford 1997; Hall 2012; Jones and Jackson 2014a; Massey 1997; Rapport and Dawson 1998).

The local and the global represent two poles in relation to how people conceive of their identities and how they live. Local constructions of identity are rooted in places, and their counterpart is a different kind of identity related to multiple places that are mediated and generalised, involving a loss of place attachment in the construction of the self. Globalisation, the development of transnational communities, and the space–time compression provided by travel and communications technologies undoubtedly produce new understandings of place that are both hybridised and contingent. Previous notions of a static distinctiveness of place are being transformed through connections to the world beyond, through labour migrations and diasporas, internationalisation of economic structures and consumer products, tourism, flexibility and mobility in labour markets, and so on. The boundaries of global cities, where they might begin or end, how far their global influence extends, become increasingly blurred and problematic. Cities are thus betwixt and between, borderlands between sameness and uniqueness – in Massey's terms, 'meeting places' (Massey 2007).

But even if the places of the city are increasingly hybrid meeting places, they are still places, and we can investigate the character of meeting and gatherings in these places, something impossible at the scale of the city itself. Appadurai (1996), Eriksen (2010), Hannerz (1996) and others have cogently argued that globalisation, rather than eroding the identities and significance of place, has instead resulted in their growing diversity and differentiation. It produces place but in a different kind of way.

Massey's brief discussion of Kilburn in north London is a celebration of its multi-ethnic diversity and hybridity (Massey 1997). A walk down its high street immediately reveals its diversity, as does the way they people dress and the activities they are engaged in. It is a place constituted by multiple personal identities related to gender, age and class, and communities within it, and its own history in terms of the outside world and what happens within. These together constitute its platial uniqueness.

In a similar fashion, Hall discusses the Walworth Road in south London as an arena in which multi-ethnic culture is visible in the street itself, its shops and signage, and in interactions between the proprietors of its small independent shops and the customers within them. Her research starts from the place itself, the street rather than a category of people within its neighbourhood. She notes that:

> People's lives and livelihoods were inevitably more complex and far more differentiated than the less cluttered logic of the theoretical frame. The value of ethnography in understanding difference is that it renders a situated and multivocal sense of people and places as they live in, respond to and shape their social worlds. (Hall 2012: 8)

Hall describes everyday life in the street from the vantage point of the cafe and the tailor's shop. From these small places within the place and the details of bodily gestures, dress and speech, everyday life is emphasised in its social performance.

While Kilburn High Street and the Walworth Road might, through an examination of the generalised population statistics in relation to ethnicity, seem pretty much the same, both have their own identities as places. The primary difference between Massey's and Hall's accounts resides partly in the ethnographic depth of Hall's study, whereas Massey's discussion is based more on a casual observations and personal reflections, but also in the conceptualisation of the character of these streets and neighbourhoods. For Massey, a global sense of the local needs conjoining with a global sense of place. But as Hall points out, this conflation of the global and the local does not really cope very well with place specificity, with sub-worlds within them that may be both bounded and introverted (Hall 2012:99).

Augé has argued that, in what he calls our 'hypermodernity', a new category of place has increasingly developed. Cities are now characterised by a proliferation of 'non-places' (Augé 1995). 'If a place can be defined as relational, historical and concerned with identity, then a space which cannot be defined as relational, or historical, or concerned with identity will be a non-place' (Augé 1995:77–8). These non-places are air, rail and motorway routes, airports and railway stations, hotel chains, leisure parks, supermarkets, and large retail outlets such as shopping malls (this perspective, it needs to be noted, contrasts curiously with his later account of the Paris Metro, which is definitely not a non-place). These non-places are characterised in terms of the journeys made in them, the discourses that take place in them and their relation to the identities of the people who use them. In these non-places, referring to de Certeau's discussions of everyday life, it is an abstracted notion of space that dominates. The non-places are constructed in relation to certain ends, transport, transit, commerce, leisure and the relations that individuals have with them (Augé 1995:94). This is a matter of passing through rather than dwelling, of fleeting, transitory and vicarious experiences and relations people have with them. In the big supermarket, 'the customer wanders around in silence, reads labels, weighs fruit and vegetables on a machine… then hands his credit card to a young woman as silent as himself – anyway, not very chatty – who runs each article past the sensor of a decoding machine before checking the validity of the customer's credit card' (Augé 1995:100). The user of a supermarket or an airport is essentially both alone but also one of many, but in a contractual relation with it, manifested in presenting their boarding card at the check-in desk of the airport or payment in a supermarket. The space of non-place 'creates neither singular identity nor relations. Only solitude and similitude' (Augé 1995:103).

Augé only conceives his non-places in terms of the person who passes through them, and here one can see a certain veracity in the argument. But for the people who work in the airport or the shopping mall or travel on the underground, it becomes a familiar place that they know intimately and so forms part of their biography and identity. Even the most recent of non-places has its history and its own materiality. Shopping malls can instead be argued to be new meeting points and gathering places for identity construction in place (see Miller et al.'s 1998 discussion of the Brent Cross shopping mall in north London and Wood Green in relation to family structure, household provisioning, ethnicity and class). The manner in which people think about themselves and their situation is not simply a matter of the mind, and people do not usually think about the city or anywhere else in terms of abstractions but in terms of their embodied experiences, which are always materially situated. Places are thus a highly variable resource for personal and collective reflection. Different experiences of places give rise to varying emotional and personal responses. Places are not inert, and their sheer materiality means that we cannot think about them in any way we like. They provide sensuous resources for thought and understanding, discussed below.

Sensory engagement in place

Our bodily perceptual experiences are both the medium and outcome of research that takes place in and through our own bodies and those of others in relation to place. The sensing and sensed body itself is our primary research tool. We take our bodies into places and learn from them. Put another way, this is to intermesh fleshy corporeality and bricks, concrete and stone, people and things, emotions and practices, being and becoming, the material and the immaterial, the virtual and the tangible.

In the process of either living or doing research, we do not go about seeing the world around us or hearing, tasting and smelling it, or feeling it externally through reaching out or internally through the kinaesthetics of our bodies. All our perceptual senses mingle in and through our engagement in the world and all at once. Perception, affect, emotion, and habitual or discursive consciousness are all simultaneously part and parcel of our entangled immersion and co-presence in the material and social world that we inhabit. Therefore, all our sensory experiences cannot be neatly extracted or abstracted from each other, except of course in the limiting cases of blindness, loss of smell or hearing, or other modes of sensory disablement and deprivation.

Our engagement with and participation in the world always involves all our senses and all at once. I have always found two consistent and repeated claims or analytical and methodological positions in some of the growing literature on the senses as rather odd. The first is that the senses can be isolated from each other in packaged studies of vision, taste, touch, sound and smell that do not consider or that sideline the others (e.g. Bull and Back 2003; Classen 2005; Dikovitskaya 2005; Korsmeyer 2005). We may need to write about these different sensory perceptions separately, simply because of the sheer flux of sensations that bombard us all at once for analytical convenience, but to isolate them is a fundamental mistake. The second is the notion that certain senses are more important than the others historically or cross-culturally (e.g. Classen, Howes and Synnot 1994). Neither of these claims can be maintained from the standpoint of a phenomenological position of embodied being in the world. They in fact potentially limit our understanding, through their concentration on one sense and relative lack of consideration of, for example, visual engagement in taste, the smells of sounds, the touch of colours, the taste of smell or the sounds of vision. These are normal and universal human capacities for perceptual experiences, although of course the particular form that they take inevitably varies between individuals and groups within different cultures and through time. Such studies are not phenomenological, to their detriment, because they fail to take embodied multi-sensorial experience seriously enough in trying to claim that one rather than another sensory dimension of experience is fundamental in a culture or a historical epoch.

Our own contemporary culture has, over and over again, been claimed to be one in which the visual and visual culture dominates, and vision itself has been commonly regarded as the 'noblest' and by far the most significant of the senses (for excellent discussions, see, among many others: Burnett 1995; Jay 1994). But as everyone who has actually experienced living knows, this is simply an abstracted analytical academic vision that dangerously simplifies and rarefies our full multi-sensorial being and relationship to the world, which comes to us all at once rather than in partitioned sensory experiences.

There can, therefore, be no such things as cultures of vision or cultures of sound, although in different social and material consequences one or a few of our perceptual senses may dominate and appear to be far more important in reaching an understanding of how people relate to their worlds than others in particular contexts.

The aim of phenomenological multi-sensory research is deceptively simple. It is to produce a richly nuanced and evocative description of the world that people inhabit, to convey an understanding of the sensorial ordering of cultures and subcultures, the smells and sounds and tastes, touch and visual aspects of social being *in place* (Classen 1993; Helliwell 1996; Howes 2005; Howes 2005a; Rhys-Taylor 2017; Serres, Sankey and Cowley 2008; Sutton 2001). It is to try and bring forth into words that which is never normally said, through participant observation, to produce a richly textured and nuanced account.

From this perspective, cities are beginning to be understood not only in terms of their obvious visuality, but in relation to their multi-sensorial characteristics (Degen 2008, 2014; Edensor 2006, 2014) or in terms of a focus on their particular soundscapes (Adams, Hoelscher and Till 2001; Back 2007; Bull 2000), design and their tactile characteristics (Sasaki 2000) and their tastes and smells (Diaconu 2016; Henshaw 2015; Rhys-Taylor 2013, 2014, 2017).

Recent work by Rhys-Taylor in his sensory ethnography of east London (Rhys-Taylor 2017) is particularly pertinent to highlight here. Rhys-Taylor has shown the huge potential for understanding the city in a strikingly different manner through the medium of the senses. Specifically, Rhys-Taylor discusses how the city can be understood through its smells and tastes, and how these sensory dimensions powerfully constitute the multicultural aspects of city life in the markets and streets through which he walks and senses. In doing so, he underlines the critique that the lack of attention to the actual experiences of those who dwell in the city is severely detrimental to understanding the problems faced by those living in them and finding solutions to those problems. Rhys-Taylor's book concerns itself with the 'heat of chilli peppers, the brackish tang of jellied eels and the warmth of Japanese curry sauce to the oily herbs and spice of fried chicken takeaways' (Rhys-Taylor 2017:9).

Rhys-Taylor demonstrates how sensory dimensions themselves play a powerful role in shaping sociality itself, class, culture and multi-culture. A focus on the fine-grain detail of everyday life reveals far more about the city as a lived space than any amount of macro-spatial theorising. The politics of our multi-sensorial experiences are integral to an understanding of the distinctions of class and multi-culture, ethnicity, race and gender, social inclusion and feelings of belonging and exclusion, them and us.

Discussions of the synaesthetic sensuous engagement of people and place form a fundamental element of all the individual chapters that make up this book, from the descriptions of the places themselves to the discussions of the manner in which people dwell in and materially inhabit them.

Walking the city

Another powerful strand in the kind of research undertaken in this book is the humble act of walking to acquire knowledge of places through our limbs. All the field research undertaken in the various chapters has involved walking in between and out of places. Knowing the city through walking it, like phenomenology in general, and platial analysis in particular, has a long history in social research, going back to Baudelaire and the work of Benjamin and his meditative wanderings and reflections on urbanism in relation to mass consumption as an emerging new way of city life in the nineteenth century (Benjamin 1973, 1979).

Benjamin, somewhat in the same spirit as Aron's conceptualisation of the apricot cocktail, was interested in exploring the city both from the small nuances and overlooked details of place, and the manner in which the past interpenetrates the present. For example, in *One Way Street*, he writes of the central obelisk in the Place de la Concorde in Paris.

> What was carved in it four thousand years ago today stands at the centre of the greatest of city squares. Had that been foretold to him – what a triumph for the pharaoh! The foremost Western cultural empire will one day bear at its centre the memorial of his rule. How does this apotheosis appear in reality? Not one among the tens of

thousands who passes by pauses: not one among the tens of thousands who pause can read the inscription. (Benjamin 1979:70)

Benjamin's perspective on the city stresses the relationship between the materiality of its built environment, personal and collective memories and the historical past. The stress is on the urban fabric as perceived, and in this respect he is close to de Certeau's and Lefebvre's notion of spaces of representation or perceived space (Lefebvre 1991).

Benjamin's aphoristic portraits of Naples, Moscow, Marseilles and Paris stress the particularity of these cities, their constant ability to surprise, rather than their spatialised sameness. He was sensitive to their auratic qualities, involving the tactile sensing of the city through the body. He was interested in the everyday processes by which flesh and stone interact and through which knowledges of the city are gained and lost. We encounter in Benjamin the figure of the *flâneur* who moves:

> ... through space and among the people with a viscosity that both enables and privileges vision... The *flâneur* possesses a power, it walks at will, freely and seemingly without purpose, but simultaneously with an inquisitive wonder and an infinite capacity to absorb the activities of the collective – often formulated as 'the crowd'. (Jenks 1995:146)

The *flâneur* acquires knowledge through being there, strolling, looking, feeling, touching, feeling, smelling. To be effective, the *flâneur* must dissolve into the crowd. He (and for Benjamin the *flâneur* was always male) is simultaneously visible and invisible. He dwells and participates within urban life as an observer, a witness of the unexpected. Wandering and losing himself in the city, he is most productive in his apparent indolence. He is a spectator of urban life. Restless and constantly wandering, he goes in search of the new experiences and spectacles the city throws up.

Walking has until recently been little discussed in either anthropology or urban sociology as a means of knowing and researching, but there is now a growing literature (Bates and Rhys-Taylor 2017; Chambers 1994; Chen 2016, chapter 4; Horowitz 2013; Ingold 2007; Ingold and Vergunst 2008; Richardson 2015; Solnit 2002; Tilley 1994, 2004, 2008, 2010, 2012; Tilley and Cameron-Daum 2017) forming another set of resources on which individual contributors draw in their accounts.

Walking is central to city life in London. It is perfectly aligned with a phenomenological position in which one takes one's body into place and with sensory scholarship. In this respect, I have put forward the notion of the 'phenomenological walk'. This is the walk of the walk.

> It is a participatory understanding produced by taking one's own body into places and landscapes and opening up one's perceptual sensibilities and experience. Such a walk always needs to start from a bracketing off of mediated representations of landscapes and places. It is an attempt to learn by describing perceptual experiences as precisely as possible as they unfold during the course of the walk. As such it unfolds in the form of a story or narrative that needs to be written as one walks. Walking and writing become synonymous acts as language and knowing are synonymous. This is simply because the act of writing slows experience down and focuses attention… So one walks in order to be able to write and one writes in order to be able to walk. (Tilley 2012: 28)

Various contributors to this book write and walk in this general spirit. Through this process of research, perspectival experience arises both from the body and, in the city, from the active material agency of the built environment in relation to it and the other people, situations and events encountered along the way. Perception is intimately related to material presences and sensations that unfold in the passage of time. Walking becomes embodied in one's being and ultimately allows a comparative understanding of places in the urban landscape. There is always sensory overload. One always has to select from it to make sense of anything, but there is no substitute for the sensing and sensed carnal body in place for which the recording technologies of vision and sound (none exist for tactile experience, bodily kinaesthetics, taste and smell) are always inadequate because of their very disembodiment. In the walk, the small intimate details of everyday life may be pieced together like so many bits of a jigsaw puzzle to provide the broader picture – the rough sleeper in the doorway of a fashionable shop, the lady carrying multiple bags, graffiti on the walls, the pollarded tree, the smell of the curry house, shop window decorations, Christmas tree lights in December, the sirens of the police car, the diesel hum of black cabs, the asphalt and the flagstones, the colour of the bricks, gleaming shafts of sunlight highlighting a tree.

Pulini's account (chapter 1) of a central London street is derived from both sitting in it on a step and observing and walking it. Yates (chapter 3) takes us on a walk from Hounslow West underground station through suburban streets of semi-detached houses to enter the housing estate that is the focus of his analysis, and then leads us in and around the estate itself. Jeevendrampillai's discussion of Surbiton (chapter 4) shows how the inhabitants make it their own through collective practices of walking. Tilley explores Holland Park through walking in and around it at different times of the day, on different days of the week, and during different seasons of the year (chapter 9).

Of course, there are other ways to experience the city: from the perspective of a bicycle (Cox 2015; Tilley and Cameron-Daum 2017, chapter 7; Vivanco 2013), from a train or a bus or a car (Adams 2001; Thrift 2010), or from a skateboard (Borden 2003). Urry has explored the general theme of mobilities as experiential modes (Urry 2007). Experiencing the city on a boat provides another alternative experiential relationship. As Malkogeorgou shows (chapter 5), a boater's experience of the city from the water is entirely different from that of those who dwell on the fixity of the land. Living on a boat affords both relative social isolation and new kinds of transitory, yet at the same time repetitive, social bonds.

The rhythms of the city

Lefebvre puts forward another perspective for understanding the practices of everyday life: the analysis of rhythms and their intersection with the biological, psychological and social aspects of dwelling (Lefebvre 2004). The notion of rhythm is one that embraces a non-linear notion of time and repetitive practices. Rhythms always depend on repetitions materialised in the space-time of places in the city. They are linear and cyclical flows and tempos that are constitutive of life. They embrace the repetitive time of the body rather than chronometric time, a strong phenomenological theme, space-time as lived through the body.

The musical analogies that Lefebvre uses – melody, harmony, rhythm – are key to understanding this approach. Melody is a sequence of notes, harmony is these notes sounding sympathetically together, rhythm is about the placement of notes and their relative lengths. The human body has its internal corporeal rhythms, and each organ has its own rhythm but is part of a spatiotemporal whole. This body in the world is the site of interaction between the biological, physiological and the social (Lefebvre 2004:81).

Rhythms link time to space in a localised time or temporalised space. The rhythm analyst thinks through his or her body not in the abstract but in the lived time-space of the body. There is always a plurality of rhythms in social life that can thus be characterised as being polyrhythmic in character, composed of diverse rhythms (Lefebvre 2004:89). The sensing and sensed body itself relates to a sensory world of rhythms, the odours of the morning and of the evening, the diurnal repetition of darkness and light, of rain and sunlight, and so on (Lefebvre 2004:21).

Looking out from a window at a junction of roads in Paris, Lefebvre discusses the multiple rhythmic characteristics of the street. These consist of the soundscape of rhythms of traffic starting and stopping at a traffic light, coupled with the stench of fumes, the flows of pedestrians walking up and down the street, the rhythms of shoppers flowing into and out of the street, in and around and among the cars at the junction, and the tourists who walk and explore the city at a different pace and time. There are the habitual repetitive rhythms of people going to and from work in the morning and the evening, of children going back and forth to school, the rhythms characterising the social life of the hours of the day and night, a weekday and a weekend, related to the repetitive passage of the seasons (Lefebvre 2004:19–26). Rhythms are thus always synaesthetic in character.

Lefebvre suggests one might best understand these rhythms from above, from the window looking down. A phenomenologist of rhythm would instead want to experience them in the street itself as part of the polyrhythmic flow. This is where rhythms are materialised in the interactions of people and things, in and through the built fabric of place: 'the crowd is a body, the body is a crowd' (Lefebvre 2004:42). The body is thus both singular and multiple. The biological rhythms of the body are linked to the day and the night and to the rhythms of capitalist production and consumption in the city.

The rhythms of the city arise from life itself, not just its immediacy but life in all of its thickness, in the multiple relations between the human and nonhuman, the corporeal and the inorganic, the phenomenal and the epiphenomenal, between the most banal and most intense of human experiences of the everyday. City rhythms orientate and direct the lives of those who dwell in them. Different places in the city have their own rhythmic intensities and order in relation to the governmentality and institutionalisation of city space, such as congestion zones and traffic rules, opening and closing times, restrictions on smell and noise, freedom of movement.

Lefebvre's rhythmanalysis does not provide a methodology for studying the urban any more than Benjamin's *flâneurie* does. Instead, it provides an orientational metaphor for understanding urban life in terms of rhythms and flows. Some of the general ideas have been taken up and developed in some recent urban studies (e.g. Chen 2016; Schlör 1998; Smith and Hetherington 2013).

Schlör (1998) discusses the night-time rhythms of Paris, Berlin and London between 1840 and 1930 and their link to the material technologies of lighting, policing, and changing normative moral codes in relation to state regulations, providing a rich set of interpretations that could be taken forward in a study of contemporary London in relation to, for example, attempts to further stimulate a night-time economy, the recent night-time running of parts of the underground system, and the relaxation of drinking hours.

Smith and Hall (2013) discuss the 24-hour city in relation to the night-time rhythms of contemporary Cardiff in relation to a range of urban patrols – those of street cleaners, the police and outreach social workers coping with the homeless – and through which street-level politics of place, time and movement are negotiated. This is a one-day snapshot of the city, and such an analysis could be considerably extended. As often as not, the rhythms of places within the city during the day are inverted during the night. They are thus composed of contrasting temporalities.

Revill (2013) links rhythm to the sonoric spaces of the railway station. Rhythms are not just about movement, they have their own repetitive soundscapes that effectively become part of the embodied relationship of people to railway terminals. One might also note here that all other kinds of sensory perceptions have their rhythmic patterns – rhythms of smell and taste, touch and visual perception.

Chen (2016) emphasises the materiality of rhythms of walking in east London: 'the assemblage constructions of pedestrians, vehicles, wind, rubbish bins, a ticketing machine, a traffic island and stairways continually weave street rhythms… traffic lights, yellow lines, parking metres, road signs and zebra crossing' (Chen 2016:75). Arranged sequentially and repetitively along the street, their materiality is in part constitutive of the rhythms of the feet and bodies along it, rhythmic agents in the process of walking. However, Chen's account of east London is not that of its contemporary street rhythms but rather a more generalised 'rhythmic' cultural history of the walking of its inhabitants, generated by considering the representational discourses of texts and films.

A number of contributors to this book incorporate a discussion of rhythms in their accounts. Pulini (chapter 1) begins her contribution with a consideration of the social rhythms of a street. Rhythms of movement back and forth along the river and canal system of north-east London form a fundamental part of the experience of living on a houseboat in Malkogeorgou's account (chapter 5). Rhythms are discussed in Tilley's account of a park that socially self-segregates itself (chapter 9). They are the centre of analysis in Young's account of a taxi rank (chapter 8).

Temporalities and the storied character of place

An obvious connection can be made between the rhythms of place, a place's embodied temporalities and stories of place. Young draws this out forcefully in his account of the storied temporal and historical characteristics of the Harrington Road taxi rank (chapter 8). Tilley (chapter 9) discusses the manner in which prestige, power and social distinction are reproduced in a London park over the *longue durée*.

Temporalities are part and parcel of place making and their construction as 'other' in relation to other places. Various cultural historical and biographical discussions and historical ethnographic accounts of cities in general and London in particular have explored the ordinary everyday life in the city in form of more embodied perspectives on the meaning and significance of place, emotions and the urban experience. Examples include Raban's *Soft City* (Raban 1974), works by Ackroyd (2000), Sennett (1992, 2006, 2018) and Campkin (2013), Marcus's apartment stories (Marcus 1999) and White's social history of a tenement block in east London, the Rothschild Buildings (White 2003). Recently, such storied historical accounts of the city have been explicitly linked to methodological practices of walking in place in the city. Back (2017) incorporates stories of place in walking the streets in east London that also play a significant role in Rhys-Taylor's account of the sensory dimensions of urban multi-culture (Rhys-Taylor 2017).

Places have their own temporalities, or their timed platial identities and meanings (Lynch 1972). This is not a simple matter of continuity and change in terms of an empty chronometric time of dates and events. Instead, the pasts of places can be considered to be, in important respects, coeval with their presents. The idea is that time is not uniform, a kind of universal measuring scale that is homogeneous and linear in character, but subjective and made up of different human temporalities: some short-, some medium-, and some very long-term indeed that intermingle and criss-cross. There is no present divorced from a past that is supposedly gone for ever.

The past is always a material presence, and we are always surrounded by things of the past that, in fact, are constitutive of our present. There are different ways in which we can conceive of the importance of cultural traditions and collective memories of the past. One form is the recall of traditions and memories that sit in the mind and is linked to individual and collective experiences of the past in the present. Another approach is to place emphasis on memories that sit in the body in the world – that is, they are embodied and do not require acts of recollection (Casey 2000; Connerton 1989; Ricoeur 2004). The memories instead involve the manner in which bodies engage with the materiality of landscapes, places and things. Such bodily memories borne out of bodily experiences transcend time and directly link past and present through the medium of embodied interactions, producing an active habitual immanence mediating relationships between people and things and places.

The notion of time informing the individual chapters in this book is phenomenologically understood as *temporality*, the times of bodies, sensual relations and human experience. This time of the body and of intersubjective material relations is a time of the self and a time of others, a lived time and one of the multiple times of places. The temporality of social life, produced in concrete practices that actively produce space-time rather than taking place in space and in time, has been stressed by a number of anthropologists (Bourdieu 1977; Hirsch and Stewart 2005; Munn 1992; Tilley 2017). Time has thus been understood as fluid and in flux, and multiple rather than singular in character.

Bergson (1991) influentially stressed time as *la durée* or duration. The carnal human body exists in time; it fuses through its material being past, present and future, which interpenetrate each other. The body experiences a flux of sensations in time, linking matter to memory. How we understand the world therefore links matter to memory. Our understanding is embedded in the manner in which we encounter and remember the world through our embodied experience of it. Time is embodied through memories. These memories may either be consciously recalled or a product of inscribed corporeality and habit (Bergson 1991:81–2). Through the moving corporeal body, past and present interpenetrate each other and lead to the future. Both duration and simultaneity constitute the self. Through the body the present passes at the same time as it is present. The paradox is that the past becomes contemporary with, or is in the same time as, the present that it once was part of. Different times can coexist with each other; some are deep and are of a very long-term nature, others are much shallower and of shorter duration.

In the ordinary life of the street, the past has an active and performative immanence. Pulini (chapter 1) in her discussion shows, in relation to the social history of a street for over 100 years, that while radical changes have occurred in its social composition and use these are entangled with long-term continuities in the social characteristics of this place. One change was the early development of boarding houses, transforming individual family dwellings to those with multiple occupants.

A second was the overwhelmingly female social composition of the street, initially in terms of servants servicing the family dwellings, later in women who worked in the surrounding shops and service sectors. A third was the dominance of one-person households. These significantly structure an understanding of the street today. In Heideggerian terms, buildings are prerequisites for dwelling, and some of the dwellings in the street are effectively in the same time as the past but exist in the present. In other words, the street is characterised by multiple temporalities. It does not just exist in one time, in one place.

Communities

One recurrent theme that occurs in some of the accounts in both sections of the book concerns the question of communities in place and the manner in which they are realised in everyday life. This is one of the most difficult and fractured topics in the entire literature on urban culture. A large number of contemporary writers agree that old traditional notions of community have been significantly eroded, and sometimes have vanished entirely, in the modern city. This is the general theme of Augé's notion of non-places, discussed above. For Bauman (2000), a new world has arisen characterised by fragile and ephemeral social relationships linked to migration and displacement, globalisation and transnational and cosmopolitan connections and senses of belonging enabled by the new communication media in the fabric of daily life. In an era of risk and uncertainty people no longer know who or what they are or how to live. Giddens links this theme to the evacuation of tradition in our 'late modernity' (Giddens 1994). Once we start asking identity questions with regard to who we are, how we should relate to others and how to live, we have lost all that was previously important in identity formation: tradition and the routinisation of that tradition in daily life. We increasingly live in an atomised 'land of strangers' in which care and concern for others has all but vanished (Amin 2012).

In relation to the city, Amin (2012) explores, conceptually at least, the manner in which 'the many local separations, dispersed geographies of attachment and qualified proximities between strangers that characterise modern urban living make it difficult to build urban commons based on care for the other' (Amin 2012:78). His solution is to systematically construct a politics of togetherness, making connections and dependencies between people visible and so hopefully revealing the value of a shared and functioning commons. But Amin's conceptualisation is not based on any first-hand evidence. It remains just an assertion.

Amin (2012) argues that to promote an ethics of the city (a theme also explored by Sennett 2018) we need to include consideration of the habituated experiences of the city, between prosaic usage of places and public articulation of what this adds to personal and collective life. This requires systematic proliferation of:

> ... the sites of shared living through which a dispersed sense of the plural communal can emerge... the associations, clubs, meeting places, friendship networks, workplaces and spaces of learning that fill cities, where habits of being with others and in a common space... take shape. They include the physical spaces – streets, retail spaces, libraries, parks, buildings, public services and collective institutions [and]... the city's public sphere – symbolic, cultural discursive and political. (Amin 2012:79)

But all these somewhat utopian assertions that one can somehow socially engineer a new kind of city that enhances the social lives of its inhabitants should surely be predicated on a grounded in-depth knowledge of such places and whether they do indeed produce urban conviviality or instead, frequently, a contested landscape infused by a politics of exclusion, privilege and hierarchy (see chapter 9 of this book).

Combining Bourdieu's concepts of habitus and social field, Savage and colleagues have proposed a notion of 'elective belonging' to characterise neighbourhoods (Savage, Bagnall and Longhurst 2005). This is intended to resolve two poles in a consideration of urban communities mentioned above: roots and routes, stasis and mobility. They argue that residential place is chosen in relation to life trajectories of individuals. The fixity of place counterbalances global flows by providing 'new kinds of solidarities among people who choose to live in particular places' (Savage, Bagnall and Longhurst 2005:53). People moving into a neighbourhood both adopt it and adapt to it. Thus the 'aura' or 'aesthetics' of the place are more important than any traditional notion of community belonging and interaction between people. The neighbourhood can thus become an arena in which class distinctions can be marked, a form of symbolic capital in which patterns of inequality are materially marked out.

Butler has related this to changing residential patterns of the middle classes (Butler 2007), while Watt uses the term 'selective belonging' in both urban and suburban places to refer to more fine-grained distinctions within neighbourhoods (Watt 2010, 2011).The suburbs as much as the inner city are increasingly becoming places of migratory flows, places in between characterised by multiple senses of belonging (Watt and Smets 2014).

The more general theme here is of communities and places as being process, rather than in terms of stable and enduring relationships between friends, family and neighbours, and places themselves as multiple and relational. Jones and Jackson describe the particular type of belonging where 'people experience different places at different times or several places at once, as "cosmopolitan belonging"' (Jones and Jackson 2014a:5). Again, what is missing in these considerations of what community might mean to the residents of the contemporary city is a consideration of the materiality of these symbolic practices and narratives, elective and selective belongings in place. They are primarily conceptualised as being a matter of mind rather than body, a fragmentary immaterial sharing of an imagined sense of belonging.

Blokland's fine-grained ethnography of three adjacent areas of the Hillesluis neighbourhood in Rotterdam (Blokland 2003) provides, in contrast, an excellent ethnographic account of grounded research in an urban community in transition. Blokland begins her account with a fictional walk along the streets as they were in 1995 (Blokland 2003:28ff.), discussing their history, layout and the character of the built architecture, the gardens of some of the houses, whether they are dilapidated or renovated, and so on. The picture painted is of a wide variety of building styles and arrangements of public space. The focus is on community in relation to a distinct and bounded place in the built environment.

Following Hannerz (1980), Blokland discusses social roles in relation to age structure, and the life cycle and ethnicity in relation to public space. She then analyses personal networks, intimate bonds between family, friends, neighbours and colleagues, networks of social relations, community understood in terms of interpersonal relations and whether these are localised or extent far beyond the limits of the place as physically defined. Her focus then shifts to the manner in which people define themselves and others in terms of transactions, attachments and personal bonds – what community affiliations people have or do not have. Blokland notes that over time, from the 1920s, social changes in Hillesluis have led 'less to the loss of communities than to privatisation in which familiarity in the neighbourhood progressively loses its significance... [It] no longer offers a framework for reference groups and social distinctions' (Blokland 2003:89). Interdependencies between people become increasingly anonymous.

Four general patterns emerged in the way in which people understood themselves in relation to their neighbourhoods: people who associated no particular significance in relation to place; people who just used the neighbourhood for practical purposes; people who focused on symbolic neighbourhood use, largely elderly with an emotional involvement with the place mentioned in their stories; and those who associated living there with a particular lifestyle and patterns of consumption (Blokland 2003:157). The strongest local orientation was among peer groups, largely displacing the historical role of the family that had previously been all important:

> … the shopping street, the community centre where they played bingo and the pavement in front of their doorsteps were the peer group's socialising sites in the built environment. Since the peer group members considered visiting each other's homes inappropriate they did much of their socialising on the street. The street thus became "their" street and the square "their square"… Embedded rituals had evolved at the locations where they experienced events together. The built environment reminded them of these events. (Blokland 2003:159)

Place and locality were extremely significant to them and were expressed in terms of distinctions between 'us' and 'them'.

Blokland (2003) suggests that the community she studied was characterised both by binding and divisive attitudes (Blokland 2003:86). These were related to politics, clashes of religious values and practices (Protestants versus Catholics), and ethnicity in relation to a recent influx of immigrants from Turkey, Surinam and Morocco. In the new politics of place, the white Dutch minority (constituting now only a third of the population) still dominated culturally, drawing on the past and a nostalgic and selective remembering of that past to assert their own identity and rights to the place. In the words of one of her informants: 'we established Hillesluisians who have lived here our whole lives and *the rightful owners of this neighbourhood*, had a better time together when it was just us here. You newcomers… couldn't possibly have known how cosy it was here' (Blokland 2003:199; emphasis in original).

Blokland's general conclusions are that community today is to be best understood as a form of social imagination that is realised in urban practices producing shared symbolic practices and narratives: 'they exist as impressions of thinking and feeling that "we belong together" and as everyday social practices in which we express with whom we belong and where we include others with "us", or in fact exclude them from "us"' (Blokland 2003:209). What community may be supposed to be can be interpreted in any number of different ways by the individuals involved.

Imagined communities and relational belonging

Exploring the way communities imagine themselves further, in a later book Blokland argues that in the contemporary city human affiliations are made up by a complex web of ties – social networks, durable engagements, fluid encounters, bonds, attachments and interdependencies. These create 'relational settings of belonging' between people (Blokland 2017:86). Sociologically, a connection between community and place does not have to be made any more. She examines this in terms of poles of a continuum between public and private, anonymous and intimate relations (Blokland 2017:89). Practices of belonging do not necessarily involve any community, nor may such belonging contribute to it: 'community is not local; community is not a matter of personal networks either; and we can experience belonging on very many scales' (Blokland 2017:165). Community has then vanished in this account to be replaced by a sense of belonging that may be experienced to a greater or lesser degree by different individuals and who they identify with and the manner in which they think they belong. Essentially, this is a matter of choice, a personal option. In symbolic practices of belonging, communities become imagined entities. It should be noted that Blokland's later book is not based on any ethnography, but is rather theorised in relation to recent sociological literature, an imagining of what the real might be like for people and groups. Her new 'informants' with regard to community and place in the city are not people, but the writings and representations of other urban sociologists.

It is notable, in this respect, that the surviving multicultural inhabitants of the Grenfell Tower disaster in west London clearly felt a very strong sense of identification and place attachment to a specific place and locality, so much so that most still remained in temporary or hotel accommodation a year later because they did not wish to be rehoused in another place and area of the city. One of Blokland's informants in Hillesluis told her 'everybody has to live somewhere' (Blokland 2003:58). For those living in the tower, it was their home and that was precisely why the fire was so devastating and traumatic. The fire not only wiped away lives but destroyed homes and the personal and social memories connected with the material things with which these people lived out their lives. The inhabitants of Grenfell Tower did not conceive of themselves of living in an anonymous world of global flows and diffuse fluid urban belongings, decentred from place. They did not think that they were living among Amin's land of strangers, but still in terms of family, friends and neighbours. Are we to suggest that they are deluded? Have they no understanding, or a false consciousness of their own lives? There appears to be a systematic mismatch between many academic accounts of what urban communities have become today and how ordinary people think.

The protests following the fire, outside the town hall, and subsequently, essentially involved the objectification of identity politics in the face of adversity. This brought out a positive evaluation and sense of community, of living together in a neighbourhood, that was normally lived through their bodily routines and everyday practices rather than verbally expressed. It involved an attachment to others that they felt were like themselves. The protestors in opposition to a right-wing Conservative council and its neo-liberal policies of outsourcing and privatisation were firstly saying that those who died did so because they were poor, but also that those who survived had nothing more than the clothes they stood up in. In the immediate aftermath of the fire, volunteers amassed a huge assemblage of things for redistribution. This was not just about a functional need for things. It was rather an expression of the comfort the things themselves would provide as people began to rebuild their lives.

Constructing place and community

Place identities are always fragile. They require active production and reproduction through continuous situated social acts that produce subjects and moralities. Places are not given and static but in the process of being and becoming. Neighbourhoods are contexts for the production of local subjects: 'existing places and spaces, within a historically produced spatiotemporal neighbourhood and with a series of localised rituals, social categories, expert practitioners, and informed audiences, are required in order for new members… to be made temporary or permanent subjects' (Appadurai 1996:185).

It was to the London suburbs that the middle classes increasingly moved post World War 1, and, following that, back into the inner city from the 1960s, resulting in its gentrification. The suburbs were a product of both planning and speculation linked to the extension of transport systems, principally the underground in the north of the city. The suburbs promised and were represented as a kind of pastoral and rural ideal, allowing both easy access to and escape from the inner city to live in a calm green and leafy place (see Matless 1998:32ff. for an excellent historical discussion of this and the sexualised 'hermaphrodite' qualities of suburbia).

In his account of Surbiton in chapter 4, Jeevendrampillai explodes the standard representational myth of the surburb as a place that is boring, conservative and conformist in terms of the manner in which people live their lives, coupled with the uniformity of their dwellings and lifestyles, the 'desperate housewives' territory of the media, film and some academic writing. The suburbs as represented become endless and relentless plots of houses, each an individual dream, but each the same as the others. Relph, for example, tells us that the office blocks of the inner city are:

> ... reoccupied daily by armies of clone-like organisation men and women, issuing from the suburban blandscape wherein lives a race of uniformly bland suburbanites, striving to indulge their materialist tendencies in the latest model of a video-recorder, a package tour to Spain, or, at the very least, in the ineffable sameness of the umpteen-billioneth hamburger. (Relph 1981:13)

The surburban dweller in this account is essentially a clone living in a uniform flat-scape with no sense of belonging. This fear and critique of a homogenised world has haunted much urban thought. But when we talk to people and observe their place-making activities, an entirely different picture emerges. The suburbs when we examine them closely enough prove to be every bit as vibrant and architecturally differentiated as the inner city, each with its own character and sense of place.

The public ritualisation and objectification of identities in the form of public parades, spectacles, performances and practices is a common theme in the anthropological literature on place. People reveal themselves to themselves and rethink themselves in the process (e.g. Cohen 2013; Guss 2000).

Jeevendrampillai discusses the manner in which local people celebrate their relationship to the south London suburb of Surbiton through rituals and parades of urban identity construction in a celebration of the distinctiveness of this place drawing on and reinterpreting the historical past in the process. The material sensuousness of the suburbs offers a rich set of stories for the construction of place. These invert the myth of the soulless suburb lacking in any real identity of its own and equivalent to any other. The 'Seethingers' of Surbiton actively rework symbols and histories of place into new stories and materialise these stories in events and parades to construct a vibrant sense of place and neighbourhood through which community identity and meaning are created. Humour and irony, entirely overlooked in urban studies, are part of this. This form of the active creation of suburbia is by no means uncommon or unusual in London. For example, the inhabitants of Walthamstow and South Norwood perform similar work in the construction of their suburbs (see their 'unofficial tourist boards': http://www.walthamstowtourism.co.uk and https://southnorwoodtouristboard.com).

Households and streets

Miller has argued in relation to the biographies of the inhabitants of the south London street that he studied with regard to their home possessions (Miller 2009) that the street was essentially a series of unrelated households, so a focus on the individual was the only way to understand the lives of its householders. This work arose from a dissatisfaction with the manner in which the social sciences try to treat people as 'representative' tokens of broader social categories in terms of their gender, ethnicity, nationality and social class. Instead, Miller writes that:

> These households were radically unconnected with either community or neighbourhood. But, apart from some older isolated males, there was no particular sense of alienation or anomie; both presupposed by holistic traditions of social analysis as conditions which follow in the absence of these wider relationships of belonging. (Miller 2009:7)

Miller adds that the inhabitants of the street did not identify either with living in London or the UK. Only 23 per cent of the inhabitants of the 100 households studied were born in London. Many households consisted of people from entirely different backgrounds and nationalities; community did not exist. However, what Miller has missed out and did not consider was the materiality of the street itself and its location in a neighbourhood and how this can be part of an embodied construction of identity and community that becomes habituated, leading to a feeling of being at home, something that by its very nature is not usually verbally expressed.

Pulini (chapter 1) argues that you do not need to know someone's name or talk to them in the street or attend community meetings to establish a sense of a shared identity in place. The whole process is far more subtle than that. It involves the repetitions and rhythms of life as lived, recognising the faces of others that live in the street, the material characteristics of the house doors, the multiple door bells of the flats on the outside, the metal railings and the basements, the birch trees on the street corner, regularly visiting the shops in the neighbourhood in the provisioning of the household, a shared soundscape and smell-scape, looking out from the windows of your flat and seeing sisters performing pedicure on the balcony opposite, the changing diurnal cycles of light and shade and darkness and the manner in which the rhythms of daily life change at the end of the working week. All these and other materialised realities create a sense of social being and belonging to place. People's relationships to their streets are materially grounded in these ways and they are not part of some grand scheme or design. They arise from life itself.

The street discussed by Pulini (chapter 1) in the London Royal Borough of Kensington and Chelsea is well within a 10-minute walking distance of Kensington Palace. This is an area of London that has the most desirable postcode (W8). It is consistently characterised in the sociological literature on class as being the heartland 'territory' of the super-rich (Savage et al. 2015; Webber and Burrows 2015), who have glitzy and glamorous lifestyles, spending money like water. This is the clichéd image of the place that occurs over and over again in texts and is derived from the aggregate social statistics and consumer survey data. Compared with the poorer neighbourhoods of east London that have been extensively studied over a 30-year period (Butler and Hamnett 2011), this area of the city has been ignored by social researchers until very recently. Elite areas of the city were apparently not worth studying, as their social composition could more or less be taken for granted.

Pulini's detailed examination of the residential structure of the street, undertaken on the ground, reveals a far more complex pattern of residential use in which some of those who dwell there are living on or just above the minimum wage in small barely furnished single rooms and using communal toilets and washing facilities.

Writing the city

Phenomenological accounts, based as they are on participatory lived experience among people, inevitably result in a representation in text. The accounts try to say the unsaid, pick up on the habitual routinised relations of people to place and to the materiality of the urban world, the manner in which people in their daily lives relate to the affordances and constraints of urban life. The 'deep hanging out' (Geertz 2000:107) of participant observation needs to be realised in the form of richly nuanced description. Inadequate as our language remains, we must attempt to put into words the city as felt, a structure of feeling and emotion, delight and disgust, fear and loathing, contest and conflict, or a sense of well-being and relative harmony. This means exploring the tropic or metaphoric character of language to communicate meaning, rather than a dull or deadened literalism (Gibbs 1994; Lakoff and Johnson 1990; Tilley 1999) to link, as Merleau-Ponty puts it, the flesh of our bodies to the flesh of the world (Merleau-Ponty 1968:142). This is the manner in which we both touch and are simultaneously touched by the things around us – touched by the feel of things, the sight of things, their smell and taste, their sounds, their surfaces, colours and textures and through the kinaesthetic of our bodies – that are always in place.

The language used thus flows from an embodied relation to place. In the bulk of academic literature, it is quite striking how disembodied written landscapes and places become as textual representations. This is in part because much that is written about the city is not only written on paper, it is principally derived from paper, from maps, paintings, archives, texts or alternatively from highly structured and framed representations of photographic images and in film. All the individual authors in this book make a return to the real an essential part of their studies – places as lived, rather than representations of them.

There has been a long tradition of writing and representing the city in a more evocative manner. There is much to be learned here from the literary styles of novelists and journalists and their representations of place in text. The surrealists and situationists attempted to grasp the city through various non-conventional mappings, artistic and poetic attempts to evoke and rethink the urban (McDonough 2009) leading on to more recent attempts to produce psychogeographies of emotions, thought and feeling (Coverley 2006; Richardson 2015; Self 2007; Sinclair 2003a, 2003b, 2009).

Sinclair's best writings are about Hackney (2009), where he has himself lived and walked since 1968. He provides a vivid and, in many ways, extraordinary perspective on the borough, written and researched for over a decade. The book is part fact, part fiction, part memory work by himself and those he talked to. The central theme is the story of Sinclair's life in Hackney from the late 1960s, combining observations, events, personal reminiscences and taped interviews. He talks and listens to local radicals and gentrifiers, elderly Jews, ex-ravers and previous residents who have moved away, among others. From the stories of others and his own personal involvement – from living in a communal house, to labouring jobs, to dealing in secondhand books, to becoming a popular author – he creates an alternative fragmented and engaging social history of place, charting its pubs, street markets, petty crime, schools, supermarkets, barber's shops, bus routes and much more. Sinclair is a master of observational detail, which is evocatively written:

> The supermarket had a space platform glow. WE'RE open 24 HOURS: a thorium luminescence… Malformed pigeons, feathers the colour of sodden bog paper, mobbed the spiked TESCO sign, scratching their parasites on anti bird spikes. The canted roof was slick with droppings. Everybody parked here, it was free and the rest of Hackney was impossible, residents only: patrolled, taxed, clamped, dragged away, crushed. Tesco tried barriers, but these were rammed, dismantled. They tried uniformed patrols, but that only stepped up paranoid levels… The crunching of metal, shivering of glass. Alarms trilling at disputed parking bays… A bright place in the Hackney night of blind walkers who decorate privet hedges with cans of Foster's and Red Bull. White plastic forks and spoons like the regurgitated bones of extinct fish. (Sinclair 2009:237–8)

Part of the narrative involves Hackney's transformation from decaying neighbourhood in industrial decline to its current gentrifying state. If you want to learn about Hackney through Sinclair's eyes and in terms of his social networks, this is an extraordinary book. Sinclair's accounts and discussions are personalised and perhaps ultimately, one might suggest, narcissistic narratives. They frequently resonate with a nostalgia for the traces of a lost past in the contemporary city (see Bonnett 2009 for a discussion of this). This is also a prevalent theme in other writings about material and social change concerned with the gentrification of places and neighbourhoods (see, e.g., Jacobs 1961 and discussions in Zukin 2010). On the other hand, the book is a major contribution to the understanding of this place. Place matters to Sinclair, and his knowledge of the place is through his involvement in it, living it, breathing its air, smelling its vapours.

A gap between words and things, people and texts can in fact only be bridged by the poetic and evocative use of language, involving what Geertz refers to as the 'thick description' of the ethnographic text (Geertz 1973). Such descriptions aim to clarify, illuminate and through their inevitably selective nature (no descriptions can ever be exhaustive) perform a process of conceptual analysis. Arising from the real, they inevitably re-describe it from a point of view, an orientation, an intervention.

This book consists of a series of platial stories and material accounts of London. The contributions deliberately do not start with a theory to apply, a methodology to be followed, or a series of research objectives to be fulfilled, with answers provided in the conclusions, in the standard academic mode. This entire apparatus puts research into a straitjacket, moulding its contours and dooming its interpretative creativity and veracity from the outset.

The contributors start their accounts instead by describing the particular place under discussion, asking a deceptively simple question: what kind of place is this? The answers provided are as varied as the places described. These introductory descriptions of place have the purpose of attempting to evoke something of their character, 'aura' and feel in text. Above all, what is being emphasised in these accounts is the sensuous materiality of these places, whether it be the concrete A-frame structure of the Brunswick Centre, a hotel and a taxi rank on the Harrington Road, the green and wooded space of Holland Park, the interior and exterior spaces of Smithfield and Bermondsey markets, or graffiti and street art in Shoreditch. This is another way of telling, going against the grain of standard academic accounts.

To take one example from the book, Wilson's evocative account of Smithfield meat market (chapter 6) begins with the manner in which the carcass of a lamb is expertly cut in three minutes. She describes the relationship between knife and bone and wooden cutting board, the visceral sound of the work, and the embodied movements of the cutters, who do not need to think about what they do. She then describes the crumbling structure of the market itself, its buildings and its incongruous juxtaposition in relation to the surrounding fabric of the built environment. It is a market of the night, characterised by whiteness and the harshness of fluorescent light, a bitter coldness, the constant hum of the refrigeration units, a raucous chorus of lorries and vans, trolleys, thuds of cleavers on meat and bone, the all-pervading smell of flesh and blood and offal. Still and silent during the day, when the surrounding commercial buildings come alive, it inverts the normal rhythms of urban life.

Structure of the book and scales of analysis

The particular places in London discussed are shown in Figure 0.1.

The book is divided into two parts. The first part considers the domestic and residential social sphere at different scales of analysis.

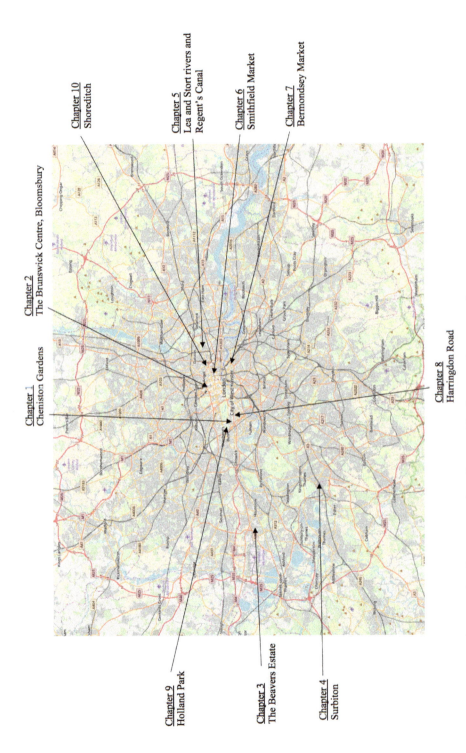

Fig. 0.1 Map showing the places in London discussed in the text. Source: author

Taking a London street as a place for study is exemplified by Miller's anthropological studies of shopping for things to provision home and household (Miller 1998b) and of the manner in which people objectify their identities, memories and social relationships in their homes in relation to material things, revealing the significance of material forms for understanding the manner in which ordinary people construct through the medium of the things themselves meaning and significance for their lives (Miller 2008). Pulini (chapter 1) considers one residential street in west central London consisting of brick-built, late nineteenth-century terraced family houses that have subsequently been converted into flats and altered and haphazardly extended beyond recognition of the original architectural scheme at the back.

Melhuish (chapter 2) considers the modernist and 'brutalist' architecture of the Brunswick Centre, also in central London – a huge tiered concrete and glass structure consisting of streets in the sky subdivided into 600 flats dating back to the 1970s, originally designed to provide social housing.

Yates (chapter 3) discusses another social housing estate, in Hounslow on the western suburban periphery of the city, built of prefabricated concrete blocks and also completed in the early 1970s, but radically different in plan and design, consisting of low-rise grey buildings subdivided into flats, with walkways on the upper levels and flats with small gardens on the ground floor. The central theme here is social isolation and the effects that are created by this isolation, although ironically the estate is situated right next to the global hub of Heathrow Airport.

Jeevendrampillai's paper (chapter 4) discusses Surbiton, another suburb, but in south London.

In these studies, we move from place considered at the level of a single street to increasingly larger scales of platial analysis. All these studies consider the manner in which the material fabric of these very different architectural places becomes embodied in quite distinct ways as part of everyday life. In the suburbs of Hounslow and Surbiton, the experience of the city and its places and the affordances and experiences it offers are of a very different character to those of the people who live in the city's centre.

Malkogeorgou's study (chapter 5), by contrast, concerns itself with the everyday life of people who live on the water rather than the land, in a floating 'linear village' of houseboats, each moored for two weeks and then moving from one place to another along the canal and river systems of north-east London. The inhabitants of these boats, people who are always on the move, have a very different platial relationship, both to the city itself and to where they temporarily live. Their essentially migrational relationship to the city, quite literally going with the flow, contrasts in significant ways to the relationship to the city of those whose identities are fixed on the land.

All the chapters in part I explore relations between local communities and the places discussed above. The chapters in part II of the book consider a variety of different kinds of places in the public sphere: markets, a park, a taxi rank and gentrified streets replete with graffiti and street art. These places in the city are discussed below.

Markets

Markets form the focus of the chapters by Wilson and Yates in part II of the book. Wilson (chapter 6) and Yates (chapter 7) discuss two very different kinds of meeting place, both markets in the centre of the city: Smithfield Meat Market and Bermondsey Antiques Market. London is well known for both the diversity and ubiquity of its markets, from general street markets to those with specialised commercial niches. Both the markets considered are specialist in character: London's largest wholesale meat market, and Bermondsey, one of the principal antiques markets of the city. Both are currently under threat and operate under the spectre of redevelopment. They have become in different ways sites of resistance related to their own histories.

The dominant perspective on markets in the literature is rather narrow, and markets are routinely regarded as primarily economic institutions. Discussions are usually related to a distinction between the physical marketplace itself, where goods are bought and sold, and market principles of supply and demand (Applbaum 2005). Markets have become today increasingly networked in the form of global commodity chains or the links through which a product passes and the manner in which it is fabricated, distributed and marketed along the way, between sites of production and consumption. Mintz (1986) and Roseberry (1996) provide excellent case studies. Markets have become more broadly conceptualised in terms of transnational 'ethnoscapes', 'technoscapes', 'finanscapes', 'mediascapes', 'ideoscapes' and transnational trade flows (Appadurai 1996). In this perspective, place becomes of little interest and all the emphasis is put on the fluidity of exchange.

These are not the kinds of general issues discussed by Wilson and Yates. They instead follow an alternative anthropological and ethnographic perspective in understanding markets as distinct places linked to the identities and practices of those who trade in these markets and those who use them, social relationships among and between market traders and customers, and histories of markets in particular places (see Bestor 2004; Geertz 1979; Mayol 1998:107ff.; Richardson 2003; Rhys-Taylor 2013; Stoller 1997, chapter 5; Watson and Studdert 2006). The issues of interest here go beyond these social relationships to the material characteristics of what is being sold and how this impacts on those who work in and visit the markets. This involves the physical infrastructure of the marketplace itself, its relationship to the surrounding area, the manner in which goods are displayed and presented to give them their own aura or material aesthetic, the character of the market stalls and shops themselves and the spaces in between them, and the sensory environment of the market.

Bestor's analysis of Tsukiji, the world's largest fish market, exemplifies this alternative perspective well. He discusses Tsukiji as a focal point for global commodity chains and as a central node in global seafood, but more importantly in terms of social and material relationships (Bestor 2004). This involves consideration of Tsukiji's complex social institutions, the everyday reproduction of Japanese cultural practices within it, the relationship of the market to the city and in terms of its sensuous qualities, the sights and sounds and smells, tastes and textures of the market itself in which fish are transformed into food and meanings created. Bestor's rich discussion of the market is punctuated with details such as these.

> Eels wriggle in plastic buckets; a flotilla of sea bass stare bleakly from their tank; live shrimps and crabs kick tiny showers of sawdust onto stall floors; mussels and clams spill across wide trays as if the tide had just exposed them; tubs of salted fish roe glitter. (Bestor 2004:10)
>
> Merchandise spills out from the tiny stalls into the aisles… Passage is difficult and a leisurely stroll impossible. Buyers lugging square wicker baskets may temporarily block an aisle while they make a purchase, but they are politely yet impatiently pushed aside by other buyers… An old woman with a rectangular bamboo basket slung across her bent back selects miniscule amounts of shrimps, octopus, mackerel and tuna for her tiny retail shop on a backstreet downtown residential neighbourhood. (Bestor 2004:81)

This study of the fish market from the bottom up significantly contributes to an understanding of both Tokyo and the global fish trade from such material details and discussions of the social identities of those who work in this place, in a manner that more abstracted top-down discussions fail to do. From the prism of a microcosm of the market, we can better reflect on the macro-economics of the global market for fish and understand it better in the process.

Favero's account of the competing sensuous cacophony of the Japath street market in central New Delhi, its traders, customers, tourists and visitors, similarly approaches general issues of globalisation, place and identity. The starting point is a layered phenomenological description of the material and sensory characteristics of the place. The market, as depicted, is pastiche. It now apparently lacks any cultural distinctiveness or local or national authenticity. As a result of commercialism and deterritorialisation, it thus becomes a kind of 'non-place' in that respect. However, Favero explains that contrary to what might be thought:

> In a market where global and local, tradition and modernity, past and present merge and blur the boundaries that separate them, is an arena for understanding the importance of imagination in everyday life. It offers a window on India's active production of imaginings about the 'West' in relation to its own history. (Favero 2003:574)

Wilson, in this volume (chapter 6), discusses issues of identity politics in relation to the male, predominantly white working-class social environment of the Smithfield Meat Market in central London. The market workers are people who cannot afford to live in the city but migrate to their place of work during the night. Wilson discusses how those who work in the market conceptualise themselves in opposition to their surroundings, the authority of the City of London and its regulatory activities, to people who do not eat meat, and to the real and imagined history of the market itself as a place and in its connections with slaughtering and burnings and executions, industries and activities that historically could not take place within the perimeter of the old city walls.

Strong bonds occur between those who work in Smithfield Meat Market. The workers conceive of themselves as a social body with a shared identity or fictive kinship transcending family ties, in which the market is their primary home, with their tools extensions of their bodies. Wilson shows how body, work and the building are co-constitutive of the social body of the market workers. The market workers are initiated into the place, married to it in arcane ceremonies of place that are pervaded by a sense of the carnivalesque and mockery, combining disorder and violence, comedy and humour.

Yates's account of the Bermondsey Antiques Market (chapter 7) shows how the market actively constructs the meanings of the things themselves in the context of a particular institutional framework. Selling antiques is understood in terms of a social network whose primary characteristic involves the active selection and representation of both people and things as having value within the particular market context itself. The place – the market – co-presences things of value in relation to valued persons.

Anthropological studies of value show over and over again how value is a relative concept, defined and redefined by local communities, each having its own cosmology and type of value. Things considered valuable in one context may have little or no value for people in another (e.g. Appadurai 1986; Graeber 2001; Gregory 1982; Munn 1986). Most things of value to people today, in a market economy, in their everyday lives, are valuable precisely because they have no price – they are too valuable to be priced, and wealth and notions of what is *of value* are conceptually separated. This is because most cultural values are drawn from social relationships and personal experiences, notions of what makes a good life, and not from general economistic mental abstractions in which value is to be solely understood in terms of the kind of value created by exchange. Value instead relates to sentiment, thought and feeling, constituted relationally through living and experiencing the world with others. Value relates to the biographies of people and the biographies of things that are always entangled (Hoskins 1998, 2006; Kopytoff 1986). The production of commodities is part of a cultural process; they are marked as being a certain kind of thing in relation to social networks that create value in distinctive ways through systems of classification and practical taxonomies. Bestor's study of the Tsukiji fish market exemplifies this point forcefully (Bestor 2004). Things, like people, have life trajectories relating to their production, exchange, consumption, discard use and reuse. Rubbish can be turned into a valuable thing overnight.

Yates discusses this selective and biographical construction of value in the context of the antique market in relation to the selection of the traders in it and the relationship between the traders themselves and the things that they value and sell. Regular buyers purchase antiques in the market because of the people there rather than the goods themselves. Relationships of trust are fundamental to this; people buy from people, and the things themselves are intermediaries in this social relationship that acquire value as part of this process.

A taxi rank

Young (chapter 8) discusses a completely different kind of public place – a taxi rank on the Harrington Road in central London. He shows how the flows of people and vehicles become an integral part of the character of this place, which has its own rhythmical sensory characteristics and differing diurnal rhythms of movement and flow and pause. Young discusses the manner in which these flows are intimately related to much broader socio-economic and political issues. One of these is the increasing use of digital technologies and the increasingly fraught and conflictual relationship between officially sanctioned and regulated black-cab taxi drivers and those driving Uber taxis. Another is a sense of an erosion of community, the loss of a way of life and conviviality among cab drivers supporting each other so that they can collectively make a living. This change extends to affecting the cab drivers' pride in what they do – the erosion of the significance of their three-year training and of their encyclopaedic knowledge of the city streets and the best routes to follow according to the day of the week and the time of day, made increasingly redundant by satellite navigation technologies.

The life and community of black-cab drivers is threatened by fragmentation, new technologies, a breakdown in regulation and cut-throat unwelcome competition undercutting wages. Following Lefebvre's consistent linkage of rhythms to the politics of identity, Young connects the issues to wider features of capitalism and the manner in which these are the politics of place on the Harrington Road. The Uber app, technology itself, erodes the significance of the taxi rank, for it is possible to call for a taxi anywhere and everywhere in the city without even needing the simple ritual of raising a hand. Young discusses how in reality both black-cab and Uber drivers share a similar predicament, both struggling with a precarious way of life and low wages. They are both part of a neoliberal political economy, replacing specialist by unqualified labour, and institutionalising distinctions between the working classes, splintering them and creating competition between similar socio-economic groups, providing a distraction from the injustices that capitalism itself creates.

Parks

London is famous for its parks, garden squares and green spaces. It is now being marketed and rebranded not as a city with parks but as a city *within* a park. The Ordnance Survey (the mapping agency of the UK) published, in October 2017, a new map showing over 3,000 parks, woodlands, playing fields, woodlands, city farms, rivers and canals, as part of the launch of National Park City, which aims to re-frame London 'as a connected and natural landscape' (see https://www.ordnancesurvey.co.uk/blog/2017/10/beautiful-new-map-london-created-celebrate-outdoors). Such a green city will encourage tourists and foreign investors and make Londoners care for and appreciate their city and encourage norms of public civility.

Parks have long been regarded as ameliorating city life, the green lungs of the city. Victoria Park in Hackney was the first purpose-built public park, opened in 1845 and created as a project aimed at morally uplifting the working poor of London's East End. Public parks in the city have since been regarded as meeting places for different social classes and ethnicities to interact or at the very least be co-present in the same place. In the city, parks provide major sites for childhood socialisation. Almost every child has fond memories of being taken to a park and playing in a park, and almost all parks have their playgrounds. They are places to meet other people, to picnic, to relax and stroll, and learn about 'nature' and horticulture. Most, apart from those in central inner London, are used almost entirely by local communities and play an important role in establishing and maintaining social bonds between those who live in their vicinity. Some, like Holland Park, discussed by Tilley (chapter 9) have now become informal cemeteries for remembering the dead, with their numerous inscribed benches and signs beneath trees. They provide an entirely different sensory environment in the city, and with their cafes and bandstands and concerts are places of entertainment. These large open green spaces are of fundamental significance for dog walkers, for health and well-being (green therapy) and for keeping fit in the city. Besides these positive aspects, they may also be places to be feared and avoided by different ethnic and marginalised groups and by others, especially women, during the night and sometimes in daylight (see Branson (1978) for a personal account of some north London parks, and Elborough (2016) for a recent popular history). It is hard to overestimate the significance of parks as prisms for understanding everyday life.

Yet despite these detailed studies of urban parks, investigations of these and other issues are surprisingly rare in the academic literature, and studies of the material culture of parks are virtually non-existent. The anthropological study by Low, Taplin and Scheld of five parks in the USA (Low, Taplin and Scheld 2005) is an exception. These studies were commissioned by park management or government agencies aiming to understand the needs of users and how proposed changes to the park environment might impact on them, including in relation to local democratic changes. This is very much applied research and does not go into any detail about the sensuous character of parks as places or their social and cultural meanings. The same is true of three British studies: Greenhalgh and Worpole (1996), Holland et al. (2007) and House of Commons (2017). The main issue explored is how parks can contribute to democratic values and promote social inclusion, dominated as they are by hegemonic white middle class values in their management and maintenance, even in multicultural neighbourhoods (Low, Taplin and Scheld 2005:16). Other studies of parks are almost exclusively concerned with the psychological benefits of green space in the city (see, e.g., Beck 2016; Carrus et al. 2014; Taylor and Kuo 2009).

Tilley's analysis is of Holland Park in west central London. This, like Pulini's street, is in 'alpha-rich' territory, except that here there are no shabby houses in its vicinity. Holland Park is surrounded by luxurious mansions, smaller houses and flats that retail for staggering prices. Their proximity to the park substantially boosts their market value in an area of London with the highest population density and the least green space.

The chapter explores Holland Park from a materialist phenomenological perspective, in terms of its social rhythms and conflicts with regard to who and what it is for, and what it should become in relation to London: a park for locals or a tourist destination, a park for peace and relaxation or a place for public entertainment, a place in which people should be allowed to go anywhere they like or a place for nature conservation in which public access to large areas is restricted. The contested character of the park goes far beyond these general issues. It also concerns rights to use the park and its governance and how people should use it and be regulated and controlled by disciplinary means. This involves different user groups: joggers and fitness trainers, dog walkers, cyclists, sports enthusiasts, people with horticultural and botanical interests, mothers and children, the frail and the elderly.

The chapter explores the social rhythms of the park in relation to times of the day and days of the week, the ebbs and flows of people into and out of it, and the way it becomes transformed from being an essentially white park used predominantly by locals during weekdays to a multicultural meeting place at the weekends, predominantly used by 'outsiders', when many locals absent themselves because they no longer feel it is their place. In this manner, the park subtly and silently becomes a socially segregated place, primarily maintained for, and enjoyed by, a social elite.

Gentrification on the streets

Sociological and geographical studies of gentrification in general, and in London in particular, have proliferated over the last 30 years (Bridge, Butler and Lees 2012; Butler 1997; Butler and Lees 2006; Hamnett 2003b; Hamnett and Williams 1979; Jackson and Butler 2015; Lees, Slater and Wyly 2010; Slater 2011). Gentrification has generally been understood as the colonisation and transformation of the inner city by affluent middle-class professional groups that more or less takes the same form everywhere, leading to the devastating displacement of working-class communities from home and neighbourhood. This is related to the shift from production to consumption and new forms of urban living involving a reinvestment in fixed capital. The brute social realities of displacement, the material inequalities and social injustice involved, are often disguised by referring to the regeneration and rejuvenation of these places in the city.

It is now understood in the growing literature on this topic that initial gentrification may lead, over time, to a new form of super-gentrification of neighbourhoods in which locality plays a crucial role (Butler and Lees 2006). High-middle-class professionals, particularly those working in the financial sector, are now displacing the initial gentrifiers, creating new ghettos of wealth and privilege. This argument is supported by census data, information about household income and occupation, and house price data.

However, despite the fact that processes of gentrification substantially alter the material character of the built environment of the neighbourhood, of homes and domestic interiors, and patterns of household consumption, these key *material* characteristics have been largely overlooked in the literature. It is, apparently, enough to spot the presence of a vegetarian restaurant or the presence of a gastropub on a shopping street to confirm gentrification has materially taken place. This dematerialised approach has obvious difficulty coping with either the material or social specificity of gentrification, because they are interlinked processes that are always geographically specific and linked to different places in the city.

Gentrification scholars have been more recently interested in trying to distinguish between the different styles, types and forms of gentrification in different areas of the city (e.g. fully gentrified, socially mixed but gentrifying, gated community, suburban, exurban (Jones and Jackson 2014b; Jackson and Butler 2015), or initial gentrification and subsequent super-gentrification (Butler and Lees 2006). Studies have continued to distinguish gentrification only in terms of a very broad social optic in which the everyday lives of the gentrifiers are not considered in any detail. In order to produce a more fine-grained, nuanced and textured perspective on the relationship of gentrification to place, the suggestion here is that studies need to observe the streets themselves and go behind closed doors.

An in-depth, bottom-up materialist approach to gentrification would instead begin with the buildings themselves, the manner in which they are furnished and designed, styles of lighting, the colours of the doors and the choice of the paint used, the ornaments on the dressing table, which frame and constitute everyday life (see Samuel 1994, part I, for some general discussion of the built environment, and Attfield 1989, 2000; Blunt 2008; Dovey 2010, chapter 5; Frykman and Löfgren 1987; Gregson 2011; Halle 1993; Miller 2001, 2009 for discussions of the material culture of the homes and their biographies).

Schacter (chapter 10) returns us to the streets themselves, in this spirit, to consider gentrification from a critical and political material culture perspective in a study of graffiti and street art in Shoreditch in east London over a 15-year period. He discusses the multiple platial characteristics of graffiti and street art in east London and examines its changing temporal character and socio-political character. Schacter charts the temporal transformation of graffiti and street art's material inscription on the buildings and walls from being initially transgressive, the illicit creative ephemeral artefacts of a clandestine act of resistance and rebellion to the city authorities, to something done openly and deemed acceptable and institutionalised. Originally 'dirt', matter out of place, it has been purified.

The power of these images to make any difference as an act of rebellion and resistance becomes defused. The images now become part and parcel of the re-presentation of this place as somewhere that is distinct and different because of their presence. It can thus both be packaged, marketed and sold to tourists by the London Tourist Board and equally appeal to the influx of new urban hipsters. The political and social impact of these images becomes hijacked and is intimately linked to the gentrification of this area of the city. The art becomes part of a new spurious heritage of the place, valued in terms of the additions it now makes to property prices, lifestyle shopping and consumption on the streets, and tourist revenues. Schacter argues that the performative material agency of the images, their possibility to make a difference, has become defused in the process. Now drained of political content, the appropriated subversive look and feel of these images is now considered 'cool', forming the increasingly commercialised and commodified urban landscape that Shoreditch has become.

The new arbiters of 'taste' and the social acceptability of once dirty images to be scrubbed away and removed are now the council authorities. The council sanctions and blesses their inscription in place. The images thus become part of the planning process in the creation of a theme park in which the streets themselves become an outdoor museum for an aestheticised experience rather than a critical interrogation of the city.

Conclusions

Anthropologists always work at the small scale. There is no prospect or possibility of producing an ethnography of the city in its totality, but we may hope to provide it by considering in detail the constellation of places within it that make it up. A defining characteristic of an anthropological participatory and phenomenological ethnography of place is that it necessarily requires a fine-grained focus. It eschews the abstractions of many urban studies in an attempt to return to the materiality of the real. We might imagine, in the future, an entire programme of such studies discussing and describing in comparative research the fine-grained detail of London as performed and lived: studies of football stadiums, art galleries and museums, restaurants, different public squares and parks, walks through shopping streets and malls, investigations of residential streets and neighbourhoods in different parts of the city and the interiors of people's homes.

This book aims to further encourage such an approach and project in the belief that if we are ever to develop a more nuanced and sophisticated understanding of the entangled intersections of the materialities and socialities of everyday life in London, such a perspective provides the only realistic possibility of doing so. The city touches people physically, sensually, socially and culturally. They in turn are touched by it. This is the other way of telling that this book aspires to stimulate and promote.

References

Abram, D. 1997. *The Spell of the Sensuous*. New York: Vintage.
Ackroyd, P. 2000. *London: The Biography*. London: Chatto and Windus.
Adams, P. 2001. 'Peripatetic Imagery and Peripatetic Sense of Place'. In *Textures of Place*, edited by P. Adams, S. Hoelscher and K. Till, 186–206. Minneapolis: University of Minnesota Press.
Adams, P., Hoelscher, S. and Till, K. (eds) 2001. *Textures of Place*. Minneapolis: University of Minnesota Press.

Amin, A. 2012. *Land of Strangers*. Cambridge: Polity.
Amin, A. and Thrift, N. 2002. *Cities: Reimagining the Urban*. Cambridge: Polity.
Amin, A. and Thrift, N. 2017. *Seeing Like a City*. Cambridge: Polity.
Appadurai, A. 1986. (ed.) *The Social Lives of Things: Commodities in Cultural Perspective*. Cambridge: Cambridge University Press.
Appadurai, A. 1996. *Modernity at Large. Cultural Dimensions of Globalization*. Minneapolis: University of Minnesota Press.
Applbaum, K. 2005. 'The Anthropology of Markets'. In *A Handbook of Economic Anthropology*, edited by J. Carrier, 275–89. Cheltenham: Edward Elgar.
Atkinson, S., Fuller, S. and Painter, J. (eds) 2016. *Wellbeing and Place*. London: Routledge.
Attfield, J. 1989. 'Inside Pram Town: A Case Study of Harlow House Interiors 1951–61'. In *A View from the Interior*, edited by J., Attfield and P. Kirkham. London: The Women's Press.
Attfield, J. 2000. *Wild Things: The Material Culture of Everyday Life*. Oxford: Berg.
Augé, M., 1995. *Non-Places: Introduction to an Anthropology of Supermodernity*. London: Verso.
Augé, M. 2002. *In the Metro*. Minneapolis: University of Minnesota Press.
Bachelard, G. 1969. *The Poetics of Space*. Boston: Beacon Press.
Back, L. 2007. *The Art of Listening*. Oxford: Berg.
Back, L. 2017. 'Marchers and Steppers; Memory, City Life and Walking'. In *Walking Through Social Research*, edited by C. Bates and A. Rhys-Taylor, 21–37. Abingdon: Routledge.
Bates, C. and Rhys-Taylor, A. (eds) 2017. *Walking through Social Research*. Abingdon: Routledge.
Bauman, Z. 2000. *Liquid Modernity*. Cambridge: Polity.
Beck, H. 2016. 'Understanding the Impact of Urban Green Space on Health and Wellbeing'. In *Wellbeing and Place*, edited by S. Atkinson, S. Fuller and J. Painter, 35–52. London: Routledge.
Bender, B. (ed.) 1993. *Landscape: Politics and Perspectives*. Oxford: Berg.
Bender, B. 2006. 'Place and Landscape'. In *Handbook of Material Culture*, edited by C. Tilley et al., 303–14. London: Sage.
Bender, B. and Winer, M. 2001 (eds) 2001. *Contested Landscapes. Movement, Exile and Place*. Oxford: Berg.
Benjamin, W. 1973. *Charles Baudelaire: A Lyric Poet in the Era of High Capitalism*. London: New Left Books.
Benjamin, W. 1979. *One Way Street and Other Writings*. London: New Left Books.
Bennett, T., Savage, M., Silva, E., Warde, A., Gavo-Cal, M. and Wright, D. 2009. *Culture, Class, Distinction*. London: Routledge.
Bergson, H. 1991. *Matter and Memory*. New York: Zone Books.
Bestor, T. 2004. *Tsukiji. The Fish Market at the Center of the World*. Berkeley: University of California Press.
Blokland, T. 2003. *Urban Bonds: Social Relationships in an Inner City Neighbourhood*. Cambridge: Polity.
Blokland, T. 2017. *Community as Urban Practice*. Cambridge: Polity.
Blunt, A. 2008. 'The 'Skyscraper Settlement': Home and Residence at Christodora House', *Environment and Planning A* 40: 550–71.
Bonnett, A. 2009. 'The Dilemmas of Radical Nostalgia in British Psychogeography', *Theory, Culture and* Society 26(1):45–70.
Borden, I. 2003. *Skateboarding, Space and the City*. Oxford: Berg.
Bourdieu, P. 1977. *Outline of a Theory of Practice*. Cambridge: Cambridge University Press.
Bourdieu, P. 1984. *Distinction: A Social Critique of the Judgement of Taste*. London: Routledge.
Bourdieu, P. 1992. *The Logic of Practice*. Cambridge: Polity Press.
Branson, G. 1978. *The Ungreen Park*. London: Bodley Head.
Bridge, G., Butler, T. and Lees, L. (eds) 2012. *Mixed Communities: Gentrification by Stealth?* Bristol: Policy Press.
Buchli, V. (ed.) 2002. *The Material Culture Reader*. Oxford: Berg.
Buchli, V. 2013. *An Anthropology of Architecture*. London: Bloomsbury.
Bull, M. 2000. *Sounding Out the City*. Oxford: Berg.
Bull, M. and Back, L. (eds.) 2003. *The Auditory Culture Reader*. Oxford: Berg.
Burnett, R. 1995.*Cultures of Vision*. Bloomington: Indiana University Press.
Butler, T. 1997. *Gentrification and the Middle Classes*. London: Ashgate.
Butler, T. 2007. 'Re-urbanizing London Docklands: Gentrification, Suburbanisation or New Urbanism?', *International Journal of Urban and Regional Research* 31(4):759–81.

Butler, T. and Hamnett, C. 2011. *Ethnicity, Class and Aspiration: Understanding London's New East End*. Bristol: Policy Press.
Butler, T. and Lees, L. 2006. 'Super-Gentrification in Barnsbury, London: Globalization and Gentrifying Global Elites at the Neighbourhood Level', *Transactions of the Institute of British Geographers* NS 31:467–87.
Butler, T. and Robson, G. 2003. *London Calling: The Middle Classes and the Re-Making of Inner London*. Oxford: Berg.
Buttimer, A. and Seamon, D. (eds) 1980. *The Human Experience of Space and Place*. New York: St Martin's Press.
Campkin, B. 2013. *Remaking London: Decline and Regeneration in Urban Culture*. London: I.B. Tauris.
Carrus, G., Scapelliti, M., Fornara, F., Bonnes, M. and Bonaitou, M. 2014. 'Place Attachment, Community Identification and Pro-environmental Engagement'. In *Place Attachment*, edited by L. Manzo and P. Devine-Wright. London: Routledge.
Casey, E. 2000. *Remembering: A Phenomenological Study* (second edition). Bloomington: Indiana University Press.
Chambers, I. 1994. *Migrancy, Culture, Identity*. London: Routledge.
Chen, Y. 2016. *Practising Rhythmanalysis: Theories and Methodologies*. London: Rowland and Littlefield.
Classen, C. (ed.) 2005. *The Book of Touch*. Oxford: Berg.
Classen. C., Howes, D. and Synott, A. 1994. *Aroma: The Cultural History of Smell*. London: Routledge.
Clifford, J. 1997. *Routes*; *Travel and Translation in the Late Twentieth Century*. Cambridge, MA: Harvard University Press.
Cohen, A. 2013. *The Symbolic Construction of Community*. London: Routledge.
Connerton, P. 1989. *How Societies Remember*. Cambridge: Cambridge University Press.
Coverley, M. 2006. *Psychogeography*. Harpenden: Pocket Essentials.
Cox, P. 2015. 'Cycling Cultures and Social Theory'. In *Cycling Cultures*, edited by P. Cox. Chester: University of Chester Press.
Cresswell, T. 2004. *Place; A Short Introduction*. Oxford: Blackwell.
Csordas, T. 1990. 'Embodiment as a Paradigm for Anthropology', *Ethos* 18(1):5–47.
Davis, M. 2007. *Planet of Slums*. London: Verso.
de Beauvoir, S. 1965. *The Prime of Life*. Harmondsworth: Penguin.
de Certeau, P. 1984. *The Practice of Everyday Life*. Berkeley: University of California Press.
de Certeau, P., Giard, L. and Mayol, P. 1998. *The Practice of Everyday Life. Volume 2: Living and Cooking*. Minneapolis: University of Minnesota Press.
Degen, M. 2008. *Sensing Cities: Regenerating Public Life in Barcelona and* Manchester. London: Routledge.
Degen, M. 2014. 'The Everyday Life of the Senses'. In *Cities and Social Change: Encounters with Contemporary Urbanism*, edited by R. Paddison and E. McCann. London: Sage.
Desjarlais, R. and Throop, C. 2011. 'Phenomenological Approaches in Anthropology', *Annual Review of Anthropology* 40:87–102.
Diaconu, M. 2016. 'Chartings Smellscapes'. In *Engaged Urbanism: Cities and Methodologies*, edited by B. Camplin and G. Duijzings, 205–210. London: I.B. Taurus.
Dikovitskaya, M. 2005. *Visual Culture: The study of the Visual after the Cultural Turn*. Cambridge, MA: The Mitt Press.
Dorling, D. 2013. *The 32 Stops*. London: Penguin.
Dovey, K. 2010. *Becoming Places*. London: Routledge.
Edensor, T. 2006. 'Sensing Tourist Spaces'. In *Travels in Paradox' Remapping Tourism*, edited by C. Minca and T. Oakes, 23–45. Lanham: Rowland and Littlefied.
Edensor, T. 2014. 'The Social Life of the Senses: Ordering and Disordering the Modern Sensorium'. In *A Cultural History of the Senses in the Modern Era*, edited by D. Howes. London: Bloomsbury.
Elborough, T. 2016. *A Walk in the Park*. London: Jonathan Cape.
Eriksen, T. 2010. *Small Places, Large Issues* (third edition). London: Pluto Press.
Favero, P. 2003. 'Phantasms in a "Starry" Place: Space and Identification in a Central New Delhi Market', *Cultural Anthropology* 18(4):551–84.
Feld, S. and Basso, K. (eds) 1996. *Senses of Place*. Santa Fe: School of American Research Press.
Frykman, J. and Löfgren, O. 1987. *Culture Builders: A Historical Anthropology of Middle Class Life*. New Brunswick: Rutgers University Press.

Geertz, C. 1973. 'Thick Description and the Interpretation of Culture'. In *The Interpretation of Cultures*, edited by C. Geertz, 3–31. New York: Basic Books.

Geertz, C. 1979. 'Suq: The Bazaar Economy of Sefrou'. In. *Meaning and Order in Moroccan Society: Three Essays in Cultural Analysis*, edited by C. Geertz, H. Geertz and I. Rosen, 123–314. Cambridge: Cambridge University Press.

Geertz, C. 2000. *Available Light: Anthropological Reflections on Philosophical Topics*. Princeton: Princeton University Press.

Gell, A. 1998. *Art and Agency*. Oxford: Oxford University Press.

Gibbs, R. 1994. *The Poetics of Mind*. Cambridge: Cambridge University Press.

Giddens, A. 1994. 'Living in a post-traditional society'. In *Reflexive Modernization*, edited by U. Beck, A. Giddens and S. Lash. Cambridge: Polity.

Graeber, D. 2001. *Toward an Anthropological Theory of Value: The False Coin of our Own Dreams*. New York: Palgrave.

Gregory, C. 1982. *Gifts and Commodities*. London: Academic Press.

Gregson, N. 2011. *Living with Things: Ridding, Accommodation, Dwelling*. Wantage: Sean Kingston Publishing.

Greenhalgh, L. and Worpole, K. 1996. *People, Parks and Cities: A Guide to Good Practice in Urban Parks*. London: HMSO.

Guss, D. 2000. '"Indianness" and the Construction of Ethnicity in the Day of the Monkey'. In *The Festive State*, edited by D. Guss, 60–89. Berkeley: University of California Press.

Hall, S. 2012. *City, Street and Citizen. The Measure of the Ordinary*. London: Routledge.

Halle, D. 1993. *Inside Culture: Art and Class in the American Home*. Chicago: University of Chicago Press.

Hamnett, C. 2003a. *Unequal City: London in the Global Arena*. London: Routledge.

Hamnett, C. 2003b. 'Gentrification and the Middle-class: Remaking of Inner London, 1961–2001', *Urban Studies* 40:2401–26.

Hamnett, C. and Williams, P. 1979. *Gentrification in London 1961–1971: An Empirical and Theoretical Analysis of Social Change*. Birmingham: University of Birmingham, Centre for Urban and Regional Studies.

Hannerz, U. 1980. *Exploring the City: Inquiries Towards an Urban Anthropology*. New York: Columbia University Press.

Hannerz, U. 1996. *Transnational Connections: Culture, People, Places*. London: Routledge.

Harvey, D. 1973. *Social Justice and the City*. London: Edward Arnold.

Harvey, D. 1989. *The Urban Experience*. Oxford: Blackwell.

Harvey, D. 2001. *Spaces of Capital*. Edinburgh: Edinburgh University Press.

Harvey, D. 2011. *Rebel Cities*. London: Verso.

Heidegger, M. 2003. 'Building, Dwelling, Thinking'. In *Basic Writings*, edited by D. Krell, 343–64. London: Routledge.

Helliwell, C. 1996. 'Space and Sociality in a Dayak Longhouse'. In *Things as They Are: New Directions in Phenomenological Anthropology*, edited by M. Jackson. Bloomington: Indiana University Press.

Henare, A., Holbraad, M. and Wastell, S. 2007. *Theorizing Artefacts Ethnographically*. Abingdon: Routledge.

Henshaw, V. 2015. 'Route Planning a Sensory Walk: Sniffing out the Issues'. In *Contemporary British Psychogeography*, edited by T. Richardson, 195–2010. London: Rowman and Littlefield.

Hirsch, E. and Stewart, C. (eds) 2005. 'Ethnographies of Historicity', *History and Anthropology* 16(3).

Holland, C., Clark, A., Katz, J. and Peace, S. 2007. *Social Interaction in Urban Public Places*. Bristol: Policy Press.

Horowitz, A. 2013. *On Looking: Eleven Walks with Expert Eyes*. London: Scribner.

Hoskins, J. 1998. *Biographical: How Things Tell the Stories of People's Lives*. London: Routledge.

Hoskins, J. 2006 'Agency, Biography and Objects'. In *Handbook of Material* Culture, edited by C. Tilley, W. Keane, S. Küchler, M. Rowlands and P. Spyer, 74–84. London: Sage.

House of Commons 2017. *Public Parks: Seventh Report of Session 2016–17*. Communities and Local Government Committee. https://publications.parliament.uk/pa/cm201617/cmselect/cmcomloc/45/45.pdf (accessed February 2019).

Howes, D. (ed.) 2005. *Sensual Relations. Engaging the Senses in Culture and Social Theory*. Ann Arbor: University of Michigan Press.

Howes, D. (ed.) 2005a. *Empire of the Senses. The Sensual Culture Reader*. Oxford: Berg.
Ingold, T. 2007. *Lines: A Brief History*. London: Routledge.
Ingold, T. and Vergunst, J. Lee. (eds) 2008. *Ways of Walking: Ethnography and Practice on Foot*. Aldershot, Hants: Ashgate.
Jackson, E. and Butler, T. 2015. 'Revisiting 'Social Tectonics': The Middle Classes and Social Mix in Gentrifying Neighbourhoods', *Urban* Studies 52(13):2349–65.
Jacobs, J. 1961. *The Death and Life of Great American Cities*. New York: Random House.
Jay, M. 1994. *Downcast Eyes: The Denigration of Vision in Twentieth Century French Thought*. Berkeley: University of California Press.
Jenks, C. 1995. *Visual Culture*. London: Routledge.
Jones, H. and Jackson, E. (eds) 2014a. *Stories of Cosmopolitan Belonging*. Abingdon: Routledge.
Jones, H. and Jackson, E. (eds) 2014b. *Stories of Metropolitan Belonging*. London: Routledge.
Korsmeyer, C. (ed.) 2005. *The Taste Culture Reader*. Oxford: Berg.
Kopytoff, I. 1986. 'The Cultural Biography of Things: Commoditization as a Process'. In *The Social Life of Things: Commodities in Cultural Perspective*, edited by A. Appadurai. Cambridge: Cambridge University Press.
Lakoff, G. and Johnson, M. 1990. *Metaphors We Live By*. Chicago: Chicago University Press.
Lees, L, Slater, T. and Wyly, E. (eds) 2010. *The Gentrification Reader*. London: Routledge.
Lefebvre, H. 1991. *The Production of Space*. Oxford: Blackwell.
Lefebvre, H. 2004. *Rhythmanalysis*. London: Continuum.
Lovell, N. (ed.) 1998. *Locality and Belonging*. London: Routledge.
Low, S. and Lawrence-Zúñiga, D. (eds) 2003. *The Anthropology of Space and Place*. Oxford: Blackwell.
Low, S., Taplin, D. and Scheld, S. 2005. *Rethinking Urban Parks: Public Space and Cultural Diversity*. Austin: University of Texas Press.
Lynch, K. 1972. *What Time is this Place?* Cambridge, MA: The MIT Press.
Manzo, L. and Devine-Wright, P. 2014. *Place Attachment*. London: Routledge.
Marcus, S. 1999. *Apartment Stories*. Berkeley: University of California Press.
Massey, D. 1997. 'A Global Sense of Place'. In *Reading Human* Geography, edited by T. Barnes and D. Gregory, 315–23. London: Arnold.
Massey, D. 2000. 'Living in Wythenshawe'. In *The Unknown City: Contesting Architecture and Social Space*, edited by I. Borden, J. Kerr and J. Redell, 458–75. Cambridge, MA: MIT Press.
Massey, D. 2007. *World City*. Cambridge: Polity Press.
Matless, D. 1998. *Landscape and Englishness*. London: Reaktion Books.
Mayol, P. 1998. 'Part I: Living'. In *The Practice of Everyday Life. Volume 2: Living and Cooking*, edited by M. de Certeau, L. Giard and P. Mayol, 5–114. Minneapolis: University of Minnesota Press.
McDonough, T. (ed.) 2009. *The Situationists and the City*. London: Verso.
Merleau-Ponty, M. 1962. *The Phenomenology of Perception*. London: Routledge.
Merleau-Ponty, M. 1968. *The Visible and the Invisible*. Evanston, IL: Northwestern University Press.
Miller, D. (ed.) 1998a. *Material Cultures: Why Some Things Matter*. London: UCL Press.
Miller, D. 1998b. *A Theory of Shopping*. Cambridge: Polity Press.
Miller, D. (ed.) 2001. *Home Possessions*. Oxford: Berg.
Miller, D. 2008. *The Comfort of Things*. Cambridge: Polity Press.
Miller, D. 2009. 'Individuals and the Aesthetic of Order'. In *Anthropology and the Individual: A Material Culture Perspective*, edited by D. Miller, 3–25. Oxford: Berg.
Miller, D. 2010. *Stuff*. Cambridge: Polity Press.
Miller, D., Jackson, P., Thrift, N., Holbrook, B. and Rowlands, M. 1998. *Shopping, Place and Identity*. London: Routledge.
Mintz, S. 1986. *Sweetness and Power: The Place of Sugar in Modern History*. London: Penguin.
Munn, N. 1986. *The Fame of Gawa*. Cambridge: Cambridge University Press.
Munn, N. 1992. 'The Anthropology of Time', *Annual Review of Anthropology* 21:93–123.
Raban, J. 1974. *Soft City*. London: Picador.
Rapport, N. and Dawson, A. 1998. *Migrants of Identity: Perceptions of Home in a World of Movement*. Oxford: Berg.
Relph, E. 1976. *Place and Placelessness*. London: Pion.
Relph, E. 1981. *Rational Landscapes and Humanistic Geography*. London: Routledge.
Revill, G. 2013. 'Points of Departure: Listening to Rhythm in the Sonoric Spaces of the Railway Station'. In *Urban Rhythms: Mobilities, Space and Interaction in the Contemporary City*, edited

by R. Smith and K. Hetherington, 51–68. Oxford: Wiley Blackwell (Sociological Review Monographs).

Rhys-Taylor, A. 2013. 'The Essences of Multiculture: A Sensory Exploration of an Inner-city Street Market', *Identities* 20(4):393–406.

Rhys-Taylor, A. 2014. 'Intersemiotic Fruit: Mangoes, Multiculture and the City'. In *Stories of Metropolitan Belonging: Emotion and Location*, edited by H. Jones and E. Jackson. London: Routledge.

Rhys-Taylor, A. 2017. *Food and Multiculture: A Sensory Ethnography of East London*. London: Bloomsbury.

Richardson, M. 2003. 'Being-in-the Market versus Being-in-the plaza: Material Culture and the Construction of Social Reality in Spanish America'. In *The Anthropology of Space and Place*, edited by S. Low and D. Lawrence- Zúñiga, 74–91. Oxford: Blackwell.

Richardson, T. (ed.) 2015. *Walking Inside Out: Contemporary British Psychogeography*. London: Rowman and Littlefield.

Ricoeur, P. 2004. *Memory, History, Forgetting*. Chicago: University of Chicago Press.

Roseberry, W. 1996. 'Yuppee Coffee and the Rejuvenation of Class in the United States', *American Anthropologist* 94(4):762–75.

Samuel, R. 1994. *Theatres of Memory*. London: Verso.

Sasaki, K.-I. 2000. 'For Whom is City Design: Tactility Versus Visuality'. In *The City Cultures Reader*, edited by I. Borden, T. Hall and M. Miles, 36–44. London: Routledge.

Savage, M., Bagnall, G. and Longhurst, B. 2005. *Globalization and Belonging*. London: Sage.

Savage, M., Cunningham, N., Devine, F., Friedman, S., Laurison, D., Mckenzie, L., Miles, A., Snee, H. and Wakeling, P. 2015. *Social Class in the 21st Century*. London: Pelican.

Schlör, J. 1998. *Nights in the Big City*. London: Reaktion.

Seamon, D. (ed.) 1993. *Dwelling, Seeing, and Designing; Toward a Phenomenological Ecology*. Albany: State University of New York Press.

Self, W. 2007. *Psychogeography*. London: Bloomsbury.

Sennett, R. 1992. *The Fall of Public Man*. New York: W. Norton and Company.

Sennett, R. 2006. *Flesh and Stone: The Body and the City in Western Civilization*. London: W. Norton and Company.

Sennett, R. 2018. *Building and Dwelling: Ethics for the City*. London: Penguin.

Serres, M., Sankey, M. and Cowley, P. 2008. *The Five Senses: A Philosophy of Mingled Bodies*. London: Continuum International Publishing Group.

Sinclair, I. 2003a. *Lights Out for the Territory: 9 Excursions in the Secret History of London*. London: Penguin.

Sinclair, I. 2003b. *London Orbital*. London: Penguin.

Sinclair, I. 2009. *Hackney, That Rose-Red Empire: A Confidential Report*. London: Penguin.

Slater, T. 2011. 'Gentrification of the City'. In *The New Blackwell Companion to the City*, edited by G. Bridge and S. Watson, 571–85. Oxford: Blackwell Publishing.

Smith, R. and Hall, T. 2013. 'No Time Out: Mobility. Rhythmicity and Urban Patrol in the Twenty-four Hour City'. In *Urban Rhythms: Mobilities, Space and Interaction in the Contemporary City*, edited by R. Smith and K. Hetherington, pp. 89–108. Oxford: Wiley Blackwell (Sociological Review Monographs).

Smith, R. and Hetherington, K. 2013. *Urban Rhythms: Mobilities, Space and Interaction in the Contemporary City*. Oxford: Wiley Blackwell (Sociological Review Monographs).

Soja, E. 1989. *Postmodern Geographies. The Reassertion of Space in Critical Social Theory*. London: Verso.

Soja, E. 1996. *Thirdspace*. Oxford: Wiley-Blackwell.

Solnit, R. 2002. *Wanderlust: A History of Walking*. Harmondsworth, Penguin Random House.

Stoller, P. 1997. *Sensuous Scholarship*. Philadelphia: University of Pennsylvania Press.

Sutton, D. 2001. *Rememberance of Repasts: An Anthropology of Food and Memory*. Oxford: Berg.

Taun, Y.-F. 1974. *Topophilia*. New York: Columbia University Press.

Taun, Y-F. 1977. *Space and Place*. Minneapolis: University of Minnesota Press.

Taylor, Andrea F. and Kuo, Frances E. 2009. 'Children with Attention Deficits Concentrate Better after Walk in the Park' *Journal of Attention Disorders* 12(5):402–9.

Thrift, N. 2010. 'Driving in the City'. In *The Blackwell City Reader* (second edition), edited by G. Bridge and S. Watson, 152–8. Oxford: Wiley-Blackwell.

Tilley, C. 1994. *A Phenomenology of Landscape: Places, Paths and Monuments*. Oxford: Berg.

Tilley, C.1999. *Metaphor and Material Culture*. Oxford: Blackwell.

Tilley, C. 2004. *The Materiality of Stone: Explorations in Landscape Phenomenology I*. Oxford: Berg.
Tilley, C. 2007. 'Ethnography and Material Culture'. In *Handbook of Ethnography*, edited by P. Atkinson, A. Coffey, S. Delamont, J. Lofland and L. Lofland, 258–72. London: Sage.
Tilley, C. 2008. *Body and Image: Explorations in Landscape Phenomenology 2*. Walnut Creek, CA: Left Coast Press.
Tilley, C. 2010. *Interpreting Landscapes: Explorations in Landscape Phenomenology* 3. Walnut Creek, CA: Left Coast Press.
Tilley, C. 2012. 'Walking the Past in the Present'. In *Landscapes Beyond Land*, edited by A. Arnason, N. Ellison, J. Vergunst and A. Whitehouse, 15–32. Oxford: Berghahn.
Tilley, C. 2017. *Landscape in the Longue Durée*. London: UCL Press.
Tilley, C. and Cameron-Daum, K. 2017. *An Anthropology of Landscape*. London: UCL Press.
Tilley, C., Keane, W., Küchler, S., Rowlands, M. and Spyer, P. (eds.) 2006. *The Handbook of Material Culture*. London: Sage.
Urry, J. 2007. *Mobilities*. Cambridge: Polity Press.
Vivanco, L. 2013. *Reconsidering the Bicycle: An Anthropological Perspective on a New (Old) Thing*. London: Routledge.
Watson, S. and Studdert, D. 2006. *Markets as Sites for Social Interaction: Spaces of Diversity*. London: The Policy Press.
Watt, P. 2010. 'Unravelling the Narratives and Politics of Belonging to Place', *Housing, Theory and Society* 27(2):153–9.
Watt, P. 2011. 'Selective Belonging: Fear and Avoidance in Urban and Suburban Neighbourhoods', *Lo Squderno: Explorations in Space and Society* 21:55–9.
Watt, P. and Smets, P. 2014. *Mobilities and Neighbourhood Belonging in Cities and Suburbs*. Basingstoke: Palgrave Macmillan.
Webber, R. and Burrows, R. 2015. 'Life in an Alpha Territory: Discontinuity and Conflict in an Elite London 'Village', *Urban Studies* 53(15):3139–54.
Weiner, A. 1992. *Inalienable Possessions: The Paradox of Giving while Keeping*. Berkeley: University of California Press.
White, J. 2003. *Rothschild Buildings: Life in an East End Tenement Block 1887–1920*. London: Pimlico.
Zukin, S. 2010. *Naked City: The Death and Life of Authentic Urban Places*. Oxford: Oxford University Press.

Part I
The domestic and residential sphere

1
Change and continuity in a central London street
Ilaria Pulini

'Rhythm must have meaning.'

Ezra Pound

Life starts early in Cheniston Gardens (CG) on weekdays. People begin to come out from the Victorian buildings at 6.00a.m., heading to the underground station where the Circle and District lines will distribute them all over London and beyond (fig.1.1). Residents mix with other people taking CG as a shortcut towards High Street Kensington (HSK): male and female adults, no children. Many check their smartphones on the way; a few emerge from the basement flats with a dog, quite likely heading to Kensington Gardens or Holland Park. The flux of pedestrians moving out of the street reaches its peak between 8.00 and 9.30a.m.; meanwhile, in the nearby Wrights Lane (WL), a busy thoroughfare with modern residential and commercial premises leading to HSK, traffic becomes congested. By 10.00a.m. the outward rush is over, motorcycles have left their racks, and bicycles have been unlocked from the railings enclosing the lower ground floor flats. Now a different rhythm, made of short-term activities performed by residents and outsiders, takes place in CG until the late afternoon counter-wave brings people back home.

An uninterrupted flux of tourists pull creaking wheeled luggage along WL from the tube station towards the two hotels at the bottom of the street. Some stop at The Muffin Man, a tea room at the corner between CG and WL, enthusiastically recommended by TripAdvisor reviewers as a quintessential English experience: 'very British', 'a quaint little shop', 'a microcosm of Kensington society', 'a cosy alternative to your usual Starbucks or Costa' (Tripadvisor n.d.) (fig. 1.2). The tatty atmosphere

Fig. 1.1 Cheniston Gardens (encircled in red) and the surrounding area of Kensington. Source: Ordnance Survey open data, 2017

Fig. 1.2 The Muffin Man at the corner between Cheniston Gardens and Wrights Lane. Source: author

of the tearoom, and the aroma of freshly baked muffins mixed with the smell of toasted bread and fried eggs with bacon evoke the Victorian character of the neighbourhood and enhance the British appeal of the place. Reproductions of old black-and-white photographs of the surroundings are strategically deployed on the walls to tickle the customers' fancy and add visual awareness to their experience (fig. 1.3). Some of the pictures predate the construction of CG and show how green and airy this area was before major property speculation changed the urban layout of West London in the course of the last three decades of the nineteenth century. The evocative appeal of the old pictures adds meaning to an immersive British re-enactment performed in the 'true' atmosphere of the tearoom, culminating in the ritual 'selfie' with CG in the background, showing the regular alignment of four-storey Victorian townhouses on the sides of this peculiarly L-shaped street.

During the day, the noise of a broom reveals that Pedro, the caretaker of no. 9, is sweeping the pavement in front of his building. No. 9 is in a dreadful condition: the once creamy stock bricks of the facade are covered with a thick, blackish layer of dirt, creating a sharp contrast with the buildings nearby, whose facades have been renovated recently (fig. 1.4). Although no other house in CG shows a comparable degree of shabbiness, the overall look of the street is undeniably rather patchy. Some facades have been fully or partially coated with white or

Fig. 1.3 View of Wrights Lane from north, before 1881. The brick wall enclosed the rear gardens of houses facing High Street Kensington. The small cottage at the bottom, used as a stable or a warehouse, was later incorporated into the northern sector of the Cheniston Gardens development. © RBKC Local Studies & Archives department

Fig. 1.4 Nos 7–11 Cheniston Gardens – contrasting facades. Source: author

Fig. 1.5 Examples of doorbells in Cheniston Gardens. Source: author

grey paint to conceal a long-lasting negligence; window frames, front doors and tiled steps have different finishing and colour; quite a few doorbells are of a poor quality (fig. 1.5), with labels carelessly scribbled, and dozens of aerial cables are hanging loose along the facades.

On weekdays, most of the residents are away between the rush hours. Apart from Pedro and the owner of The Muffin Man, the only people left in CG are a few housewives and aged people, the employees of the Armenian Embassy at no. 25, three priests in charge of the residence of the Catholic Order of the Augustinian Recollects at no. 14, and the doorman of an extensive apartment mansion at the bottom of the street.

All day long, delivery vans try to find their way among the rows of cars parked on both sides of the street; they always come with two drivers, one remaining in the unparkable vehicle, the other delivering the parcels. The postman arrives at 2.00p.m., after any sort of junk mail has been dropped through the slots of the front doors. Every Tuesday and Friday, waste collection is announced by three bin-men in their high-visibility vests, who swiftly and silently take the rubbish bags out of the basements' vaults and pile them up by the street lamps; for half an hour, the street is transformed into an open-air dump until the bin lorry comes along and voraciously swallows all the waste up. Male voices from behind a scaffold, regular hitting of hammers, persistent screeching of drills, the soft daubing of a paintbrush, indicate that renovation works are going on somewhere on the street. Near and distant sounds: tenacious noises from burglar alarms, the sudden slamming of a doorway. A siren approaches from HSK and fades down towards Cromwell Road; wheels of a pram pushed by a young mother; an old lady trudging past, carrying a heavy shopping bag. Overall, there is a quiet atmosphere in CG on weekdays, almost untouched by the incumbent rhythms of nearby WL, where traffic goes on intermittently, in tune with HSK traffic lights. High above, the sky is congested with airplanes flying in the direction of Heathrow airport. They come across the CG skyline exactly every 60 seconds, and by the end of the day more than 300,000 people have been flying over this stretch of sky. These gigantic jets do not 'sing' like those of the humanised London skyline of Virginia Woolf, nor do they scare people, as did the German Luftwaffe flying over London in World War 2 (WW2) (Woolf 1976:8; see also Beer 1990; Britzolakis 2011). Each new rumble overlaps the previous in a see-sawing rhythm that goes on unrelentingly from 6.00a.m. until the flight ban starts at 11.30p.m. Nevertheless, airplanes come across the sky almost unnoticed, until their sudden disappearance, just before midnight, gives way to an archaic and disorienting silence; paradoxically, it is their very absence that makes people aware of the dull, penetrating sound they have been exposed to during the day.

The Muffin Man shuts at 8.00p.m., the Thai restaurant, situated opposite to it, around 11.00p.m. Before midnight, most of the lights facing CG are being switched off one after the other. For the rest of the night CG sleeps until dawn, wrapped up by the spectral light of old-fashioned-style lamps. Such a quiet atmosphere is typical of CG nights except for Friday and Saturday, when posh cars approaching the nightclub at the bottom of WL rumble along the street looking for a parking space, and a shouting boozy population goes on messing around through the small hours.

At weekends, rhythms and routines are different. Open windows along the facades disclose the jingling and clinking of kitchenware that mingles with indistinct conversations, laughing and coughing. In a first floor flat, a cat pointlessly seeks to open a gap in the wire mesh wrapped around and above the balcony to prevent it from jumping into the neighbouring flats. At no. 9, a woman pampers her plants on a tiny, cosy balcony, unquestionably the prettiest among the almost uninterrupted row of balconies that run along the first floors of the buildings. Two women in their fifties set the table for a Sunday lunch with guests, but no hint of what they are preparing can be guessed from any smell in the street; in the afternoons during good weather the women come out on the balcony, next to the cosy flowered one, where they sometimes treat each other to pedicure sessions.

Meanwhile in the street, car boots are being filled up and emptied, people either alone or as couples walk out of CG, others come back with shopping bags – a predominantly white milieu, with a conspicuous presence of Asians and just a few people of black heritage. Conversations are in English for the most part, to a lesser extent in some European language (particularly French, Spanish and Italian) or in different (although undistinguishable to my comprehension) Asian and Arab languages. It is a multicultural soundscape that hints directly at the wide geographical network connecting CG to the rest of the world. Apparently no music is associated to such a soundscape, although a wider composite symphony is likely to go on within the privacy of individual earphones. An exception to this lack of music is the Sunday morning liturgical tunes – the hymns attuned to the notes of an organ from the First Church of Christ Scientists on WL at 11.00a.m. and the bell from the spire of St Mary Abbots, the Anglican Parish Church on Kensington Church Street, that clangs intermittently for almost an hour from 8.45a.m. St Mary Abbots' bells have been regulating the rhythms of the surroundings for many centuries. Ezra Pound, who lived in a flat behind the church at the beginning of the twentieth century, was literally obsessed by their regular striking, to the extent that 'the Vicar of St Mary Abbots and his bells' ended up in the list of 'those to be lambasted' in the manifesto of Vorticism, the avant-garde movement he founded in 1914, providing a genuinely peculiar and rather unorthodox interpretation of the 'meaning' of that 'rhythm' (Pound 1971:49; Wyndham Lewis 1914:21).

An ordinary street in the 'alpha territory'

Altogether, the rhythms and routines observed in CG convey a sense of the 'ordinary' that stands at odds with the 'extra-ordinary' character of Kensington, known for being one of the wealthiest sectors of the city, where property prices are among the highest in the UK. So, to what extent does this ordinary street comes to terms with the cliché of Kensington as the London elite neighbourhood par excellence? Actually, although the key role of the 'elite' in the London socio-economic context has been widely acknowledged (Atkinson 2015; Atkinson, Burrows and Rhodes 2016; Atkinson, Parker and Burrows 2017; Hay 2013; Savage and Williams 2008; Savage et al. 2015), until recently the analysis of this social group has been dealing at large with abstract conceptualisations and statistics rather than with the actual places where the super-rich live (Birtchnell and Caletrio 2014; Capgemini 2016). Meanwhile, the spatial mapping of this sector of the population has remained ascertainable only at the level of macro areas (Atkinson et al. 2017; Beaverstock, Hubbard and Short 2004; Cunningham and Savage 2015; Hay and Muller 2011; Savage et al. 2015:281) and information about the residential distribution of the London elite still relies largely on the mainstream representations given by the media and the property market or on the descriptions of the so-called 'alpha territories' provided by geo-referenced consumer classification systems such as Mosaic or Acorn (Burrows and Gane 2006; Parker, Uprichard and Burrows 2007; Webber and Burrows 2016). Apart from notable exceptions (Butler and Lees 2006), only in the last few years have the academic focus on localised sectors of the 'alpha territories' been advocated as an urgent priority and new site-specific investigations making extensive use of ethnography been launched (Burrows and Glucksberg 2016; Glucksberg 2016; Knowles 2017; Webber and Burrows 2016). Under these circumstances, qualitative research focusing on a single street represents a new perspective to the study of the spatial dynamics of the London elite. It may uncover contingent specificities and peculiarities and at the same time provide insights for broader generalisations.

CG has much in common with other exclusive Kensington addresses, starting with the uniformity of the Victorian architectural features still preserved throughout this area of London, yet it differs from the surroundings in its slightly rundown character. If in large sectors of the borough the wave of 'super-gentrification' (Butler and Lees 2006) in the last 20 years has cancelled the traces of previous neglect and disrepair, CG is somehow midway through. Such a unique character makes this street a perfect case study to investigate changes and discontinuities in residential space. It provides the opportunity to look through the grain of the material world, searching for traces, absences and disappearances that reflect changes in dwelling habits and reveal the inherent tension between the longevity of the buildings and the transiency of the dwellers over time.

For the study of CG residential patterns in a diachronic perspective, two methods of investigation have been used: documentary research and ethnography. Maps, public records and demographic data (censuses, directories, electoral rolls), photographs, literary sources, local magazines and newspapers have been dug up to find relevant information dating back to the end of the nineteenth century, including surveys conducted for Charles Booth's social map of London (Booth 1891, 1902), that provide invaluable early examples of street observation. Ethnography has been backed by a broadly phenomenological approach (Tilley 1994, 2012; Tilley and Cameron-Daum 2017) that emphasises the profound significance of human perceptions, interactions and negotiations in relation to the place where people live (Back 2007; Bates and Rhys-Taylor 2016; de Certeau 1984; de Certeau, Giard and Mayol 1998; Lefebvre 1991; Massey 2005; Pink 2012, 2015; Silva and Bennett 2004). Drawing from the conceptual and methodological perspectives of *flânerie* (Benjamin 1979) and *rhythmanalysis* (Amin and Thrift 2002; Lefebvre 2014), street observation has been extensively employed to generate thick descriptions of the built environment and everyday routines in CG. This type of information has been complemented by the stories that emerged in the course of semi-structured interviews with the local residents who have been also engaged in sketching their mental maps of the CG neighbourhood and in taking pictures of its surroundings, thus adding the evidence of their bodily experiences to the verbal narratives. In the course of these conversations, it was possible to explore the manifold ways CG people deal with mobility and place-belonging within the wider scenarios of transnational connections that emerged from their stories.

Residential patterns in Cheniston Gardens

CG and its immediate surroundings along WL have been cut out from the boundaries of the Kensington conservation areas established in the 1970s and 1980s. With regard to this, the question arises: what are the reasons for such exclusion? No doubt CG's architectural forms might not be as aesthetically appealing as in other streets of the borough. Surely, its houses are 'squeezed-up, gardenless, very dry and bleak enough' in their appearance (Survey of London 1986:107), yet unattractiveness alone cannot be a reason for exclusion, as other unattractive streets in the borough are nonetheless included in the conservation areas. Likewise, CG was already rundown and shabby in the 1970s and 1980s when the conservation areas were drawn, but its degree of decay was not much different to that elsewhere in those years. A possible alternative explanation can be found in the high concentration of small flats and bedsits that has characterised the street throughout the twentieth century and to a lesser extent still continues today with the complicity of the local council. By keeping CG out of the conservation area, the council gives de facto free rein to a lucrative renting business of small dwellings, which is hitherto justified and encouraged as a strategy 'to resist the loss of existing small, self-contained flats of one or two habitable rooms' that are regarded as a 'typical Kensington feature' (RBKC 2015:212). Such a strategy reflects a double-faced building control action that on the one hand justifies and encourages the development of small units in the streets excluded from the conservation areas, and on the other hand allows the super-rich to dig underground 'pits' to expand the volumes (and the values) of their properties in the conservation areas – a 'fair' deal attempting to reconcile a chronic housing shortage with building speculation. As a result of this policy, today in CG it is much easier to obtain permission to upgrade existing bedsits into the same number of modern units than to convert them into fewer flats or, even more difficult if not impossible, to bring them back to the original Victorian layout of a single independent house, as was attempted unsuccessfully with no. 17.

The majority of CG bedsits have been upgraded into fancy studios with independent cooking and toilet facilities during the last 10–15 years, but still a few look, or have looked until recently, quite rundown. A survey of no. 17 CG carried out in December 2014, just before the building was sold by public auction for £4.5 million (Allsop 2014), revealed a state of disrepair below any acceptable standard: 19 rooms, including one in the basement without any window at all, with cramped shared toilets and showers arranged in the hallways under the communal staircase. Intensive multiple occupation of this building had been going on since the end of WW2, when it was converted from flats into bedsits. During the 1980s, no. 17 was an unauthorised hostel for international students, and short-term letting was carried on uninterruptedly for 30 years under different owners without any substantial improvement to the building. In 2010, an application to re-convert no. 17 into a single house was rejected by the borough on the grounds of the need to 'resist the loss of small units'. After being auctioned, the property underwent a complete refurbishment that reduced the number of rooms of just two units from 19 to 17, which are now advertised on the property market as luxury studios for short lets at £4,500 per month by a discreet company operating for a foreign owner (figs 1.6 and 1.7).

Fig. 1.6 Bedrooms at no. 17 before the auction of the building (2014) and after renovation (2016). Source: author

In contrast to no. 17, no. 9 has remained to date unchanged and looks as if it is 'suspended in time'. No authorised renovation seems to have occurred since the house was built in the early 1880s. From the 1950s, after more than 50 years of occupation by members of the same family, the building started being used as a boarding house; since then, intensive occupation by people of different nationalities (mainly Irish,

Fig. 1.7 Kitchens at no. 17 before and after renovation. Source: author

Greek, Maltese and Indian) went on until the arrival in the 1980s of a 'colony' of Galicians, who still live there today in independent rooms with shared toilets and showers. They have low-paid jobs, mostly in the caring and service sectors. One of them, Pedro, acts as unofficial house caretaker during his time off from his job as a night watchman in Knightsbridge; he is in charge of collecting the rents on behalf of the British proprietor: 'When you have to collect the money,' he explains with a complicit wink, 'you have to speak the same language.'

Some of CG bedsits are advertised as student-friendly accommodation. These are self-contained studios with bathing and cooking facilities. They are comparatively cheap for the area (from £150 to £220 per week including bills), but usually very small and the furnishing extremely basic. Monica, a 31-year-old Slovakian woman, lived in a bedsit at no. 16 CG for five years and moved away in 2015; she arrived in London as a student, and now works for an estate agent in Chiswick: 'When I came here the building was half empty. The Arab agent told me that the new owner, an Armenian investor, had just completed the refurbishment.' CG Middle Eastern property agents are usually very efficient in filling up bedsits; for example, a young single mother from Martinique and her teenage son were approached just on their arrival from Paris at St Pancras station by a man with a visiting card advertising lettings in CG. Behind these small entrepreneurs there are wealthy investors whose identities most of the time are shrouded in mystery, as the account of Rose, an American student on a one-year contract at no. 6, points out: 'There is a story going around that this house was gifted a couple of years ago to an Arab guy by his multimillionaire family for his 28th birthday.'

In CG's dwelling geography, the world of bedsits coexists with larger residential units that can be afforded only by people with substantial assets. Fred, a US citizen and CEO of an American media company, rented a luxury maisonette at no. 30 for more than two years, paying £3,350 a month. Thomas, a retired Swiss banker, occupied a sober, classical two-bedroom flat with antique paintings and a tiny balcony for 30 years. He is back in Switzerland now, and his flat was sold for £1,195 million to an international investor from Medellin (Colombia).

Basement apartments provide an opportunity to stay conveniently located in the city with relatively smaller budgets, particularly if you have a pet. Emily, a divorced middle-aged lady with an interest in building history, has lived in the basement flat at no. 14 since 1994: 'I was looking for something affordable in the area and I found this flat that was cheap because of its dreadful condition.' She thoroughly transformed her basement from dark and bleak into a bright cheerful burrow for herself and Rufus, her pet dog. Two houses away, Glenda, another dog owner and a lecturer in economics in her late 50s, comes to her basement flat in her red sports car only on the days she has to teach courses at the university. Her flat had been kept shabby and dark for more than 30 years until a cheerful neighbour working in the building sector renovated it to a fairly decent standard.

The shabby appearance of the street is likely to be the reason for the relatively 'lower' average price of CG properties (£1,359 million) compared to the average property value for W8 (£2,758 million) (Zoopla, n.d.). However, as anybody who has invested in a central London location has experienced, those who bought a property in CG two or three decades ago have seen the properties' values at least double, if not increase three to ten times from their original price, thus becoming de facto millionaires. Maria bought her two-floor maisonette at no. 21 CG in April 1992: 'We bought the flat with a mortgage when the previous owner, an old lady, died. I had fallen in love with it at first sight.' Maria is a retired primary school teacher and a widow now and she lives at no. 21 CG with two of her three sons. Together with her elder son, a filmmaker, she volunteers with young adults with disabilities and refugee and immigrant families. Their flat is one of the largest in CG, more than 150 square metres split over two floors. The living room on the ground floor is screened from the street by dozens of plants placed against the large bay window that looks like an indoor greenhouse. Though unpretentious and unsophisticated, the home is cosy and atmospheric and conveys an overall sense of inclusiveness. Nothing is there by chance; furniture and accessories tell a lot about the life story of the family, the places they had previously lived in or visited, their tastes and beliefs. The miniatures and butterflies framed on the walls, the tribal mask on the side table, the ethnic sculpture on the fireplace and the poster of a Ken Loach film are fragments of personal biographies – messy, temporary and precarious, as human lives are.

The human richness of Maria's interior contrasts strikingly with the anonymity of CG furbished homes available on the rental market. In these homes, immaculate fitted kitchens are combined with living areas where the banal becomes manifest through touches of exoticism mixed with a zest for vintage and a flavour of Britishness. A reproduction of a photograph chosen within a predictable range of subjects invariably complements these interiors, usually placed above the fireplace. Fireplaces are highly appraised and, together with bathtubs, represent the material and symbolic objectifications of the divide between flats and studios, no matter whether real fires are actually forbidden in central London or showers have replaced baths in the accelerated rhythms of everyday life. There are many flats of this kind in CG. They are almost identical to each other and to the vast majority of the flats on the rental market in central London. Estate agents label them as 'fully' or 'newly' 'refurbished to a high standard', as opposed to the properties described as 'with a lot of character and potential', hinting at a long-standing lack of substantial renovation.

The diversified array of accommodation available in CG, from bedsits to flats of various sizes, either newly refurbished or in disrepair, reflects the economic diversity within the social milieu of the street. In CG one can find British people like Maria who have been upgraded to be millionaires by the market living next door to rich foreign investors and to a mostly transient, less affluent multicultural population of students, professionals, skilled and unskilled workers. From this point of view, the characterisation of CG that emerges from an empirical approach to the study of its residential patterns discloses peculiarities and specificities that stand out in partial contradiction to the mainstream representation of prime central London locations as territories uniformly occupied by a fleeting and inaccessible elite of super-rich, and suggests the existence of wealth gaps in Kensington that collide with the depiction of this borough as the quintessential 'alpha territory' of the super-rich.

Filling up

Currently, the CG Victorian development accommodates a population that can be roughly estimated at 400/450 people distributed over 293 dwellings. These figures, obtained by comparing and contrasting the 2011 census data at the level of the local area (NOMIS 2017) with the results of street observations, indicate a densely occupied neighbourhood, matching the data reported by the census for the whole Borough of Kensington and Chelsea, which scores the second-highest population density and the highest household density in London and the UK (ONS 2011). While the extremely high figures in terms of population and household density come as no surprise, what is indeed surprising is the comparison of such figures with the demographic data provided by the historic censuses. In 1901, when the CG compound was in full occupation, it accommodated a population of 254 residents living in 57 independent dwellings. This means that over the course of 116 years, the number of residents has almost doubled, and those very houses that were created to accommodate a few dozen households are now parcelled up in a number of units that is five times bigger than the number foreseen in the original development. For a thorough understanding of the present residential pattern, this section will focus on the process that underpinned the transformation of the CG built environment from self-contained Victorian townhouses to boarding houses/bedsits and flats, demonstrating how such a process had already started at the beginning of the twentieth century in connection with major changes in the socio-economic milieu that are reflected in the composition and organisation of the household (fig. 1.8).

The CG Victorian development was built on a plot of approximately 7,000 square metres on the western side of WL previously occupied by a Georgian villa with a pleasure garden that was demolished (fig. 1.9). The new compound and the L-shaped street that cuts through it were given the fictional name Cheniston Gardens, passing it off as an old English version of Kensington (Loftie 1888:13–15). Thirty-nine high-rise terrace-houses were ready for occupation in 1882, together with three semi-detached artists' studios hidden in the corner where the street bends southwards (fig. 1.10). A fancy redbrick cottage, Cheniston Lodge, was attached to the western row of townhouses three years later, and in 1895 a mansion with 12 apartments was built next to it (fig. 1.11). The houses were erected over five levels, including a lower ground floor, using as building material a creamy stock brick pointed with reddish lime mortar that is typical of many Victorian buildings. Two architectural styles merged in the layout of the facades: small windows with red terracotta friezes on the two upper floors, classical stuccoed porticos and large bay windows on the levels below, quite likely an aesthetic artifice in an attempt to minimise the visual impact caused by the lower ceiling heights of the two upper floors. The difference in style of the two lower floors was accentuated by two rows of cast iron balustrades at street level and along the first floor, where they encapsulated small balconies running on the top of the patios and bay windows of the ground floor.

Each townhouse was meant to fit the needs of one family with a few servants. Each building was subdivided into 10–14 rooms over the four floors and the basement. On the lower ground, accessible via the external staircase but also connected internally to the upper floors, there were a kitchen, a pantry, a scullery, a cellar, the servants' toilet and two storage spaces for coal in the external patio. The ground and first floors were used as living spaces: a dining room and a library or smoking room on the

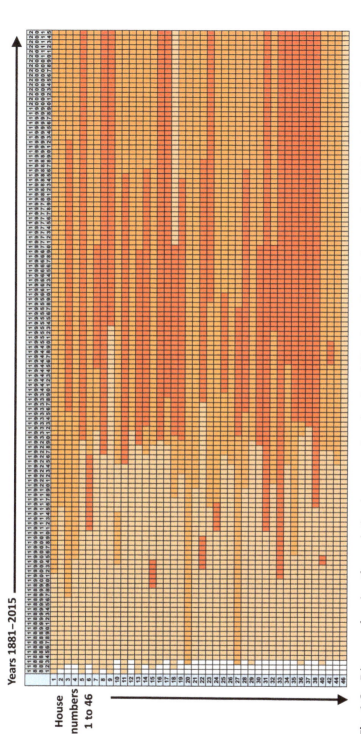

Fig. 1.8 Diagram showing the variation in occupation density of Cheniston Gardens houses from 1881 to 2015. Pale orange: single family dwellings; orange: flats; red: boarding houses, bedsits, studios. Source: author

Fig. 1.9 Map of the area before Cheniston Gardens was developed. Source: Ordnance Survey Map 1871, Sheet 74 Kensington

Fig. 1.10 Entrance to Cheniston Gardens studios nested among two rows of townhouses. Source: author

Fig. 1.11 Cheniston Gardens, view from south. To the left Cheniston Lodge and the apartment house that were added to the row of townhouses in 1885 and 1895. Source: author

ground floor, a landing and a drawing room on the first floor. The second floor accommodated three main bedrooms and a bathroom. Four smaller bedrooms on the top floor were meant for the servants but could also accommodate children if needed. Each floor was equipped with four fireplaces.

From the early 1880s to the turn of the century, CG townhouses became the homes of the families of well-to-do civil servants, army officers and professionals (solicitors, businessmen, doctors, engineers and architects). A large majority had colonial connections either by birth or by career, including quite a few retired officers who had spent part of their life in the colonies either in the army or in the civil service. A lively artistic community congregated around the three studios, adding a touch of bohemian atmosphere to the prevalent bourgeois character of the street: some were minor artists who left little track of their activities, yet a few were among the most successful portraitists of the Victorian aristocracy. In those days, CG residents were exclusively of British origin with roots in central or southern England, where many returned to spend part of the year in their family country estates, coming back to London for the 'season' (from October to the end of April).

While away, some residents rented out their houses on short-term agreements; others simply left them vacant for a substantial period of time: in 1891, 14 out of 42 households registered in the census were reported as being temporarily vacant or the properties occupied just by servants. An Irish enclave was formed by a group of houses next to each other on the northern stretch of the street, a residential pattern that unveils the contradictory feelings of the elite sector of the Irish migration, whose members on the one hand tended to group together to preserve their ethnic identity, and on the other hand were keen to mix with the English upper class to mark their status and at the same time act as ambassadors of Irish cultural values within British society (Swift and Gilley 1999).

A substantial number of spinsters and widows 'living on their own means' provide clues to the existence in CG already in 1891 of small yet prosperous renting businesses. The most renowned house in this respect was that of Mrs Vernon, who ran an unofficial boarding house at no. 32. An artist involved in the Women's suffrage movement, a lieutenant, a clerk at an insurance office, a student at the National Health Society, a retired army general and a retired engineer are just a pale reflection of the varied community she accommodated at her premises in the course of almost 40 years.

In Charles Booth's social map of London of 1889, CG is represented in yellow, a colour employed for the 'Upper-middle and Upper class' (Booth 1891). Yellow areas are not uniformly widespread in Kensington, and CG stands out in the map among less affluent areas that are represented in red, confirming its character as an exclusive elite neighbourhood (fig. 1.12). However, according to the census carried out two years later, the members of the wealthy families amounted to just 74 out of the 169 people living in CG, and the rest of the population were servants. Except for a footman, a page and a valet, all the servants were women, in large majority from southern England and London, aged from 15 to 60 according to their tasks. Their overwhelming presence was crucial in shaping CG everyday rhythms as highly gendered. Husbands were away at work for most of the day, while teenaged sons were spending part of the year in college elsewhere. CG, therefore, was the absolute domain of women: housewives with their daughters, spinsters, widows and servants (fig. 1.13).

With the new century, an increase in the number of boarding houses began to undermine the stability that had characterised the CG social milieu during the previous 20 years. The shift towards a more structured renting business is hinted already in 1901 in the field notes of

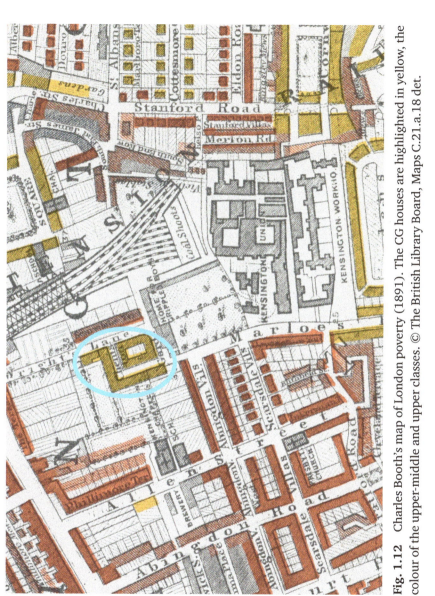

Fig. 1.12 Charles Booth's map of London poverty (1891). The CG houses are highlighted in yellow, the colour of the upper-middle and upper classes. © The British Library Board, Maps C.21.a.18 det.

Fig. 1.13 Maid on the front door of a Cheniston Gardens townhouse. Photo by Edward Linley Sambourne, 29 July 1906. © The Royal Borough of Kensington and Chelsea, 18 Stafford Terrace

Inspector King, a police officer in charge of the survey of Kensington for the new edition of Charles Booth's social map, who observes that CG 'looks like lodging houses' and suggests to represent CG as 'red to yellow' in the map, where the red stands for 'a hardworking sober, energetic class' (Booth 1902:33–62). A substantial change in the CG social milieu is confirmed 10 years later by the number of official boarding houses recorded by the new census. Gradually, the typical Victorian family with servants was giving way to a different kind of household, centred on the housekeeper. A woman in most cases, she was responsible for accommodating the boarders and for their lodging. In-house servants were not necessary, since the housekeeper was also directly in charge of domestic services or hired cleaners living elsewhere. Together with her family, she usually occupied a small portion of the house either in the basement or on the ground floor. The housekeepers and the members of their families – a jobbing paperhanger, an upholsterer, a clerk in a coach-building firm, a bookbinder, a milk carrier, a carpenter and joiner, just to mention a few – had little to share with the upper-class people who had been dominant in CG during the previous three decades. The change in the social milieu was also favoured by an increasing number of boarders. These were in the vast majority young people in their 20s: some had come to London to study at the university; many were music students or professional musicians, quite likely in connection with the nearby Royal Academy of Music; others were foreigners who had come to London to improve their English; a few young girls were aspiring actresses seeking their fortune on the London stage.

At the same time, the gradual displacement from CG of the upper-middle class was facilitated by the aspirations for change of that very elite. By the turn of the century, bearing the costs for the maintenance of a large Victorian property with live-in servants came to be considered unaffordable, and new types of dwellings appeared more suitable to a modern lifestyle, from self-contained flats to smaller detached or semi-detached houses in the new London suburbs, where people could benefit from more greenery and much cleaner air. The lack of green space became a particularly crucial issue for CG residents when it was announced that a massive development of six-storey mansions was to be built just behind the street on the last bit of green space in the surroundings of WL. The opposition of several CG householders did not succeed in stopping or changing the project of Iverna Court, which was completed in 1901. In the meantime, an increasing number of commercial premises were altering the original residential character of the street, bringing a further reason for the progressive estrangement of the upper class. At the beginning, these were essentially dressmakers' workshops, which worked to supply the fashionable department stores – Barkers, Derry & Toms, and Pontings – that had started their fast-growing expansion on the High Street, but over the course of the years other businesses joined in: schools of dance and music, care homes, a kindergarten, private clubs with restaurants, therapists and masseurs.

During the inter-war period, the scale of conversion of the original Victorian homes into smaller units became massive in connection with the needs of a new type of dweller looking for affordable accommodation, no matter how small it was. In view of this, many houses were converted into one- to three-bedroom flats or into cheap bedsits, where any available space was turned into a place to sleep equipped with a washbasin. Renovations implied in most cases extensions to the rear of the buildings in order to fit bathrooms and toilets on all floors and to create extra space for new bedrooms. Bit by bit, internal courtyards and patios disappeared, replaced by messy brick boxes, piled up one on top of the other without any planning criteria and with the complicity of loose building controls that followed the overarching principle that anything can happen to the interior as long as it is not visible from the outside. The massive transformation into smaller living units is likely to have been favoured by the compressed design of the buildings, which implied simple readjustments rather than reshaping; without spare spaces in excess, a bedsit could be created by just shutting a door. Likewise, inexpensive extensions for additional rooms were just as easily carried out, particularly in the central building compound, where the backyards of the townhouses are encapsulated inside four wings of facades and therefore totally concealed from view (fig.1.14).

Again, in this new phase, a vast majority of residents were single women, now flocking to live in central London as the result of major transformations in the labour market during the first decades of the twentieth century. The first to arrive had been young girls from poorer areas of London, hired as live-in apprentices by the tailoring shops that had opened their businesses in CG. A second wave of women arrived after World War 1 (WW1), coming from all over the country to work in London as typists, receptionists, shop assistants, or employees in the civil service. Some CG boarding houses accepted exclusively women, as it was at the Perks', which accommodated female boarders throughout its 60 years of activity at no. 30. When the Perks had moved to CG in 1911, John Perks was a clerk at the stock exchange and Elsie, his wife, a dressmaker/employer. Like all other CG tailors, Madame Elsie shut down her business by the end of the 1920s and turned her workshop into a boarding house. Elizabeth, who recently passed away, was one of the boarders in 1943. She was 22 years old, had just graduated in English from Oxford, and had found a job in London as a civil servant at the Ministry of Information in Senate House. Between air raids, she was carrying on a fair routine, working until 6.00p.m., taking typing lessons at Pitmans, and going out with friends in the West End in the evenings. She recalls her stay at the Perks' as a substantial improvement compared to her previous accommodation in North London, where she had to climb up five floors to reach the toilet: 'In CG my room was on the first floor, not far from the bathroom. There was a partition dividing the bed from the stove and the sink. Apart from the bed, there was no other furniture in the room, and when I had friends visiting me, we used to sit on the floor.'

Alongside boarding houses and bedsits, sectors of townhouses were converted into flats of various sizes, some occupying one single floor, others extending over two floors into large maisonettes. Better-off families, predominantly British, but also American and Australian, from

Fig. 1.14 Aerial view of the rear extensions of the central group of Cheniston Gardens townhouses. © Google Earth

more advantaged social and economic backgrounds were living in these larger dwellings. At no. 17, a maisonette on the second and third floor was the home of the offspring of two business partners of the renowned department store Fortnum & Mason. Emma, a current resident at no. 12, recalls that the Sewells, distant relatives of her husband, lived there from the 1930s to the end of the 1950s: 'They had created a large dance studio that occupied the whole first floor; it was still there with part of its decoration, its mirrors, an empty, magnificent open space when we moved here thirty years ago.' That was the studio of Edna Morton Sewell, the world champion ballroom dancer known as Edna Deane, famous for being the 'girl who danced with the Prince of Wales nine times in a row' (*New York Times* 1995).

In the aftermath of WW2, London was hit by a severe housing crisis as a consequence of the shortage of new homes and of the heavy damage to the housing stock from air raids. The Kensington 'Great Sunday Squat' on 8 September 1946, when more than a thousand people took over empty flats in the district, lasted only two weeks but led the central government to act with new social housing measures (Burnham 2004). These measures implied that many unoccupied buildings in central London were to be turned into council houses. In CG, no. 25 was confiscated and converted into a house for destitute old ladies. A few years later, the Cheniston Court Hotel that extended over two buildings was transformed into temporary accommodation for homeless families. Even the once-praised Cheniston Lodge, which had been home to rich merchants and professionals, became a council property and, after being used as air raid precaution depot during the war, was turned into the registrars' offices of the borough (Murphy 2010). However, differently from nearby Earls' Court and Notting Hill, Kensington was not targeted by the post-war massive migration of people forcibly displaced from their countries or voluntarily seeking asylum. A limited effect of such a phenomenon in CG is hinted at by a few Eastern European names (Polish, Russian, Yugoslav and Armenian) listed in the electoral rolls.

During the 1950s and 1960s, the whole of Kensington was being transformed into what has been labelled the 'land of the bedsitter' (Miles 2010:82), a world that Muriel Spark efficaciously represented in her best-selling novel *A Far Cry from Kensington* (Spark 1988). Bedsits in CG were now used on a corporate scale: a prominent dealer in antiques accommodated his many American customers at no. 23, no.18 was a staff hostel for Sainsbury's employees, no. 38 a nursing home.

While during the inter-war period, the coexistence of bedsit occupants and apartment householders had been apparently rather peaceful, the situation was different after the war: particularly from the 1960s, tensions among neighbours became a common affair, reflecting not only social differences but also generational conflicts. Complaints were made from the traditional households about groups of young people living together in rundown properties; sharing flats was in fact a fashionable habit among the youth counterculture gathered around the catch-all term of 'swinging London', which had in the nearby High Street one of its most iconic temples, the fashionable Biba shop. From the 1970s, bedsit landlords were largely people of foreign nationality, either well-off Middle Eastern investors or expatriates from Eastern European countries, as was the case with the Serbian owners of a bed and breakfast at no. 28 CG, who had started as cleaners and caretakers in the 1960s ending up in the 1980s with a financial empire in the hotel business. The aggressive approach of this new wave of speculators was the origin of complaints from many flats' householders; the director of a well-known London museum, who was living in CG in those years, was literally obsessed by the growing number of 'disguised hotels' and by the intensive letting out of rooms that was transforming the residential character of the street.

The count of the people registered in the electoral rolls suggests a specific demographic trend for CG, showing constant population growth from the 1930s to at least the 1960s, in stark contrast with the census figures relating to Kensington, which are conversely characterised by a substantial population drop (GB Historical GIS 2017). During this period of time, CG residents were, in the vast majority, white British, with the addition of a few Europeans, Australians and Americans, but from the 1980s foreign migration, particularly from European countries, became significant both in CG and in the wider neighbourhood. This was the time when the Galicians came to live at no. 9. Bedsits and flats were quite rundown in those days, due to a lack of renovation for many years, and provided cheap accommodation to a multicultural population often from disadvantaged backgrounds. Emily has a vivid memory of the tenants who lived in her basement flat before she moved in: 'There by the toilet's door there was a hole on the floor where he [a drug dealer] used to hide the dope. He shared the flat with an Argentinian prostitute who was claiming she was doing the job part-time just when her husband was away.' Maria remembers the 'filthy curtains reeking of cigarettes' she found when she moved to no. 21; 'We stripped everything away; under the carpet we discovered a whole layer of old newspapers reporting on the Vietnam war.' Some dwellings were available under a social housing scheme that, in a few circumstances, was in force until not long ago:

'A Scottish cleaner was still living in this house after it was renovated; the agent told me it was hard to make her vacate the room,' explains the American art student at no. 6. In 2001, more than a dozen residents from African and Afro-Caribbean backgrounds were still renting under a social housing scheme. These types of dwellings, run down and for this very reason 'affordable', existed until very recently in CG, and in a few cases still exist today, alongside flats that have been renovated to the highest standards. Just a few yards away from no. 9, where the Galician enclave is squeezed in cramped bedsits, the three Cheniston Studios have been the home of well-off arty types and celebrities all the way into the new millennium, the late Robin Gibb of the Bee Gees being just the last of a long list of renowned names.

Dwelling inequalities ultimately explain the current uneven appearance of CG, yet they are scarcely visible from the outside. As on a theatre stage, the Victorian facades with their repetitive architectural patterns act as brick curtains, keeping out of sight what is going on behind the scenes. Only the long lists of numbers on the doorbells, in the majority carelessly scribbled, hint at what is concealed behind the front doors. Inequalities have been at work in CG since the first occupants settled in the street more than 130 years ago; at the very beginning it was the distinction between servants and members of the affluent Victorian families, then among bedsit tenants on short-term contracts and long-term flat occupiers, then between migrants and wealthy white British. Through the act of dwelling, the less affluent and the better off have been ceaselessly living side by side in a social milieu that, far from being the exclusive terrain of a consistently wealthy class, has been characterised over time by people with pronounced economic disparities: between the poor and the affluent, the well to do and the wealthy and, in more recent times, between the rich and the super-rich. In this perspective, the analysis of residential patterns over time transcends the minutiae of the historical reconstruction and provides a powerful lens for understanding the complexity of contemporary urban inequalities (Atkinson, Burrows and Rhodes 2016; Butler and Watt 2007; Dorling 2014; Hamnett 2003; Minton 2017; Savage et al. 2015).

The neighbourhood

The most recent comprehensive update on the CG population has been provided by the Office for National Statistics through the neighbourhood statistics area-based web service, NOMIS, where 2011 census data have been released at the level of preset small geographical output areas (NOMIS 2017). CG data are included in an output area referring to 198 households constituting a total of 281 residents. Although this area does not match exactly the CG compound (a part of the southern stretch of the street is cut out), the data associated with it provide a fairly accurate picture of the CG neighbourhood at the time of the last national census. They show that 60 per cent of the dwellings are one-person households; two-person households represent 25 per cent, while those with more than two people 15 per cent. The picture that emerges is of a population of singles (either unmarried or separated/divorced) and couples without children. The number of women is slightly lower than that of men (47 versus 53 per cent), according to a countertrend that started with the new millennium and is now consistent all over the borough. Age records show that 65 per cent of the residents are between 25 and 44 – a fairly young adult population compared to the figures available for the borough as a whole, where the same life stage is represented by 39 per cent of the residents. Many are graduates and work in professional or managerial occupations, and their incomes are well above the national average and, although less dramatically, above the London average. In the geo-demographic segmentation of socio-economic types developed by Acorn, the vast majority fit into the category of 'metropolitan professionals', while the so called 'metropolitan money', whose homes are worth over £1 million, are under-represented as compared to other Kensington neighborhoods (http://acorn.caci.co.uk). In other words, CG is a street where the 'ordinary rich' prevail as opposed to the 'super-rich' gathered in other more exclusive areas of the borough.

The contrast with the borough figures is particularly remarkable when it comes to people's ethnicity and country of origin. Although Kensington, and CG with it, are traditionally white areas with a white population above 70 per cent, the ratio between white British and 'other Whites' shows an almost reversed pattern: British and Irish represent 42 per cent of the population in Kensington and 27 per cent in CG, while the 'other Whites' are 29 per cent in Kensington and 50 per cent in CG. Compared to the figure for the whole city of London, where they represent only 13 per cent, the 'other Whites' stand out as a robust component of the Kensington population, but their presence in CG is well over the average for the borough. The same applies to the country of birth: those born in the UK/Ireland are 50 per cent in Kensington and 31 per cent in CG, while Europeans (European Union (EU) and non-EU) are 20 per cent in Kensington and 36 per cent in CG (fig. 1.15). Zooming in on the census records for the output area, there were 102 Europe-born residents

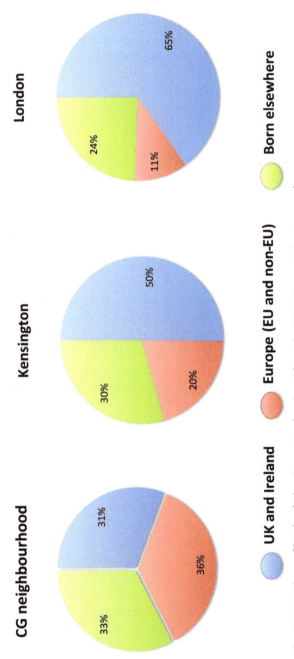

Fig. 1.15 Place of birth of Cheniston Gardens' residents in 2011 Census. Source: author

in 2011: 17 from Spain, 12 from Italy, 10 German, 9 French and the rest from Poland, Romania, Portugal and Turkey. The availability of small accommodation in rented bedsits and studios is likely to have acted as a catalyst for a growing wave of Europeans favoured until now by free movement within the EU, to the extent that at present European-born residents represent by far the largest component of CG multicultural environment. Besides the Europeans and the British, this includes to a lesser extent people from all over the world; according to the census records, 31 different languages apart from English are actually spoken in this small area.

Altogether, the picture provided by the census adds further evidence to what the analysis of the residential patterns has so far highlighted: that is, the unique character of CG, whose population on the one hand shares features with the wider borough, but on the other hand stands out for its own distinctive traits – a younger multicultural population with a far higher number of Europeans who live in this street on either a permanent or temporary basis.

However, although statistics and geo-referenced consumer classifications are undoubtedly helpful to spot peculiarities and suggest trends, they may easily lead to stereotyped generalisations. They give detailed evidence of a multicultural environment in CG, but they do not unravel the dynamics of diversity, rootedness and mobility that underpin it. They suggest forms of transnationalism that make class distinctions meaningless, but at the same time they do not provide explanations of how people connect to the place and the meanings they attach to it, as situated ethnographic research can do.

To understand the CG neighbourhood, it is necessary to focus on the habits and values of its residents and on how these are reflected in their relationship with the street, the borough, the city and the wider world. Adopting a broad phenomenological perspective, this research on the CG social environment wittingly moves away from abstract conceptualisations about neighbourhood and their multiple relationships with the idea of community that still enlivens the sociological debate about place (see Tonkiss 2003; Watt and Smets 2014) and focuses instead on the 'sensuous and sensory dimension of social experience and community life' (Back 2009:14). Neighbourhoods and communities in London are fleeting, fragile and constantly reworked. Yet bonds exist (Andreotti 2014; Blokland 2003; Blokland 2017) and the notion of neighbourhood cannot be simply dismissed as irreconcilable with contemporary London, as is suggested by Daniel Miller, who refers to the 'unprecedented coherence' and the 'unique configurations' at the level of individuals and households that are revealing of 'an internal holism and order set against the overall diversity of London' (Miller 2008; 2009:7–11).

Investigating the CG neighborhood should not necessarily mean searching for ties that justify its existence, or looking for its borders (Watt and Smets 2014:8). It rather means unravelling how near-dwellers coexist 'in place' and what meaning they ascribe to it. In CG, near-dwellers hardly know each other but they feel each other's presence: along the street or from the windows of their flats, their proximity is marked by gazes, gestures and rarely by words; a soft concurrence of signs and non-verbal exchanges defines the style of an 'imagined' neighbourhood, 'whose members will never know most of their fellow-members, meet them, or even hear of them, yet in the minds of each lives the image of their communion' (Anderson 2006:5, 6). From this point of view, CG provides a grounded example of the often cited 'London conviviality' (Gilroy 2004), where 'indifference to difference' is the key word to understand human relationships (Amin 2012; Valluvan 2016).

Cognitive maps

The investigation of a residential neighbourhood is challenging, because it lacks the vibrancy of human relations that, conversely, can be found in commercial streets, where social interaction is more overtly disclosed. A residential street is to a certain extent 'sanitised', and its sensorial lure more difficult to grasp compared, for example, to a market, where a phenomenological approach involves the whole sensorial spectrum (Rhys-Taylor 2013, 2017). In CG, smells and tastes remain behind closed doors, apart from the mixed aroma of baked muffins and fried eggs coming from The Muffin Man. In addition, the homogeneity of the Victorian architecture muffles the visual details and makes specificities not immediately ascertainable.

In such a context, the information about individual experiences and practices provided by the residents' interviews (table 1.1) and by their pictures and sketched maps of the neighbourhood becomes crucial for the understanding of CG everyday life. Photos and maps reflect individual and differentiated topographies that help one in disclosing habits, tastes, affects, encounters and activities that form part of the everyday routine of people. Liza, a CG resident since 2000, represents her neighbourhood as a series of routinised encounters: the aged newspaper man at the kiosk by the underground station entrance, the bank clerk

Table 1.1 List of the people interviewed in Cheniston Gardens

People	M/F	Age	Nationality	Place of birth	Sector of activity	Type of dwelling	In CG
Maria	F	46–60	British	Addis Ababa	education	maisonette	1992–
Emma	F	46–60	British	Gloucestershire	yoga teacher and artist	maisonette	1985–
Monica	F	31–45	Slovakian	Slovakia	real estate	bedsit	2010–14
Yussuf	M	46–60	Iraqi/British	Iraq	IT development	flat	1987–
Lenny	M	15	French Caribbean	Martinique	high school student	bedsit (with mum)	2012–14
Liza	F	over 60	British	Hampshire	healthcare	flat	2000–
Glenda	F	46–60	British	south of London	academic	basement flat	1984–
Kate	F	31–45	Australian	Australia	housewife	apartment	2014–
Emily	F	46–60	British	London	living on own means	basement flat	1994–
Thomas	M	over 60	Swiss	Switzerland	retired banker	flat	1990–2016
Rose	F	18–30	American	USA	MA student	bedsit	2014–15
Father Felipe	M	over 60	Spanish/British	Spain	priest	house	2007
Alice	F	46–60	American/British	USA	PR	flat	2008
Dominique	M	31–45	French	France	IT	flat	2012

(Continued table 1.1)

(Continued table 1.1)

People	M/F	Age	Nationality	Place of birth	Sector of activity	Type of dwelling	In CG
Fred	M	46–60	American	South Africa	IT CEO	maisonette	2013
Pedro	M	over 60	Spanish/British	Spain	watchman/housekeeper	flat	1985
Rob	M	Over 60	British	UK	doorman	flat	2000
Anthony	M	Over 60	British/Lebanese	Lebanon	owner of coffee shop	coffee shop	not known
Elizabeth	F	93	British	UK	retired	bedsit	In 1943

sitting behind his office window, the chocolate seller, the people at her gym in WL, and to the east, past her favourite charity shop, Waitrose where she buys her groceries. The neighbourhood topography that Emma draws traces her daily itinerary with her dog towards Kensington Gardens (fig.1.17), less than 10 minutes to the north-east of CG. This park is mentioned also by other residents as a place for a walk, either with dog or without, or to cycle through, often coupled with Holland Park, but most often in opposition to it: Emily starts her daily routine at 8.30a.m. by going for a walk with Rufus to Holland Park; Glenda takes her dog exclusively to Kensington Gardens; Liza goes cycling every day through Kensington Gardens, as in Holland Park cycling is forbidden. In the mental maps of many CG residents, these two extensive parks represent the eastern and western edges of neighbourhood interaction, compensating for the lack of green spaces in the immediate surroundings of CG, where the only form of greenery is provided by two slender and battered birch trees planted some 20 years ago on the inner corner of the street (fig. 1.16). Most of the residents' on-site routine takes place on the stretch of HSK between the two parks where a vast array of fancy, posh and expensive retailers and department stores are lined up. Shopping for groceries is a selective activity and may vary according to affordability, personal attitudes, interests and moods. Marks & Spencer, the closest supermarket to the tube station, is easily reachable 'in the days you are lazy or in hurry' (Emily), but at Waitrose 'the food is more fresh' (Liza); the Americans and the Italians prefer the alleged natural and organic products of the even more expensive Whole Foods. Dominique, a young French professional in the IT sector, goes to Whole Foods just for the 'small everyday grocery', and for the 'big stuff' he shops online; a sporty type, fond of rock climbing, cycling and jogging, he is also a regular client of the retailers of outdoor and mountain equipment that are aligned on the northern side of this stretch of the High Street at a stone's throw from each other. Five residents extend their maps of the neighbourhood to Stratford Road, a small alley to the south of CG, but their acquaintance with this location varies according to tastes and habits: Kate, a young Australian mother of two who lives in the apartment house at the end of CG, goes there for its pharmacy; Glenda because of its good pub; Emma for the tea room; Thomas for its grocery shops that create a village atmosphere; Lenny, the teenager from Martinique, because there he buys snacks and nibbles on his way to school. In the course of the interview, Maria, Dominique and Yussuf, an IT consultant living at no. 7, disclose their 'secret places' far from the crowd and hidden from view: for Maria, it is the roof garden of the iconic Barker's building on the High Street; for

Fig. 1.16 Cheniston Gardens – view towards the central corner of the street with the birch trees from a top-floor flat. Source: author

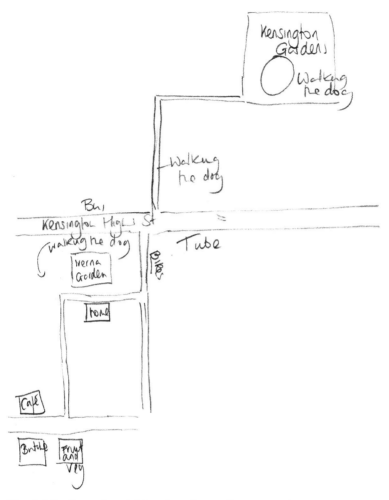

Fig. 1.17 Emma's neighbourhood map. Source: author

Dominique, the secluded alleys behind St Mary Abbots, those very streets that Ezra Pound hated for the noisy bells; Yussuf took me behind the parish to show me his little green corner with a bench by the old churchyard.

Belonging in contemporary Cheniston Gardens

Altogether, the phenomenology of everyday routines and bodily experiences suggests that the people who live in CG sense their local environment in manifold ways. Following on from that, the idea of neighbourhood that emerges, rather than univocal and unambiguous, takes a variety of configurations, all of them precarious and unstable, that reflect personal and contingent choices as well as different forms of social belonging. Particularly, the narratives of the rooted residents, often also homeowners, disclose a strong attachment to their CG homes: 'I have been knowing CG for a long time; there was a special memory attached to it, as we had married here at the register office just opposite this house in 1977; we were living in Earls Court before and the landlord was very nasty with my kids and when this house came on the market I literally fell in love with it' (Maria). 'CG is my home. I like it for its diversity, its location and for being a little scruffy' (Emily). And again: 'It's the last scruffy street in this part of Kensington, but it has a lot of character' (Emma). 'Scruffy' is a recurring adjective in the descriptions of CG, and, in contrast to 'shabby', it entails an implicit loving indulgence for this 'idiosyncratic' street (Glenda). Those who have been living in CG for a long time seem to love it even more precisely because of its rundown character, like a mother who shows a particular care for a sickly child.

If these are tangible examples of what has been described as 'elective belonging' that reflect the intentionality of a residential choice (Savage 2010; Savage, Bagnall and Longhurst 2005; Watt and Smets 2014), positive forms of attachment to CG are manifested also by the transient population: 'This is one of the best places to live in London, it is a safe area, but my accommodation was so tiny, the supermarkets so expensive, and also the neighbours so noisy […]. I moved with my sister to Ealing Broadway, it is more liveable there, and now I am pregnant, I could not live here with a child, but I keep coming here, I like the surroundings, there is Holland Park, The Muffin Man and so many cute little streets to walk around' (Monica, in a bedsit, two years in CG). But in general, the attitude of the transient residents is more detached, if not negative: 'I moved to CG from east London because I liked this residential area, particularly its quiet position, close to the parks and to the South Kensington museums, but I do not know anybody here' (Dominique). For Fred, an American CEO, CG is 'just a place to live, with a convenient location by the tube station, close to grocery shops and to London cultural centres, but the area is too snobbish and people are not all friendly'. In 2016, Fred finally left his luxury maisonette in CG and moved to Notting Hill: 'I prefer Notting Hill to Kensington, it has a more diverse economic and racial mix. Anyway, I stop two or three times a month at Whole Foods in Kensington on my way home, then hop on the bus from there to Notting Hill, and I can still run on weekends in Kensington Gardens.'

The number of years necessary to become a 'rooted' resident varies from one situation to another, but, ultimately, a proactive attitude is helpful in speeding up the process. This is what happened with Alice, who was already a soundly rooted resident two years after her arrival at no. 10 CG in 2006. American by birth, but prompted by a genuine interest in British heritage, she decided to launch a CG residents' association in order to foster joint actions on communal goals: 'The residents' feedback went beyond my expectations and I realised that the wish to bring CG back to a decent standard was a shared aspiration.' 'The association' echoes Thomas, the Swiss banker, 'could do a lot to help improving the character of the street, for example we could persuade bedsits owners to instruct their tenants to dispose of their rubbish in the set collection days.' But in spite of the good start, the association has been inactive since 2011.

Although a few CG residents declare to have good relationships with some of the people living in the street, and stories of communal solidarity are provided to support evidence of proactive neighbourhood relationships, the logic of collective action is absolutely temporary and volatile. Relations among 'near dwellers' are not revolving around the dynamics of negotiation among tied social groups – outsiders versus insiders or between those 'on the move' and the rooted residents – neither can we observe the polarisation between newcomers and an established white British community being forced 'by necessity' to move out from its elective location that has been observed elsewhere in the affluent west London neighbourhoods (Glucksberg 2015, 2016:250; Minton 2017:7–9).

Within the debate about communities and neighbourhoods in urban contexts, we find multiple explanations of the lack of cohesiveness and the concurrent increase in anonymity and alienation in what seems to become more and more a society of strangers (Amin 2012; Tonkiss 2003). Whatever specific explanation is put forward, there is an almost general consensus to consider the looseness of social and cultural bonds as a typical condition of post-modernity and a consequence of the flows of globalisation and of accelerated mobility (Bauman 2000; Elliott and Urry 2010; Giddens 1990; Urry 2007). Particularly, David Harvey (1989, 2001:124) has articulated the concept of 'time–space compression' to deal with the uncertainty of being in a place as a constituent element of post-modernity. Yet, in the specific case of CG, things seem to work slightly differently. As we have seen in the previous section, the wealthy British elite started moving out of CG 'by choice' at the beginning of the twentieth century, and the transformation of the neighbourhood was accelerated by the concurrent increase in boarding houses and bedsits that favoured different social configurations. Apart from a few stable residents, a relentless turnover of people had already started in CG in the inter-war period, and since then the pace of change in residential patterns has been and keeps being too fast to allow any stable form of aggregation among people. In other words, by analysing the residential trends over time, we can argue that in CG 'space–time compression' was having an impact on the social life of the neighbourhood long before postmodernity, suggesting that a detailed analysis of household mobility over time might shed new light on social trends that are considered integral to the contemporary society.

In CG, the idea of community endures in idealised narratives of past events but does not apply to the present: 'When we moved here [1992] there was a different atmosphere, people sitting outside on the doorsteps, chatting and laughing, I do not know, perhaps it was because it was a very hot summer that year, everybody seemed to know each other' (Maria). Proactive behaviour recurs in the form of a shared neighbourhood mythology, as in the story of the night when a hardened group of neighbours convinced the car-clamping truck man not to remove the car of a disabled resident who had left CG before the temporary parking ban had been implemented, or of the voluntary care offered on various occasions to an old lady living in a top floor flat. In practice, on the rare occasions when soft and volatile forms of neighbourhood relations occur, these take the shape of hybrid and contingent configurations rather than enduring alliances, and they might involve tastes and sensibilities or intersect issues of gender, age and ethnicity. For example, female residents share a recurrent narrative in which three male rooted 'personalities' emerge: Anthony, the owner of The Muffin Man, Pedro, the Galician caretaker, and Rob, the doorman of the apartment house, whom they describe as the watchdogs of the street. The crucial role of these three people as unofficial guardians of CG is confirmed also by male residents either verbally or by their drawings of the neighbourhood, but what makes women's descriptions unique is the charisma embedded with the paternal authority they bestow on these three male figures, a charisma that is reminiscent of pristine logics of self-sustaining patriarchal communities. On the other hand, looking at the three CG guardians from another angle, the fact that they are from three different ethnic backgrounds – a Spanish Galician (Pedro), a Lebanese (Anthony) and a white British (Rob) – is paradigmatic not only of the transnational urbanity of contemporary London, but also of how the often-cited 'multicultural drift' (Hall 2000) is today a taken-for-granted scenario in this west London street. Multiculturalism started unfolding as an incremental process from the 1980s in CG and it is today an uncontroversial reality. Of course, in the case of CG, as in the rest of central London, the smoothness of the process has been facilitated by the economic prosperity of the residents and by the character of their 'migration', driven, in the vast majority, by 'lifestyle' aspirations (Benson 2009, 2014; Benson and Osbaldiston 2014) rather than by necessity.

However, even if multicultural relations are easy and smooth, different cultural sensibilities occasionally emerge, particularly in connection with building maintenance. When asking the residents what was the thing they disliked most about CG, quite frequently the answer was one of their fellow tenants; when investigating the reasons, distressing stories emerged including trials, tribunal notifications, prying and harassment in relation to the properties. Such harsh conflicts are likely to be generated by different sets of values and meanings that are ascribed to the idea of 'conservation'. For the conservationists, the material properties of the ancient buildings and the skills implied in their construction are enshrined as sacred: 'the bricks themselves […] are treated as art objects and proof of authenticity' (Samuel 1994:119–20). Conservationists in CG invest the Victorian creamy stock brick with almost human qualities: they describe it as tactile, textured and grainy, individual, quirky, warm. They refer to it as to a human body that needs to breathe and that matures and improves with the passage of years. Such an extremely sectarian attitude hardly reconciles with the practical strategies of those who think of refurbishment exclusively in terms of modernisation and simplification and propose to coat the brick surface of the building with grey paint to make it look clean for longer, or to substitute the original window frames with plastic ones so they will not deteriorate. Moreover, when the material practices of renovation are called into question, the Europeans in general, but particularly the Italians, seem to have a totally different approach from British residents. For the British, the imperative is the external look – and for this reason they do the least possible work, ultimately cheap and scruffy, provided the bad quality of the finishes is appropriately concealed. At the other end of the spectrum, the Italians are driven by a deep-seated *habitus* for durable works of the best possible standard: 'That bloody Italian and his works, he broke through my ceiling and now he wants to get rid of my water tank on the roof; he is absolutely arrogant, I want to report him for bullying […].' Liza's belligerent words are echoed by Maria's more composed opinion about the couple who recently bought the top-floor flat in the same house where she lives: 'They are Swiss you know, their posh architect wants us [the people living in the other flats] to engage in massive communal works; we do not care, we just let them talk.' Ultimately, two different visions of the built environment are at stake: a soft one, pointing at the fleeting and unstable nature of the buildings, and a hard one that is keen to invest financially and emotionally in the longevity of the home.

Mobility and the 'other place'

CG is the place where people have their homes, but it is a fact that in contemporary society the time people spend at home, and the relations revolving around it, take just a limited proportion of their lives. Sociality is increasingly 'deterritorialised' both at the level of individual desires and aspirations and of the embodied practices of the everyday (Appadurai 1990). The way people connect to a place is unavoidably entangled with the way they connect with the 'outside', whether real or virtual. In such accentuated dynamics of deterritorialisation, mobility plays a crucial role (Urry 2000, 2007).

'Convenience' is invariably the answer I was given by CG residents when I asked why they chose to live here: the convenience of a well-connected underground line at a stone's throw from their homes that frees them from the use of the car even when they own one: 'I take the car only when I need to go outside the Circle line or to shop for heavy stuff at Tesco on the Cromwell Road' (Emily). Living by the underground station increases the quality of their lives and pays them back in terms of 'discretionary' control over time and ultimately in an individual sense of freedom (Wajcman 2015:65). Using the underground, they move around London leading to their workplaces (mostly eastwards to the City or to the western media and technology hubs), but during their leisure time they are doggedly local, just rotating around the two parks or other venues situated in Kensington and its immediate surroundings, more rarely along the river by Southwark, the Tate Modern and the Borough Market. On weekends of good weather, they may jog long distances or cycle further westwards along the Thames towards Richmond, but they do not seem at all keen to go east beyond the City, providing evidence that the traditional distinction between west and east London is not just a residual legacy of the past, but is still working as a social and cultural divide, although with different patterns and under different social conditions than in the past.

The trajectories that drive residents out of CG occasionally intersect wider diasporic landscapes: 'Every weekend I go to Elephant and Castle where we have one of the branches of our Chaplaincy' says Father Felipe of the Augustinian Recollects; his mission and his social encounters are there, beyond the river, among one of the largest Latin American communities in London; for him, CG is just a place to live and to host a few Latin American Catholic students; the only other people he knows in the street, besides those staying at the residence, are the Galicians, because 'they are catholic and speak the same language'. The Galicians, in turn, have connections with the northern fringes of Portobello Road: 'When we arrived,' Pedro remembers, 'many of us already lived there; we have the Spanish School in Portobello road [the Instituto Vicente Cañada Blanch], it is not far from here, just one stop on the underground.' While Father José and the Galicians need to go out from Kensington to connect with other expats, by contrast, the Armenians, who are concentrated in the London boroughs of Ealing, Hounslow, Brent and Haringey, every year at the middle of July flock to Iverna Court, the large garden square that was built just behind CG, for the Armenian Street Festival. In the CG surroundings there are no traces of an Armenian community – not a single Armenian apparently lives in CG – yet the Armenians converge here from all over London to pay tribute to the ethnic, political and religious legitimation of their contested nation, symbolically embodied by the presence in this area of two centres of power and resistance: the church of St Sarkis, whose construction was financed in 1923 by Calouste Gulbenkian, a British Armenian who had amassed a huge fortune in the petroleum business, and the Armenian Embassy, which opened at no. 25 CG in 1961, despite the resistance of the UK government, thanks to the passionate efforts of an Armenian dentist living in CG in those years (Amit Talai,1989; George 2009).

CG residents' mobility follows inwards and outwards trajectories that expand concentrically throughout Kensington, across London and beyond towards the rest of the world, mingling with the entangled network of disembodied connections enabled by digital information and communications technologies (Castells 1996). Material and virtual mobility are crucial to facilitate social relations and to connect to places afar. The existence of a meaningful 'other place' is a feature shared by many residents in CG, a place that acts as a counter-landscape as it stands out in dialectical opposition to the place of abode and at the same time complements it. The 'other place', either near or distant, wide or enclosed, is where people actually spend or have spent part of their life or they plan, look for or just dream about returning to sooner or later. In the experiences of the transnational residents, the 'other place' reconnects to the 'ethnoscapes' (Appadurai 1996) where global and local processes intersect. Through its juxtaposition to 'the place of abode', the 'other place' generates different forms of place attachment within the wide scenario of what has been described as 'cosmopolitan belonging' (Amit and Gardiner Barber 2015; Andreotti, Le Gales and Moreno-Fuentes 2015; Jones and Jackson 2014).

A first type of 'other place' is that of the transient transnational residents, the young cosmopolitan professionals who live their life 'on the move', or the international students who stay in CG for a short period of time. For them, 'the other place' is a special place in their homelands to which they are linked by strong familial and social bonds. They have a life suspended between two places, their temporary London address and a home in their country of origin; their emotions are connected to both place of origin and place of arrival (Andreotti, Le Gales and Moreno-Fuentes 2013), and their identification with two places can produce emotional complexities (Schiller and Caglar 2011). Their contacts with the 'other place' are on a daily or weekly basis and involve regular connections via social media and travels. When they meet with other expats in London, they mix with the multicultural population of the city, but when they receive visits from their relatives, they invariably wish them to experience the 'true' British atmosphere of The Muffin Man. Sometimes, transiency may turn into a rooted habit, as for Thomas and his wife, who went back to their 'other place' after 30 years spent in CG: 'We moved to Lugano mid March [2016]. We had spent over 20 years here before coming to London and we have still some friends. Life here is just the opposite than London. It is provincial, quiet, lovely weather. Obviously we miss London but we often visit our son and four grandchildren who live in Camden.'

Of a totally different type is the 'other place' of the long-established migrants – the Galicians, the Iraqis, the Lebanese – who came to London more than 30 years ago and are now fully rooted British citizens. For these people, the bond with the country of origin transcends the physical, political and cultural forms of that very land and becomes part of an individual mythology which is usually shared with other expats living in London and the UK: 'Galicia is a beautiful green land, very different from the rest of Spain, there is good wine and food' (Pedro). Their attachment to their homeland is usually quite loose, particularly when they belong to a nation currently afflicted by political and social instability: 'There are quite a few Iraqis in Kensington, the owner of the Thai restaurant is Iraqi too, but we prefer not to think of what is going on in our country, we live here now' (Yussuf). But in extraordinary circumstances, roots can be temporarily revived: Emily, who describes herself as a white British

Kensington resident, suddenly rediscovered her Christian Lebanese origins on the occasion of the 7/7 terrorist attack: 'I talked a lot with Anthony [the owner of The Muffin Man]; he is Lebanese and Christian. We cried together. I lived in Beirut as a child; I am half Jewish and half Lebanese, but Christian like him.'

The 'other place' in CG exists also at a different level, based on the contrast between the urban and the rural: Emma's 'other place' is her cottage on Exmoor, where she also has her artist's studio; for Glenda, it is her mother's house in the south, where she cultivates her passion for horse riding; for Emily it is her retreat on the Isle of Wight; for Alice, her cottage in Sussex, where she can express her love for gardening. The recurrent characterisation of this otherness is 'nature' in its phenomenological dimension of a place where the body can live, move and breathe differently than in the city, where the only available green spaces near CG are represented by two very urban parks. The opposition of urban and rural, particularly between London and the English countryside, has a long history (Matless 1998), and conceptually it can be argued that these rural retreats are the modern version of the country estate of the Victorian family – a place where individual rhythms and routines are reinvented with the complicity of a different landscape.

Conclusion

Fine-grain ethnography combined with documental research has revealed that CG is not wholly consistent with the cliché of social exclusiveness that broadly applies to the Kensington district and more generally to the wider western area of central London, suggesting the existence of wealth gaps behind the Victorian facades that are unexpected in the quintessential 'alpha territory' of the super-rich. By exploring narratives and notions of belonging in contemporary CG, this chapter suggests that social distinctions in contemporary Kensington seem connected with forms of cosmopolitan belonging rather than with hierarchies based on class and wealth.

By extending the analysis of the residential patterns over time, this chapter has argued that the cultural and social distinctions that are at work today in CG are grounded into the process of conversion of the Victorian family houses into smaller independent units that started at the beginning of the twentieth century when two contrasting dwelling styles – one based on larger flats, and the other on bedsits with single occupants – began to attract to this street people of different socio-economic and cultural backgrounds. Overall, the research on CG shows how 'local' examples can be used to explore broader questions in connection with the spatial distribution of the elites in contemporary London, suggesting that the history of places plays a crucial role in steering their residential patterns.

Since observation of the street started in 2013 and residents' interviews were carried out in 2014, many things have changed in CG: a few facades have been cleaned, others repainted; the Galician townhouse is still there, but even more dilapidated; the lady with the nice balcony left and took her plants with her, and the cat on the first floor balcony has also gone; Glenda retired; Thomas returned to Switzerland; other interviewees left their CG homes. The result of the 2016 referendum that has ratified the exit of the UK from the EU is likely to impact heavily on the geography of CG and of the whole of Kensington, and new residential configurations are likely to occur before 2020. One year later, the devastating Grenfell Tower fire, which left more than 70 people dead and hundreds homeless, has dramatically pointed at the striking juxtaposition within the same neighbourhood between outright winners and vulnerable losers in the battlefield of social and housing inequality. Turbulence can be forecast in the 'alpha territory', and once more the new will add to the old in a dialectic continuum where the present is just 'the latest episode of the ever-same' (Benjamin 1974:673; Savage 2000:40).

Methodological note

The archival research on CG has been based on extensive use of the household data collected for the 1891, 1901 and 1911 censuses, and on the street directories and electoral rolls available from the Local Studies collection of the Kensington and Chelsea Library. Interviews with CG residents were carried out in the summer 2014 and involved informal talks with 19 people, who also provided sketches and pictures of the neighbourhood. Ten are female and nine male; their age range, nationality, sectors of activity, type of house and length of stay in CG are given in table 1.1. Although I (the author) have obtained informed consent to publish the results of the interviews, names have been changed. All the photographs of CG except otherwise specified have been taken by me.

References

Allsop. 2014. Catalogue of residential auction, 17 December 2014. http://www.auction.co.uk/residential/home.asp?JP=LDE&A=881&ID=881000023

Amin, A. 2012. *Land of Strangers*. Cambridge: Polity Press.

Amin, A. and Thrift, N. 2002. *Cities: Reimagining the Urban*. Cambridge: Polity Press.

Amit Talai, V. 1989. *Armenians in London: The Management of Social Boundaries*. Anthropological Studies of Britain no. 4. Manchester: Manchester University Press.

Amit, V. and Gardiner Barber, P. 2015. 'Mobility and Cosmopolitanism: Complicating the Interaction between Aspiration and Practice', *Identities* 22(5): 543–50.

Anderson, B. 2006. *Imagined Communities: Reflections on the Origin and Spread of Nationalism*. London: Verso.

Andreotti, A. 2014. 'Neighbourhoods in the Globalized World', *Sociologia Urbana e Rurale* 105:7–19.

Andreotti, A., Le Gales, P. and Moreno Fuentes, F.J. (2013). 'Transnational Mobility and Rootedness: The Upper Middle Classes in European Cities', *Global Networks*, 13 (1): 41-–59.

Andreotti, A., Le Gales, F. and Moreno-Fuentes, F.J. 2015. *Globalised Minds, Roots in the City: Urban Upper-Middle Classes in Europe*. Oxford: Wiley, Blackwell.

Appadurai, A. 1990. 'Disjuncture and Difference in the Global Cultural Economy', *Theory, Culture & Society* 7:295–310.

Appadurai, A. 1996. 'The Production of Locality'. In *Modernity at Large: Cultural Dimensions of Globalisation* by A. Appadurai, 178–99. Minneapolis: University of Minnesota Press.

Atkinson, R. 2015. 'Limited Exposure: Social Concealment, Mobility and Engagement with Public Space by the Super-rich in London', *Environment and Planning A:* 1–16.

Atkinson, R., Burrows, R. and Rhodes, D. 2016. 'Capital City? London's Housing Markets and the "Super-rich"'. In *Handbook on Wealth and the Super-Rich* edited by J. Hay and J.V. Beaverstock, 225–43. Cheltenham: Edward Elgar Publishing.

Atkinson, R., Burrows, R., Glucksberg, L., Ho, H., Knowles, C. and Rhodes, D. 2017. 'Minimum City? The Deeper Impacts of the "Super-Rich" on Urban Life'. In *Cities and the Super-Rich: Real Estate, Elite Practices, and Urban Political Economies* edited by R. Forrest, B. Wissink and S.Y. Koh, 253–72. London: Palgrave Macmillan.

Atkinson, R., Parker, S. and Burrows, R. 2017. 'Elite Formation, Power and Space in Contemporary London', *Theory, Culture and Society,* 34(5, 6): 179–200.

Back, L. 2007. *The Art of Listening*. Oxford: Berg.

Back, L. 2009. 'Researching Community and its Moral Projects', *21st Century Society: Journal of the Academy of Social Sciences* 4(2): 201–14.

Bates, C. and Rhys-Taylor, A. (eds.). 2016. *Walking through Social Research*. London-New York: Routledge.

Bauman, Z. 2000. *Liquid Modernity*. Cambridge: Polity.

Beaverstock, J.V., Hubbard, P. and Short, J.R. 2004. 'Getting away with it? Exposing the Geographies of the Super-rich', *Geoforum* 35:401–7.

Beer, G. 1990. 'The Island and the Airplane: The case of Virginia Woolf'. In *Nation and Narration* edited by H.K. Bhabha, 159–62. London: Routledge.

Benjamin, W. 1974. *Gesammelte Schriften,* I, edited by R. Tiedemann and H. Schweppenhauser. Frankfurt: Suhrkamp.

Benjamin, W. 1979. *One-Way Street and Other Writings*. London: New Left Book.

Benson, M. 2009. *Lifestyle Migration, Expectations, Aspirations and Experiences*. London: Routledge.

Benson, M. 2014. 'Trajectories of Middle-Class Belonging: The Dynamics of Place Attachment and Classed Identities', *Urban Studies*, November 2014, 51(14): 3097–112.

Benson, M. and Osbaldiston, N. (eds). 2014. *Understanding Lifestyle Migration: Theoretical Approaches to Migration and the Quest for a Better Way of Life*. Houdsmill, Basingstoke: Palgrave.

Birtchnell, J. and Caletrio, J. (eds.). 2014. *Elite Mobilities*. Abingdon: Routledge.

Blokland, T. 2003. *Urban bonds: Social Relationships in an Inner City Neighbourhood,* Cambridge: Polity Press.

Blokland, T. 2017. *Community as Urban Practice*. Cambridge: Polity Press.

Booth, C. 1891[1889]. *Descriptive Map of London Poverty*. Maps first published as appendix to *Life and Labour of the People in London* by C. Booth. London and Edinburgh: Williams and Norgate.

Booth, C. 1902. *Life and Labour of the People in London,* Vol. 1. London: Macmillan.
Britzolakis, C. 2011. '"The Strange High Singing of some Aeroplane Overhead": War, Utopia and the Everyday in Virginia Woolf's Fiction'. In *Utopian Spaces of Modernism: Literature and Culture, 1885–1945* edited by R. Gregory and B. Kohlmann, 121–40. Basingstoke: Palgrave Macmillan.
Burnham, P. 2004. 'The Squatters of 1946: A Local Study in National Context', *Socialist History* 25:20–45.
Burrows, R. and Gane, N. 2006. 'Geodemographics, Software and Class', *Sociology* 40(5):793–812.
Burrows, R. and Glucksberg, L. 2016. 'Family Offices and the Contemporary Infrastructures of Dynastic Wealth', *Sociologica* 2:1–23.
Butler, T. and Lees, L. 2006. 'Super-gentrification in Barnsbury, London: Globalization and Gentrifying Global Élites at the Neighbourhood Level', *Transactions of the Institute of British Geographers* 31(4):467–87.
Butler, T. and Watt, P. 2007. *Understanding Social Inequality.* London: Sage.
Capgemini. 2016. *World Wealth Report* 2016. https://www.worldwealthreport.com (accessed April 2017).
Castells, M. 1996. *The Rise of the Network Society.* Vol. 1, *The Information Age: Economy, Society and Culture.* Oxford: Blackwell.
Cunningham, N. and Savage, M. 2015. 'The Secret Garden? Élite Metropolitan Geographies in the Contemporary UK', *The Sociological Review* 63:321–48.
de Certeau, M. 1984. *The Practice of Every Day Life.* Berkeley: University of California Press.
de Certeau, M., Giard, L. and Mayol, P. 1998. *The Practice of Everyday Life.* Vol. 2: *Cooking and Living.* Minneapolis: University of Minnesota Press.
Dorling, D. 2014. *Inequality and the 1%.* London: Verso Books.
Elliott, A. and Urry, J. 2010. *Mobile Lives.* Abingdon, Oxon: Routledge.
GB Historical GIS. 2017. GB Historical GIS University of Portsmouth. Kensington and Chelsea District through time | Population Statistics | Total Population, *A Vision of Britain through Time.* http://www.visionofbritain.org.uk/unit/10085573/cube/TOT_POP (accessed: April 2017).
George, J. 2009. *Merchants to Magnates, Intrigue and Survival: Armenians in London 1900–2000.* Noida: Taderon Press.
Giddens, A. 1990. *The Consequences of Modernity.* Cambridge: Polity Press.
Gilroy, P. 2004. *After Empire: Melancholia or Convivial Culture?* Abingdon: Routledge.
Glucksberg, L. 2015. 'London Élites are also being Priced Out of their Homes – Here's why it Matters', *The Conversation,* 20 October. https://theconversation.com/london-elites-are-also-being-priced-out-of-their-homes-heres-why-it-matters-49175 (accessed February 2019).
Glucksberg, L. 2016. 'A View From the Top: Unpacking Capital Flows and Foreign Investment in the Alpha Territories of London', *City: Special Issue on the Global Housing Crisis* 20(2):238–55.
Hall, S. 2000. 'Conclusion: The Multi-cultural Question'. In *Un/settled Multiculturalisms: Diasporas, Enlightenments, Transruptions* edited by H. Barnor, 209–41. London: Zed Books.
Hamnett, C. 2003. *Unequal City: London in the Global Arena.* London: Routledge.
Harvey, D. 1989. *The Condition of Postmodernity: An Enquiry into the Origin of Cultural Change.* Cambridge, MA: Blackwell.
Harvey, D. 2001. *Spaces of Capital: Towards a Critical Geography.* New York: Routledge.
Hay, I. (ed.). 2013. *Geographies of the Super-Rich.* Cheltenham: Edward Elgar Publishing.
Hay, I, and Muller, S. 2011. '"That Tiny, Stratospheric Apex That Owns Most of the World"' – Exploring Geographies of the Super-Rich'. *Geographical Research* 50(1):75–88.
Knowles, C. 2017. 'Walking Plutocratic London: Exploring Erotic, phantasmagoric Mayfair', *Social Semiotics* 27:299–309.
Jones, H. and Jackson, E. (eds.). 2014. *Stories of Cosmopolitan Belonging: Emotion and Location.* London: Routledge.
Lefebvre, H. 1991. *The Production of Space.* Oxford: Blackwell Publishers Ltd.
Lefebvre, H. 2014. *Rhythmanalysis: Space, Time and Everyday Life.* London: Bloomsbury.
Loftie, W.J. 1888. *Kensington Picturesque and Historical.* London: The Leadenhall Press.
Massey, D. 2005. *For Space.* London: Sage.
Matless, D. 1998. *Landscape and Englishness.* London: Reaktion Books Ltd.
Miles, B. 2010. *London Calling: A Countercultural History of London Since 1945.* London: Atlantic Books.

Miller D. 2008. *The Comfort of Things*. Cambridge: Polity.
Miller, D. (ed.). 2009. *Anthropology and the Individual: A Material Culture Perspective*. Oxford: Berg.
Minton, A. 2017. *Big Capital: What is London for?* London: Penguin Books.
Murphy, K. 2010. *Cheniston Lodge, Heritage Appraisal*. Report commissioned by Avida Ltd, London.
New York Times. 1995. *Edna Deane, Dancer and Inspiration, 90*. Obituary published in the *New York Times* on 26 November 1995. http://www.nytimes.com/1995/11/26/world/edna-deane-dancer-and-inspiration-90.html.
NOMIS. 2017. Official labour market statistics, Office for National Statistics, local output area E00014063. https://www.nomisweb.co.uk/reports/localarea?search=W86tq (accessed April 2017).
ONS. 2011. Census 2011, Office for National Statistics. https://www.ons.gov.uk/census/2011 census.
Parker, S., Uprichard, E. and Burrows, R. 2007. 'Class Places and Place Classes: Geodemographics and the Spatialization of Class', *Information, Communication and Society* 10(6):902–21.
Pink, S. 2012. *Situating Everyday Life*. London: Sage.
Pink, S. 2015. *Doing Sensory Ethnography* (second edition). London: Sage.
Pound, E. 1971[1915]. Letter to Harriet Monroe. In *The Selected Letters of Ezra Pound 1907–1941* edited by D.D. Paige, 48–50. New York: New Direction Publishing.
RBKC. 2015. *Royal Borough of Kensington and Chelsea: Consolidated Local Plan*. July 2015.
Rhys-Taylor, A. 2013. 'The Essences of Multiculture: A Sensory Exploration of an Inner-city Street Market', *Identities: Global Studies in Culture and Power* 20(4):393–406.
Rhys-Taylor, A. 2017. *Food and Multiculture: A Sensory Ethnography of East London*. London: Bloomsbury.
Samuel, R. 1994. *Theatres of Memory*. Vol. 1: *Past and Present in Contemporary Culture*. London: Verso.
Savage, M. 2000. 'Walter Benjamin's Urban Thought. A Critical Analysis'. In *Thinking Space* edited by M. Crang and N. Thrift, 33–53. London: Routledge.
Savage, M. 2010. 'The Politics of Elective Belonging', *Housing, Theory and Society* 27(2):115–61.
Savage, M., Bagnall, G. and Longhurst, B.J. 2005. *Globalization and Belonging*. London: Sage.
Savage, M., Cunningham, N., Devine, F., Friedman, S., Laurison, D., McKenzie, L., Miles, A., Snee, H., Taylor, M. and Wakeling, P. 2015. *Social Class in the 21st Century*. London: Pelican.
Savage, M. and Williams, K. (eds.). 2008. *Remembering Elites*. Oxford: Blackwell.
Schiller, N.G. and Caglar, A. (eds.). 2011. *Locating Migration: Rescaling Cities and Migrants*. Ithaca, NY: Cornell University Press.
Silva, E.B. and Bennett, T. (eds.). 2004. *Contemporary culture and Everyday Life*. Durham: Sociology Press.
Spark, M. 1988. *A Far Cry from Kensington*. London: Constable & Co.
Survey of London. 1986. *Southern Kensington: Kensington Square to Earl's Court*. Survey of London, Volume XLII. London: The Athlone Press.
Swift, R. and Gilley, S. 1999. *The Irish in Victorian Britain: The Local Dimension*. Dublin: Four Courts Press.
Tilley, C. 1994. *A Phenomenology of Landscape: Places, Paths and Monuments*. Oxford: Berg.
Tilley, C. 2012. 'Walking in the Past in the Present'. In *Landscape Beyond Land: Routes, Aesthetics, Narratives* edited by A. Arnason, N. Ellison, J. Vergunst and A. Whitehouse, 15–32. Oxford: Berghahn Books.
Tilley, C. and Cameron-Daum, K. 2017. *An Anthropology of Landscape: The Extraordinary in the Ordinary*. London, UCL Press.
Tonkiss, F. 2003. 'The Ethics of Indifference: Community and Solitude in the City', *International Journal of Cultural Studies* 6(3):297–311.
TripAdvisor. n.d.. Reviews of The Muffin Man tea shop. https://www.tripadvisor.co.uk/Restaurant_Review-g186338-d1134350-Reviews-or20-The_Muffin_Man_Tea_Shop-London_England.html#REVIEWS (accessed February 2019).
Urry, J. 2000. *Sociology beyond Societies: Mobilities for the Twenty-First Century*. Abingdon, Oxon: Routledge.
Urry, J. 2007. *Mobilities*. Cambridge: Polity.
Valluvan, S. 2016. 'Conviviality and Multiculture: A Post-Integration Sociology of Multi-ethnic Interaction', *Young* 24(3):204–21.

Wajcman, J. 2015. *Pressed for Time. The Acceleration of Life in Digital Capitalism.* Chicago: The University of Chicago Press.

Watt, P. and Smets, P. (eds.). 2014. *Mobilities and Neighbourhood Belonging in Cities and Suburbs.* Basingstoke: Palgrave Macmillan.

Webber, R. and Burrows, R. 2016. 'Life in an Alpha Territory: Discontinuity and conflict in an élite London "village"'. *Urban Studies* 53(15):3139–54.

Woolf, V. 1976. *Mrs Dalloway.* London: Grafton Books.

Wyndham Lewis, P. (ed.). 1914. *Blast 1: Review of the great English Vortex,* 20 June.

Zoopla. n.d. http://www.zoopla.co.uk/house-prices/london/cheniston-gardens/ (accessed April 2017).

2
Towards a phenomenology of the concrete megastructure: Space and perception at the Brunswick Centre, London
Clare Melhuish

Introduction

More than a decade has passed since the first writing of this work, and much has changed in London's physical and social landscape since then. Indeed, the pace of change and alteration to the face and shape of the city has been unexpectedly dramatic, notwithstanding the financial crash of 2008 and accompanying political and economic instability. In the view through the window at my desk, the once open skyline marked only by the dome of St Paul's cathedral and the Canary Wharf tower has been filled in with stark, illuminated building blocks and the dotted red lights marking the tops of construction cranes – 24 at the last count – which indicate the transformation is not yet complete. Such radical interventions in the urban fabric echo the transformations of London's post-war landscape, in which modernist housing projects such as the Brunswick, the subject of this chapter, played such a significant part, significantly changing the shape and texture not only of the built fabric but also of the lived experience of the city's inhabitants across a richly interconnected network of urban neighbourhoods. Between the 1960s and 70s, parts of the city changed spatially and aesthetically in ways that could hardly have been imagined before the destruction brought by World War 2, and in doing so had a dramatic impact on patterns of urban life at local level and through networks of social interaction spread across a constellation of urban places and spaces. Today, many of those developments – typically large-scale sites of local authority housing, such as the Heygate and Aylesbury estates in Elephant and Castle – are themselves the subject of demolition and replacement. These projects remake the city in equally far-reaching ways, re-affirming the highly contested and politicised nature of these disruptive processes of physical and social displacement, driven by even larger global forces – flows of capital and people and shifting political alliances.

In this chapter on the Brunswick, I take one such example of radical urban intervention as a case study through which to consider the impact of urban change embodied in built form on the city's inhabitants, focusing on an ethnographic investigation of architecture as social setting, and a phenomenological framing of urban experience. This approach seems all the more relevant in light of both the far-reaching economisation of the urban landscape and its inhabitants, which has gathered pace through the implementation of neoliberal economic policies and politics in London, and the significance of the capital as a focus for grounded research on the diverse experiences of post-colonial, cosmopolitan urbanites – elite and underprivileged alike (Rabinow 1986). An anthropological perspective re-centres personal and social lived experience in understandings of the city and the far-reaching effects that globally circulating urban and planning policies have on communities, notably the privatisation of urban development and commercialisation and heritagisation of city centres. Furthermore, this approach addresses the more recent 'affective turn' in geography and architecture theory, and the associated concerns that have arisen regarding its splitting of the sensuous and experiential from the mental imaginaries and thinking processes that impel action (Spencer 2016). Instead, it posits an integrated and holistic understanding of phenomenological urban experience as a fusion of body–mind–imagination. Such a perspective helps to make sense of a lengthy history of engagement between residents and the building they inhabit in this case study on the Brunswick – a structure that anchors their experiences of city dwelling and frames a tangible, emplaced aesthetic of social identity.

The Brunswick is a concrete megastructure comprising a shopping precinct and flats, built near Russell Square in central London between 1968 and 1972, listed by English Heritage (Grade II) as a building of architectural and historical significance in 2000, and refurbished in 2006 to implement some significant alterations to the public and retail space at its heart. This chapter, presenting a re-reading of its spatial characteristics, is concerned with revealing the layers of cultural meaning invested in a building typically classified as a work of abstract modernism, or stark brutalism, until softened by its 10-year-old refurbishment, through a process of architectural objectification conducted by architectural experts. It sets out to develop a reinterpretation of the building as a social setting embedded in and interconnected with the city fabric, articulated by an array of urban voices within 'a continuum of sociospatial attachments' (Clifford 1998: 367). It does so through a multidimensional exploration of its design and occupation, bringing to the fore issues of perception and embodiment, or 'being-in-the-world', at individual and collective level.

The Brunswick: material and social context

The Brunswick is a long, formerly open-ended shopping precinct in the heart of Georgian Bloomsbury, bordered along its east and west edges with monolithic concrete A-frame blocks housing some 600 flats from first to seventh floor level, and 677 people, as recorded in the 2001 census. It was designed by the architect Patrick Hodgkinson (1930–2016) during the 1950s and 60s as an alternative low-rise model of high-density housing, representing an inspired challenge to the prevailing high-rise housing policies of the time.

The complex has a monumental porticoed entrance (fig. 2.1) onto Brunswick Square, on the east, under which the Curzon cinema (formerly

Fig. 2.1 View from east through Brunswick Square's porticoed entrance, O'Donnell Court. © S. Stone

Fig. 2.2 View of winter gardens, O'Donnell Court, prior to 2006 refurbishment. Source: author

Renoir) is located, but the better-used, if more modest, entrance into the precinct was for much of its history on the west, from Marchmont Street, a shopping street in decline, and more recently from the south. However, the most distinctive external feature of the development, apart from its sheer scale and its unabashed use of exposed concrete, is the cascading glass terraces on both sides of each block (fig. 2.2) – the famous 'winter gardens' to the flats, which glint in the light on a bright day and give a view of the sky from within. Inside, the housing blocks are characterised by long perspectives down access galleries passing through the heavy concrete of the distinctive internal A-frame structure (fig. 2.3). The view down into the broad, shadowy concourse at podium level contrasts with sudden views out at the upper levels (the sixth and seventh floors) across rooftops and cityscape, while the monotonous linear sequence of front doors on each floor is brought to life by personal details colouring the thresholds between common parts and private domestic space (fig. 2.4).

The development was originally designed to create an upmarket shopping environment with a grand, civic presence, and public gardens were planned for the terraces looking over it at second-floor level. However, the terraces were closed to the public early on, the grand external staircase leading up to them removed for security reasons, and a large percentage of the flats, originally intended for mixed-income

Fig. 2.3 View through A-frame structure, Foundling Court, first floor level. © S. Stone

Fig. 2.4 Front door, Foundling Court. Source: author

occupancy, designated as sheltered accommodation for the elderly or fragile. During the 1980s and 90s, the shopping precinct looked neglected and decaying, most of the retail units behind the colonnades of concrete columns standing empty, and the whole development acquired a ruinous aura and reputation to match: 'They should do something about it. It's been neglected. Keeps being sold,' said my respondents in 2000. Both the public and private spaces of the complex became host to social interactions and activities deemed inappropriate and transgressive, including rough sleeping, prostitution and drug consumption, coexisting with the everyday patterns of regular residential life – provisioning, schooling, earning a living and socialising in the city (fig. 2.5).

A major retail refurbishment completed between 2004 and 2006 (fig 2.6) transformed the atmosphere and public spaces of the complex, arousing mixed emotions on the part of those who knew the Brunswick from the inside, as reported by the residents I interviewed at the time and recorded in my field notes (see postscript on methodology). 'Mary said a wonderful thing when somebody asked her about living in the Brunswick Centre… she said, "It's wonderful, I never see anybody." I suddenly realised along with that, that the emptiness of the place is actually one of its attractions… you'd think it was slightly menacing. But it's not…'. Mark bought his flat on the sixth floor in 1994 and moved in with his partner, Mary, her teenage daughter and a dog, which became a much-loved companion: 'there were three – four really – of us' and he

Fig. 2.5 Brunswick Centre shopping precinct, view from south, prior to 2006 refurbishment. Source: author

Fig. 2.6 'A high street for Bloomsbury': view through shopping precinct after refurbishment, showing new supermarket at northern end. Source: author

'would have to find whatever little space there was'. At the time of my research, Mark lived in the two-bedroom flat alone, using one room as an office where sometimes an assistant would come and work with him. Social relationships and interactions were evidently important, and the flat was full of objects and images that prompted a ready verbal narrative about different people and places, extending back many years. But he loved the emptiness inside the Brunswick: 'I think I'm much more appreciative of it now than I was when I first moved in.' The fact that the atrium spaces at the heart of the housing blocks remained quiet, uninhabited zones was a great relief to him in comparison to the busyness of the newly refurbished shopping centre – an effective buffer from the hubbub of people he describes as shopaholics and caffeine addicts (a not so oblique reference to the alcoholics and drug addicts they have replaced) around the new retail and restaurant outlets he could see from his windows.

Mark disliked the fact that the newcomers were people 'who you don't know'. The relationship between the precinct space and the living-room windows of the flats looking over the precinct is acoustically very intimate, even though the line of vision is across towards the windows of the opposite block or towards the upper storeys of the older buildings on Bernard Street and up to the sky, not down. To get a view of the precinct, you need to stand up and look down with some deliberation. For these reasons, it had become a special pleasure for Mark to be able to walk out of his flat into the empty space of the atrium where he was unlikely to bump into anybody that he didn't know, nor even anyone that he did know. As a person who did not depend on chance encounters or 'gossip opportunities', as another resident put it, to sustain a social existence, it suited him very well. Moreover, it generated an extended zone of privacy and belonging around his flat, which perhaps compensated to some extent for the small size of the flat itself. His sense of proprietorship within his own territory was effectively extended by his awareness of his own flat as part of a more global scheme, which, as a design professional and someone very familiar with the plans of the Brunswick, he was particularly able to visualise and hold in his mind's eye. He also appreciated the emptiness of the atrium space as a sign that security was working and that undesirable intruders had been successfully excluded. One of his main points of disagreement with the original design of the building was the idea of the permeable 'internal street' connected to the public spaces outside via numerous open access points, which he believed to have been a big mistake.

Stephanie, however, who was largely housebound, told me that she used to enjoy the atrium space as well, precisely because it felt like being 'outside' without going out. Then the council sealed up the view-holes to the outside and secured the entrances, and now in its current internalised form she finds it oppressive. She told me she was lucky to live on the 'outside' of the Brunswick, because it looks over the street and the pub rather than onto the precinct and the opposite block, and so gives her some sense of connection to the city without having to go anywhere.

The floor on which Mark lived, together with the top floor above it and the floor below, were perceived by others who lived there as having a strong sense of community compared to the lower floors of the Brunswick, where Stephanie lived. In fact, there were a higher proportion of newcomers on the upper floors. Some of these people, who tended to have professional jobs and wide social networks extending beyond the immediate locality, had chosen to invest in the local community they believed they had found at the Brunswick as a kind of project, partly because they had not previously experienced that kind of life, lived at local level within the global city. Susan, who initially shared her flat with a flatmate but had now established a more conventional household set-up with her boyfriend and their baby, said that 'we genuinely didn't know our neighbours' where she lived before in another part of London. By contrast, she described the drawn-out, unusually intimate, process of buying the Brunswick flat from the elderly couple who lived there as like 'buying a flat from your granny', and she also referred to her neighbour, Elsie, who would invite them round for meals and ask favours of them, in the same terms. She reported that when she took her maternity leave and started to see her Brunswick neighbours in the street during the day, for the first time, there had been much excitement at the realisation she was going to have a baby, because, they said, 'We haven't had a baby up here [on the upper floors] for years!'

Susan never spoke of 'empty' spaces at the Brunswick, and was enjoying the busyness of the precinct, especially since giving up work to look after her baby. She would regularly meet up, outside the new Starbucks, with other new mothers for whom it provided a meeting place. Released from her office away from the Brunswick, her world had become geographically more localised, and simultaneously the precinct, which she would not formerly have used that much, had become a more attractive and less obviously 'local' place to be, compensating for that loss of daily engagement with the wider city.

The apotheosisation of the everyday and the local in the form of the Brunswick estate by some of those newcomers who had ready access to other, non-local social networks, was evocatively embodied in the narrative of one long-term resident, Gloria, who was part of a highly 'emplaced' family network going back several generations: 'Basically my roots are here, and deep are the roots', she told me. In common with many other first-generation residents, she had been relocated by Camden Council to O'Donnell Court at the Brunswick from her home in a local street, along with neighbours and relatives including her aunt and her mother. Her three immediate neighbours from the old street lived 'across the landing, and… up the stairs', she explained, evoking a notion of the Brunswick as a big house; her aunt lived 'over the way' in Foundling Court. But notwithstanding the close presence of friends and relatives, she noted that 'You could live here for a year and not see anybody', which she attributed to 'the nature of flats'. She defined her neighbours as people who were 'there if you need them', but not necessarily to interact with on a daily basis.

Modernism and anthropology

Richard Sennett (1993) described the Brunswick Centre in Bloomsbury in terms that epitomise a view of modernist architecture and urban intervention as abstract, alienating, over-scaled and largely devoid of cultural reference. His sentiments echo through Daniel Miller's sweeping reference to 'the social disaster of the new built environment', identified as 'the major expression of modernity' – 'modernity as alien abstraction so brilliantly described by Simmel' (Miller 1987). Indeed, there is a large body of literature that presents modernism as a condition of breakdown in social cohesion and collective belief. As such, it implies a negation of the very concept of culture, and this perhaps explains the problems of developing a discourse about modern architecture as material culture within the wider context of anthropology.

The classic critiques of modernism posit a condition of alienation between the individual and the external material world that fundamentally affects the individual's sense of, and ability to realise, self-identity, particularly in an urban context – but at the same time may offer positive new opportunities for freedom and fulfilling experience. Baudelaire, Benjamin and, indeed, Simmel all explored the possibilities offered by the modern city for the freedom of the individual and for fulfilling experience in a highly personal, rather than collective, dimension, precisely because of the loosening of traditional social bonds and the fragmentation of a holistic cultural framework triggered by the conditions of modernity – notably a compression of time and space brought about by changes in labour, production and commodity exchange, driven by new manufacturing and communication technologies.

Modernist architecture, art and literature enthusiastically embraced the possibilities generated by the new ambiguity concerning notions of place and localised identity that were generated by these economic changes, and the processes of spatial and cultural integration that they prompted. Giddens (1991) underlines the fundamental distinction between modern life and 'most of human history [when] people lived in social settings that were fairly closely connected with each other' (Giddens 1991:257) and the local community was dominant. By contrast, 'the settings of modern social life are much more diverse and segmented' (Giddens 1991:257), and lifestyle choices thus become a primary means of structuring social stratification, as analysed by Bourdieu (1977), as well as representing the results of class differences in the realm of production.

The very foundation of the modernist project in architecture was an explicit engagement with notions of cultural alienation and disintegration that are quite opposite to the project of traditional anthropology, rendering the modernist architectural artefact not only uninteresting but even distasteful. Anthropological studies of modernist architecture (Attfield 1989; Boudon 1972; Miller 1988) have tended to focus on the ways in which the alien, 'imposed' forms of modernism have been privately or covertly modified by individuals during the life of such buildings, as part of a necessary (and arguably subversive) process of 'appropriation' or 'sublation', while failing to acknowledge the origins and development of such buildings in a complex social and cultural fabric, and the extent to which they may play a role in concretising and objectifying collective identities and belief systems.

Yet anthropological research into the architectural material culture of traditional, small-scale societies also offers fruitful directions for the study of modern architecture. Levi-Strauss's structuralist analysis highlighted the role of the individual house building in certain societies as the acknowledged embodiment and objectification of a specific form of social organisation, and, building on his work, Carsten and Hugh-Jones (1995) emphasise the significance of the house as 'a prime agent of socialisation. Through habit and inhabiting, each person builds up a practical mastery of the fundamental schemes of their culture' (Carsten and Hugh-Jones 1995: 2). Bourdieu's study (1977) of the Kabyle house in Algeria, embodying this approach, is well known, but Bloch's work (1995) on the Zafimaniry house in Madagascar is of particular interest to the following discussion, because it shifts the focus onto the actual materiality of the building. Bloch suggests that other anthropologists are mistaken in trying to pin down the 'meaning', in a strictly symbolic or semiotic interpretation, of traditional carvings on the timber elements of the houses, and suggests a looser, alternative approach, which might be considered more synaesthetic or phenomenological in character – notably, one that highlights the carvings as a natural continuation of the progressive hardening of the materials used to build the house during the progress of a marriage, representing its success and fruitfulness. Bloch's analysis acknowledges all the senses as the equipment of perception and, moreover, the dynamism and vitality of material phenomena, which might otherwise be considered inert and passive.

Merleau-Ponty (1962) argued for 'sense experience' as 'that vital communication with the world which makes it present', forging a bond between 'the perceived object and the perceiving subject', termed 'intentional tissue.' However, as Thomas Czordas points out (1999), 'the notion of "experience" virtually dropped out of theorising about culture' during the 1980s, because of the great emphasis on structuralist analysis, involving the methods of literary criticism and semiotics. He draws attention to the fundamental paradox in this, for: 'The very possibility of individuation, the creation of the individual that we understand… as at the core of the ideological structure of western culture, has as its condition of possibility a particular mode of inhabiting the world as a bodily being.' But Czordas also stresses that the process of perception, the 'deployment of senses and sensibility, and not only their content, is emphatically cultural' – that is, the way that individuals use their senses, and their particular responses to phenomena – is highly determined by cultural context and conditions.

Czordas's perspective offers particular potential for a study of modern architecture capable of revealing depths of cultural meaning at individual and collective level that have been largely dismissed as a result of a prevailing discourse of alienation, abstraction and cultural fragmentation, and an emphasis on the notion of imposed, individual authorship. In order to explore this perspective, I therefore adopted the ethnographic method offered by anthropology, privileging the active personal engagement of the anthropologist with individuals and groups at the site of the research in order to understand their relationship with the modernist built environment.

Rationalism or existentialism

In 2000, the government finally decided to list the Brunswick, on the grounds of its architectural and historical significance, as a megastructure. However, the listing decision was challenged by DOCOMOMO-UK (the organisation for documentation of Modern Movement buildings), which asserted that '[the] definition [of megastructure] contains only half the concept (Cooke 2000). The other half is the idea of a framework that accepts and assumes change within it over time… The great space-making structure that accommodates the communal spaces and the fundamental relationships of parts is a fix, and the detailed pattern of uses and components within it reflects change.'

DOCOMOMO feared that if listing were to take place, future change and development would be frozen. Its position highlights the problems inherent to a form of architectural discourse that serves to establish fixed, closed interpretations and meaning – in this case those of the megastructure and a brutalist ideology of materials (concrete), which cannot begin to reflect the multi-faceted complexity of meaning embodied in an architectural artefact, or any other material artefact, and in its existence over a period of time. This is especially true of the material culture of the twentieth century, due to the sheer pace of cultural change.

Buchli (1999) argues that 'most of our interpretative tools [predicated on generally Marxian materialist assumptions within a 'foundationalist' tradition of western thought] leave us somewhat at a loss to understand' the 'superfluity of meaning' with which the 'physical architectural artefact and its attendant metaphors are confusingly and painfully pregnant…'. His viewpoint is, in fact, echoed in the outlook of much contemporary architectural theory, defined by Mary McLeod (2000) as a preoccupation with the concept of 'other' or 'otherness'. But she also points out that there is a continuing neglect of the notion of everyday spaces and everyday life as the significant arena of cultural meaning – the concern of Lefebvre and de Certeau (de Certeau 1998; Lefebvre 2008). McLeod summarises this concern as 'not only to depict the power of disciplinary technology, but also to reveal how society resists being reduced by it, not just in the unusual or removed places but in the most ordinary'. This involves a focus on 'the intensification of sensory impressions, the freedom and positive excesses of consumption as experiences that counter the webs of control and monotony in daily life'.

In the case of the Brunswick, such an approach may be viewed as fundamentally opposed to the 'closed' modernist framework of thought within which the building is conventionally located. Furthermore, this interpretation of the Brunswick as the clearly defined product of a strictly rational, functionalist and scientific approach to architecture, planning and social organisation can be shown to be essentially flawed, even at its origins.

The project to redevelop the Brunswick site, initiated by the developer E. Alec Coleman, was founded on a vision of a thorough-going rationalisation of space and traffic circulation, regardless of the social fabric, which was prevalent in the post-war era (Buchanan 1963). At that time, the site consisted of war-damaged Georgian terraces and small ancillary buildings. Between 1958 and 1960, Coleman made a series of planning applications, which were rejected, but in February 1963 an outline planning scheme by Leslie Martin and Patrick Hodgkinson for a different type of mixed-use, low-rise development housing 1,800 people in five-storey linear blocks was finally approved, following which Hodgkinson was appointed sole architect.

Hodgkinson believed 'The Foundling Estate presented an opportunity to again bring together living, work and recreation to stimulate each other, against normal practice of the time' (Hodgkinson 1992) – a view that evokes the beginnings of a sea change in attitudes towards redevelopment and an implicit acknowledgement that, as Tilley (1994) writes, 'space does not and cannot exist apart from the events and activities within which it is implicated… Socially produced space combines the cognitive, the physical and the emotional… A social space, rather than being uniform and forever the same, is constituted by differential densities of human experience, attachment and involvement.' Hodgkinson attributes his views to the influence of Sartre's existentialism. He felt strongly that a modern architecture should concern itself with the psyche of the individual, rather than being a vehicle for socialism. He entertained an essentially romantic imagination about the possibilities of modern architecture as vehicle for living, which challenges the conventional interpretation of the Brunswick as an expression of rationalist abstraction inspired by Le Corbusier.

The early schemes for the Brunswick were socially idealistic, intended to incorporate a wide mixture of people from different social strata, within the equalising framework of a common building type framing a common public space, or 'town room'. Hodgkinson (1972) described it as 'a liner without class distinctions on its promenading decks…' While the image of the ocean liner was also used by Le Corbusier (1923) in his evocation of a new architecture – along with the 'airplane' and 'automobile' – Le Corbusier was more interested in the aesthetic of these constructions, 'a beauty of a more technical order', than in a concept of social structure, or an aesthetic of social identity.

Hodgkinson's first scheme was for a series of brick courtyard buildings on an elevated plinth, creating an open-ended configuration of buildings and sheltered spaces capable of redefining a physical and cultural territory suited to the conditions of modern life that could also support and nurture both the collective and the individual psyche. The scheme proposed an existential engagement with a notion of being-in-the-world that had more in common with Heidegger than with Le Corbusier and classic modernism, and had a refinement at odds with the 'raw' approach of British brutalism. The stepped section, providing balconies for every flat, was 'about looking up' towards the sky – precisely the feature of the Brunswick flats that Sennett interprets as severing the connection between life inside the flats and everyday street-level activities, and a form of alienating abstraction. For Hodgkinson, however, the possibility of living 'in the clouds' was something to aspire to, allowing an escape from 'the frightful buildings around the Brunswick', including a number of university institutions and various hotels. In other words, it allowed an engagement with an existential awareness of self in the world, in much the terms of the 'phenomenological reduction' defined by Merleau-Ponty (1989 [1962]): man's capacity, as a 'meditating Ego', to distinguish himself 'from the world and things' and to reflect upon it and wonder at it – a process, which though impossible to achieve completely, 'reveals that world as strange and paradoxical'.

The use of the 'winter garden' concept in the Brunswick scheme was fundamental, then, to the 'existential' programme of the project, insofar as it can be defined in such tangible terms. But it is clear that the existential dimension of the design does not work for everyone. Mrs X, who has placed a big table in the glazed area (fig. 2.7), says she can't believe how lucky she is: 'The sun in the flat makes me feel so bright.' Ms Y, on the other hand, has thermally lined curtains permanently closed across the windows, not only to keep the flat both warm and cool, but also to shut out the view of the terraces opposite. She says, 'I'm not convinced I like the view' and 'I don't want forever to be thinking about it.' A number of residents stress the importance of the view down into the precinct, because, as one says, 'The view down "humanises" me and other tenants, as we can see people wandering around', and others lament the lack of a view of people passing by the kitchen window overlooking the access galleries, suggesting an unfavourable comparison with the traditional street environment.

During the construction of the Brunswick, graffiti was painted on the site hoardings, dubbing it the 'Bloomsbury Prison', and certain critics

Fig. 2.7 Interior view looking across the precinct from O'Donnell Court, 2006. © S. Stone

fiercely condemned the scheme. But not everyone was antagonistic. A year later, the *Daily Telegraph* described it as reminiscent of Mediterranean shores – a stylish, imaginative and exotic intervention that restored the 'Bloomsbury of a century ago, as a centre for the professional classes'. It reported that the first tenants 'find it provides a sense of identity. It's not a question of just living in another block.' In 1990, the chair of the tenants association, looking back, said, 'It was an honour to live here, as it was a very elegant block. We thought it was paradise…' (Johnstone 1972).

It seems clear that many people did, and do, respond to the architect's ideal of a place that could, in some way, transcend the more banal and depressing aspects of everyday life and provide the possibility of a liberation of the psyche. In 1989, critic David Hamilton Eddy summed up this liberating and magical dimension of the scheme as 'a dream world, familiar and entrancing and disturbing at once' which allowed a freedom from the strict social order of Georgian and Victorian London, where 'everyone is "placed" and knows their "place"; the magic is to do with the escape from the quotidian grind into a poetic and paradisal world' (Hamilton Eddy 1989).

Christian Norberg-Schulz (1980) set out a theory of a 'phenomenology of architecture' based on a definition of architecture as 'a concretisation of existential space'. He argued that this condition was generated through the transformation of nature into a 'cultural landscape' by man-made elements and settlement patterns, so that construction technology itself became a crucial mediator in the relationship between man and environment and the realisation of its existential dimensions. The 'existential purpose of building' is, therefore, to make a site become a place by uncovering its latent and potential meanings. The key referent in Norberg-Schulz's argument is Heidegger's concept of dwelling as being-in-the-world, but Merleau-Ponty's influence is also clearly evident, particularly in the latter's argument that: 'For most of us, Nature is no more than a vague and remote entity, overlaid by cities, roads, houses and above all by the presence of other people… The "human world" ceases to be a metaphor and becomes once more… the seat and as it were the homeland of our thoughts…'

Such a concept of building and the purpose of architecture, suggesting a blurring of clearly defined boundaries between subject and object through the notion of place as 'a qualitative totality', is fundamentally distinct from the deterministic, functionalist programme with which the Brunswick is often identified, and offers a far more revealing insight into the conception and subsequent evolution of the project. As Norberg-Schulz writes, 'most modern buildings… live their abstract life in a kind of mathematical–technological space', identifying lack of enclosure and density, loss of imageability, and weak 'presence' of new buildings as typical characteristics of 'place today', which drain it of existential meaning. The following discussion seeks to make clear that these are not characteristics of the Brunswick, analysed as a 'concrete totality' of phenomena, or manifestation of embodied cultural meaning in various aspects.

Phenomenology

Norberg-Schulz defined a clear set of criteria by which, he suggested, the phenomenological identity of architecture could be analysed. He proposed that any study of man-made place should take as its point of departure its relationship to the natural environment, then proceed to an examination of its formal articulation and the ways in which basic temporal structures are translated into spatial properties. He stated that the matter of structure must be examined in concrete terms, to give the phenomenology of architecture a 'realistic basis', focusing on enclosure, 'standing and rising' (structure, proportion, relationship to ground and sky) and materiality (Norberg-Schulz 1980).

Norberg-Schulz's approach is interesting for its aspiration towards precision and the continuing evidence of an interest in establishing a scientifically respectable footing for a 'phenomenology of architecture' – even though he states that he has moved away from the 'methods taken over from natural science' which he used in his earlier book, *Intentions in Architecture*, and he makes it clear that the notion of 'existential space' is 'not a logico-mathematical term'. He asserts the urgency of returning to 'a qualitative, phenomenological understanding of architecture', but nevertheless, the terminology used in identifying the purpose of the book as 'the conquest of the existential dimension' suggests a lingering sense of scientific mission (Norberg-Schulz 1980).

The methods that Norberg-Schulz outlines continue to emphasise the visual, aesthetic and symbolic qualities of architecture as the basis for a structuralist type of interpretation, with particular attention paid to identifying archetypal symbolic forms representing man's place in a cosmic order. He does not really begin to address a concept of synaesthesia, or multi-sensory experience of the world, which Merleau-Ponty (1989 [1962])described as the 'rich notion of sense experience', generating the 'connecting tissue between perceived object and perceiving subject'.

The architect and writer Juhani Pallasmaa complained in 1994 that 'The architecture of our time is turning into the retinal art of the eye' (Pallasmaa 2005), proposing seven realms of sensory experience as the framework for perception of architecture: acoustic intimacy, silence, scent, touch, taste, physical movement, and scale and gravity. He asserted the need to acknowledge the 'language and wisdom of the body', but, as Czordas (1999) points out, individual and collective bodily experience and perception are in themselves strongly coloured – if not actually determined – by cultural factors, which have to be taken into account. And, as Abram (1996) has proposed, the imagination too must be understood as 'an attribute of the senses... Not a separate mental faculty', which is a fundamental part of the perceptual apparatus: 'the perceiving body... lending its imagination to things in order to see them more fully'. Mind and body together, then, tie a person to the natural and built environment in, as Seamon (n.d.) puts it, an 'intentional relationship' which can be analysed in three dimensions – 'lifeworld, place, and home' – underlining the phenomenological significance of architecture.

The discussion so far has touched on two crucial factors governing the design of the Brunswick, namely the importance of the view of the sky, or the bodily relationship with an infinite realm of light above, and the concept of the site as an open-ended, permeable terrain of solids and voids, continuous with the surrounding urban and cultural landscape, as opposed to one large, enclosed and impermeable block. I would suggest that both factors demonstrate the architect's awareness of the phenomenological dimensions of the project. However, they must also be understood as developing out of a complex web of cultural and economic influences and conditions that defined both the brief and the response, and are not simply the result of an act of individual authorship. Indeed, this understanding represents a fundamental premise of any analysis of architecture that proceeds on the basis of a wide-ranging understanding of materiality and embodiment, as opposed to a narrowly defined, aesthetic and intellectual concept, and should become evident from the following discussion of a community's direct experience and perception of the Brunswick, and the cultural dimensions of that experience.

Spatial hierarchy: layered realms of existence

Ethnographic field work at the Brunswick revealed that the architecture establishes a spatial hierarchy that is experienced by residents, at a physical and psychological level, as a clear layering of distinct realms of existence within both a localised and globalised world. In other words, it seems that the experience of living in this set piece of modern architecture does have the potential to generate a meaningful sense of self-identity and place within a larger urban and cultural order, which has little relation to the notion of alien abstraction embedded within the discourse around modernist material culture.

One of the epithets most frequently used by residents to describe their experience of living in the Brunswick was that of the 'concrete jungle'. This metaphor suggests a maze of routes and a proliferation of different concrete elements – a spatial hierarchy that is not easily deciphered, and a mass of material components that is overwhelming in its sensory impact. Yet, at the same time, the use of the word 'jungle' suggests a certain grandeur of scale and conception that provokes some kind of admiration. The lofty verticality of the A-frame structure from within is undeniably impressive. Furthermore, the flats themselves were repeatedly described as 'beautiful', setting a standard of 'luxury' compared with the standard of other rented council housing. As a result, there has been a lively market in private sales, particularly on the top floors with the best views, to professional middle-class incomers.

While residents' experience of the grandeur of the Brunswick is strongly shaped by its vertical qualities, users of the shopping precinct below get a very different impression. Here, the complex reads at an almost exclusively horizontal level as a pedestrian route across the precinct and a line of vision firmly directed along the horizontal lines of the ranked glazed terraces of housing, glinting in the light. Experienced in this way, the Brunswick precinct was often described as too wide to be comfortable: a prairie of a piazza, rather than the 'town-room' evoked by Hodgkinson, a space which the angled set-back of the housing terraces above allowed to 'escape' rather than enclosing adequately. This perceived failing was addressed by bringing forward the columns of the arcade in 2006 to create a more contained public space.

By comparison, the upstands of the A-frame structure framing the centre of the residential blocks are comparable in scale to ancient forest trees or the soaring buttresses and vaults of medieval cathedrals. Framed by this tall, narrow space, at level C (the internal street), a person is revealed as a small figure, while the stacked access galleries overhead host small clusters of people around front doors on different levels, who appear to be clinging to the sides of the walls like crustaceans on the bows of a ship.

When Mrs A's friend suggested that the Brunswick was like a 'big ship', the metaphor completely changed Mrs A's feelings about living in the Brunswick, which had been mainly negative. Initially she found the fact that the front doors to the flats did not open onto the precinct, where her young son used to ride his bicycle, very problematic in terms of meeting people, and she felt generally 'very detached' from the building. But ironically, it was the threat, as she saw it, to the building itself in the 1990s which led her to become more involved. She was incensed by what she calls the 'lean-to' scheme for a block of new flats built across and in the space of the Brunswick Square portico, and in her letter of objection described the Brunswick as 'one of the most wonderful pieces of architecture'.

Mrs A described the 'fight-back' against the developers as one of the most important events in her life. In a sense it created an idea of a real and viable community threatened by the freeholder. But at the same time it drew out divisions. Residents of Foundling Court queried why support should be given to O'Donnell Court over the 'lean-to' building, when O'Donnell had not supported Foundling in its battle to stop the hotel opposite building additional storeys which would block light and views out towards the horizon from the upper levels. This perceived division was crystallised by Mr M when he referred to 'the two estates'.

In the original scheme, the continuity of the terraces around the roof of the central shopping hall should have created a sense of unity between the two buildings, but as it was built, without the shopping hall, the sense of connection between the two sides was sustained only by two narrow footbridges, which have now been removed altogether.

For Mrs C, Foundling was definitely inhabited by 'a better class of people', on account of its direct relationship with Marchmont Street, its shops and post office, where people meet and consolidate social relationships. O'Donnell Court, by contrast, addresses the relatively abstract, even though more beautiful, space of Brunswick Square. For years, the shops of the precinct itself were too specialised, except for the old supermarket and perhaps one of the cafes, to provide a regular common meeting-ground for both sides of the complex – and many of the retail units stood empty for some time before the 2006 refurbishment.

Even within each block, there was a clear sense that the spatial design structured and differentiated the Brunswick 'community', so that perceptions of it as either 'cliquey', or lacking in any sense of community at all, were voiced. The vertical grandeur of the common internal space underlines the hierarchical layering of floors towards the light and views at the top of the main block, but the obstruction of the line of vision upwards by the concrete upstands means there is no view of what happens on each floor, and therefore little integration between them. Each floor then tends to operate as a separate community, with the top floors regarded as considerably more desirable than the second to fourth floors, where more burglaries are reported to take place because of the comparative lack of daylight. The tangible effect of this ordering is that the flats on the top floors have sold better on the private market, establishing a distinct, socially differentiated group at the top of the building. Some of this group described themselves as 'refugees' from other areas of the city, especially in west London, gentrified in advance of Holborn and Kings Cross, who came in search of 'real neighbourliness' and 'a sense of humanity', as one respondent put it. Many were architects and designers, buying in to the building's architectural significance. Some, however, found the necessity of social mixing imposed by the vertical access through the building painful and unwelcome, such as Mrs E, who stated that she would prefer not to be forced into proximity with, and awareness of, the 'creeping working classes'. Others noted with dislike but resignation the high maintenance bills charged to 'home-owners' by Camden's Housing Department in order to subsidise its tenants.

In this scenario, the lifts (fig. 2.8) played a crucial integrating social role in the building's history. Mrs E described them as important meeting-points, where conversations between neighbours on different floors could take place, albeit briefly, and acquaintanceships were initiated. Yet at the same time, they were places of confrontation and risk. 'Nobody wants to get in a lift with someone they don't know', explained Mrs D. Stories of muggings were rife, involving strangers

Fig. 2.8 View of internal circulation spaces, Foundling Court, 2001. Source: author

pushing through the entrance doors and into the lifts behind residents, and a prevalent discourse of security, or lack of it, and fear in the blocks crystallised around the vertical mechanism of the lift, often judged unreliable in itself.

Such narratives and perceptions seem to confirm the often-cited judgement that 'streets in the sky' do not work at a social level, even though they may make striking architectural compositions. Mrs E said she felt as though she was always seeing the long access gallery leading from the lift to her front door, and way beyond it past many other front doors (fig. 2.9), through the lens of a camera. But the spatial language of the street itself was also often used – so-and-so is 'across the road' – and most respondents seemed to be familiar and on reasonably friendly terms with their neighbours, usually known to them by name. The aspect of the spatial order that was most commonly criticised is the lack of a proper outlook onto the 'street'. As the site superintendent put it, 'The front door is at the back of the flat', and, 'On your balcony you only see your immediate neighbour.' He said, 'The community spirit was lost in the design'; but, nevertheless, 'The mix here is brilliant', and it is 'a city sitting in itself'. He said, 'Everything was here… it was good… living on top of the high street.'

The tension between the private domestic and public domains within the building is tangible. Sharon Marcus (1999) has outlined the

Fig. 2.9 View through second floor access gallery to flats (perimeter block, Foundling Court) 2001. Source: author

discourse of the apartment building and identified the apartment building as an undesirable building type in nineteenth-century London, for the reason that multi-occupancy of subdivided buildings was seen to fundamentally transgress values of permanence, stability and moral rectitude that could only be sustained against the amoral values of the market place within the insulated cocoon of the family. The very concept of the shared apartment building was considered to undermine the sanctity of the private, introverted family unit. The spatial design of the Brunswick, however, seems to generate a condition of privacy within the flats themselves that was spoken of by occupants in both positive and negative terms. On the one hand, the lack of acoustic seepage between dwellings was noted as a benefit, but on the other, respondents spoke of feeling 'cut off' in their flats – of the building as 'alienating', 'a shambles, far too big', with 'no camaraderie'. One described it as 'a very cruel building', where people 'watch and listen, but don't do anything, and then gossip' – a building of invisible eyes and ears and whispering, but no visible community spirit, manifested most strikingly in the empty public spaces of level 2 – the internal street, and the terraces.

These evidently discreet dwellings are, however, by no means congruent with the family unit, and the unsuitability of the Brunswick for family life is often spoken of, despite the fact that Brunswick does house numbers of families, some, particularly immigrant families, with four or more children. Since none of the flats has more than two bedrooms, many of the first, local, generation of residents moved out when their children, if they had two of different sex, became too old to share a bedroom. Mrs X also suggested that the kitchen was too small to eat in as a family, and most people felt it should have taken up some of the unnecessary space allocated to the living room. The shoulder-height partition between the two spaces was 'good', because she could look over while working in the kitchen to keep an eye on her boys playing in the living room, but she closed the gap off with glass in her flat, apparently finding the ambiguity of the spatial segregation troublesome. Several respondents also referred to an antipathy on the part of many residents towards children, which resulted in the use of the terraces as play areas being forbidden, and their resulting virtual redundancy as public space.

The former estate manager described the limited spatial range of accommodation at the Brunswick as a serious problem for the cohesion of the community, in that it provided no scope for people to stay in the building throughout their lives, thus eroding family connections and placing undue pressure on the council's community welfare services. She wrongly claims that the original speculative design was not meant to accommodate families at all, but only 'business people' – a misconception echoed in another respondent's claim that the Brunswick was built as 'holiday flatlets' – but both claims underline a pervasive attitude towards the Brunswick as not being designed with families in mind.

On the other hand, the Brunswick provides a structure for a different sort of community, one in which people without family ties can, by all accounts, make themselves at home within a loose, relatively anonymous framework that also allows a sense of communal identity. Half of the housing accommodation is designated 'sheltered', so 50 per cent of residents live independently in their flats, within easy reach of a 'warden'. The wardens themselves assert that 'the best thing about the Brunswick is that you can remain anonymous'. Although most of the elderly are housed in one-bedroom flats and studios on the ground to second floors (opening onto the internal street and terraces), which are clearly identified with the elderly community, other people may be housed anywhere within the spatial hierarchy, avoiding any immediate identification with the 'sheltered' population. In this case, it seems apparent that it is precisely those spatial characteristics of the Brunswick prompting its description as a 'shambles' or a 'concrete jungle' that provide the possibility of an anonymous existence in the crowd and freedom from gossip for those whose existence in a more spatially integrated, close-knit community could be difficult.

But it is also this dimension of the Brunswick community – the possibility and awareness of free-floating, unaccountable elements – that has generated a powerfully pervasive discourse of security during its history. The lack of protection from confrontational transgressive behaviours was graphically perceived in terms of a building that was too permeable, full of odd crevices and leftover hidden spaces and underused public spaces that attract colonisation by 'undesirables'. The most dramatic expression of this dimension of the 'community' was the underground world of homeless residency and transgressive activity that developed early on in the two basement levels of the complex on a basis of such permanence that many 'residents' would give their address, for social security purposes, as The Ramp, and receive their post there. The site superintendent detailed in precise terms the material characteristics of the buildings that facilitated such occupation, and noted the social segregation between the east and west sides of the service ramp, the east side benefiting from the 'hot air from the Safeway freezer extract': 'They also used the fire hoses to shower under and wash their clothes, the clothing was then hung up to dry under the hot air.' But this level of domestic harmony, as it might be perceived, began to break down during the 1980s as the underground community became increasingly violent and aggressive, resulting in an 'attempted murder' charge and a destructive invasion of the whole labyrinthine area, including switch and plant rooms.

This dark realm of urban existence beneath the Brunswick seems to represent the inverse of the realm of light, reaching towards the sky above, but also seeping into the whole building. A tenant of the 'professional chambers', now studio units, on the terrace level, summed it up as a problem of 'uncontextualised places being taken over by uncontextualised people'. Yet the first generation of residents at the Brunswick were predominantly local; they had been born and brought up on or near the site, had watched the building being erected and, in many cases, had specifically requested to be rehoused in the new flats. For Mrs X, who moved in when newly married and pregnant, there was nothing 'uncontextual' about the Brunswick; everyone was local, and many of her new neighbours had known her as a child. Mary, in her 90s at the time of the research, was living nearby when the Brunswick was being built; she used to talk to all the builders, and was determined to see what the new flats were like to live in. When she moved in, she knew lots of people – 'We'd have cups of tea round each other's flats.'

Most respondents suggested that problems with social cohesion and order at the Brunswick had less to do with the architecture of the building than with the housing policy of the local council, widely perceived as 'moving anybody in' – people 'who don't come from London' – without due consideration for the community there already. Yet at the same time, there was a pervasive sense of reliance, even dependence, on the council as an institution, not only for the welfare of the residential community, but also, in some sense, for its very identity as a cohesive group. This is clearly revealed in a discourse of 'domestic complaint', which closely parallels that identified by Marcus (1999) as a persistent feature of the literature of housing and the leasehold system in nineteenth-century London. The institution of the council itself, via the estate manager, is constantly criticised and even reviled for its lack of reliability, promptness and general failure to bring such problems under control. Mr M thought there was a problem with a 'dependency culture', insofar as the council's tenants could be divided into two types: those who were not particularly happy to be council tenants, but were obliged to accept their situation because of their circumstances, like himself (living with his disabled sister), and those who were 'determined to be for their whole lives'.

This perception of the council, suggesting a dimension of kinship, was reflected in the attitude of some tenants and their children who, according to one respondent, regard their parents' flats as their 'birth right'. While Mr M believed this relationship between tenants and their landlord derives from an outdated notion of councils as 'universal providers', it is also arguably, and perhaps more potently, rooted in a very real sense of a geographical, or spatial, identity under threat. The council effectively represented and activated an expression of locality and community which, in many ways, has been eroded by the transient nature of London's population and the influx of outsiders, many of whom do not consider their London residences as their primary homes. According to a community worker, most of the Bangladeshi families who had recently arrived in the borough and been allocated flats in the Brunswick and other local authority blocks regarded their accommodation as 'somewhere to stay', while 'home' continued to be in Bangladesh. Such people, she suggested, may have very little idea about the terms of their tenancies and their everyday responsibilities for maintaining their accommodation and common areas in good condition; this in turn leads to tension with other residents who distinguish themselves by the longevity of their residence in the building and their status as long-term council tenants.

Yet the level of spatial identification between the building of the Brunswick, the institution of the council both as landlord and welfare provider, and a notion of localised community is confused by the historic division of the complex into two ownerships in 1965, when the housing in its entirety, plus the professional chambers on the terrace level, were leased by the council, leaving the commercial parts of the building in private ownership. The situation was described by a council tenant of the studio units as 'upstairs, downstairs': a spatial description with a strong implication of social hierarchy. The ambiguities of the relationship between the upper, middle and precinct levels emerged as a key issue in the identity of the building as a whole when the freehold and commercial components were sold in 1999. Most respondents expressed a view that the new freeholder had a moral obligation to consult with the residential tenants of the Brunswick about their plans for upgrading and refurbishing the commercial areas of the building, and to proceed with work as soon as possible for the benefit of residents. There was a clear sense that the precinct and its shops existed primarily to serve the needs of residents, a view significantly at odds with that of the developer.

For the freeholder, the public and commercial space of the Brunswick represented much less a space of local and domestic identity than a site of engagement with a far broader community of users, including tourists, students, office workers and commuters, symbolically located at the historic centre of a cosmopolitan city on a globalised stage. Their perception of the Brunswick as a localised focus of universal interests, and the corresponding execution of plans to upgrade the complex, aspired to resurrect the original intention of the development as a grand, formal axis and public space between nodes of mass transportation, which even, at one stage, included a passenger terminal for Heathrow. In a very real sense, the tense relationship between the two landlords and their tenant communities has symbolised a conflict between spatially defined identities – the local and the global – which is embodied in the very fabric of the Brunswick as a building, and is manifested in the 2006 alterations.

The Brunswick can thus be read as a strongly contested site or series of territories embodied in clearly differentiated spatial realms or layers of existence. The spatial ordering of the building may therefore be understood not simply as a condition of its architectural conception and aesthetic, but also as an active framework for the social ordering and evolution of the complex in close relation to political and economic circumstances and other urban processes such as gentrification and migration. The question of how it 'concretises' the community or communities that inhabit 'existential space' through its architectural spaces is complex and full of subtleties that are disallowed by conventional architectural discourse in its concern to establish a fixed interpretation of form.

One of the newer tenants introduced to the commercial precinct prior to the refurbishment was Myrtle – an advertising and media agency instantly recognisable as 'other' in the context of the more established retail uses of the complex – which has now moved on. Myrtle wanted to be 'somewhere which reflected the people we deal with on a daily basis', and which allowed it to 'be in touch with a real community'. At the same time, Myrtle described the Brunswick as being 'like some giant spaceship landed in genteel Bloomsbury, really cool': a carefully defined, media-generated image that had little relation to the perceptions of the people who lived there, or indeed to the original intentions of the development and its architecture, but which has made it attractive to film-makers (including Antonioni, who set a scene from *The Passenger,* 1975, on its steps) on numerous occasions during its lifetime. It is clear then that the Brunswick, understood as a complex of material and spatial phenomena rather than as a fixed intellectual imposed idea, offers the possibility of multiple readings and meanings to different groups of people, framed by the cultural conditions of any given moment.

Conclusion

One of the most significant signs of the Brunswick's legitimacy and vitality as a vehicle of cultural meaning has been the evident extent of its appeal to the imagination of both the immediate community – evoked in the use of metaphors of the ship, paradise, Mediterranean shores, Gardens of Babylon, and others – but also of the wider society that produced it, and continues to live through it, manifested most obviously in the numerous films that have been shot within its boundaries. Abram (1996) stresses the importance of recognising the imagination as a fundamental part of the perceptual apparatus that allows the body to see things more fully. The Brunswick's appeal to the imagination, both at an individual and a collective level, may be interpreted as a significant measure of its success as a channel of 'sense experience' and, through that, 'communication with the world', as defined by Merleau-Ponty (1989 [1962]).

Notwithstanding Camden Council's explicit socially motivated agenda in acquiring the housing at the Brunswick as part of an initiative to reinstate family life in the Holborn area, and regardless of the estate's long-standing and well-documented problems in functioning properly as a viable mixed-use development incorporating both public and private spaces, the experience of life 'inside' the Brunswick has not really entered the public domain as the subject of discourse in its own right. As a place in the urban landscape, perceived from within as a container of disparate people linked (or not) in space by many different threads rather than observed from without as an external profile or aesthetic form, the Brunswick represents a multi-layered, multi-vocal social setting with its own internal dynamic that exists autonomously of the evaluation of the building both as a significant work of architecture within a particular European strand of modernist architectural history, and as a landmark of national post-war cultural and urban heritage. Nevertheless, the architecture of the Brunswick also provides an expressive and inescapable environmental framework for the social life that subsists within it, infused with material agency. It not only outlines, but also dramatically draws attention to, a particular territory and offers a certain definition – an aesthetic of social identity – to the lives and relationships of the people who inhabit and invest it with meaning in the wider context of an increasingly commercialised yet contested city.

Methodological note

The material for this study was generated from a study of historical archive material, combined with numerous observation sessions and personal semi-structured interviews carried out between August 2000 and June 2001, then again between 2004 and 2006, both on and off the site of the Brunswick. These included tenants' meetings and interviews with the architect, Patrick Hodgkinson, residents of the flats, tenants of commercial premises at the Brunswick, and various people having an official involvement with running and making decisions directly and indirectly about the future of the Brunswick.

The archive material held at the Holborn Library Local Archive Centre and by the Planning Department at Camden Council included a very large number of revealing letters written by residents and non-residents during the course of the planning consultations held in connection with two earlier proposals for refurbishment during the 1990s. Another valuable source was the press cuttings file, dating back to the start of the project, held by Patrick Hodgkinson, which included most of the key architectural critiques published over the Brunswick's lifetime. In addition, I was given access to the uncatalogued archive of Hodgkinson's drawings and documents relating to the project, which he had recently gifted to the RIBA Drawings Collection, and which was to be slowly put in order during the course of my own research.

During the periods of field work, I passed through the Brunswick Centre almost daily in my comings and goings around the local area, and registered my impressions of a building I already knew well at different times of day and in contrasting lights and weather conditions. I used the underground car park, shopped in the precinct, and stopped at one or other of the cafes to observe the everyday activities on the site, until the radical disruption of construction work made that impossible and created a different kind of environment to negotiate. I installed myself for a two-week period, house-sitting a flat in Foundling Court, so that I could experience the Brunswick from the inside, at first hand, and familiarise myself with its semi-public and private spaces. In July 2005, the even more radical disruption of the bomb blast at nearby Russell Square tube, followed by local street closures and appeals for information on the missing, many pictured in photographs fastened to the Brunswick's site hoardings, cast a terrible pall over my field-site. Yet, by the following year, the building had been transformed into a new 'high street for Bloomsbury', its stained concrete facades gone for ever under a thick veneer of cream paint, and the re-glazed winter gardens sparkling more brightly than before as a new Waitrose supermarket opened its doors to the public, blocking off one end of the formerly open precinct.

I was aware that my resident respondents were almost equally split between a long-standing 'indigenous' community of council tenants, some of whom who had subsequently bought their flats under 'right to buy' legislation in the 1980s, and a more recent incoming professional community of owner-occupiers (accounting for only one-sixth of total occupants in 2001). There was a predominance of female respondents. While the former included tenants who were anxious about being displaced by the refurbishment, the latter were anticipating a significant increase in the value of their property and equity. My evidence for the experience of newer incoming tenants housed by the council, including a significant proportion of ethnic minority households (particularly Bangladeshi), people with physical and mental health problems, and ex-offenders, was largely gleaned at third hand through official parties, due to a mix of communication and translation problems and people's fears of being reported to the social benefits authorities.

Over time and successive interviews, I got to know some of these people quite well. In 2006, I put on a slide exhibition of our photographs of the interiors of many of their homes, a constellation of unique little domestic worlds concealed behind the external public face of the Brunswick and within its industrial-scale concrete structure. The exhibition was mounted in a basement service space of the building, providing a glimpse inside the everyday lives of the people who knew it best. It also provided an unlikely backdrop for the developers' official re-opening of the shopping precinct, which was framed by a rhetoric of regeneration in which a resounding critique of architectural modernism and urbanism was implicit. That encounter between life subjectively experienced on the inside and the dispassionate, objectifying view from outside encapsulated the value of bringing an anthropological perspective to bear on the impact of the modernist legacy on urban experience.

References

Abram, D. 1996. 'The Mindful Life of the Body'. In *The Spell of the Sensuous: Perception and Language in a More-than-human World*, by D. Abram. New York: Vintage Books.
Attfield, J. 1989. 'Inside Pram Town: A Case Study of Harlow Interiors 1951–61'. In *A View from the Interior: Feminism, Women and Design History*, edited by J. Attfield and Pat Kirkham. London: Women's Press.
Bloch, M. 1995. 'The Resurrection of the House amongst the Zafimaniry'. In *About the House: Levi-Strauss and Beyond*, by Janet Carsten and Steven Hugh-Jones. Cambridge: Cambridge University Press.

Boudon, P. 1972. *Lived-In Architecture: Le Corbusier's Pessac Revisited*. London: Lund Humphries.
Bourdieu, P. 1977. 'The Kabyle House, or the World Reversed'. In *The Logic of Practice* by Pierre Bourdieu. Cambridge: Polity Press.
Buchanan, C. 1963. *Traffic in Towns*, London: Ministry of Transport.
Buchli, V. 1999. *The Archaeology of Socialism*. Oxford: Berg.
Carsten, J. and Hugh-Jones, S. 1995. *About the House: Levi-Strauss and Beyond*. Cambridge: Cambridge University Press.
de Certeau, M. 1998 [1980]. *The Practice of Everyday Life*. Minneapolis, London: University of Minnesota Press.
Cooke, C. (2000). Letter from Chair, DOCOMOMO-UK (UK branch, International Working Party for Documentation and Conservation of Buildings, Sites and Neighbourhoods of the Modern Movement), to Kenneth Humphreys, Buildings, Monuments and Sites Division of the UK Government Department of Culture, Media and Sports, 15 March.
Clifford, J. 1998. 'Mixed Feelings'. In *Cosmopolitics: Thinking and Feeling beyond the Nation* by P. Cheah and B. Robbins, 362–70. Minneapolis: University of Minnesota Press.
Czordas, T. 1999. 'Embodiment and Cultural Phenomenology'. In *Perspectives on Embodiment: The Intersection of Nature and Culture*, edited by Gail Weiss. London: Routledge.
Giddens, A. 1991. 'The Trajectory of the Self'. In *Modernity and Self-Identity* by Anthony Giddens. Cambridge: Polity Press.
Hamilton Eddy, D. 1989. 'Castle Mythology in British Housing', *RIBA Journal* December, pp. 28–33.
Hodgkinson, P. 1972. 'Notes', *Architectural Review* October.
Hodgkinson, P. 1992. Speculation with Humanity? Architect's objection to Tranmac's planning application, 10 July.
Johnstone, V. 1972. 'Another London "Barbican", custom-built for Bloomsbury', *Daily Telegraph*, 27 June (CLSC np).
Le Corbusier, Charles Edouard Jeanneret. 1970 [1923]. *Towards a New Architecture*. Translated by Frederick Etchells. London: Architectural Press.
Lefebvre, H. 2008 [1947–1961]. *Critique of Everyday Life*, volumes 1–3. London: Verso.
Marcus, S. 1999. *Apartment Stories: City and Home in 19th-Century Paris and London*. Berkeley; London: University of California Press.
McLeod, M. 2000. 'Everyday and Other Spaces'. In *Gender Space Architecture: An Interdisciplinary Discussion*, edited by Jane Rendell et al. London: Routledge.
Merleau-Ponty, M. 1989 [1962]. *Phenomenology of Perception*. London: Routledge. New Jersey: Humanities Press
Miller, D. 1987. 'Towards a Theory of Consumption'. In *Material Culture and Mass Consumption* by D. Miller. Oxford: Blackwell.
Miller, D. 1988. 'Appropriating the State on the Council Estate', *Man* 23:353–72
Norberg-Schulz, C. 1980. *Genius Loci: Towards a Phenomenology of Architecture*. London: Academy Editions.
Pallasmaa, J. 2005. *The Eyes of the Skin: Architecture and the Senses*, Chichester: Wiley Academy. First published as 'An Architecture of the Seven Senses' [1994], *A + U Questions of Perception: Phenomenology of Architecture*, July: 27–38
Rabinow, P. 1986. 'Representations are Social Facts'. In *Writing Culture: The Poetics and Politics of Ethnography* by J. Clifford and G. Marcus, 234–61. Berkeley: University of California Press.
Seamon, D. n.d. 'Phenomenology, Place, Environment and Architecture: A Review'. In *Environmental and Architectural Phenomenology Newsletter*.
Sennett, R. 1993. *The Fall of Public Man*. London: Faber.
Spencer, D. 2016. *The Architecture of Neoliberalism: How Contemporary Architecture Became an Instrument of Control and Compliance*. London: Bloomsbury.
Tilley, C. 1994. *A Phenomenology of Landscape: Places, Paths and Monuments*. Oxford: Berg.

3
Isolation: A walk through a London estate

Dave Yates

In this chapter, we are going to take a trip west to a small estate at the edge of London in the borough of Hounslow, which sits at one end of the Piccadilly line. The only other destination further west from the centre is Heathrow. The airport represents access to over 1,400 national and international flights a day. Over the skies of Hounslow, some 10 miles from Charing Cross, a plane passes every 45 seconds – over 1,400 planes per day (Wicks 2014).

Introduction

Travelling on the dark blue of the Piccadilly tube line heading west, the underground first fills with people heading across the centre of town and then slowly empties as it breaches out into the open air. Hounslow, despite its distance from the centre of the capital, has three beautiful art deco stations: Hounslow East, Central and West. Straddling the main street – the Bath Road – and supported by a car park large enough to cater for the suburban commuters stopping here before heading east, Hounslow West was built in 1884 and was named 'Hounslow Barracks' after the cavalry on Beavers Lane (Rose 1983).

As I walk from the station on one visit, the summer heat hits the pavement outside and the area feels sparse, deserted; yet it is far from either. The streets are full of stalls, shoppers, commuters and all the life of a busy, and diverse, London town.

In the 2011 census, the borough of Hounslow was reported as being 53.3 per cent white and 34.4 per cent Asian (taken from the 2011 census data, where 'white' is a combined reference to white: (English, Welsh, Scottish, Northern Irish, Irish; white; Irish); White Other and Asian (Asian British; Indian/ Pakistani/Bangladeshi/Chinese and other) across a population of around 265,000. The numbers and proportions of each group (and subgroup) vary greatly between areas such as Chiswick (majority white British) and west or central Hounslow, where there are a higher proportion of those who identify as Asian. On the Bath Road, retail outlets and stalls along the street appear to mimic these statistics, provisioning for a largely Indian or Pakistani customer and owned and operated by the same. Perhaps it is both this diversity and lack of performance of 'traditional' English retail that make this feel like a very British, or perhaps just a very London, high street.

Hounslow West

Leaving the underground station and walking south across the road, we enter the suburban residential area of Hounslow West. The noise of the main road drops behind and the silence of these quiet and bare streets envelops you. Turning a corner around a wide street, it is clear that this is no leafy district like Islington or Camberwell (fig. 3.1).

Fig. 3.1 Rosemary Avenue looking west. Source: author

The roads here are wide, and the streets and houses quiet, giving the impression that all who usually reside here are at work and away from home during the day. The houses are mainly red brick, grey or beige, with white window frames – the tones a stark contrast to the vibrancy of the high street. Their white PVC windows and grey/white net curtains are framed by pebble-dashed walls and red-tiled roofs. Few trees line the cracked pavement streets, and even fewer gardens have survived the need for off-road parking enforced by the council's control of parking in the area. Despite the warmth of the day, very little stirs. The gardens do not appear to desire attention, and few appear to be tended regularly. Most of the spaces in front of the homes have been given over to pavement and concrete. While they remain empty during the day, they fill with family cars come the evening. All is quiet, all stark and deserted of street life and noise.

Then it happens. The first of many planes roars over the roof tops, appearing to scrape the red tiles of the nearby houses before thundering off towards its destination. It is followed, unceremoniously, by another and another. The planes here either take off over the neighbourhood or they queue along landing patterns waiting for their slots. At night, their headlights can be seen forming an orderly queue in to the night sky. The effect on the neighbourhood is clear: every window in the area is double glazed, and although not visible, every loft is likely to be insulated. Heathrow offers a widely adopted scheme to help reduce the impact of the planes' noise (Heathrow Community Relations Team 2014), which is now helping reduce the impact of noise for over 40,000 homes in the surrounding area. Despite the near-constant nature of the sound intrusion into the neighbourhood, people respond more quickly than you might expect. At first these monstrous metal dragons pierce every mental space as they tear off to one location or another. Yet over time even the barking engines of the larger Airbus planes that come and go at Heathrow fall into the background as you eventually get used to the intrusion.

As you can see from the satellite image (fig. 3.2), as you walk down past the large and well-kept Beaversfield Park (bottom right), this area of Hounslow West is a loose-grid layout (Hounslow 2015) markedly different to the leafy layout of the estate to the left, the target of our attention. But it is not until you turn into Vincent Road (centre left) and look down to the end of the street towards the estate to the west that you notice how different it is. From the sparse gardens and beige and grey streets, the colour changes as large mature trees mark the entrance to the estate (far left). Getting closer, you instantly notice the grey walls and

Fig. 3.2 Hounslow West – station to the far right, with the Beavers (the Meadows) Estate to the left visible by the trees (Google Maps, 2016 – accessed 14 December 2016)

Fig. 3.3 Entrance to the Beavers Estate from Vincent Road. Source: author

dark-tiled roofs, but much of the view of the estate is hidden, at least during the warmer months, by large soft, green leaves (fig. 3.3).

Plans for the building of the Beavers Estate started in 1968, but the estate was not completely finished until 1971. The Greater London Council records of the construction of this estate are patchy. Archives such as the London Metropolitan hold several records of the estate, but much of the original planning and works were carried out within the Department of Housing and thereby undertaken by the in-house architect at the time. What is clear is that the original plans were for the estate to be a temporary solution to house families leaving sites across London. Predominately, these people came from Hammersmith, Hackney and Maida Vale, where major redevelopments were in process. If you spend enough time speaking to people on the estate, you can still hear the stories of what it was like when they arrived. There are still enough of these first residents for them to have formed their own group; collectively, they call themselves 'the beginning ladies'.

When they first arrived on the site, the ladies recall loving it instantly. They came from high-rise apartments with no space outside, and with shared toilets and kitchens – sometimes shared between up to five families. It is not too much of an exaggeration to call the blocks of housing they left behind slums. Many of the families were offered locations further afield or simply just not large enough to house their growing families. For some this was a last hope, a hope gratefully received. All in all, the low-rise flat-roofed buildings, the trees and the multiple open and landscaped areas gave the estate the feeling of a holiday home:

> When I first came here it was like being on holiday. I said to my mum, 'Are you sure they are not going to send us home?' (resident from 1971)

On the new estate they had '[…] central heating, hot water, a real kitchen, good size outside space, and a bathroom of our own – we were in heaven.' They were told when they arrived that the estate was designed to last only 15 years, but many of those first residents, and now their families, are still there some 45 years later. Below are a set of images taken in 1971 (fig. 3.4). The low-rise buildings, clear open areas and lack of dense traffic gave the estate a chalet feel.

The images in fig. 3.4 show the estate just after completion – long before the trees had matured or the new pitched roofs were added. The type of construction of the building is known as 'bison frame', and despite the name no frame was required. The apparent lack of recorded information on the decision to use this technique may be down to the speed required to produce new residential properties. The technique

Fig. 3.4 Beavers Estate C1971–3. © London Metropolitan Archives 2016 (GLC/AR/PL/17)

had gained some popularity at the time. It was known to reduce construction time and costs, and as such enjoyed a large period of popularity in the UK (Georghiou et al. 1986). Despite this apparent success, it was only two years after completion that residents started to complain about condensation and damp. While there are records to 1990 of the problem still being discussed, it was not for almost 10 years after that (in around 2000) when pitched roofs were added and the asbestos was removed from the properties (UK Parliament, 1990).

Fig. 3.5 shows images from the estate as it is now. Today, damp is only one of the problems that residents have had to contend with. The estate forms the majority of a lower layer super output area (LSOA) comprising 1,755 people (Hounslow, 2013). The only residential properties that are not part of the estate are several houses along Beavers Lane, to the south-west. This LSOA, labelled as 016B, sits within 20 per cent of the most deprived in England, the top 10 per cent most deprived in London, and the second most deprived in the Borough of Hounslow itself (Hounslow 2015). Despite this, Hounslow has high employment rates – 75.8 per cent – compared to the London average of 70.1 per cent (City of London 2016). Given these damning statistics, the Borough of Hounslow initiated a piece of research with the public policy think tank, the Royal Society for the Encouragement of Arts, Manufacture and Commerce (RSA), to better understand the complexities of the problem within the LSOA (RSA 2014). This chapter is based on the research I undertook while working for the RSA on the completion of the project (Parsfield and Yates 2015; this project undertook quantitative

Fig. 3.5 The 'bison frame' blocks today. Source: author

questionnaires, ethnography and social network analysis; together they confirmed anecdotal reports of isolation on the estate).

Despite such apparent deprivation, historical issues with antisocial behaviour, and continuing problems of dogs fouling the pathways, many residents speak very fondly of the area and the estate in general. The unique nature of the buildings, the maturity of the trees and even the very physical and geographic isolation of the estate itself may provide a strong benefit to the residents, not least a strong sense of identity. But, as this chapter will explore, this identity is more than difference, but also an insulation from the external world. Be it from noise pollution or the ethnic 'difference' that some feel 'encroaches' on their world, the estate affords an element of differentiation that its material location and physicality enforces. The theme of isolation, as discussed later, has been drawn out from observation and from the views of the individuals who live on the estate. For them, the site is home and as such affords protection, but it remains disconnected from its surroundings. This separation is in stark contrast to the character, ethnicity and apparent economic success of the area, but perhaps more so this disconnection stands in highest contrast to the constant noise of one of the world's busiest airports. Such insulation can reinforce separation – removal from new influences and changes that are key for growth and adaptation. In short, isolation can be distinction, it can be insulation and it can also become stagnation. From the very day people arrived on the estate, the built environment made the space feel like a 'holiday home'. 45 years later this 'home from home' remains isolated.

Isolation as distinction

In the data from the 2011 census, it is possible to clearly discern a difference between the Beavers Estate and the surrounding area, especially to the east. The web portal datashine.org.uk makes this difference visually clear. Specifically, we see a marked difference in the level of education obtained, economic activity, length of residence in the UK and even health. The population of the estate is not less educated, or struggling to find or keep work, but has been in the UK longer and suffers some significantly lower levels of health. It also has a higher rate of those identifying as white British than the rest of Hounslow West. On the one hand, the estate benefits from a strong identity and sense of internal community. On the other hand, its separation keeps it removed from change and external influences that may shift negative patterns towards more beneficial outcomes. This accidental distinction differs from forced or conscious acts of segregation, but many of the same secondary results are the same. Isolation, it appears, is a double-edged sword.

Another plane, another roar, and my face turns from concrete grey walls to grey sky filled with noise. They pass over here so often that the residents no longer notice. In conversations, in gardens, in the street and even in their homes with the windows open they hardly lift their voices and they never pause speaking to let the plane pass. Here the isolation of the estate feels like a bunker, protecting the inhabitants from the pollution of the sky travellers. Few of the residents have used the airport, although the nearest bus stop west is sponsored by Heathrow. After all, it transports many people needed to make the airport run.

Circumnavigating the estate is a single-lane road that fails to completely loop back on itself in a prescriptive but useful way, and instead passes only one way around the estate. The road's name is Chinchilla Drive. All the roads here are rodents or small mammals: Mink, Ermine, Raccoon, Badger, Opossum, Sable and Marmot. Although a clear reason for this remains elusive, it is likely that, like the estate, the roads were simply named in reference to the farm that sat on the site before – Beavers. Barring the limited options of Chinchilla Drive, there are only two other routes in and out of the estate. One is a small alley leading north, and another a painted tunnel leading to Beavers Lane to the south (more on these later).

Despite this holistic approach to the naming, the estate has recently gone through something of a (largely failed) identity makeover. In the late 1990s the estate was suffering greatly from fly tipping and drugs and antisocial behaviour from teenagers. At the time the local council had trouble moving low-income families into the estate due to its bad reputation. Many residents recall this time in reference to how things are much improved now. The site has since been transformed into the 'Meadows Estate', yet despite talking to over a hundred people on the estate, I never once encountered anyone who did not scoff at the name change.

> MEADOWS! HA! It is the Beavers, and will always be the Beavers. You can't shake off the past by changing the name. Anyway, things are better now anyhow. ('Rachael')

Nearing the north edge of the estate, we come across the new healthcare centre and pharmacy, which opened in 2011 and cost £5.7 million (MyLondon, 2013). Despite the centre having quite up-to-date facilities, the local people continue to use their own surgeries located in Hounslow Central. When asked, they often say that they waited too long for the service on the estate – and now it sits, underutilised. The centre was built on the site of an old car park that for many years brought more trouble than many thought it was worth. Rather, it attracted those who sought a hidden location to gather or meet, often for illegal purposes. A covered site, away from passing eyes, the car park itself was rarely used for parking cars, as many of the residents did not own them.

To the side of the centre lies a small alley, north of four lanes of busy A30 traffic. Sitting at the end of the long thin alley way, and away from the protection of the large leafy trees, the constant noise and obvious danger of the road feels like a barrier against movement. Defra record the noise from this road at 70–75 dBm, matched only by similar noise from the air (Lee et al. 2017). This is a useful connection point; if you wish to catch one of two routes towards Staines, it takes some 45 minutes by bus; to Heathrow T5, only 25 minutes. But if you want to get to Hounslow West, or even Central (your nearest large high street), you need to cross four lanes of busy traffic. Alternatively, residents can walk 200 yards in either direction to the safety of an underpass (fig. 3.6).

Back down the alley way and along the street named after a South American rodent, we come across the only other exit, barring the two ends of Chinchilla Drive: a small tunnel that connects the estate to Beavers Lane and the school on the other side. Here someone took the time, care and attention to paint the walls of the tunnel with the names

Fig. 3.6 The Beavers Estate tunnel. Source: author

of the streets found within the estate. It did nothing for the aesthetics, and apart from the school trip, does little for access to other amenities, transport hubs or retail outlets. The tunnel is a stark reminder of how disconnected the estate is. Further, as we wander through the estate, it becomes clear how inwardly facing it is, not only in the physicality, but also in the protection that the physicality brings people to have focused on what is near. In many places, this has meant a focus on their gardens.

In stark contrast to the gardens along the path we took to the estate from Hounslow West station, where many lawns have been replaced with paving stone for driveways, the green and grey of the Beavers Estate is littered with plush and beautiful gardens. Not every home has a piece of land, either front or back, to call or work for their own. The flats in the second-floor blocks have neither garden nor the more modern fashion of an external balcony. But where the homes hit the streets, there is a clear trend towards attention in the garden. Some gardens are marked out by large and luscious roses of many colours. These mark out places where residents clearly spend time and attention. Most of the front gardens are bordered by small wooden or metal fences and gates. Depending on the layouts of the flats, the front gardens are sometimes nothing more than a porch – a fenced-off location big enough to place a single chair in the sun during summer or to have a small raised bed of flowers. Yet almost every garden is tended to one degree or another. At times, this tending means only to keep the area clear of weeds, sometimes by the drastic measure of keeping the porch area cemented over and freshly painted. But others use even the smallest area to grow flowers, bushes, shrubs and even small fruit trees. Some gardens have broken out of their barriers and taken over small patches of common grass that, unlike the estate buildings and layout, were formally designed by an external landscape architect and were designed to give the area a sense of adventure. The outside spaces are tended and enjoyed by the residents of the estate. Perhaps, in part, this is due to the ageing population and their ability to spend time in such pursuits. Certainly, many of the younger respondents had the flats on the second floor, with no outside space to worry about, barring the balcony that provided access to the flats. Here children store their collections of wheeled vehicles, while others make varied use of the space, filling it with plant pots and even deckchairs.

As we walk along Chinchilla Drive, down towards the small shopping area and local 'hub', the estate stays ever to the left. Once it may have been grey and abstract, but now mature plane trees give it a sheltered and natural feel. On the right is only the back of a fence or a blankness of a brick wall from neighbouring estates. This reinforces the bounded, isolated, and insular character of the estate. Practically speaking, it is hard to find and even harder to leave. A one-way drive around Chinchilla Drive leaves you facing south and exiting into the light industrial outskirts of Heathrow. To the south-east are the cavalry barracks, ring-fenced by high walls and barbed wire, which is far from inviting, and to the north the 'delicate' four lanes of the A30. The Beavers Estate is isolated, not by the attitude of its residents, but almost, it appears, by design. While few records are still held as to why the estate was built, or even why it was designed in quite this way, we might assume that much of it was purely functional. Indeed, what we do know was that the choice of construction, bison frame, was probably chosen out of the practicalities of constraint, namely time and money.

Isolation as insulation

The buildings on the estate were constructed out of precast concrete slabs. These were moulded offsite and shipped to the location, and then simply craned in. The method gained quite some attraction in that time, and the construction firm that installed the units, Concrete (Southern) Ltd (Now 'Bison Ltd': BML 2016), won the Queen's Award for Industry in 1967, so was certainly on the radar of the Greater London Authority's (GLA) in-house architecture team. The landscape of the area, on the other hand, was tackled by an external architect, Michael Brown.

Michael Brown's architectural practice reached its heights in the late 1960s and early 1970s. Although Brown died in 1996, his career is marked with some reverence among landscape architects. The excerpt below is from his obituary in the Independent.

> His schemes were always impeccably detailed and introduced a human scale to the landscape, often in contrast to an intimidating surround of deck access housing. He used sinuous paths, scattered groves of trees and subtly contoured brick surfaces or grass banks to achieve a quiet sense of adventure. A small sandpit in the office helped envisage the effects of proposed land modelling. (Stuart-Smith 1996)

Immediately, this description holds true for the landscape around the estate. Perhaps even more evocative of Michael Brown's interests is what remains of the records of discussions between the Housing Department at the GLA and his own office. In stark contrast to discussions held about the construction and layout of the (intended) temporary estate, there remains full correspondence between the office and Brown's own practice. One fact runs clearly throughout the pages of memos, invoices and reports: the shape, size, maturity and number of trees was of great importance to Brown. So much so that most of the discussions between the offices focused around the budget and sourcing of just the right number of trees. Looking down on the estate from the comfort of a satellite view (fig. 3.2) or walking to the entrances from Vincent Road or Beavers Lane (or even from the A30), it is immediately clear how important this battle, hard fought and won, was to Michael Brown.

When first arriving on the estate, armed with little more than a camera, notepad and a background of the statistics of deprivation in the area, I was stunned by how impactful the trees are (fig. 3.7). They give the estate life and movement, with the sound of birds filling the gaps between planes. The estate is far more beautiful and serene than one might, externally, assume. Returning, as I have, at different times throughout the year, I cannot help but be struck by the contrast with Hounslow West, and by the impact of the mature trees. Some trees, now more than 45 years old, do so much more than soften the precast walls and tarmac roads. Here Brown's vision of this estate is held in the canopies of the tallest – they reach out over the estate, touching each other and the very roofs of the tallest blocks – they join to form a roof, a cover that protects, insulates and isolates the estate from noise, from concrete and from misery.

Fig. 3.7 The play park in the centre of the estate. Source: author

Leaving Chinchilla Drive and walking into the estate, through the soft paths and past grass verges and play areas, the sounds from nearby roads are dampened into the background. Even the planes appear more distant when you are under one of the larger sycamores. At the centre of the estate by the newly renovated play park, the estate feels peaceful, calm and almost tranquil – an island surrounded by the noise and movement of the city, but peaceful and safe within. The strong sense of family, community and safety is present here. Everyone nods and says hello as they pass each other. In the summer, children run from open doors across the quiet and car-less paths to the green spaces for football or simply to chase each other. There is an openness here that I do not feel when I return to my own neighbourhood.

> It feels safe here. It always has to me, even when there was trouble when I was younger. I like the space inside – I feel my kids can run and play. ('Natalie')

This notion of an island of calm emerged from the very grounded reports of the residents who, while recognising the problems the estate has, also know that this isolation brings safety, security and (between planes) peace. This estate, through accident or design, has developed a strong sense of identity – one that not even a name change could alter.

It is with some regret that I found that many of the residents feel less that romantically about the trees. They, much like the dog-fouled paths, are a constant call of complaint in the context of living conditions. Residents call for the trees to be removed or, at the very least, heavily pruned. The problem is twofold. Firstly, these stunningly large trees are so close to the flats that they often block out the sun. In the summer months, this forces people to keep lights on around the house, with a distinct knock-on effect of this on electricity bills. It is a clear and honest concern for many in the higher flats especially. Secondly, some of the larger trees are so close to the buildings that the roots cause problems to the very foundations of the buildings. It is important to remember that this temporary housing estate was not meant to last so long. Nor, I would hazard a guess, was the protective nature of its isolation meant to be so strong. Michael Brown fought hard for these trees, but perhaps he did not guess how long they would have to grow and develop.

> God, I wish they would sort them out. Don't get me wrong, I like the trees, but they are just too big! They cover my windows so much that I have noticed it in my bills. They used to manage the

trees here much better. There was a groundman, a permanent guy, who would come 'round and sort the trees out throughout the year. Then cut backs and now it has gotten so bad they are just taking them out completely. Cheaper that way I guess. ('Robert')

Life on the estate is far from easy. Battling leaves and roots from the trees are just one of the many gripes that the residents have, but perhaps one of the easiest to solve. Many of the occupants struggle with drugs, ill health, and finding or keeping regular work. Despite these struggles, the estate offers a feeling of community strength and camaraderie. So much so that for those families strong enough to be able to express their needs at the local residents' association meeting, one of the largest problems is finding houses on the estate for their children's young families.

During my time on the estate I met many people, and some I met again and again. One such individual, 'Francis', has lived on the estate nearly 20 years. She and her husband have four children and six grandchildren. To their continuing delight, all of them live on the estate – occupying four other properties in the area. Far from being a happy accident, this is a hard-won development by Francis and her partner. By articulating their situation well and making good use of a (now defunct) 'community stream' set out by the council, they have managed to keep their family together. All four of their children are either working full time or are full-time carers for their own children. During the summer months, the front door of Francis's home can often be seen open, with children and grandchildren playing outside. It feels homely and safe, and the family often recall how lucky they feel. Indeed, not everyone has found such luck on the estate.

Many who stay on the estate have had time in other locations or have moved away, only to return to a place of refuge and safety. Others have had to move away, but often return to see family and remain resolute that they would return if a suitable place became available. One such mother of three, 'Sam', recalls the time where she left the estate after the birth of her eldest son. Although the new location was better for the shops, being closer to Hounslow Central, she found herself constantly returning to the estate. Here there was never a problem with finding someone to watch the kids or borrow the archetypal 'cup of sugar' from. Here she knew people, not least of all her mother and the father of her three children. Leaving the estate meant leaving the community. While leaving the estate also meant new opportunities and chances for employment, it meant travelling away from the very people needed to support her. Sam moved back just a few months after she left.

The community here, her family, help her get by. They, and the estate in general, protect her from harm, but they also insulate her from change.

Such protection on the estate comes in many forms, not all of them easily recognisable. Despite the great improvements in the reduction of antisocial behaviour on the estate in the last few years, many still find problems with young adults, usually men, who have little better to do than hang out at the local betting shop and drink lager before going home for lunch. Collectively, the small group of people are known as the 'the boys', and while the name is gender-accurate for most of this little group, the age specificity is not. Some of its members are far more mature than the rest. The health of one member has confined him to an electric chair – another reason that makes it hard for him to leave the well tarmacked estate.

Spending time on the estate you start to bump into the same people. One such person was 'Jane', a mother of three and the daughter of a woman who had been on the estate since the late 1970s. Both Jane and her partner, 'Sam', were on disability and income support at the time I met them. They both struggle to find and keep work due to their own issues with mental health and drug addiction. For them the estate is home, in every sense of the word. Sam is one of 'the boys', and while he is young, fit and rather handsome, he has not taken easily to fatherhood – of the youngest, and only, daughter. In the few months that I knew the young family, I saw Sam work hard with his own demons and find work. His efforts, unfortunately, were not supported by his environment. Jane recounts with pride Sam finding work.

> You should see him, Dave! He is so much happier and confident. You said it yourself, didn't you mum!? ('Jane')

Sitting on the toy-covered sofa in one of the small two-bed flats in a first-floor flat, I follow the given cue and turn to Jane's mother for confirmation. She sits with her six-week old granddaughter in arms and, her focus largely on her, she nods some agreement.

> He even started talking about sorting the house out. He wants to get stacking boxes for the toys, and to throw out the old ones. He didn't manage to work yesterday, but he did tidy up! (Jane's mother)

Evidence of Sam's efforts to clean the flat hours before are lost now. Jane's other two children (boys aged seven and nine) have spread toys across every surface available, like the detritus of youth. They now run around the house fighting for attention, sibling power, or just a few precious moments of fantasy in play. Dirty-faced and bare-chested in the warm summer months, the boys may not be clean, but they are happy, healthy and not hungry. The public moral maze here is that Sam should not be claiming benefits if he is working. By definition, he is a benefits cheat, but in reality what he is doing is trying his best for his family despite the problems. For him, some part-time labouring (offered by someone on the estate) has allowed him to think more of the future, focus on his family and be more confident. If he informed the council of his productivity, it would remove the safety net of the whole family's support. While this new confidence helps, Sam is not ready to take the whole strain, not to risk the children's food if he loses another job. Sam is trapped between poor mental health and the possibility of escape in narcotics. Much like the two boys he is a father figure to, he searches for the moment of fantasy in play.

Jane is supported on the estate by her mother and the decades that have brought a tight community. Her rent is 'affordable', and while she recognises the problems on the estate, and her own shortcomings, she knows that outside there is more to fear in the unknown. She feels little strength in leaving and when she does need to leave for shopping or for a meeting with the council, it is not done without a certain level of logistical planning. Three children, spare clothes, nappies, buggies (up and down stairs), scooters, and purse – getting everything in one place, let alone to the destination, is a feat.

> I can't talk today. I have to get to the food bank. I have a token, and one for a friend. Hey actually, do you think you could give me a hand?

Of course, I could, but the moment doesn't arrive.

> Sorry, just got to the bus stop and had to come back. The bailiffs are at the door. If I get back quick, I can stop them turning off the electricity. But I will have to be quick. Hope they don't take too long as the bloody fridge is empty!

Getting out of the estate, even leaving the house, at times can be risky. Today it means that they will miss out on a weekly jaunt for food. Hopefully they will get out tomorrow, but nothing about Jane's demeanour suggests that this is a certainty. Simple distance to the nearest useful public transport is enough to cause issues. Many of the more important meetings for benefits need to be had in Hounslow Central, a 40-minute walk (30 minutes if you manage to get the buggy and three kids on the bus with the money for the fare). Leaving the estate is a mission and one not done unless there is a very good reason.

As a stranger to the estate, I was often given more attention than I either wanted or always felt comfortable with. Yet as time moved on and I met 'the boys' at different times and in different circumstances, the air eased between us. By the end I was being invited to buy them some beer and join them outside the shops for a smoke. The faux aggression and awkward behaviour appeared to do much to keep unwanted attention at bay. But more than this, it helped them get by with the knowledge of their own existence, as much (at least) as the lager or the moment of chance at the betting shop did. This small group, various in number but consistent in behaviour, was recalled differently by many: to some, a problem of drugs and crime; to others, a reassuring presence at the gate of the estate. Indeed, local community lore would have it that on more than one occasion 'the boys' had turned back a small child from leaving the estate or had come to support a resident in the face of an external threat. 'The boys' were insulated from the outside world, from passing police or troublesome work. In turn, they helped to insulate and protect those within, their environment affecting their own behaviour and reinforcing that which functions to support/benefit those within.

Isolation as stagnation

Isolation is a form of distinction, a separation of one thing from another to keep it separate. While the estate sits within the urban landscape, much like any other residential development, there are strong design and situational elements that have kept the estate distinct from its surroundings. Such obvious isolation on the estate may have been purposefully functional: that isolation, itself, may have been the goal; in the creation of this sealed (even though intentionally temporary) burrow of rodent named streets, the actors involved looked to shield the residents within, housing them together, protecting them from the noise above and the chaos around. After all, isolating a community may, indeed, drive the development of strong community ties. Despite this most laudable of possible acts, isolation is also separation from external forces. Isolation from harm can also be isolation from change and from growth.

As researchers, when we first entered the estate, we engaged with community groups as a way of engaging with the residents. We quickly found that those groups were often quite well established and demonstrated a strong sense of identity and wellbeing. As we stayed longer, we realised that in order to approach and understand those people who were struggling on the estate, we needed to reach out beyond members of a group; soon we found ourselves knocking on doors. During the day, behind the majority of the doors it remained silent, and when some sound came from within, more often than not the doors remained closed. On one such occasion a curt reply to a knock came through a letterbox, and after gentle reassurance that I was neither selling nor collecting, the door opened and I was ushered in. Behind this closed door, was a world of life and colour. The hallway carpet, walls and shelves were covered with brightly coloured objects, materials and pictures. What space was left was taken up by plants. The front room was cluttered with objects and green foliage so much that the seating area in the middle was squashed in from the sides. Inside this house of colour lived a single woman, alone and quite afraid.

> Sorry about being rude. I don't usually answer the door. Sometimes people knock. Sometimes they kick the door! I thought you were the council. They keep coming… they want this or that – usually money. I'm too old to cope with these things anymore. I used to be the youngest here. Now I am the oldest. ('Hilda', resident of Beavers Estate)

Hilda lives in the small one-roomed apartment on her own. She is married, but her partner lives in Brighton now. She loves her plants, and despite attending the residents' association meetings and appealing to the council, she has never managed to get a flat on the ground floor so she can extend her love of plants to a whole garden. She stays here, on her own, almost every day. At the weekend, her estranged husband brings her food and, if she needs it, fixes the things that have broken. But then he leaves, and she is alone again.

> I love my plants – they are all I have really. I never speak to anyone else any more. If something breaks, I either fix it or my husband does at the weekend. I don't bother calling the housing people any more. They don't answer, or the people there are so rude. They are so young!

Hilda's own home has become a place of refuge but also a prison that she is both too scared to leave and yet too comfortable to need to step out of.

Fig. 3.8 Shopping area at 'the bottom'. Source: author

This is in stark contrast to the attitudes of people at the community meetings.

This agency of community creation, or at the very least its attempted facilitation, can be seen physically as we walk down Chinchilla Drive to the small, semi-derelict shopping arcade known locally as 'the bottom' (fig. 3.8). At the time of my last visit to the estate, over one-third of the shop fronts here were boarded over with signs of long-term developmental goals. Such goals have taken years, and the shops are still free of commercial tenants. What remain of the commercial facilities are just the essentials: a cafe, a post office, a newsagent, a pharmacy, two takeaways (Chinese and kebab) and a betting shop. Sadly, the local public house (AKA 'The Beaver') has closed – trashed by constant crime and a lack of serious revenue. More recently, the pub has been reincarnated into a competitor to the local newsagents. The streets here, quite unlike the clean, well-kept gardens elsewhere on the estate, are strewn with litter and signs of frequent fly tipping. Perhaps this is a product of its location, so near to the edge of the estate and a main route in and out. Here leaves mix with crisp packets, and faded beer cans pile up in small alleys and around the car park, which has room for 40 or 50 cars in front of the shops. While the car park is often occupied during the day, many of the vehicles do not seem to change. Several of these are missing windscreens, wheels or in otherwise disrepair. Residents inform me that the owner of the shopping arcade uses this site to store cars he is in the process of selling. Many of the cars look like they have been here for months, if not years.

Such signs of disrepair should not be regarded as a lack of effort or attention by the local council, nor indeed as a mark of disrespect by residents. As mentioned before, their gardens, houses and the wider streets are mostly very well kept. Since the 2011 census indicated the area is of such deprivation, the council has made clear attempts to support the community and alleviate some of the issues. In the last 15 years, money has been pumped into the estate in the form of renovated play parks, murals, tree clearances and, not least of all, the new healthcare centre.

Regardless of these financial and heartfelt attempts of the local council, few things seemed to have made an impact. One such failed story is that of the community library, the 'Hub' (fig. 3.9). This large, single-floored building is fronted by blank and unwelcoming corrugated iron sheets. The initial faded red paint has been repainted in the last couple of years and now boasts leafy designs and the large letters of a name above the door. While this remains an improvement, the iron-sheeted front is cold and industrial. It sits next to the shopping arcade at 'the bottom' and comes complete with a sport cage marked for football and basketball. Inside the building, it is clean and offers services as a children's centre and library, and houses a youth and community officer.

Despite the money and the breadth of the services, many of the residents I spoke to stated that they never used the library nor visited the building. Some of this may be down to the opening hours, which are admittedly short (9a.m. to 3p.m. five days a week, and closed every

Fig. 3.9 The Hub. Source: author

Friday and Sunday). Some offered no answer as to why the Hub offered such little attraction, just that there was not a reason to go there. Others stated clearly that they felt the community centre was not for them. Unfortunately, this last statement only made sense when several visits demonstrated that many of the clientele were Indian or Pakistani, rather than the white British who made up the majority of my respondents. For those using the facilities, the centre offers nothing more than a place to entertain the children, giving parents a much-needed sit down, a rest and a chat with people in similar situations. It seems an obvious shame that this building could not be a place for social groups to mix and engage in difference. Yet despite the strong benefit of having such a facility on the estate, it has become an indicator of separation rather than a place where different people can sit and share. Many events at the site (dog micro-chipping, mother and toddler mornings, free financial advice) are often well attended, but the Hub, like the healthcare centre, remains greatly underutilised.

Opposite the Hub, behind tall pine trees and towering over the estate by at least 12 floors, is the Vista building. For many on the estate, this building, despite its closeness, is simply part of the airport's external reach. Full of mid-range offices and a gym, it offers locations for businesses making use of the nearby airport. Car rental, investments, freight, technology, recruitment, accounting and regulation; the firms here do not provide services for the community on the estate. Despite the many conversations I had with people on the estate, not one recalled anyone who worked there. Many the stories that included the Vista building involved the local police office that was stationed there a few years ago. Many recall how officers would walk through the estate to and from the building on patrol or going about other duties. That office has left the building now, and the locals see the police far less. Instead, many cars related to Heathrow's mobile offices for the various chauffeur and taxi firms take up space along Chinchilla Drive, making parking for residents difficult. Some have complained, and there has been a council response, but the issue remains.

Like everywhere on the estate, at 'the bottom', the feeling of isolation is palpable. Even when you are leaving the estate, it is like leaving a leafy oasis of safety for barren streets and high fences. Heading south out of the estate you are faced with tree-lined streets which border low-impact industry buildings, including the Heathrow Corporate Park. The park is a collection of large low-rise buildings that house important partners for Heathrow's activities, such as one of their data centres. The buildings back onto the estate, leaving the surrounding streets lined with bare fence and bush barriers. Facing south and off to the west lies Beavers Lane Community School and a few other scattered red-brick houses that face the back side of the corporate park. To the east, it is much the same – houses facing the back of the park – until the corporate park unit finishes. Then, a little further down the road, the stark barrier swaps sides, and the new barrier, white walls and barbed wire, demarks the local military barracks, a site so shielded from view that Google blurs the image of the gateway and leaves the description blank. South of the estate feels barren, devoid of the large mature trees and children playing. Yet even at the edges, life from the estate remains.

'The boys'

Back by the shops and standing outside the betting shop with the collection of young men – 'the boys'. Smoking, drinking and taking regular trips to the betting shop, or around the corner in the alley, for relief. 'The boys' take life on the estate in their stride. As mentioned, their presence is not universally disliked and is even welcomed by some who are reassured by their obvious antagonism to strangers. One lady recalled that she felt reassured that they were there, and they often greeted her warmly. Regardless, some find their numbers threatening and have reported them for antisocial behaviour. But while it may appear easy to condemn these individuals for not working, for their drug abuse, or for their loud behaviour at weekends, we might consider another position. Rather than worry about their threat to the estate, perhaps the estate is what threatens them.

One reported story of the boys illustrates this less obvious position nicely. It occurs back near the centre of the estate, where the trees and nearby flats shield those within from external view. There are two large green and leafy areas inside the estate. The first, and previously mentioned, is the children's park. The second lies to the eastern side and is, in many respects, a microcosm of the estate itself. Having only two entry points and backed onto by fenced gardens from the rear of flats sit a circle of a dozen large trees accompanied by large stones (fig. 3.10), each easily big enough to accommodate two or three people sitting. As with other named locations, this one has the suitably functional name 'the stones' (fig. 3.10). This area of the estate is a favourite for a Friday night gathering. Often groups gather here after the pub and away from the eyes of outsiders. Come the morning, signs left around the stones talk of drink and drug use, the back fences of the local residents smell of

Fig. 3.10 'The stones'. Source: author

urine. Indeed, it is often this last fact that is complained about the most. Those attending the gatherings are not often residents in the immediate flats, but live elsewhere on the estate. As the saying goes, you don't 'shit in your own front garden'.

Rather than the idyllic image of the garden square or green common shared by all, and a centre of community activity, this site has become a shielded place of mischief and perhaps a little too much relaxation. Despite the surrounding flats and the twitches of net curtains, 'the boys' behave as if this is a safe place where they can entertain themselves legally, or otherwise. Interviewing one specific resident whose flat boarders the space, she tells me how her complaints fall on deaf ears. When she does manage to get through to a sensitive ear, attendance by police rarely effects a change in behaviour. She recalls how, no matter when she calls, by the time the police get through the estate, those gathering have dispersed back to their own flats or elsewhere. The police, who drive to the nearest road, are spotted early from others on the estate and the warning goes out. With no one else left to arrest, and only cans and rubbish in evidence, the police leave. The following weekend or even that same night, the groups might return.

The estate blocks engagement by the outside world. Even when outside influence arrives to adjust an event that might not be socially suitable, the estate's own physical and social structure mediates the impact of the change. It reduces the risk to the social norms of behaviour and actively allows behaviour usually requiring more secluded space. In short, the estate's very isolation protects the estate from change and allows those within to stagnate. Rather than seeking change, those on the estate manage nicely by staying on the estate. In other words, behaviour and social norms that would otherwise be tempered by external pressures are left to flourish – leaving behind the social staleness of deprivation.

Conclusion

There is a considerable literature on the contemporary city, conceptualising it in terms of anonymous and increasingly socially isolated lives in which place identities are no longer significant (see e.g. Amin 2012; Bauman 2000; Blokland 2017 and the discussion in the introduction to this book). In this chapter I have explored isolation in relation to a particular housing estate, and the picture that emerges of what isolation is, how it occurs and what it means is rather different and more complex. Taking the walk down from Hounslow West station, through the brown and sparse streets towards the small estate that appears will forever be known as the Beavers, we can see how urban landscapes have a profound influence on the communities that reside within. The Beavers Estate might be high on indicators of deprivation, making it the target of research and community development projects, but not everything about this LSOA is deprived. Indeed, while the physicality of its isolation has kept it from change, it has helped create a site of remarkable peace, inward respect and a strong (if insular) community. Efforts to alleviate the very real problems on the estate by the local council appear to have failed, yet perhaps their effects are rather shielded from causal influence.

What we have seen is that the estate, either through purposeful attention to the built environment intended to help shield the residents from noise, or through accidental restrictions of time and money, has developed strong factors of isolation – factors that are not demonstrated through simple linear cause-and-effect models but through more complex sets of relationships. In other words, rather than thinking of the isolation as simple protection from the surrounding noise of Heathrow, with a corresponding effect of a strong sense of identity, we have seen that isolation produces many effects, both positive and negative. Furthermore, despite goodwill and good intentions, urban landscapes remain part of the wider environment, and, as such, isolating a place or space from its surroundings limits opportunities for change.

Literally building in a function or characteristic with purposefully intentional and positive goals will always create multiple and varied effects. Many of these effects are likely to go beyond the intended in unpredictable directions. Many are likely to combine to form emergent properties – the effects of which will probably remain invisible for many years. The constructed, and accidental, isolation on the estate does many things. On the Beavers Estate, it increases the sense of place and a corresponding sense of belonging for the residents. It aids the building and development of a community, the individuals all having a strong sense of identity. Yet such identity combined with the physicality of isolation that drives attention inwards and keeps other attention away can limit opportunity for change, which in turn may drive a sort of stagnation. Closing an estate and protecting it from the external world also reduces its ability to be affected by external influences. Focusing on the singular and the protective also creates the isolated and reduce chances for adaptation. Ultimately, without adaptive change, people and places lack the ability to be resilient in the face of external forces; they can fall into destructive and insular patterns and behaviours that are both caused by and reinforced because of the very (over) protection that is provided by their environment.

Identity itself can be understood as an indicator of the level of resilience. In the strong sense of self that confidence brings, we also find a lack of adaptive change, while being 'open-minded' to be able to admit fault and to shift position appropriately, we can be seen as resilient. When we try and build confidence in a community, we need to also allow that community to change. Likewise, when we are planning the development of an estate, we must appreciate that the surrounding area, and even the estate itself, is unlikely to remain fixed. Instead, estates require integration and connectivity as much as they need distinction. Indeed, when the Beavers Estate obtained a reputation that many disliked, a shift in name appeared a simple solution. Yet without acceptance of or even desire for this from those whom this identifier means the most, change remains difficult if not impossible to enact. Few if any on the estate refer to it as the Meadows, and without this change coming from within it appears unlikely that few ever will. Without forces of the external world to facilitate local change and the structure within to accept this change by connecting it to pre-existing structure, larger-scale adaptation on the estate will always be more difficult. We experientially select from our environment to build our understanding of the world around us and to help maintain a sense of agency. Without new and different experiences and observations of such changes, we are left to select from what we already know. We reinforce fallacies and push opinions, characteristics and behaviour further to extreme positions.

Methodological note

Initially, this research came through some freelance ethnographic research undertaken at the RSA. At the time, I was in the final year of my PhD write-up, and taking three to six months out of this appeared to be a good idea. The project was funded through Hounslow Borough Council under the project title of 'Cranford, Stronger Together'. The project focused on indices of high reliance on social care, low economic output, low mental and physical wellbeing and low understanding of the causes and issues therein. The aim was to understand the complexities of the problem and explore whether there was an opportunity to understand how low–medium health issues could, at least to some degree, be understood through the strength of community relations. Before the research had begun, it was clear that this fitted the RSA's focus on 'connected communities' and, more broadly, on how community engagement might help alleviate stress on the already very strained NHS.

As an ethnographer, I was requested to engage on the housing estate and reach out to the groups therein. The goal was to gain deeper, nuanced information about the lives of the people who self-identified as 'struggling' (having low–medium mental or physical health problems). I was given three months to engage the community and collect information – rather a short time in terms of ethnography, but it was illuminating as to what can be achieved when you have a deadline. The ethnographic work, although only making the appendix of the final report, was said to be a key element of the story. It was to work in conjunction with quantitative analysis on surveys and social network analysis undertaken from the corresponding data. A total of 170 interviews were undertaken (representing 13.85 per cent of the population of the LSOA). The copy of the final report is available, and links can be found in the bibliography (Hounslow 2015).

For the ethnographic interviews, we found three individuals who were happy to be engaged over a longer period and for several days. I spoke for many hours with them at their homes on the estate, taking trips to the housing office, hospital and other excursions. I observed the issues their physical and mental conditions caused and, importantly to this later project, how their own position on the estate helped or hindered their access to amenities and support or other communication. Alongside these in-depth interviews with respondents, we also conducted participant observation with 'the boys' and the 'beginning ladies'. Alongside drinking many cups of tea, I also sat with 'the boys' outside the betting shop and drank a can of 'lager' (once) as they smoked and joked either at my expense or about the project's wider goals. While these two groups were often said to be at odds (especially over concerns at 'the stones'), I never witnessed any hostility from 'the boys', and on more than one occasion I saw members of the two groups speaking cordially to each other.

After completion of this project I returned many times to the site, to collect personal images of people, families and groups I had met during the time, but also to undertake more descriptive analysis of the landscape and surrounding areas. These two separate periods of research covered a time of over two years. In addition to the semi-structured interviews, participant observation and photographic work, I conducted some archival research to explore the idea that the estate was built as a temporary location. The goal of that research was to try and understand whether the isolation on the estate was created intentionally (as it felt) or whether the isolation had developed more organically and the corresponding results were accidental. As discussed above, I could not find any confirmation either way in this regard, other than that the site was developed quickly and the overall plans and use of the bison frame happened off the record or that such records (unlike the dealings with the landscape architect) were in-house, and therefore no minutes were held as to design.

Acknowledgements

Thank you to the RSA for helping me to confirm some of the information, and to Matthew Parsfield. Also, thank you to all the staff at the London Metropolitan Archives (LMA) for their support in my archival research. I would also like to take the opportunity to thank the kind people of the Beavers Estate (the Meadows) for their time and their patience at my annoying questions. While there are a few people I would like to thank specifically, all personal details of respondents have either been changed or not recorded here to maintain their anonymity. Despite the history, reputation and isolation of the estate, I found the residents helpful, friendly, kind and compassionate to those in need. Despite their struggles and obvious poverty (in some circumstances), I found them welcoming and open to newcomers wanting to help. Thank you.

References

Amin, A. 2012. *Land of Strangers*. Cambridge: Polity.
Bauman, Z. 2000. *Liquid Modernity*. Cambridge: Polity.
Blokland, T. 2017. *Community as Urban Practice*. Cambridge: Polity.
BML. 2016. Heritage. http://www.bison.co.uk/about-us/heritage/ (accessed 28 December 2016).
City of London. 2016. 'Deprivation in London', briefing paper. https://www.cityoflondon.gov.uk/business/economic-research-and-information/research-publications/Pages/Deprivation-in-London.aspx (accessed 14 December 2016).
Georghiou, L., Evans, J., Ray, T., Metcalfe, J.S. and Gibbons, M. *Post-Innovation Performance, Technological Development and Competition*. Palgrave Macmillan.
Heathrow Community Relations Team. 2014. Noise insulation schemes. Available at: http://www.heathrow.com/noise/what-you-can-do/apply-for-help/noise-insulation-schemes (accessed 14 December 2016).
Hounslow, London Borough of. 2013. Census 2011. https://www.hounslow.gov.uk/info/20110/open_data_and_information_requests/1322/census_2011 (accessed 10 January 2019).
Hounslow, London Borough of. 2015. Intelligence Briefing: Indices of Deprivation. https://democraticservices.hounslow.gov.uk/documents/s121856/ (accessed 14 December 2016).
Lee, J., Cebrian, G., Edmonds, L., Patel, J. and Rhodes, D. 2017. *Noise Exposure Contours for Heathrow Airport 2015*, ERCD Report 1601. Civil Aviation Authority, Environmental Research and Consultancy Department. https://assets.publishing.service.gov.uk/government/uploads/system/uploads/attachment_data/file/582641/heathrowairport-noise-2015.pdf (accessed 19 December 2018).
MyLondon. 2013. Beavers Estate Health Centre Opens for Business, 30 September. https://www.mylondon.news/news/health/beavers-estate-health-centre-opens-5981570 (accessed 28 December 2016).
Parsfield, M. and Yates, D. 2015. *Cranford Stronger Together*. London: Royal Society for the encouragement of Arts, Manufactures and Commerce (RSA). http://democraticservices.hounslow.gov.uk/documents/s115121/Cranford%20Stronger%20Together%20project%20-%20Final%20Report%20not%20for%20printing.pdf (accessed 14 December 2016).
Rose, D. 1983. *The London Underground: A Diagrammatic History*. London: Capital Transport.
RSA 2014. 'Hounslow: Cranford Stronger Together'. https://www.thersa.org/action-and-research/rsa-projects/public-services-and-communities-folder/hounslow---cranford-stronger-together (accessed 14 December 2016).
Stuart-Smith, T. 1996. Obituary: Michael Brown. *The Independent*, 7 March. http://www.independent.co.uk/news/people/obituary-michael-brown-1340740.html
UK Parliament. 1990. 'Beaver Estate, Hounslow', Hansard. http://hansard.millbanksystems.com/commons/1990/oct/19/beaver-estate-hounslow (accessed 14 December 2016).
Wicks, R. 2014 *Heathrow Airport Manual: Designing, Building and Operating the World's Busiest International Airport*. London, UK: J H Haynes & Co.

4
The making of a suburb
David Jeevendrampillai

Introduction

When one imagines life in central London, one might think of the grand historic buildings or perhaps some form of gritty inner-city aesthetic of graffiti and concrete. However, the majority of London's residents dwell in the outer regions of the capital in the leafy, distinctly un-grand, un-gritty suburbs. According to Vaughan et al. (2009), around two-thirds of London's population and over 80 per cent of the UK's population live in suburbs. The cultural imaginary of such places is one that conjures an image of dull, lifeless middle England; as Jim McClellan of *The Big Issue* magazine reports, suburbs are 'where the life of the mind curls up in front of the fire in a comfy pair of M&S slippers, it's a brain-dead blizzard of matching carriage lamps and mock Tudor details' (McClellan 1999:16–7). Surbiton is known as the queen of this imagery; as David McKie writes, 'The name sounds so much like "Suburbia". When some joker on the stage or the television screen says Surbiton, what we all subliminally hear is Suburbiton' (McKie 2014).

Suburbs were once seen as the great retreat from the urban, as a paradise found. As Bourne notes, suburbia was a fine intermingling of the city and the countryside. It represented a return to a simpler, less polluted way of life without cutting the economic and cultural umbilical cord of the city (Bourne 1996:180). With the rise of the modern city, so rose a popular disaffection for the overcrowded, polluted and cramped city. People did not want to live right by their workplace, nor did they want the 'cheek by jowl' closeness of the inner city (Clapson 2003:51). However, the notion that the suburbs represented a utopian vision of post-war living has given way to a much bleaker dystopian discourse, as Rowen Moore reports: 'All these ideas we have about leafy suburbs have changed. They are losing their distinctiveness and reasons to be. Family homes have been denatured. They have been made into mini apartment blocks and their gardens torn up and turned into car parks for all their residents. The high streets are declining. They are turning into dormitories – and not very nice dormitories at that' (page cited in Moore in Duncan 2014). It appears that one vision, dream and myth of suburban living has been replaced by another, much more aggressive, representation of the suburbs. The image of the monotonous, dull suburb abounds in the popular discourse of modern residential landscapes. TV programmes and films such as *American Beauty* (Mendes 1999), *The Good Life* (Esmonde and Larbey 1975) and *Desperate Housewives* (Cherry 2004) have portrayed suburbs as 'inauthentic consumption centres and conformity factories' (Muzzio and Halper 2002:543). If this is the true character of the suburbs, then why do so many people live there?

This chapter demonstrates that life in the suburbs is vibrant, fun and optimistic; it shows that people not only enjoy living there, but revel in the stories the suburbs offer – including the tale of being dull and lifeless, which works to enliven place and develop community. Some of my informants told me of the local history, while others knew nothing of it; what mattered was that all had a story to tell. Usually this was a combination of tales about people and memories of events, often infused in the local geography. These stories of the suburbs almost always related to some sensory aspect of place – the light at dusk, the sound of birds – while some explained how much the teller enjoyed kicking autumn leaves that showed 'the passing of the seasons'. There are as many reasons for liking the suburbs as there are people living there, but what this chapter shows is that, as well as the mix of location relative to the city, green space and the feel of the suburbs, it is the sense of community that suburbs allow which is appealing. Suburbs, in the words of my informants, allow space for people to play, to mix with others and have fun. This sense of community is not produced through historical societies or nature groups, but through a shared love of place and the mingling of people and place into local stories and narratives which are distinctly local. This production of the local, both in the sense of a local place and a local subjectivity, occurs not only despite the myth of the dystopian suburb, but rather through playing with that myth – mixing facts, fictions and imaginations into the local, suburban, sensibility.

The historical emergence of the suburbs

Historically, cities have always had activities located on their outskirts. In medieval Britain, 'dirty industries' such as tanneries, butchery and charcoal making were done outside the city walls (Bourne 1996). Peter Ackroyd notes that London's suburbs are 'as old as the city itself' (Ackroyd 2001:727) emphasising the historical truth behind the old adage that London is 'a city of a thousand villages'. Ackroyd describes how many of the places we know as suburbs today were, at one point, distinct villages apart from the city. It is a common misconception that the city spread from the centre to swallow such places; however, in his 1966 work, Harold James Dyos did much to rescue the historical story of the suburbs, outlining how they have grown into each other, co-evolving with London's centre in a symbiotic social and economic relationship (see also Jackson 1985; McManus and Ethington 2007). Dyos notes that by the sixteenth century, the dispersal of industry to the suburbs had become quite marked (Dyos 1966:34) and by the 1700s, the suburbs started to take on a definite character. Bourne (1996:167) states that across the UK, 'The modern suburbanization process is generally said to have started on a significant scale in the mid-19th century'; but this was most pronounced in London. The major drivers of rapid growth were initially provided by advancements in roads and motor vehicles. However, most people still used walking as the predominant way of getting around, and it was not until the 1860s, with the development of rail and the removal of road tolls, that large-scale movement started to occur. The 1883 rail act saw the introduction of cheap rail fares and allowed people to 'escape the city' and 'delocalise' (Clapson, 2003:25) as they found work and entertainment elsewhere. Clapson notes that economy and infrastructure were not the only driving forces behind suburban expansion, but that social and cultural factors, such as the dream of countryside life, were extremely influential. By the 1900s, the ideal of the countryside was manifest and typified through such things as the Garden City Movement, which saw new settlements planned around the ideal balance between industry, residence and agriculture. By 1919, the Housing and Town Planning Act increased the role of local authorities in providing housing for their constituents. It was estimated that up to 700,000 homes were needed to replace slums and house those returning from war. It was in these inter-war years that the UK, specifically England and London (see Clapson 2003), saw a housing boom that was predominantly suburban. Such was the scale of the boom that huge residential areas of the city were built with a similar architectural style, typified by vernacular aesthetics of pitched roofs, brick cavity walls, covered porches and a range of styles from mock Tudor to neo-Georgian. The similarity of the housing styles contributed to the idea that suburbs everywhere were alike. J.B. Priestly describes a typical road he travelled in his tour of England as 'the standard new suburban road of our time, and there are hundreds of them everywhere all alike' (Priestley 1934:21–2).

Suburbs have been described as a 'non-place urban realm' (Clapson 2003:159 following Augé 1995) and are seen as key protagonists in the discourses of community decline. This is most recently manifested in the declaration of the death of the high street (see Duncan 2014) across media reporting of the suburbs. A government review of the future of suburbs called for interventions into perceived decline through changes to the high street (see Portas 2011). Griffiths et al. argue that the traditional focus on the residential nature of suburbs has 'distorted our conceptions' of what they should and can be (Griffiths et al. 2008:899), and that suburbs often conceal 'more variegated activities' (Griffiths et al. 2008:3).

It is the ability of suburbs to adapt to different social and economic conditions, argue Vaughan et al. (2009), that will see them endure, but perhaps not in their current forms. This endurance and adaptation is not only economic, but also social. People are in constant dialogue with their suburbs; they move through them, animate them with stories, and ascribe value and meaning to the landscape. In the next section I trace how suburbs emerged not as the sprawling commuter belt of a city but from distinct places that continue to be infused with a particular local character. Focusing on Surbiton, a southwest suburb of London, I unpack its historical emergence and outline how walking and narratives help make a sense of place, community and belonging.

The history of Surbiton

Surbiton, which sits just south of its more historic big brother Kingston (fig. 4.1), has a story typical of many London suburbs. Kingston is an ancient market town in the borough of Kingston upon Thames on the southwest border of London where it meets the county of Surrey. Its name means 'in the King's manor' (Mills 2010), and Kingston is reputedly the site where Saxon kings were coronated. The symbol of the borough, comprising three fish, was derived from early recordings of the town and its three fisheries, found in the Domesday Book of 1086. Today, Kingston is a lively town with a busy shopping centre, a picturesque marketplace and a pleasant river walkway.

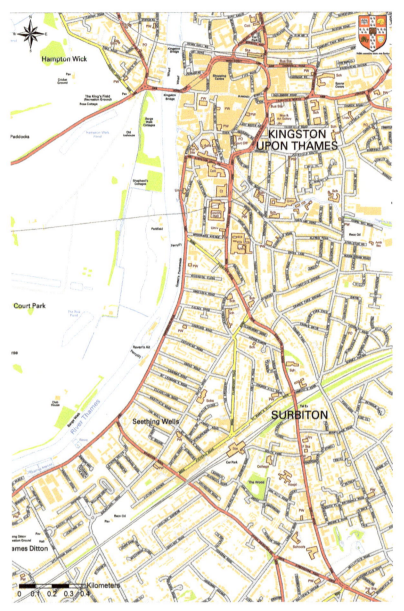

Fig. 4.1 A map of Surbiton, South West London and its relation to Kingston (map made by author using OS data copyright 2014)

Fig. 4.2 Walking by the river promenade. Photograph by Tangle Photography, reproduced with permission

On walking south along the Thames Path, one would find oneself coming onto the road by Surbiton after 15 minutes or so. Here the river promenade (fig.4.2) ends by a sizable disused water filtration site built in the early to mid-1800s (fig. 4.3), the excavated material of which made the promenade walk between Surbiton and Kingston. The site, which is very much in Surbiton, covers around 6 acres and once pumped clean water from the River Thames to the city of London. London suffered cholera epidemics in 1831, 1848–9, 1854 and 1867, and clean water was found at this site, which at the time used new water filtration methods. The site is of huge importance to the local community, as it harbours a unique history and ecology that relate to the history of cholera and clean water and the protection of endangered species (particularly Daubenton's bat). The whole Surbiton area both looks and feels much more residential and less of a buzzing urban centre than Kingston. It is served, not by a market square or shopping centre, but by a traditional high street where the usual mix of chain stores mixed with a scattering of local independent shops and charity shops (fig. 4.4) can be found. Surbiton is noticeably pleasant, and while it is not as old as Kingston it is not a new town.

At the time of the Domesday Book, Surbiton was not even recorded as a place. Its name is of unknown origin but is thought to be derived

Fig. 4.3 The filter beds and the busy Portsmouth Road. Source: author

Fig. 4.4 The high street (main shopping area) of Surbiton, Victoria Road. Source: author

from 'south of the bell tower' or to relate to South Biton, as there is also a Norbiton in the area (Statham 1996). For many years, the area was farmland serving Kingston, and by the 1800s maps of the area showed a largely uninhabited area but for Maple Farm. In 1801, the Inclosure

(Consolidation) Act was passed, accelerating the speed at which common lands, owned by all people, could be sold, and in 1806 an inclosure act was passed for 'lands in and around Kingston upon Thames and Imworth'. (Note: sometimes, these are referred to as enclosure acts.) By 1825, much of the land in and around Surbiton Hill and Tolworth, to the east side of present-day Surbiton, had been sold. Land in and around the current High Street was still being used by Maple Farm, whose owner, Christopher Terry, had no intention of selling. Around the same time, a proposal was made to build a London to Portsmouth rail line. The initial plans to route the line through Kingston were opposed by the gentlemen of Kingston, who feared it would interfere with their profitable coach trade. The nearby Earl of Wimbledon also opposed the rail line passing through his land, and as such 'Kingston by Railway', which later became Surbiton station, opened in 1836 on what was largely farm land with only a scattering of residents, around two miles from Kingston (Statham 1996), fuelling a very healthy coaching trade between 'Kingston upon Railway' and Kingston.

With the death of Terry, the land become available and was purchased by Thomas Pooley for £10,000. Pooley designed grand townhouses, often around three storeys high and with classic yellow/brown London brick; they have distinctive large stoops (a stoop is a set of steep steps up to a front entrance) and windows (figs 4.5 and 4.6). Pooley quickly made himself a fortune building much of the housing

Fig. 4.5 The town houses of Surbiton, designed by Thomas Pooley. Source: author

Fig. 4.6 A Pooley town house. Source: author

and road infrastructure that still comprises Surbiton today. However, he was never able to finish his plan fully, which would have seen him build similar houses in the area directly east of the River Thames, at the west extremity of Surbiton, close to the filter beds. As Pooley was not a gentleman of Kingston, he, and his new wealth, was much disliked by the Kingston elite; his funding was withdrawn, he was made bankrupt, and he eventually fled to France (Statham 1996). Pooley's road names were changed, and today there remains little or no direct link to Pooley in the area other than the houses he built. Pooley's unfinished second stage of house building, linking the roads leading from Maple Lane to the river, were completed in the late 1800s by William Woods. Woods built large grand houses by Kingston and workers' houses by the Surbiton filter

Fig. 4.7 The workers' cottages on a 'river road'. Source: author

beds (fig. 4.7). These 'river roads' as they are known locally, form a metaphorical ladder from Surbiton: houses range from small cottages for the workers of the filter beds to grand townhouses towards the more affluent and upper-class Kingston. Between such roads, inter-war housing of the distinct mock-Tudor, pitched-roof style has, over the years, filled in the gaps in the master plans of Pooley and Woods (fig. 4.8).

Fig. 4.8 Classic Tudor-style 'Jones' houses, typical of inter-war housing. Source: author

Surbiton today

The evening sun shines down the river roads and creates impressive red skies over the filter beds. The houses flow between Surbiton's commercial side by the rail station to the calmer, greener side by the river. The area maintains a relation to the suburban ideal of countryside through the ecology of the filter beds, the trees that line the streets and, as Sue, a resident in one of the mid-1930s houses, tells a group of fellow locals on a community walk one day, birds.

> The thing I like about this house is the swifts. I think the filter beds contribute to them liking it here; they do everything on the wing, and they don't land at all. We've got a balcony at the back and you can sit on there and they whizz past; they come all the way from Africa, just to our house.

Life in Surbiton is infused with suburban stories. I was told by a local resident that the wide, straight streets, most of which lead you to Kingston, were designed by Pooley so that a horse and carriage could turn easily. Parked cars sit easily beneath the amber London brick, watched over by gloriously large windows that allow the Surbiton sunsets, which stretch over the neighbouring Hampton Court gardens, River Thames and filter beds, to stream in. Moving from the station to the river, one passes through Pooley's townhouses until reaching Maple Road, or as the estate agents like to call it, Maple Village (it was never a village), with its cafes, gastro pubs and monthly farmers' market. One then heads down a river road, each road with its own distinct character from cottages, mock-Tudor fronts and grand townhouses. Large trees line most streets, which are scattered with small parks and green spaces and lined with well-kept front gardens. The area was graced with a large number of pubs from its earliest days in order to quench the thirst of the workers who dug the filter beds. Today, these provide a lively social scene. The area is excellent for commuting, as the train which leaves the now art deco station only takes 17 minutes to the central London Waterloo (it was 14 minutes when it was first built!).

It is a particularly pleasant place which belies its cultural image as the queen of suburbs, yet Surbiton has frequently been the target in the accusations of suburbs as dull, ahistorical and acultural. In fact, in a bid to market itself as distinctly urban and cultural, Liverpool City Council 'seriously considered adopting "Liverpool – it's not Surbiton" as a marketing slogan' in 1995 (Statham 1996). Surbiton has become a synecdoche for the ordinariness of the suburbs, and if one was to pick a place known in the popular British imagination as lacking culture, as the stalwarts of English surrealist comedy, the Monty Python collective, Chapman et al. (episode 28, BBC 1, 1972) did, then Surbiton would be a suitable place. Python parodied the anthropological investigations of the Norwegian explorer Thor Heyerdahl, who famously recreated the journey of the Kon-Tiki raft across the Pacific Ocean in order to test a hypothesis that people from South America could have settled in Polynesia. Python replace Heyerdahl with Mr and Mrs Norris, who, inspired by Heyerdahl, wanted to determine whether the people of Surbiton are related to the people of Hounslow (a similarly average suburb to the north of Surbiton). Mr Norris finds similar mock-Tudor vernacular housing, shared lawnmower technology and similar speech in both places, and decrees that the 'identical cultural background' means the areas must have been linked through a historical movement of populations. Eventually, they discover that people moved not from Surbiton to Hounslow, but rather Hounslow to Surbiton. The sketch's humour arises from the seemingly strained connections of architectural vernaculars, which are distinctly suburban or 'everywhere the same', which link two places that could be almost anywhere in suburban Britain. Further, the lack of cultural depth of the suburbs is brought to one's attention through the analogy of the exotic and dramatic tale of Heyerdahl and the everyday familiarity of the mundane Mr and Mrs Norris. What could be less adventurous, less exotic, than the suburbs?

In the next section, I outline how the cultural imaginary of the suburbs pervades the everyday thoughts of those who live, play and work in the suburbs. The notion of the ahistorical, acultural dystopian suburb as the place one goes to die a cultural death is not best countered through an assertion of the rich histories of the suburbs but rather through taking this image as the heritage of suburbs themselves (see Wickstead 2013). My informants, who all seem to love living in Surbiton, play with both the local and generic histories and myths of the suburb to create stories, and develop a sense of local belonging and community.

Festivals, events and stories of Seething

Surbiton is home to the 'Seething Villagers', a group of people who aim 'to bring people together' and build more 'resilient' communities (as stated on The Community Brain website, http://thecommunitybrain.org). Over the course of a year, Seething Villagers typically put on over a dozen events in the area, and have been doing so since 2009. The biggest annual events usually contain a similar format: a parade, a gathering in a local park, the telling of a story, and some dancing, drinking and eating, and a mini festival or fete all based around the legends and tales of Seething (see Hutchinson 2010a, 2010b, 2011, 2012).

The Seething Villagers get their name from an ancient village that, according to legend, once occupied the area (fig. 4.11). The village was to be found near a mountain upon which lived the giant, Thamas Deeton. The local villagers lived in constant fear of Thamas, who would regularly come down from Mount Seething to terrorise the village. Lefi, a goat boy who lived in a cave at the base of Mount Seething, was ostracised from the village of Seething for being different (as he was half boy, half goat). The children of Seething, who, unlike the adults, were not worn down with fear, misery and selfishness, played with Lefi and took him food. Lefi, having seen the effect the terror of Thamas had upon children as they became adults, decided to rid Seething of his terror forever. He made a bet with Thamas that if he could live on only the food passed through a small ring for one month, then Thamas would have to leave Seething for good and never terrorise Seething again. Lefi passed milk through the ring over and over until he made 29 rounds of cheese – which he ate, one a day, for the month of February. Thamas, having lost his bet, left Seething in a fit of rage and destroyed Mount Seething as he left. Rocks flew through air, and one hit Thamas. His body can still be found lying in the River Thames where it fell, now called Thames Ditton Island. Once the rocks had settled, the villagers of Seething looked for Lefi everywhere but could not find him. They felt awful about how they had treated him just for looking different; they quickly realised his kind heart and his generous spirit meant that their community was now a wonderful place to live. It is in this 'spirit of Lefi' that the Seething Villagers remember Lefi every year at the annual Lefi parade (figs 4.9 and 4.10) at the end of the month in which the 29 cheeses 'fed you and me' – or February, as we know call it (see Hutchinson 2010a).

The 'Legend of Lefi Ganderson' was first 'retold' at a local cheese night, 'Homage de Fromage', in a Surbiton pub which is known for being a key linchpin of the community. The pub frequently organised events for local charities and was nominated as Britain's most charitable pub. Since these early days, around 2009, the story has been made into a children's book. It is read at local schools and events, most notably the annual Lefi parade, where around 400 to 500 people follow a 12-foot model of Thamas through the streets of Surbiton (fig. 4.10). Local children line the

Fig. 4.9 A Seething parade along a Pooley-designed street. Source: author

Fig. 4.10 The Lefi parade on Surbiton high street (Victoria Road). Source: author

route and boo Thamas until they get to a local park where bands play and people drink from a charity bar and dance, sing and have fun together. The tale is read out in a community play, and people remember the wonderful generosity of Lefi. Today there are many Seething events which all mark different aspects of the local environment and which all embellish the local landmarks through Seething tales (fig. 4.11). Tales include 'The King's Soup', where a king was taught to share by the old lady of Seething; this is marked by a soup-sharing event. Other events include Ski Sunday, where people tie blocks of ice to their feet and ski down the only hill in the area in fancy dress, recreating the days of Mount Seething, and 'bread golf', where dough balls are hit into a floating target on the River Thames.

One event, the Freshwater Sardine Festival, marks the local relationship to the River Thames. During the annual Seething Freshwater Sardine Festival (fig. 4.12), Seethingers gather on the banks of the Thames where the walkway meets the filter beds. Hundreds watch as a boat is rowed around the bend in the river to drop a fishing net. The Seething fishermen draw no fish, and the crowd groan but then sing 'Seething sea shanties'. The fishermen then drop the net again but on the other side of the boat, and to the joy and cheers of the onlooking crowd they pull a full catch of Seething 'freshwater sardines'. The catch is then rowed ashore and placed in a cart, which is then pulled through the streets of Surbiton by four giant guinea pigs (nobody seems to know why guinea pigs) to a local park. The 'freshwater sardines' are cooked on a grill and shared out, while the villagers are entertained by local musicians and the ever-present charity bar. The book the *The Last Sardines* (Hutchinson 2012) is read aloud, and at the end of the afternoon the whole community helps clean the park and pack away borrowed tables, stages and sound equipment; many head to the pub soon after. Over time, the Seething event has grown to incorporate local food stalls into the festival to draw attention to and help start local businesses, many of which are independent from the chains found on the high street. Opportunities for new social relations are linked to, and cannot be seen as separate from, economic relations. These events give people the opportunity to try a new trade or to move from hobby cooking or craft work into making money from it. It is this flexibility in economy and lifestyle that such events encourage.

All Seething events play with the myth of the history-less suburb, the myth of a place without culture, life or vibrancy. By acknowledging the cultural imaginary of suburbs as dull, empty and ahistorical, Seethingers are able to produce their own history. There can be no expert

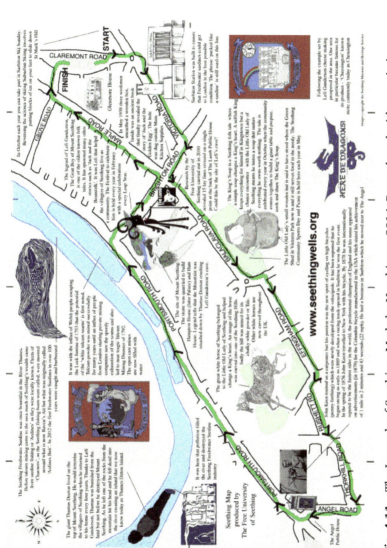

Fig. 4.11 The Legends of Seething. Made by Hutchinson 2014. Reproduced with permission

Fig. 4.12 The Seething freshwater sardine procession. Source: author

(as the history is made up) and no person who belongs more or less (as Seething is for everyone), and Seethingers make efforts to let people know that Seething is for all. A t-shirt proclaims, 'I live in Seething – it's a state of mind', playing on the idea that belonging to a place can be a sensibility. Seething takes pride in local places and local people, because it *is* pleasant, nice, leafy and green, but also because it is a place that fosters a community. By inventing their own rich myths and legends, Seethingers produce moments of fun, togetherness and community. Through such events, Seethingers produce a community pride in the local area, one that lingers in the memory of people who live in or even just visit the area. It alters the ways people perceive the suburb. No longer is it a place to curl up in front of the fire, nor is it just the butt of some surreal joke; through the Seething events, Surbiton has become known as a place to go out, to meet people, to dance, drink and start a business, or even the place with great surreal festivities.

The events interrupt the everyday rhythms of the suburbs by creating a spectacle on the high street; by people parading down the road and literally stopping traffic, everyday habits and everyday experiences of the suburb are broken (see Edensor 2010). The sight of a 12-foot high giant, a goat-boy puppet or a guinea pig pulling a cart of fish draws one in and makes one ask what is going on. People walking through streets dressed as a giant cheese, dancing in the parks and absorbing stories of fish, rivers and mountains in the local landscape seeps into the everyday sense of what the suburb is and can be. It is through moving through the suburb and telling these stories that a 'State of Seething' is performed (see Dobson 2011).

In his discussion of performing the landscape, Kenneth Olwig (2008) discusses how landscape is understood as something that is seen, to be viewed; however, this understanding was preceded by a much more performative understanding of landscape where 'what counts is not what you see but what you do' (Olwig 2008:85). Taking from Tim Ingold (1993, 2008), Olwig states that this movement to landscape as seen follows an 'inversion' where 'the pathways along which life is lived' are inverted into 'the boundaries within which it is enclosed'. This occurred through the influence of such things as Dutch landscape painting and map making that occurred with the enclosure of common land. However, Olwig argues that the 'pre-version' meaning of landscape, where one performs one's relation to the land, is still present. To understand this a little better, let us consider a practice that was common in the UK before widespread mapping: beating the bounds. This practice involved walking, or perambulating, the boundaries of a land, usually a parish, and impressing upon the memory where those boundaries lay. Houseman (1998) has noted how such impressing was often done through the taking of pains, through having a physical encounter with it. Along a route, Houseman (1998:4) describes how 'at each halting point, one of the visitants is bumped smartly against the boundary-stone, or placed head downwards against it' (quoting from Brand 1848:114; Hazlitt 1905:523). The annual perambulation would allow a deep social knowledge as to the bounds of place, and the oldest memory of such bounds would be the recourse to authority on those limits. Tilley notes that such events had 'the secular purpose of guarding against encroachments and preventing the destruction of field boundaries and the religious purpose of creating mutual respect and solidarity. Such perambulations provided the community with an embodied map of the parish which effectively became its collective memory' (Tilley 2012:26). While this practice may have faded, I argue that moving through the landscape, altering everyday rhythms and aesthetics and reimagining place through narrative and play is a way of doing landscape, of making place (see Cresswell 2004). Olwig considers the ways in which shepherds describe how sheep heft or bond themselves to various places in the land and into a social unit that becomes familiar with particular grazing places. Olwig follows the etymology of the word 'heft' and notes that it can refer to the ways in which people settle, dwell and gain a sense of belonging with place (Olwig 2008:86). Moving through the landscape, growing familiar with other people and thinking about spaces in particular way can be seen in the Seething events, where landscape is performed. In the next section, I work through how such events pervade the everyday impression of suburbs, when there are no events but the stories are still at work and interacting with one's sense of place as one moves around.

The making of a Seethinger, the making of a suburb

Over a number of years, I helped organise, and took part in, Seething events and followed Seethingers through their journeys in community life. Further to the ethnographic 'hanging out' at festivals, events and meetings, I conducted interviews with Seethingers, often while walking around the suburb, so that we could discuss their relationship to place while moving through it (see Holton and Riley 2014; Myers 2010). I asked Seethingers to keep intense diaries of all their walks around the suburb over a short period, in order to gain a sense of moving through the suburb in an everyday sense. In these diaries, Seethingers wrote down their thoughts and experiences when walking around alone. Overall, what was clear was that people really enjoyed living in their suburb; they liked the non-urbanness of it, the way in which it is green, leafy and quiet. Memories were stitched through the suburban experience, and aspects of the local landscape would often trigger an emotional response in relation to events and experiences that had happened there. Stories were not only told, but they echoed in the day-to-day experience of place and could be relived or remembered by moving through particular places. Moving through new places or revisiting places also gave fuel to new stories and curiosities. It is through moving through the landscape that the vibrancy of place and the feeling of attachment to it is developed and maintained.

For example, Hannah had moved to Surbiton after looking to live 'someplace nice' after university study. She makes her living from producing events and so, in her words, 'was free to live anywhere', but described finding Surbiton as her 'salvation' around seven years previously. Over a few hours of chatting and drinking in a bar, Hannah drew 'her' Surbiton and talked me through it. The river was a prominent feature, and Hannah explained how it felt different locally compared with in central London, yet still connects Surbiton to London; 'The river here makes me feel as if I'm in the countryside, it's peaceful [...] it's an important part of living in Surbiton, it is what makes it London but not London.' The river is her orientation; she always knows where it is in relation to her position in Surbiton or central London. Hannah often walks the river promenade, especially when going between Kingston and Surbiton. However, it wasn't the simply the pleasant suburban feel that attracted Hannah to the area: 'There is nothing in this suburb that makes me think I want to live here; if I just got off the train I wouldn't want to live here. It's "nice", Surbiton is nice. But really I should be in east London, that is where it is at.' Hannah asserts 'nice' almost as a statement of universal suburban fact – 'nice', 'pleasant' – and she contrasts this to the hip and edgy concrete graffiti of east London, the cultural home of the creative class in the capital. For Hannah, it is the people, community and friendships she has found that make it worthwhile, a distinct sense of being able to make real lasting friendships and experiment with fun and creativity: 'Surbiton is a place you can play; that's really important to have in life but easy to forget, we don't play enough. A lot of people work very hard to make living here a lot of fun.' For Hannah, Surbiton has as much creative potential to offer as other parts of London, if not more, as things can be tried out in the suburbs – it is a place to experiment. These moments of fun linger in Hannah's memories and affect not only the way she thinks of the spaces of Surbiton, but how she moves through them. Her initial impression of a local park was that, 'It wasn't an inviting space, it was full of drunks, I would often walk around it on the road on the way to the train station or bus stop.' Having felt that the park was underused, Seethingers decided to hold an event there, and it is now used for the annual Seething Trycyclingathon, which is supported by Kingston council in order to get people to try cycling. The Mayoress of Kingston noted that, 'Palace Gardens' moment has arrived […] it has been waiting to have its moment for around 100 years, and it has become a new home for Lefi.' Hannah says that until that event, she hadn't walked through that park much at all, but now she walks through it every day, as it is infused with the memories of play, fun and community – the space is animated and vibrant; she says, 'It's one of my favourite places now.'

    The ability of storytelling and Seething myths to rejuvenate place and bring vibrancy to the suburb is described well by Tom, a regular Seethinger, who is a little older than Hannah and has a family home in the area. Tom recorded all walks and his accompanying psychogeographic thoughts for a week in his diary. He noted how, upon leaving the house, he would often see the three fish of Kingston. They were on every street sign in the borough, on street furniture such as litter bins and gates, and found adorning local buildings. The council considered the symbol of the three fish with such officiousness, one Seethinger told me, that a local fish and chip shop was ordered to paint over one of three fish on its sign so as not to mimic the council symbol. Tom says that for him, the Seething Freshwater Sardine event made him feel differently about living in Surbiton. The days of fun, togetherness and sharing, such as the ones at the Seething Freshwater Sardine Festival, were remembered when he saw fish symbols around town.

> The council have fish as the nobility of royal association, power and rule, ownership of this part of the Thames, 'we conquer you with our Bridge'. It's symbolic of their will to rule us subjects not just govern us. We can't do it on our own, consensually. Instead, we have to have our royal chums close by to instil fear and to help subjugate 'those we rule'. Whereas we [Seething Villagers] have it as part of folk memory – the once-great freshwater fishing community, thriving on its relationship with nature and the democratic Thames – that's not about the literal past, but symbolic and anticipatory community future that was and once more can be. We look forward with our fish, whereas the reactionary Conservative council look back; with a prominent fish in the 'coat of arms' that is more martial than social, we hope to recover what they believe has been lost (meaning togetherness, love and balance). This too is totally different from what the council believe is lost; the council is *civic-above-citizen* – ours is more inclusive and wants it to be *civic-for the citizen*. [emphasis added]

Tom played a leading role in a community movement, distinctly separate from the Seething activities, which aimed to block a planning application to build luxury flats on the disused water filtration beds and protect the site for future community use. The filter beds, with their sunken shape, were known among Seethingers as the site of the Seething talcum mines. Having wondered why they were there, Rob, who penned the Seething stories (after some creative development by the wider community at storytelling sessions at events, schools and pubs), went to the local archive and started to uncover their real history. Finding a rich link to the story of cholera and clean water, the community won a Heritage Lottery Grant to further research the site. Tom described how the site become known and loved throughout the community through this process. A play, a website and many public talks all helped spread the story of the filter beds. So, Tom explained, when the application to develop the site came in, he felt that people were able to realise and express the value of the site as a community very quickly. They were able to mobilise support, gain press coverage and organise discussions and events.

In Surbiton, there is a careful distinction made between Seething events and the more directly political events such as objecting to planning applications. Seethingers would never make Seething events overtly political and would aim to strictly keep the events open to all. However, through telling the story of the site, either through newly discovered or revived histories or through generating myths and legends, people grow familiar with the site, connect to it and generate strong relations to it; in a sense, they have hafted themselves to the landscape and developed a sense of belonging which is intimately tied to the landscape. Through such things as the Seething events, the community were able to understand the resources and expertise available in the area that could help with the objection. They were able to quickly communicate the importance of the site to local residents by tapping into people's existing affinity with the local landscape. This affinity is developed and maintained through walking, playing and sharing stories as outlined above. Tom found the Seething events empowering and productive of a particular local identity, one that was based in knowing the landscape and the people that use it, and in moving through the landscape and imagining its narratives. It was in this sense that playing in the local landscape, exchanging stories and narratives of place, be it from the archives, word of mouth or from the Seething events, makes the suburban experience that people talk about so lovingly in Surbiton. People enjoy the space, the openness, the leaves and the trees, but also the people, the community and the ability to try things, be silly and give things a go with the support of others.

Conclusions

This chapter has outlined how people make a sense of belonging and community through moving through and telling stories about the places where they live. People are in dialogue with the rhythms, sights, sounds, histories and imagined stories of place. As people move, parade, dance, share stories, imagine giants and past lives, they bond with landscape and each other. It is the mixing of myths – of the idyllic and dystopian suburb, elements of the local history and the popular cultural image of suburbs – into the invention of new myths which mingles people, place and stories into the suburban experience. Suburban stories give a sense of belonging, a very local meaning. People would often tell me a little fact about Surbiton's history as we walked, such as why the streets were so wide, or why the train station was where it was, and often tell me how Surbiton was distinct from Kingston. People would also tell me of various events that had happened in parks, or Seething myths about the origin of place names. It matters less if the stories are fact or fiction, but rather what the stories do. Stories create memory, meaning, association and attachment. It is the combination the historical and modern myths of suburbs, of Seething and of everyday experience that make the suburb a place where it is distinctly pleasant to live for my informants. They enjoy the leafiness, the calmness – but more than this, other people, the community. However, this community requires work to make, and this making occurs during events and the everyday acts of walking around and being in the suburb.

Seethingers rework the symbols of the local landscape, such as the fish, to change what they mean, how they work. Through changing the way in which fish are associated with local governance to local community, play and togetherness, Seethingers are crafting what Web Keane calls semiotic ideologies (Keane 2005), that is the meaning of symbols and their social force. In doing so, Seethingers are crafting their experience of the suburban landscape. Here is it useful to think through the notion of affect. Originating from the Latin *affectus*, de Spinoza in *The Ethics* (1955 [1667] part 3, definition 3) notes that affect is whereby 'the active power of the said body is increased or diminished, aided or constrained'. Affect is the ability of something to create a disposition in the person perceiving it. In this way, the symbol of a fish creates an affective moment when seen by the viewer. For Tom, the nature of this disposition is different after Seething events than it was before. The index of the symbol of the fish – that is, what it means – has been changed from association with the local council, or *civic-above-citizen*, to Seething, or *civic-for-citizen*. Tom's suburban landscape is saturated with a symbolism which, for him, is empowering and enabling. If, as geographer Tim Edensor states, we live in 'geographies of heterogeneous association' (Edensor 2003:167), then I argue that Seethingers are able, to an extent, to sculpt and shape these associations in line with our socio-political needs through storytelling. Tom was able to evoke a memory of Seething tales and events and think about, or rather sense, the fish and its meaning differently after the Seething events. As Rose, Degen and Basdas (2010) discuss in relation to experiences of shopping malls, the rational human subject is able to selectively use the emotive and affective qualities of spaces. If people don't like bright lights or loud music, they are able to dynamically manipulate the affective and therefore political potential of their surrounds by 'walking away' (Rose, Degen and Basdas 2010:347).

In this chapter, I have shown that through walking in particular ways, telling stories and using the imagination, people create the landscapes through which they live. Hannah was able to reimagine the park as a place of vibrant fun after the Seething events, and regularly felt this through walking and remembering on her routine walks. In Surbiton, the Seething events allow a realignment of the meaning of the suburbs through disruptions to everyday habit (see Ahmed 2010; Bissell 2011). Performances of being 'stupid' carve new meaning in the gap between the meaning of built environment and its material form. Materiality comes to have meaning through the process and performance of telling stories of place. When these values are cohered, shared and worked up, the community can quickly unite to fight and protect spaces, such as the filter beds, from development.

Walking through the suburb, such as in a parade or while alone, works to both infuse the suburb with memories, associations and meanings and for these to diffuse back into the individual as they walk alone and reminisce and sense the memories. Hannah now takes a longer route through the park on the way to the bus, and Tom has a totally different relation to Kingston's fishy history. Through walking, notes Tim Ingold 'things fall into and out of sight, as new vistas open up and others are closed off' (Ingold 2007:87); place, he suggests, is more 'archi-textural' than architectural (following Lefebvre 1991:117–8), that is, further to sight, sense and materiality, story, play, memory and imagination play a strong role in the making of place. People gain a sense of social meaning from bodily and affective interactions with the materiality of the suburb and the stories, both fact and fictional, to craft a sense of attachment and belonging, to make place (see Cresswell 2004; Massy 2005).

Suburbs are made through the myths that both surround them and emerge through them. What storytelling, be it the facts of Pooley's demise or the myths of Seething, does is provide a way to take something that has a negative connotation, such as 'Surbiton – the little sister of Kingston' or 'Surbiton – the queen of the suburbs', and turn it into something that means something positive, something that works for locals. Surbiton, through storytelling, becomes a place infused with positive meaning for the people that live there. The landscape becomes a place rich with positive material symbols through its ability to evoke memories of feelings that occurred there. It becomes a place where people locate their social ideals and their morals, and as such a place they fight to protect.

Through storytelling, walking and imagining, people are making the suburb in the way they feel best suits the sorts of life they want to live.

Methodological note

The ethnographic research described here formed part of a PhD studentship on the UCL Adaptable Suburbs Project, funded by the UK Engineering and Physical Sciences (EPSRC: project reference EP/I001212/1). Data was collected through participant observation in the Surbiton area between 2011 and 2014. Further to ethnographic 'hanging out', I conducted around 40 non-structured interviews, many of which while walking or while drawing and narrating maps. Around 30 walking diaries were also used, where informants would keep a diary of all their local walks for one week. Names of informants have been changed and identities have been aggregated in this work to protect anonymity. Any omissions or errors remain my own.

References

Ackroyd, P. 2001. *London: The Biography*. Random House.
Ahmed, S. 2010. 'Happy Objects'. In *The Affect Theory Reader*, edited by Melissa Gregg and Gregory Seigworth. London and Durham, NC: Duke University Press.
Augé, M. 1995. *Non-Places: Introduction to Anthropology of Supermodernity*, translated by J Howe. London: Verso.
Bissell, D. 2011. 'Thinking Habits for Uncertain Subjects: Movement, Stillness, Susceptibility', *Environment and Planning A* 43:2649–65.
Bourne, L. 1996. 'Reinventing the Suburbs: Old Myths and New Realities', *Progress in Planning* 46(3):163–84.
Brand, J. 1870 [1777]. *Observations of Popular Antiquities*. Newcastle-upon-Tyre: T. Saint.
Chapman, G., Cleese, J., Idle, E., Jones, T., Palin, M. and Gilliam, T. 1972. *Monty Python's Flying Circus*, series 3, episode 28, 'Mr and Mrs Brian Norris' Ford Popular'.
Cherry, M. 2004. *Desperate Housewives*. Cherry Productions, 2004–7.
Clapson, M. 2003. *Suburban Century: Social Change and Urban Growth in England and the USA*. Oxford: Berg.
Cresswell, T. 2004. *Place: A Short Introduction*. Oxford: Blackwell Publishing.
Dobson, S. 2011. 'Sustaining Place through Community Walking Initiatives', *Journal of Cultural Heritage* 1(2):109–21.
Duncan, E. 2014. 'The Death of the High Street? Hurrah…', *The Guardian* 27 April.
Dyos, H.J. 1961. *The Victorian City: Images and Realities*. London: Routledge.
Edensor, T. 2003. 'Defamiliarizing the Mundane Roadscape', *Space and Culture* 6(2):151–68.
Edensor, T. 2010. 'Walking in Rhythms: Place, Regulation, Style and the Flow of Experience', *Visual Studies* 25(1):69–79.
Esmonde, J. and Larbey, B. 1975. *The Good Life*. BBC. 4 April 1975–10 June 1978.
Griffiths, S., Vaughan, L., Haklay, M. and Jones, C.E. 2008. 'The Sustainable Suburban High Street: A Review of Themes and Approaches', *Geography Compass* 2(10):1–34.
Hazlitt, W.C. (ed.) 1905. *Faiths and Folklore: A Dictionary*. London: Reeves and Turner.
Holton, M. and Riley, M. 2014. 'Talking on the Move: Place-Based Interviewing with Undergraduate Students', *Area* 46(1).

Houseman, M. 1998. 'Painful Places: Ritual Encounters with One's Homelands', *Journal of the Royal Anthropological Institute*, 4(3):447–67.
Hutchinson, R. 2010a. *The Legend of Lefi Ganderson*. Seething: Homage Publishing.
Hutchinson, R. 2010b. *The King's Soup*. Seething: Homage Publishing.
Hutchinson, R. 2011. *Jack and the Golden Egg, or, How the Seething Community Sports Day Started*. Seething: Homage Publishing.
Hutchinson, R. 2012. *The Last Sardines*. Seething: Homage Publishing.
Ingold, T. 1993. 'The Temporality of the Landscape', *World Archaeology* 25(2):152–74.
Ingold, T. 2007. *Lines: A Brief History*. New York: Routledge.
Ingold, T. 2008. 'Bindings Against Boundaries: Entanglements of Life in an Open World', *Environment and Planning A* 40(8):1796–810.
Jackson, K.T. 1985. *Crabgrass Frontier: The Suburbanization of the United States*. Oxford: Oxford University Press.
Keane, W. 2005. 'Signs Are Not the Garb of Meaning: On the Social Analysis of Material Things'. In *Materiality*, edited by D. Miller, 182–205. Durham, NC: Duke University Press.
Lefebvre, H. 1991. *The Production of Space*. Oxford: Blackwell.
McClellan, J. 1999. 'Everything You Think You Know about Suburbia is Wrong', *The Big Issue* 4 November.
McKie, D. 2014. 'Surbiton's Sinful Secret', *The Guardian* 14 August. https://www.theguardian.com/uk/2004/aug/19/britishidentity.comment (accessed February 2019)
McManus, R. and Ethington, P.J. 2007. 'Suburbs in Transition: New Approaches to Suburban History', *Urban History* 34(2):317–37.
Mendes, S. 1999. *American Beauty*. DreamWorks Pictures.
Mills, A.D. 2010. 'Kingston upon Thames'. In *A Dictionary of London Place Names*, 2nd edition. Oxford: Oxford University Press.
Moore, R. 2016. 'With the Good Life Over, how can Suburbia Regain its Place in the Sun?', *The Guardian* 10 July.
Muzzio, D. and Halper, T. 2002. 'Pleasantville?: The Suburb and Its Representation in American Movies', *Urban Affairs Review* 37(4):543–74.
Myers, M. 2010. '"Walk with Me, Talk with Me" 1: The Art of Conversive Wayfinding', *Visual Studies* 25(1):59–68.
Olwig, K. 2008. 'Performing on the Landscape versus Doing Landscape: Perambulatory Practice, Sight and the Sense of Belonging'. In *Ways of Walking: Ethnography and Practice on Foot*, edited by T. Ingold and J.L. Vergunst, 81–92. Ashgate Publishing, Ltd.
Portas, M. 2011. *The Portas Review. An Independent Review into the Future of Our High Streets* (Department for Business, Innovation and Skills).
Priestley, J.B. 1984[1934]. *An English Journey: Or the Road to Milton Keynes*. Carroll & Graff Publishers Inc.
Rose, G., Degen, M. and Basdas, B. 2010. 'More on "Big Things": Building Events and Feelings', *Geographical* 35(3):334–49.
de Spinoza, B.D. 1955. *Ethics*, translated by R.H.M. Elwes, The Project Gutenberg Literary.
Statham, R. 1996. *Surbiton Past*. Guildford, Surrey: Phillimore.
Tilley, C. 2012. 'Walking the Past in the Present'. In *Landscapes Beyond Land: Routes, Aesthetics, Narratives* (Vol. 19), edited by A. Árnason, N Ellison, J. Vergunst, and A. Whitehouse, 15–32. Berghahn Books.
Vaughan, L., Griffiths, S., Haklay, M and Jones, C.E. 2009. 'Do the Suburbs Exist? Discovering Complexity and Specificity in Suburban Built Form', *Transactions of the Institute of British Geographers* 34(4):475–88.
Wickstead, H. 2013. 'The Goat Boy of Mount Seething: Heritage and the English Suburbs'. In *New Suburban Stories*, edited by M. Dines and T. Vermeulen, 199–213. London and New York: Continuum. London: Bloomsbury Press.

5
The linear village: Experience of continuous cruising on the London waterways

Titika Malkogeorgou

Three Invalids – Sufferings of George and Harris – A victim to one hundred and seven fatal maladies – Useful prescriptions – Cure for liver complaint in children – we agree that we are overworked, and need rest – A week on the rolling deep? – George suggests the river – Montmorency lodges an objection – Original motion carried by majority of three to one… We drive off in great style, and arrive at Waterloo – Innocence of South Western Officials concerning such worldly things as trains – We are afloat, afloat in an open boat. (Jerome 1953 [1989])

Multiple places, alternative temporalities

Sitting majestically on the east side of the bank of the River Lee is the Olympic Stadium, now the West Ham stadium. It's not just West Ham – a small team with an oversized stadium – but the whole area that looks out of proportion. Drifting towards it in a small boat on the canal – surrounded by water – everything has a dreamlike hue. But the reality is there; slow movement, wet shoes, tired bones, humidity in the air and on the face, anxiety about the spaces, surprises in the view, muffled sounds. Holding the steering wheel, looking around and focusing close. A boater on a mission. Next to the stadium, an empty flat space, with some grass and new trees sparsely planted, curves around towards the distance. Tall new-builds and three massive cranes with their bright red lights decorate the horizon. In the twilight, not just the sky, but everything, is lit. John Lewis, a chain of upmarket department stores and one of the largest UK companies, is clearly legible from the dark towpath, an absurd reminder of ongoing shopping, encroaching commerce into the culture and nature of the canal.

The top part of the ArcelorMittal Orbit is poking its head from behind the stadium. Near John Lewis in Westfield Shopping Centre, and located between the shopping area and the stadium, is the Aquatic Centre. Neither structure is visible from the river. Yet their presence is spooking the horizon. The canal air is breezy. A vast desolate space between the towpath and the buildings in the distance looms large. Despite the seemingly convoluted effort, this place could easily be any other place if it weren't for the river. This is an ongoing project, as the rows of construction panelling suggest (fig. 5.1).

By the side of the panelling and along the river, however, people with shorts are walking their dogs. They are acoustically enhanced and audible from the boat, because of the gravelled towpath under their feet. Bicycles go by. Groups of friends chat. Half conversations sneak in the boaters' existence from land and make for very funny unstructured listening-in. Water is splashing from the river on the side of the boat. Rowers are rowing small boats. They have drifted off and they are laughing. The sound of wheeled bags sometimes breaks through the hot and stuffy evening air. Ed Sheeran's 'Shape of you' is playing repetitively in the background. It's a bank holiday in May, yet it feels wonderfully summery, and everyone knows it. This is the part of the Lee Navigation

Fig. 5.1 West Ham Stadium, Olympic Park, Stratford, east London. Source: author

Fig. 5.2 White building, art and technology called 'Space', and Sweet Toof street art, east London. Source: author

where it meets the Hertford Union Canal to the west. So, Hackney Wick to the north and north west, Stratford to the east. Boats are cruising in all directions. Oil, grease and diesel fumes mix with the smell of algae in the water, spring herbs, shrubs and bushes along the towpath.

On the Hackney side of the river it's an entirely different cityscape. No towpath for some distance. Old Victorian warehouses and post-war concrete and congregated iron buildings turned into art galleries, bars, restaurants and artists' studios line the bank. Alfred Le Roy is moored by The White Building serving cocktails (fig. 5.2). The bars are full of people. Indoors and outdoors. They are drinking. Everyone is smoking. There's a mixed murmur of people talking and traffic noise in the background. The city traffic is not visible from the canal, but its presence is in the air. Just past the bridge, towards the Hertford Union Canal, a dark towpath is busy with people and a river is thick with boats moored along the bank (fig. 5.3).

Looking towards the Hertford Union Canal from the boat heading south, there is the distinct sense of why a canal is called 'the cut'. This world that cannot be lived from the streets nor is imaginable until one is confronted by it from the water. The water is calm. It's getting dark, and the air is now still. It is truly a cut in the landscape. Rural or urban. An ancient artificial human intervention around which everything that exists today takes its character. The cut that connects and separates, unites and sets apart. That's what the whole London canal system is about (fig. 5.4).

Fig. 5.3 Political satire on display in the linear village, Lee Navigation, Stratford, east London. Source: author

Fig. 5.4 Entering the cut from the River Lee, Hertford Union Canal, Hackney, east London. Source: author

Opposite the moorings there are huge residential buildings that bear the signature of Olympic Games construction. They are at the same time new and stylistically dated, in a faux constructivist slash modern eclectic international blah, with terracotta and ochre panelling, a row of round porthole windows literally interpreting a general nautical style. The rest of the facade is glass with large windows. Most of the curtains are wide open. The lights are on. Part of the building is clad

Fig. 5.5 A quiet afternoon, leisure time and sports in Bow, Old Ford Lock No 19, east London. Source: author

in fake wood. Decking style was obviously de rigueur when this building was constructed. In fact, there aren't many styles that haven't seen their representation in this one building. In the corner of the Lee Navigation and Hertford Union Canal, and overlooking the Olympic Park, it's the cherry on the vista-pie. People are out on their balconies smoking and chatting on their mobile phones. Embarrassingly, some can be heard in the distance.

Everything moves slowly. Smells and sounds are carried by the air but channelled by the water (fig. 5.5). Cruising down the River Lee, boats are moored on the opposite side of the residential buildings, right next to where the towpath is (fig. 5.6). There are a huge variety of styles of boat. Some are double-moored. Wide-beams, narrowboats, Dutch barges, trawlers, even a sailing boat and a boat made from other boats. The river is a private, concealed world, which is at the same time surprisingly public.

And all of a sudden there is the smell of smoked sausages. Someone is having a barbecue at the back of his boat. Another boater dressed in a large towel wanders in and out of his boat. Looks like he's about to cook. Wrapped in a towel, he clearly just had a shower of some kind. Curtains are normally drawn on the side of the towpath but open on the side of the water. A fact that is quickly established. It adds to the intriguing sense of looking inside boats accidentally or through curiosity as if it's a mini stage and not someone's personal real space. But an imaginary one. Further down, a group of friends are squatting on the deck of their boat drinking and talking. Some boats are entirely dark and quiet.

Fig. 5.6 Cafes, bars, restaurants and artists' studios line the river bank, boat traffic unabated. Bow, east London. Source: author

On the west bank of the river, the tower blocks give way to more Victorian, or later, industrial buildings of various sizes. They have all become galleries, studios or restaurants now. Some are public, some are private. One extends to a floating platform on the river. People are eating around wooden tables in the candlelight. There's street art everywhere. Sweet Toof graffiti is massive and visible here and there on the side of buildings. Sweet Toof is a pseudonym for a classically trained artist whose distinctive signature street art of teeth and gums is seen extensively in and around east London. Other less celebrated street artists are competing for space too. Posters of Theresa May in satirical sketches are dotted here and there. Stuck on walls and lamp posts: 'Tories out' and anti-Trump posters, too (elections in June 2017).

Nearing Old Ford Lock 19, a great expanse of space is cleared out. It is covered by high security panels typically found on construction

Fig. 5.7 'Considerate constructors' panelling is all pervasive around Fish Island and the Olympic Park, east London. Source: author

sites – clean looking with pictures of smiling faces in hard hats and 'Considerate Constructors' written all over them. Behind is Fish Island, now a developer's paradise (fig. 5.7). A large barge for rubbish is moored on the north-west side of the lock. This is a twin lock complete with water point and Elsan (toilet pumps, etc.). The traffic is constant. Boats carrying people, plants on decks, cans of beer, cups of tea, home possessions. Some boaters wave at each other as they go past. Others are looking distinctly moody. But it's not all bars, studios and warehouses – as I just mentioned, there is an Elsan and a water point at Old Ford Lock 19, just a bit further down the River Lee (which makes it an especially popular destination). Private and public life is all there as one thing. This is the Lee Navigation in Bow. A historic part of London.

The industrial past and experience of the canal as a 'linear village'

Historically, canal construction in England dates from the eighteenth century, when it was part of a wider urbanisation and industrialisation drive. Canals were an excellent way to transport heavy goods such as coal, iron and brick, and fresh produce like milk. For economic and technical reasons, they were constructed to be narrow and were built individually without a greater plan. The workers who built the canals were also the first dwellers, as they travelled along while the canals were being built, or they travelled around the country, as they looked for work. Their reputation was similar to that of gypsies: they were mired in suspicion and there was widespread demonisation. They would eventually work on the canals as boaters or move on to build the railways; their families followed them. The family lived in the little compact cabin at the rear of the narrowboat as they all worked on the canals pulling the boats, loading and unloading the goods.

But even this way of life became increasingly difficult and eventually impossible. With the advent of railways, which run close by the canal network using the established routes, and a train network that was expanding, offering a transport system that was efficient, safe and quick – the boater families were impoverished. Struggling to cope, they became isolated from the wider community (Bowles 2015; Burton 1995). Life on the canals was lacking in chances for advancement and comfort, and was filled instead with ample opportunities for *petite* criminality. However, despite these associations of a life on the margins steeped in criminality, the imagery of those original boaters has become one of a folkloric imagery. The special dress – bonnets and wide skirts for women, and brightly woven belts for men – and narrowboats painted in the distinctly Roses and Castles style decoration evoke a much-romanticised picture of the past, the boaters' everyday struggles for survival remote from today's material reality. And included in the national narrative as workers and dwellers of the canal system faint in the historical distance, existing literature suggests that the Victorian working boater lived a physically hard life (Burton 1995).

By December 1944, when *Narrow Boat* (Rolt 1999 [1944]) was published, the canals were in disrepair and the working canal life was in total decline. But nostalgia was at its strongest for a long while. Rolt's book was to become seminal in the future of canal life, representing a sense of self that was special in the way it was embedded in heritage and a way of being-in-the-world which was physical, authentic and meaningful. In his book, Rolt recounts four months travelling around the country on his narrowboat with his wife Angela just before the outbreak of the war. He describes both making the boat – a converted wooden narrowboat – and the experience of travelling on it. He writes:

> ... it seemed to me [canal travel] to fulfil in the fullest sense the meaning of travel as opposed to a mere blind hurrying from place to place, and I feel certain that there could be no better way of approaching what is left to us of that older England of tradition which is fast disappearing... many old traditions and customs

> remain on the canals... their people are still highly individual community who have so far escaped the levelling influence of standardised thought and education... (Rolt 1999 [1944]:12)

And he was not alone. Lowenthal describes the post-war mood as one of nostalgia tinged with heavy traces of escapism across society.

> A growing rebellion against the present, and an increasing longing for the past are said to exemplify the post-war mood. Never before in all my life have I heard so many people wished that they lived 'at the turn of the century', or 'when life was simpler', or 'worth living', or simply 'in the good old days', notes a science fiction character. For the first time in man's history, man is desperate to escape the present. (Lowenthal 1985:11)

Hewison (1987) links nostalgia for the industrial past with the growth of post-modernism, while Urry (2002 [1990]) writes that heritage is seen by respondents as involving a strong sense of lineage and inheritance, as it has an identity-conferring status: 'The protection of the past conceals the destruction of the present' (Urry 2002 [1990]:99). The frenzy for preservation was slowly taking shape, not as a new idea but as something that was itself a manifestation of earlier modes of cultural expression.

> Almost everywhere and everything from the past maybe conserved... The seventeenth-century disease of nostalgia seems to have become a contemporary epidemic. (Urry 2002 [1990]:95)

MacCannell traces this nostalgia for the past, and in particular the industrial past, in a sense of loss of self and a desire to recapture this loss in the other. The objects of everyday use of others in time and space, of other lives, took on a new significance. People's routines of the past and the objects they inhabited re-emerged as bringing authenticity to life in the present.

> The remarkably rapid de-industrialisation of Britain had two important effects. It provided profound sense of loss, both of certain kinds of technologies and of the social life that had developed around those technologies. Modern 'man' is losing his attachments to the work bench, the neighbourhood, the town, the family, which

he once called 'his own' but, at the same time, he is developing an interest in the 'real lives' of others. (MacCannell 1999:91)

Within this context and revisionist tendencies, the canal system became leisure and heritage. Rolt was approached by Robert Aickman (a conservationist and fiction writer) and Charles Hadfield (a canal historian) and, after a short cruise on the canals, the three of them set up the Inland Waterways Association (IWA) (Hadfield 1981 [1968]). Shortly after, in 1948, the canals were nationalised. By now, the character of the canals had changed, as had the people who travelled on them, trading already collapsing by the 1950s. With nationalisation and the formation of IWA came the following question: what was the future for inland waterways going to be like, and who was to decide?

Robert Aickman saw the waterways as heritage. He was convinced that the only way to save the waterways was to develop the network for a multiple uses: commercial carriage, pleasure boats, fishing, water supply and drainage, the preservation of archaeological sites along the way and walking along the towpaths. The IWA's focus became towards preserving every waterway and enabling boats to move around the system. All the various authorities controlling individual navigation came under one roof: the government. In the conflict and fallout with other members of the IWA, especially Sonia Smith (one of the most outstanding people of the waterways world), who wanted to try and save selective sections of the canals in order to secure continuing commerce and better working conditions for canal people, it was the IWA that was becoming more successful; leisure boats and live-aboards were becoming the norm. Fact and fiction, romance and heritage, identity politics and economics merged to help develop a new system of canal life. Through the destruction of and nostalgia for an industrial past and the people who inhabited it – preservation and loss, development and destruction – a totally different ideal of canal life is emerging, the reality of which keeps on evolving out of the wider social and material opportunities and constraints.

Bowles, an anthropologist and a boater, writing on the London canals, states that 'it is common to speak of the waterways as a linear village'. He notes the village-like nature of the boating world and focuses on what he calls 'the close-knit community' (Bowles 2015:172), a theme alluding to the original dwellers of the canal system and the vision of subsequent preservationists like the founders of the IWA. Mostly interested in the communal aspect of people's life on the canals – dwelling, moving and socialising – he says that 'maintaining relationships across these distances is complicated' (Bowles 2015:58). Using the 'linear village' as a rhetorical construct is helpful in 'reflecting how, even though moorers are spread out in a long thin line, they are still a small and close community' (Bowles 2015:172).

But it is not a kinship 'village society', as boaters are themselves originally from various parts of the country and therefore 'from geographically separate regions…' (Bowles 2015:173). It is a village society rooted in the specific qualities of the element of water, characterised by its material condition and distinct for the shape of land that contours circulation. Its stability is in the sense of lineage that the paradox of the experience of movement creates. It takes shape by the loyalty and fluidity of the relationships that develop in time and space. A sense of belonging, not because of land ownership but of shared lives.

Flows of water: the London canals as a lived medium of action

In geography, a linear village is a settlement or a group of buildings that is formed in a long line. Many follow a transport route through some natural form, such as a road, river or canal, due to physical restriction – which could be mountains, valleys or coastlines – and often have no obvious centre. They are built in a long and narrow shape. The physical constraints of the linear village are also its character. But the river is materially much more than that in the way it is affectively experienced as a private and a public space – it is the linear aspect of its banks and dwelling spaces; it is the water that flows through; the animals, birds and fishes, as well as other boats and boaters; the trees, towpaths and houses that surround it; the intentionality of those moored up or cruising; 'Places and gazes are physically and poetically grasped and mediated through sensuous bodies' (Larsen and Urry 2011:1122). The sense of vision is the one that has been more extensively theorised and developed in social sciences and the humanities, and not just in itself but also as a medium to other senses, literally or metaphorically, before the more widespread sensory turn scholarship of recent years that includes all the senses.

Through the senses, the river is experienced as space, and as such it only has relational significance created through relation between peoples and places, because 'spatial experience is not innocent and neutral but invested with power relating to age, gender, social position and relationships with others' (Tilley 1994:10). Its 'essence' is not a metaphysical essence, 'but a set of needs and organs which become social, human, rational as a result of the power of social man over nature' (Lefebvre 2008 [1947]:173) –'"a question of the appropriation of *human reality* of the approach to the object", and this is what the "*confirmation of human reality*" consists in' (Marx 1975 [1833–4]:351). The sensuous and material aspect of real life on the canals – the boats and their particular structure as much as being in them, locks and marinas, rubbish bins and towpaths, cruising and mooring up – is not just about what happens out there, but also how it happens and what it feels like experientially.

> Travelling with an affectionate partner makes it easy to fall in love with 'romantic Paris'. And yet 'romantic Paris' can taunt the single traveller with feelings of loneliness and lost love as well as the troubled couple who realise that not even *this* place can re-establish their evaporating affection. Perhaps they secretly dream of gazing on 'romantic Paris' with someone else next time. (Larsen and Urry 2011:1117)
>
> So what is near or far, here or there, bounded or unbounded differs in relation to the body itself and its motility in the world. Past experiences feed into the present, anticipating the future. Our temporal experience 'colours' the manner in which we understand the present from the lived perspective of the body… We are not somewhere outside it, or contained by it; landscape is part of ourselves, a thing in which we move and think… it is not a blank slate for conceptual of imaginative thought but a material form with textures and surfaces. (Tilley and Cameron-Daum 2017:5).

The Olympic Park in east London can, too, be a source of conflicting views, as it is slowly approached and then left behind by the river. Dystopian Britain perhaps can be analysed elsewhere, although it does form part of boaters' everyday experience, and certainly forms part of their daily discourse. Moreover, the aesthetic merits of the Olympic Park landscape, and adjacent architecture, may or may not be one of the most troubling thoughts of those West Ham fan boaters cruising towards Old Ford Lock 19 on their way to watch a football game. But discussion is ongoing regarding, for example, access to parts of the river closed for the Olympic Games of 2012, still not available for continuous cruisers in the summer of 2017. In Lefebvre's words: 'There is no form without content, no content without form. Any separation of form and content involves a certain amount of illusion and superficiality; for form it means not an absence of formal purity, but rather a loss of content'

(Lefebvre 2008 [1947]:81). A large part of the canal around the Olympic Park has been blocked off. Whether there will be some convenient mooring space available when cruising is certainly an issue.

Other boaters, too, who are heading in that direction to use the Elsan and water point, perhaps are looking forward to having an empty toilet and full water tank. The fact that there is a water point and Elsan just in this most desirable area of east London – after all, boaters are moored and emptying their toilets opposite those marvellous postmodern super eclectic architectural constructions – is not without its meaning. And it's highly significant, as form and content cannot be separated. The Elsan and water-point service has always been in this location for when the Lee Navigation was a working canal. It is part of the history of the canal, and it is important that it is in working order. In the present, it means canal cruising is organically incorporated in the urban landscape, making it an integral part of the physical space. This is important for the social space, too. Boaters, tourists, local residents, construction workers, office workers, graffiti artists and others mingle in a rather small and often crowned space. And they all have a claim in the city. This part of the canal was created for a rather different demographic. That demographic has varied massively, and numbers fluctuated throughout. But as water points and Elsan points keep disappearing along the navigation – while they are not being replaced or others added – it appears as an integral part of the stresses of living on water. Most of the debate among boaters – and between boaters and the Canal & River Trust that manages the canal system – is focused on access to bins, Elsans and water points, the state of the locks, the banks and mooring spaces, or the lack of space.

The number of boats circulating and canal use have changed dramatically, and it's a change that has accelerated all the more in the last five years. This is the humanised space of the city that forms both the medium and the outcome of action. 'Relational thinking about cities disrupts an overly containerised view of urban space and opens up new vistas for examining cities and their wider social relationships, connections and flows' (Jonas 2015:281).

So, contextually constituted space provides a particular setting for involvement and the creation of meaning. A whole body of work dealing with leisure, space and heritage is built on the insight of Lefebvre on the production of space. Based on Marx's ideas that the 'perceptible world' is, in reality, the product of human action on the historical and social level, and that: 'as soon as the object it perceives stop being crude objects immersed in nature and become social objects, the "eye" has become a human eye' (Lefebvre 2008 [1947]:163). In his *Critique of Everyday Life*, Lefebvre proposes the undertaking of a vast survey to be called 'How we live'. And he quotes Hegel in his book: 'The familiar is not necessarily the known. Why do men go on pursuing a hidden world?' (Lefebvre 2008 [1947]:132) In his materialist analysis, Lefebvre writes:

> ... it is by means of this object, within, in and through it, that I enter into a complex network of human relations... humanised at last, this 'essence' of a man, who up until now did not exist and who can not exist in advance, is made real through action and in practice ie in everyday life.' (Lefebvre 2008 [1947]:158)

Concerned with deciphering a cosmopolitan condition in the way that growing numbers of people now appear to inhabit their world at a distance through a visual experience, an identity that involves a transformation of vision relies on remoteness, on removing oneself from immediate everyday engagement in the world. Therefore, part of the mobility of people and things is the ability to detach oneself from the environment. This is often described with reference to technology and a subsequent blurring of what is present and what is absent, what is near and what is far (Meyrowitz 1985; Szerszynski and Urry 2006). Featherstone claimed that: 'flows of information, knowledge, money, commodities, people and images: have intensified to the extent that the sense of spatial distance which separated and insulated people from the need to account all the other people which make up what has become known as humanity has become eroded' (Featherstone 1993:169).

Drawing from Lefebvre, in *The Tourist Gaze* John Urry highlights the visual as modernity's hegemony and myth. He demonstrates that looking is a learnt practice, that there is no such thing as a pure and innocent eye. The visual sense is normally the organising sense within tourist experience, but it is also performative, embodied and multi-sensuous (Tilley 2002, 2004). Lund argues in her study of walking in the Scottish hills that: 'the sense of vision and the mountaineer's gaze cannot be separated from examining the body that moves and touches the ground' (Lund 2005:40). People manoeuvre and navigate in space and around objects. And much of this debate, primarily dealing with tourism, leisure and heritage – on knowledge and an embodied 'human eye' – has led to studies on mobility.

Circulation and flow link mobility to citizenship and identity (Massey 1991). For the familiar to become known, it is through an analysis of the everyday, action and the senses. Swyndedouw's (2004) work in the Ecuadorian city of Guayaquil is a study of place and nature as socio-spatial relations. He reconstructs theoretically and empirically the socio-political and relational significance of landscape by looking at access to material elements such as potable water and how it reflects social struggles and power relations. Struggle for control of water becomes a struggle for the city itself. A number of social sciences – anthropology, geography, urban planning, history, sociology – are examining an awareness of the interdependence of other people's spaces. This kind of research looks at all forms of complex mobility and relational spaces – and how those spaces are produced through social and cultural practices such as tourism – to capture and represent various types of movement (Dudley et al. 2012; Newman and Kenworthy 2015; Sheller 2017; Urry 2007). As the mobility theme developed in social sciences, it became less about describing or explaining a mobile world and more about the effects of mobilities and immobilities as they shaped uneven spatial terrains. With a shift in emphasis from the study of spatio-temporal fixes as driven by capital to acknowledging the significance of the ordinary and mundane every day, human life invariably becomes entangled with objects – and it is recognised as such (Bialski and Otto 2015; Cresswell 2006; Sheller and Urry 2006; Urry 2011). Issues of identity, citizenship and changing ways of being-in-the-world became implicated with the complex entanglement of the visual as emblematic of all senses.

Being on the move is contingent, uneven and contested and depends upon different materialities, spatialities and temporalities that are involved in movement, meetings and access, and yet often taken for granted and not noticed. Investigating mobilities from the ground up builds on the theme of relational understanding of space and spatial processes, with an emphasis on meaning, representation, affect and embodied social practices (Adey et al. 2014; Massey 2005). Social institutions and practices presuppose some combination of mobility forms, and therefore there is little pure travel as such; it is to be understood as located within the forms in which specific social institutions and spatial practices are organised (Sheller 2017; Urry 2007).

'All the world seems to be on the move' (Sheller and Urry 2006:208) making possible institutions and practices that are corporeal. People are travelling for work or leisure. Transformation of family life, migration or escape, in addition to organised movement of objects, could be seen as physical manifestations of a world on the move (Adey and Bissell 2010; Beck and Sznaider 2006; Hannerz 1990; Harvey 1993; Urry 2007). But the world is not more mobile in the sense of more enhanced freedom of movement, because mobilities are not a free-flowing abstraction but they are also governed, tracked, controlled, under surveillance and unequal. It is relative with different historical contexts: 'These mobilities may produce relational effects of heightened intensification and speed. A record of coerced mobilities, displacement and closely controlled tracking counters discourses of mobility as freedom' (Sheller 2017).

The London canal system: 'what time is this place?'

And yet, this ever-more-elusive freedom and recapturing humanity is at the forefront of everything that life on the river embodies or represents. The two are constantly realising and de-realising each other through individuals and organisations, practices and discourses. On the representation front, it is about creating the dream of experiencing being on the canals and rivers within the urban landscape. Places indicate particular times or histories, and in that process postmodernism is important because it is localised, specific and context dependent. By contrast, modernist space is perceived as absolute, generalised and independent of context (Harvey 1989; Lynch 1972; Urry 2002 [1990]).

Experientially, there is an effort to capture this abstract dream of freedom and humanity as something actual in real life; both in its historical sense – as places indicate particular times and histories – and in what is the current official character of the London canals and rivers and how the two are connected in the daily lives of those who are part of it is examined in this chapter.

> Visit our wonderful waterways and enjoy all that they have to offer. We take pride in making sure there is something for everyone to love on their local canal or river, whether you're looking for a traffic-free route to school, somewhere to unwind at the weekend or a nearby project that would help your local community to thrive… Boaters, anglers, cyclists and walkers can find all the information they need… For memorable trips to our inspiring museums to free family days out on your local canal… But we're not just about activities. Our canals and rivers are rich in history and home to an exciting programme to arts and culture, not to mention a vast array of wildlife. (Canal & River Trust 2017a)

London is traversed by a canal system dating from the eighteenth century. Initially comprised of several independent private branches, they were all bought up, merged and eventually nationalised into the Grand Union Canal in 1948. To the west, Grand Union Canal branches link Birmingham and Oxford with London. In the east, the canal goes up to Hertford and connects with the Stort river to the east. Original plans were made for the Stort canal to go all the way to Cambridge, but the canal now ends in Bishop Stortford. The Grand Union was amalgamated at various times in the nineteenth and twentieth century with several different canals and connects with the Regent's Canal in the Paddington Basin.

The Regent's Canal, which is the central London part of the canal system, runs from Little Venice in Maida Vale through Hampstead, Kentish Town, St Pancras Basin and the Islington Tunnel to City Road, Kingsland Basin and Cambridge Heath Bridge all the way to Commercial Road, Limehouse Basin and the River Thames. Somewhere past Cambridge Heath Bridge and Old Ford Lock 8 it meets up with the Hertford Union Canal, which was built in the 1830s. At that time the whole area of east London that includes Tower Hamlets and Hackney was being developed, partly as housing and partly as industrial and gas works – all of which survives today in some form or another and creates the particular character of the area.

Within this context, the Hertford Union Canal was built (fig. 5.8). Now one of the most desirable mooring spots, it was initially a commercial failure, and for some years in the mid-nineteenth century totally unnavigable. Hertford Union Canal connects the Regent's Canal with the Lee Navigation, which stretches from the River Thames, Limehouse

Fig. 5.8 In Victoria Park, mooring is regularly two deep. Hertford Union Canal, Tower Hamlets, east London. Source: author

Fig. 5.9 Mixed mooring in Tottenham Hale, a popular destination, Lee Navigation, north London. Source: author

Cut and Bow Back Rivers and through Hackney Wick, Hackney and Walthamstow Marshes, Tottenham, Enfield and Waltham Cross, all the way to Ware and Hertford Castle (fig. 5.9) (Stiglitz 2004).

The River Stort flows into the Lee Navigation from the east near Rye House at Feildes Weir. It flows from Bishops Stortford and through Sawbridgeworth, Harlow and Roydon. The River Stort, too, is very important in this research, because London boaters tend to come to the river in the summer, or when they need to improve their continuous cruising credentials, as most of them tend to spend much of their time trying to moor around the East End of London, and in particular Tottenham, Bow and Victoria Park.

Victoria Park, which stretches across the East End of London in parts of Hackney, Bethnal Green and Cambridge Heath, is bounded on two sides by the canal. But as the canal system was being constructed, it was almost simultaneously becoming outdated and out of favour. Commercial traffic was declining and finally ceased in the 1970s (which actually makes it quite robust, all things considered) (fig. 5.10). Competition for transport of goods came first from the railways in the early 1800s and then by massive road improvements that almost completely took over in the twentieth century. Control of the canal system passed first to the British Transport Commission, then in 1962 to the British Waterways Board, then to British Waterways, and finally became a charity, the Canal & River Trust, in 2012. The Canal & River Trust inherited much of the politics and philosophy of British Waterways,

Fig. 5.10 Part of the Hertford Union canal is overlooked by private town houses and their gardens. Victoria Park, Tower Hamlets, east London. Source: author

as explained earlier in this chapter. But a fundamental change in the character and life on the canals came with the enactment of the British Waterways Act 1995. It was John Major's Conservative government that voted through an Act of Parliament (British Waterways Act 1995) that states that people may use the canals: 'without remaining continuously in any one place for more than fourteen days or such longer period as is reasonable in the circumstances', and therefore creating *continuous cruising*, the mode of being on the inland waterways that dominates canal life and around which all experiences on the canal relate to.

The argument goes as follows. Before the British Waterways Act 1995, all boaters were required to have permanent mooring. This created a lot of resentment on the canal, as many boaters moved continuously, never really accessing or making use of their mooring space and marina facilities, but still having to pay mooring fees (fig. 5.11). The system was seen as unfair and unnecessarily expensive. At this stage, the government came up with the continuous cruising idea as a workable solution. The decision is still in place today, but discussion is ongoing regarding its fairness and practicality in helping resolve canal management issues to do with funding, services, congestion and flow of movement.

As the system opened up, we can imagine life on the canal free from the constraints of a fixed abode – boaters cruising the rivers of London, sliding on the water from one location to another, taking advantage the

Fig. 5.11 Cruising and looking for space to moor can be daunting in busy areas. Hertford Union Canal, east London. Source: author

full extent of the canal network. This is the case to a certain point, and indeed it is possible, but the reality of life on the water is much more restricted, more complex and more idiosyncratic. Heraclitus is quoted in Plato as saying, 'You can never step twice into the same river', a metaphor so true exactly because it's so literal. For many boaters, much of life on the canals and rivers of London is going with the flow and according to the licence. But in everyday life, there is resistance to movement. It is paradoxical that the inevitability of never stepping twice into the same river is resisted so much by the very people who insist that movement and change are the greatest benefits about the river. In fact, continuous cruisers will invariably say that what they like most is the movement, the flux of life, change and the unknown.

Yet, in practice, London boaters navigate a specific area of the canal, try to moor in the same location, and return to that same area in regular intervals. While this is a qualitative study, it is difficult to draw great statistical conclusions to the effect that boaters not only return to favourite spots repeatedly but also share similar tastes and love of the same mooring areas. Locations appear again and again in conversations with unrelated boaters. Moreover, the Canal & River Trust promotes its permanent mooring options on a similar narrative by advertising the favourite spots. Everyone goes to the same places for quiet and the same places for socialising, shopping or partying. My own experience of living on the canal – in terms of personal preferences – certainly doesn't contest that view. But it is reinforced even more by finding certain areas overtly busy and regularly unavailable for mooring – moorings that are two and three boats deep.

In the linear village that the canal has created, continuous cruising is a form of life in its everyday existence and an identity contextualised by mooring spots in its relation to the city, as commerce was for the early boaters. It is how those spots relate to shops, markets, parks, bars, train stations, houses and even trees that makes up the character for the boater and gives lustre to the place. The canal is in constant flux because of the traffic – which is evident – and because the city itself is changing, even though 'the cut' is very clearly defined. In fact, it is contained by a bank on each side, one of which has a towpath. The towpath is not necessarily a continuation along the same side of the river. Every now and then, often where there is a lock, the towpath swaps over from one side of the canal to the other. As the canal cuts through London, it goes through a variety of cityscapes and landscapes: picturesque town houses with their back gardens opening up to the canal side, council estates with balconies, industrial buildings oddly shaped, but also marshes, parks, filter beds, nature reserves, all types of bridges and some very strange modern developments. And, therefore, continuous cruising is for people who are themselves in constant movement in a constantly changing environment, because all through London, the built environment and wherever nature creeps in, the river itself changes also – the water, the depth, the colour, the reflection of the sky and trees, the animals building their nests at the side of the canal (or inside rubber tires hanging at the side of narrowboats) and guarding it in the middle of and at regular intervals through the night.

The body as both object and subject

As with the complexity of continuous cruising, the relationship with London from the boaters' point of view is not very straightforward either. So, conflicting reports about same situations are not unexpected. Certainly, some are what one might expect given all the freedoms and opportunities cruising London from one end to another offers, with the additional bonus of stopping at all the nice spots and remaining there for up to two weeks (but not more). 'Freedom' is a concept that comes up a lot in discussion. The freedom to be in the city. The mobility to stay put. The linear village with its physical constraints opens up the city itself and draws the canal dwellers in.

Lillian has been living in her boat, which she bought with her partner about two years ago. I find her double-moored near Limehouse and struggle to get on board because of the uneven level of the two boats and the higher bank. I am carrying bags and wearing a big coat. Moreover, the humidity creates slippery surfaces on deck, and a wet atmosphere without rain engulfs the hands and face. Smoke is coming out of the chimneys of the closely packed boats and fills the air with a wood-burning smell. Other unidentified smells of burning stuff hover over the river. Lillian is 32 years old, very hospitable, working freelance and studying part-time. Inside the narrowboat, a hot coffee pot is reassuringly brewing on the stove as we speak. Everything is super-clean and tidy. There's order everywhere. It's a crisp February morning. The temperature inside and outside the boat is quite low, low enough to make taking off coats indoors rather uncomfortable. Lillian is excited and full of enthusiasm about her situation, and she puts it very beautifully as the notion of freedom is quickly evoked.

> I'd say the biggest difference [living on the boat rather than on land] is freedom in lots of different ways. So, freedom financially. But that doesn't necessarily mean that you spend less money [being] on a boat. But it just means you choose where to spend it… And other differences: I suppose I've learnt, before I was like wearing a groove between my workplace and my home. I felt like I was sort of wearing a groove in the tarmac when I was cycling to and from and nowhere else. And now I feel I've seen a lot more of the city and I understand how things join up just because I've been living in different pockets of it for two weeks at a time and a lot of it joins up. I think the main difference is the mobility and living in different places in London and living in a house where you can feel very stagnant and oppressed.

Freedom and mobility, or mobility as freedom, are qualified and not self-evident. Financial freedom can mean more of London. Freedom relates to mobility, because there is a sense of having a choice, and making a choice is empowering. Empowerment comes from mobility. The city becomes more accessible, because for one it is less forbidding financially. The ability to live in different parts of London can also mean more integration and an enhanced sense of belonging. Space is owned experientially. Lillian is thrilled with her boat and her continuous-cruiser lifestyle. She spends most of her year around Victoria Park, King's Cross and Limehouse. Other members of the family also live on a narrowboat moored further along the Lee Navigation (fig. 5.12). She's planning to venture in that direction in the summer, as she did last.

Fig. 5.12 Anchor and Hope pub opposite Walthamstow Marshes, Lee Navigation, north London. Source: author

Lillian's partner, Jonathan, is a set designer working on a rather intense and demanding day-to-day schedule that does not entail regular hours. I managed to track him down between jobs. He runs his own business, is in his early 30s and lives on the narrowboat. For him, living on the river means being able to do the rather conventional things of life like love, live and work – but do them in an unconventional way, suitable for someone with a fluctuating rather than a secure income. It is about being able to 'cheat' London, metaphorically – or, in other words, bypass the financial, social and work inequality that comes from living in an expensive city without renouncing the rewarding aspects of urban life. Ultimately, it means being with who you like, in a place you like, doing what you like. In London, this is only possible with a stable and rather large income coming from somewhere. If that's not the case, the canal can offer a solution. But how to navigate around the canal, and in terms of how the everyday works out, that is for the boater to find out for herself or himself. There is an awareness that this is different to bricks-and-mortar living. The opportunities are not just for London, but for beyond. As we sit and chat on opposite sides of a small table in front of a coal-burning stove, Jonathan very politely points towards the books stacked up on the table. They are about travel abroad. And about study abroad. Movement on the London canals is not just about movement in the city and not just an opportunity to access the city. A broader, metaphorical and literal movement is possible in the wider world. The linear village has different rules, implicit or explicit. To this extent, the Canal &

River Trust conducted a survey in 2016 gathering information regarding who is living on or using boats in the London waterways, in order to inform policy and mooring strategy. It was followed by a licence consultation (Canal & River Trust 2017b). Jonathan strikes a very similar tone to Lillian in his positivity about canal life. He describes how he imagined it from living on land and what it was actually like living in a narrowboat on water.

> I didn't imagine it in any way. I didn't come in it with any preconceptions of what it's going to be like apart from having to learn all the etiquette. I knew we had to move every two weeks and obviously the licensing and stuff like that. There is only so much you can learn before going on a boat. I feel more connected with London than I did in a house, though I've lived all over east London. I've lived in every bit now. We've been here two years, so I definitely know, I have more of a geographical connection, what's going on, where things are, how to get places. Living on a boat, it ups your logistics by a thousand per cent. All the time running a business, running a van – OK, I had it stolen – a car now, a boat, a workshop and jobs. I spend a lot of time finding where things are, planning out routes, moving things. So this morning, yesterday we came back from Kent to the workshop, a car full of stuff. I had to drive here and park after half six and unload all the stuff. This morning: meeting you, so I got up early move the car to the free car zone, had bicycle in the car, so I can cycle back to the boat. That's every day you're doing something like that... A good day is when everything is in place and maybe you have to cycle somewhere. But the bike is on the boat not the car.

The practical aspects of living on a boat appear to be much more complex compared with living on land in a specific place. And a sense of heightened alertness is evident. So there is a price to pay for freedom and movement, and it is acknowledged as such. It is an extraordinary ordinary life. Continuous cruising is nonetheless a source of excitement and a constant reminder of the city. London is much more lived in a sense, because it's lived everywhere and in every sense. For couples in their 20s and 30s living on a boat, this is not an unusual theme. Two people who want to live in London because of work, family or friends, but cannot necessarily, or who want to hold high-powered or even full-time jobs, find canal life a positive alternative – or not so much an alternative as a possibility to realise such a situation that would otherwise be out of reach. From the water, London can be lived and enjoyed on your own terms (if you are prepared to put in the work). And that is a constant reminder.

Dominic and Barbara are a couple from the Midlands in their early 30s, and each has his or her own boat. But they always move and moor their boats together, side by side, up and down the river. Moreover, each boat has a separate function and a totally different character but similar size. One is bedroom, the other is kitchen and living room. They feel that the regular friction between couples, if not absent, is diminished, although they live very different lives and have different priorities and tastes. Dominic is self-employed and works in construction. He enjoys being active and making things. Barbara works long hours for a design company in the city. They have lived on the river for about five years. Living like this doesn't come naturally. However, it means less stress over finances and a more pleasant time together. The financial aspect and the sense of freedom are recurrent themes. Financial freedom and movement as freedom. Financial freedom offers mobility, and mobility offers freedom. A common thread about canal life would also be discovering what you really like, rather than what you think you want or think you like – therefore, in many ways, what you are really like. The meaningful action is in the everyday. It's a sort of journey of self-discovery taken along the linear village that is the canal, and it appears to happen almost unintentionally. In terms of how Dominic and Barbara adjust continuous cruising to fit their working life and own time, it's been a matter of trying different ways of doing things in a mundane way.

I met Dominic while walking along the towpath with Patrick. We were on our way to buy lunch. My husband had disappeared, on the lookout for coal for the stove. It was cold, and we were desperately running out of fuel in a part of the river we were unfamiliar with at the time. Our clothes were wet. It had been raining all morning and now the sun had just come out, making everything look clean and sparkly. Blue skies and air fresh with the smells of the woods nearby. But sort of musty too. The ground soft and muddy under the feet. On the canal, the weather is more than the weather; it is the structure of life, a strong awareness of temperature, humidity, malleability, smell; and light dictates movement, mood, activity, organisation, emotion. The relationship to weather is intimate. With the change in atmosphere, people are coming out into the open as if from a long sleep. However, one should never assume that the distant sound of cars, lorries and generally vehicles of all descriptions ever leaves; an ongoing unpleasant and ever-present noise is muffled in the background. On the river, and with the change of wind, it can become more or less pronounced. The spectrum of the city is everywhere. Luckily, in the foreground, sounds of singing birds, swimming ducks and coots splashing about in the water are prominent. Swans and geese flying very loudly above are breath-taking. In the sudden sunshine, Dominic is well prepared. He has already set out his tools on the towpath and is doing his DIY despite the muddy earth and the abundance of puddles. Barbara is at work. Dominic explains how they experience movement and their own approach to living on the water (and in London).

> Yeah! Nowadays, so, in the first couple of years, we didn't move much out of central London. My girlfriend works near Liverpool Street, and I tend work in central London. And so, when we first came on the canal, we didn't move much beyond Tottenham. And then the last couple or three years, we've been coming out as far as Hertford and Ware. So, the whole of the River Lee. And, so we used to sort of moor in spots that were near train stations or near other boats. But nowadays we tend to moor in the more secluded spots. So the quieter the spot is. Nowadays, I am not really that fussed about being near the train station, even if I have to cycle a couple of miles to the station. I'd rather be somewhere nice than anywhere busy. So we tend to keep away from anywhere that's overlooked by houses – we won't stop. We stay, for the last few years, we've stayed on the River Lee. We go down as far as Hackney, the Olympic Park, and then we go up to Hertford, which is like 30 or 34 miles. And that's it really. We do that over the year. Just slowly work our way up and then slowly come back down… We don't go into central London, because it tends to get a bit busier there, and I am more worried about not being able to find a spot where we can put both boats. To be honest, if you're moving the boats, you often think it's going to be harder than it will, or that you encounter more problems, but actually most of the time you just do it, and even if you do encounter problems, they sort of are easily overcome. But I mean, central London, I'd rather be out in the countryside and near trees. I am not fussed about being in central London… if the CRT said, you need to move further, you're not moving further enough, I'd go through west London. I wouldn't have a problem with it. I really like it. I'd just move further… when I move the boats, I move them tied together, generally. Yes, we always move them together.

West London features really low in the desirability chart (for those who don't dwell there). It's seen as vulgar and rough, dominated by extremes of wealth and poverty and, for this reason, very unfriendly. Crime features as a big deterrent too. Boaters feel vulnerable to outside conditions and would rather not go where it is perceived as dangerous or not secure. However, boats are moored all the way along the canal. So that begs the obvious question: who are these boaters? And are they just passing by on their way to the country, or is there another pattern in continuous cruising that does not feature here?

Relational thinking about space and spatial thinking about social relations

Jonathan describes a very similar cruising route to other boaters. In many way it represents the root to most of the Canal & River Trust's headaches regarding congestion and circulation. It's Victoria Park, Bow, Hackney Wick, the Olympic Park, Limehouse, Tottenham, and King's Cross where there's the best Waitrose in town with wide aisles and jazz music at the weekends.

> Yeah, that's really fun. It has a cafe. Yes it's really nice and it's next to Central St. Martin's. And you're really central. It's nice to feel you're in the hub of London... I haven't enjoyed any of west. So no. King's X is nice. Paddington arm is really nice. You can book in there for a week or something and it's like a nice little place apparently. Little Venice and that: is fucking shit-hole. West London is a shit-hole. It's really rough.

Sociability, security, a scenic view – sounds a bit like a tourist's guide and a leisure weekend away (fig. 5.13). But the sense of the everyday can contain all of the special elements normally associated with the extraordinary aspects of the holiday experience. A staycation of some sort, colloquially. Moreover, what makes a place popular to boaters can vary from a large Waitrose (a chain of British supermarkets with an upmarket reputation) or even a large Tesco (a general merchandise shop and third larger retailer in the world, criticised for aggressive market behaviour), (Press Association 2011), a large field, woodland or marshland, from cool night clubs to ethnic street markets, the chance to moor next to each other with friends to the ability to moor where there are no houses in view. That is not to say that the connection to London physically, emotionally and socially – intensified by the opportunity to dwell in different parts of the city through continuous cruising – is necessarily

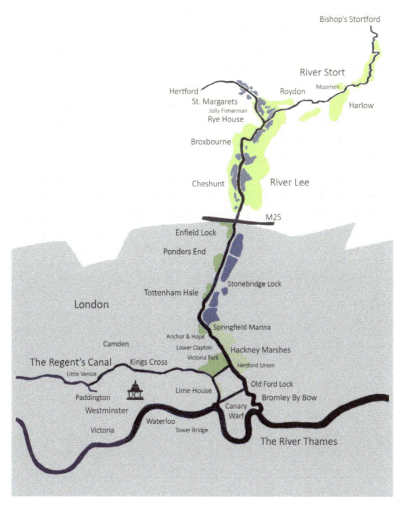

Fig. 5.13 Map of Regent's Canal, Hertford Union Canal, Lee Navigation, and the River Stort. Design by Simon Harold. Source: author

shared by all boaters. Patrick is from the west country, a 45-year-old freelance editor for a legal firm. He says he is very sociable but that he needs to spend rather a lot of time alone in his boat, because of his work, writing. The boat's interior, which is very well kept and looks new, is busy with books, papers, journals and various other items. Inside the traditional looking narrowboat space is organised around the comforts of one person only. The boat is rather large with a fireplace on one end and a drinks cabinet neatly laid out on the side. By the window a table and two chairs. The table and chair are covered with books and paper piled sky high. The other chair sits empty with a large cushion on top. I make a point about it as we are looking for space to sit. We were introduced at a party. I had several attempts at an interview with him which regularly failed. Constant cruising and other commitments got in the way. Eventually, he became a captive audience when his engine broke down and his boat was towed to the marina. There – at a fixed location – we met on my cruising down the Lee. His sister also lives in a boat, and they both have a lot of stories to tell. However, their lives' trajectory and boater experience is completely different. The calm life of the canal (though often unevenly interrupted) is ideal for Patrick in many ways. He can focus on his work, without distraction, to reach deadlines, while his boat could be moored anywhere, and he still can get on with his work without worrying about public transport or commuting (and associated time and expense), or he could work at night and travel during daytime. All that is great, except that he says: no one ever visits, which is exasperating, because it adds another layer of loneliness to a solitary existence and as such can be anxiety driven over sometimes trivial things. Patrick is florid in his description about the reality of boat life with an unconventional job (though the idea of a normal job can also be debatable) and conflicting inclination, mood or temperament:

> The thing that I least like about cruising is, as a sociable person, I can become a bit of a recluse. I'd like to have people around for a meal. I can be a bit of a recluse on the river. Because if I had a flat somewhere is easy to get to. People came around when I had a flat in London. It was a funny and shabby-glamorous penthouse on the top floor and there was always wine and tea, and cocktails! Eccentric, funny, shabby, friendly place, it was easy to get to. And for relationships and all those sorts of things: This [boat] you can slip into being cut off from life in a way. Because, especially in the winter, who wants to come out into a cold towpath? People consider it… I guess it's the pressures of London. If you're working in London, you do things you don't do on the river because you don't want to be out on a cold night. You want to come back at sunset… Last night I had a lovely night. I went to see some film with friends in London…

This is what Jonathan called 'the *logistics* of boater life are *upped*' massively. The material reality of everyday life on the canal can have an emotional as much as practical effect. And the distance to London, all of

Fig. 5.14 Lee Valley Marina, Springfield, north London. Source: author

a sudden, is increased even if you're right in the middle of the city. What was pointed out to me very graphically was the fact that you're apparently floating along the canal in a pod completely encased and absolutely detached from the world. Carrying with you all your possessions, and while you are floating about from place to place, London literary just passes you by. This physical aspect of the boat – its own materiality – which is different to living on land, shapes your relationship with the environment. Whether the landscape or built environment changes or not – leaves you, the person cruising, unmoved though you are in a state of constant movement. So the city changes, and people, and shops and bars, and special places change, but the point is that this very movement forces the boater to remain alone and unattached. Shockingly, not in London at all (fig. 5.14). A place that lacks all the localised specificity of the city. The sense of freedom associated with movement is non-existent in the static of the narrowboat's interior floating along the canal. Not just that movement feels static, but freedom to be lonely doesn't qualify for freedom but is contesting any idea of pure travel or the humanity of the canals. It also brings into focus how contingent on materialities space and movement is. Patrick goes on:

> I think the boat just adds to this isolation. Because on a boat you know, Rye House, the middle of nowhere. Isn't it? There's nothing there. So you're literally in the middle of nowhere. Maybe the boat, it's a bit more of a divide, if you don't have some sort of external. So, it's up to you to make the most of the boat really. You can have a

> very rich life on the boat if you're organised. You're not really in London in a way. You might as well be in a commuter town. You're quite far out… but that takes away the movement. A lot of it is contradictory. Cause we are more likely putting down roots than not, but we like being free as well. Because within ten, five minutes of putting down the pins in the new place, I am happy. It's the uncertainty of the journey, it's the stress, it's your home possessions. That's quite hard for me to get rid of that in a way, but by the time I get to the new place I am happy. It's amazing.

As the boat moves along with the boater and all the personal possessions, it becomes a micro-environment in itself contesting all spatialities of movement. The very fact of the boat being moored in one place or another can become abstracted from the reality of its location. As the boater becomes absorbed by every day material conditions, others are more reluctant to join in. Land visitors become rarer. Other friend or family boaters could be moored elsewhere on the waterways entirely.

Dominic and Barbara too, reflect those sentiments. Being in a couple is not necessarily a buffer against canal routine isolation and merging with one's boat. They don't appear to resent it but it comes up in the discussion. Perhaps it's more of an issue for Barbara who wants to socialise with mates from work and meet new people. Dominic instead wants to spend more time on the boat or fixing things out on the towpath. So, for him, a quiet towpath and a mooring space further away from London is preferable.

> I wouldn't say there's much of a difference [between living on a boat and a flat]. No, actually, there probably is. If you're living in one place, you're more likely to build up connections with maybe the people who live on your street, and in the same sort of area. I never had that wherever I've lived, cause I've always lived somewhere for six months, and then I moved, or I lived there for a year, and then I moved on. But I know a couple of people who have been in a flat for, maybe, ten years, and they know quite a lot of their neighbours. It's kind of different, I mean we chat to a lot of boaters. We know boaters on the canal, but we're not really massively friendly with them. And then the other thing is, because the boats are quite small, people, our friends, will come and visit us on the boat occasionally, but it's quite rare really. And because we are moving constantly, then, they feel, I don't know. I think people

don't like to travel that far... we have not got loads of friends... so occasionally people would come and see us on the boat. But it's quite rare nowadays. When we started doing it people were interested – when we were in central London we were more sociable, we see our friends more, and maybe we won't see them so much when we're out here [in Enfield].

So the magnificent connection to London through the variety of all the different locations along the canal can be superficial, fleeting, ephemeral, as one floats along the river and never establishes oneself in a specific place. There are moments of excitement in a new location. The new location can also be mundane. An inconvenience. An added layer to one's solitude. Continuous cruising can be a bit of a bore. And that visit to Waitrose and Central Saint Martins or The Anchor and Hope pub would have to wait.

And perhaps part of the resistance to continuous cruising is the act of leaving a familiar spot where the boater has stayed for two weeks probably (but certainly no more) and with it everything that makes daily routine possible. No one can ever come and visit you in the same spot because you will not be in the same spot, or even near by for some time. To go somewhere else (in the canal context), does not necessarily mean very far away. In terms of London distance, it is hardly any distance at all, unless you want it to be, but the distance can quickly add up over time. And all of a sudden everything is different, the grass, the towpath, the buildings, the coots and the moorhens. You, your boat and your possessions are still the same. Being-in-the-world is implicated in another entanglement of places and spaces.

The beholding eye: Past experiences, the present and the future

Boaters talk about the desire for an alternative lifestyle, one which exists on the canal and which offers a more authentic existence, but the drive behind getting there in the first place is often financial. Then the financial aspect would, in conjunction with other canal life elements, feed back into the person's wellbeing. Buying a house or flat in London will set the buyer back a few hundred thousand pounds. Instead, a boat would be in the tens of thousands, although of course this can grow to the hundreds of thousands for bigger and more luxurious boats – but, most importantly, it does not need to be that expensive. A typical 25-foot cruiser, which

Fig. 5.15 Dutch barge on the River Lee, Hackney Marshes, north-east London. Source: author

would be a very small narrowboat type with electrics and petrol engine, could start from £9,000. Despite its limited size, it can accommodate sleeping space for three between the bow and the stern. A traditional London narrowboat of 60 foot would come closer to £50,000. It would be in a very good condition and fitted with double-glazed windows, central heating, a stove, fridge, freezer, gas oven and hob, diesel boiler, sleeper areas, living room, bathroom, storage and wardrobes, and often solar panels. Several engine upgrades and interior updates, fashionably accessorised, and being regularly blacked, for example, can raise the price to £100,000. Instead, a 60-foot wide-beam would probably start from £100,000 and go upwards in price. Location, age, condition, size, desirability, all play a part in the price (fig. 5.15).

Moreover, as London is considered low value, in other words too expensive, boaters tend to go north to buy boats, which they then bring down to London, sometimes to resell and other times for own use. Everyone I interviewed had bought their boats from outside London. Then there are the Dutch barges. Everyone declared a love of them. Magnificent, spacious and quirky, they tend to be the more expensive and the most varied. These are also the ones seen as investment heritage boats. People pay for them to be brought over from Holland, as they are sold cheaply on the continent and their prices can escalate dramatically in Britain when they are done up. And because the Dutch canals are much wider, the boats themselves are wider and more spacious compared to the typical British canal boats.

Kenneth lives with his partner on a wide-beam type of canal boat. (Beam is a measurement of a boat's width and it's used as one of a number of ways to describe different types of canal boats.) I asked Kenneth about the structure of their boat.

> It's the terminology you use. A double-beam would be double the width of a narrowboat. A narrowboat is 6–10, 12, 13–8; this is not 13–8, so they call it a wide-beam… normally the barges are double beams. It's very rarely that you see a boat that comes up that is 13–10. If you go up the Stort, they only have 13-foot gates there, so you can't put two boats in together. If you go down the lock here, two narrowboats can get in together. They were built like that, so they can go through faster and can get to their destination quicker. And they used to make a lot of cargo barges, with no engines, no nothing on them, and then they would take up the whole width of the lock, and this way they would carry as much material as possible. And then there used to come a small tug and push them. But I don't know – I should know – why they only have 13-foot locks. It should be 14. The Stort is a small navigation… it's only about 11 miles.

Lillian again has a rather poetic take on what a boat means and how this anxiety develops in an entanglement of people, spaces and objects.

> I suppose [the worst thing about living on a boat] there's an underlying anxiety, which very rarely feels like an anxiety, but you know, about if the boat sinks. You've got everything you own, everything you love is this boat… you do see sank [sic] boats. You see them in London… it's a bit like a baby, or something you really love, say, or a mother is probably better, 'cause it gives you lots of stability, and love and freedom. But also you don't want her to die. That's a bit of a weird metaphor.

In fact, it is a powerful – if a rather unconventional – metaphor, because it shows the extent to which boaters become attached to their boats (fig. 5.16) – an attachment that evokes strong feelings, rational or not, exaggerated or modest. The complexity of their particular situation makes identifying with the boat a shared experience among boaters. The boats become in themselves a complete enclosed environment, a thing in itself which is an extension of the person, something much more intimate than a flat or a house, because not only is there the sense

Fig. 5.16 Anything can be a boat; this one is on sale for £950, down from £1,000. Stonebridge Lock 16, north London. Source: author

of waking up in it every morning or coming back to it at night in the various locations where the boaters have moored (or they might spend all their time in the boat if they're working from home or not at all), but because they take it with them to the next place. The boat is part of the person but also part of the neighbourhood, the landscape and the place. Entire areas of the canal are constantly changing as boaters congregate in certain areas, mooring and double-mooring and then abandoning those spots by cruising away. There is something unknown about the boat and her future, and that means about the boaters themselves: in practical terms, the destination. But in metaphor, it could mean much more than that. Lillian describes how it's done.

> We just move the boat until we find a spot – obviously not if it's just five minutes. But you know, half an hour of moving the boat or

more sometimes, and then we find a spot and we stop. And then because it's London, you're always going to be near somewhere… London is huge, it still feels like you're moving from village to village almost within the city. So it does feel like you are in different pockets and areas. You know, you get different things out of each place.

And this sense of moving from village to village is reassuring. The stability and love and freedom become the landscape.

In Enfield, near Dominic and Barbara's boats is Alicia's, moored close to Rammey Marsh Lock 12. Alicia has had a difficult time with addiction and recovery, and the boat has helped her reconstruct her life and make her feel much happier about her future She is a 56 years old, from London, and lives in a small boat with her dog. She approached three of us near the canal trying to cut wood for the boat stove and doing a very bad job of it. She recognised us as boaters, although she didn't actually know us, and very generously lent us her saw and gave us lots of her own wood. The saw didn't cut and the wood was too wet to burn. It was soon dark, and we were all exhausted by the effort. But in the dim light of early evening, we got talking about the river and started exchanging boater anecdotes. On the towpath there is no artificial light, only light pollution from London – which is staggering – and the nearby towns and suburbs. The next day, we meet again at the local greasy spoon for breakfast and get on with some more-detailed discussion. For Alicia, living on the canal allows her to do volunteer work on weekdays and develop her egg- and dairy-free cake-baking business for fairs and events at the weekends. She takes a rather pragmatic approach towards London, but one that is full of energy. She is positive about the river and determined to make every aspect of continuous cruising work in her favour. As with most people I have spoken to, she came to the river for financial reasons and that much-discussed elusive freedom. Alicia then discovered movement and a changed scenery that has a therapeutic effect. It certainly puts her in a better mood. She says:

> The way I see it, if you have permanent mooring you might as well be in a flat. You know, you have the same view every day, you've got the same people around you. I went to Kingsland Basin to do the Christmas market and it was marvellous. I had two nights of electrical hook-up, which was really good – but then I realised it wasn't charging up anything. I had to sort out my charger. And after two nights of being in one place, I thought: that's OK, I want to go now. I wouldn't want to stay there. I don't see the point.

Alicia has also a van, which she uses as an extension of her boat. She is full of energy and enthusiasm but also very guarded, a person who appreciates how sometimes things can get out of control, how a person can find oneself in trouble. Alicia felt more comfortable chatting in the Narrowboat Cafe rather than on her own boat. And mine was in such a state, it was totally inhospitable. Alicia was the only boater I interviewed at a place other than their boat. But the Narrowboat Cafe is an interesting place in itself. It has the worst ratings of in any place in the area – that is, for quality and service. But at the same time, it is always busy. We had cooked breakfast there. It's a place in Enfield near the River Lee and Rammey Marsh Lock, an adjacent marina and permanent moorings. The air is warm and thick with the familiar smell of cooked beans, mushrooms, sausages, etc. There is an outdoor space with benches; masks and totems decorate the entrance; inside are showers for boaters, a play area for children and a very varied clientele: locals, families, tourists, boaters and middle-aged men in Lycra, with bicycles, eating the full English breakfast. With its comfort food and exotic decoration, it appears as both a place of passage and a regular hang-out, despite the mostly negative publicity. Here everyone is in control, the customers and the hosts. In my conversation with Alicia, the word 'control' often comes up in relation to London. Sometimes it's a stand-in for qualifiable freedom. For many boaters, London is a place where you need to be vigilant not to lose control of your life in all sorts of emotional or financial practical ways, and therefore where you have to be resourceful and disciplined, careful and predictable, in order to be able to take advantage of what there is.

Normally, when something falls apart, other aspects in life follow. A failed relationship or failed health, addiction, finances. Something comes first, and total or partial collapse may follow. So, despite the isolation that often accompanies life on the canal, the boat can be the thing that links someone to ordinary life where work, home and relationships can develop in an interesting way, just as they would in any other part of the city where someone lives in a house with a garden or a flat with a view. Alicia is extraordinarily resourceful, always thinking of ideas and new schemes to make money and to socialise. Her life on the boat is primarily focused around her volunteering, and therefore part of it can be described as seasonal. In the winter, she is moored somewhere central (by central, all my interviewees mean east London, Regent's canal, Hertford Union, Stratford, Limehouse), and in the summer, somewhere perhaps slightly further out of town – like Walthamstow Marshes, Springfield and Enfield – but never too far off. A relational, embodied understanding of space in ordinary human life means there is a point of view that colours the experience, and a particular affective perspective.

> Yes, 'cause I mean you're only going to be there for two weeks. There are places where I've gone to and I thought wow this is amazing, but then after the two weeks I am like OK I've seen that kingfisher a few times, I know that woodpecker, and I've told this guy to turn his music off at 11p.m.

Continuous cruising influences in a powerful way thinking and a way of being in the everyday life, and it affects social relations and relationship to the landscape.

Space is experienced in a contradictory way: individuals act and are acted upon

The canal is not just full of young couples starting up in life or singles navigating through professional challenges or a difficult past. On the other side of the relationship spectrum there is divorce. And there can be loss, illness, shared finances, settlements and children that dominate how one experiences the canal and a life of boating. This can change the relationship to London, as personal priorities are entirely different. Pollution, public transport, crime, outdoor spaces, distance to school, doctors or family become paramount. Busy and exciting, London can be overwhelming. While younger boaters use the canal as a support mechanism to access more of the fun and growth aspects of the city, like further education, leisure, socialising, working in the arts or other notoriously risky and underpaid endeavours, for others it's a lifeline in recovery from cancer, addiction or a broken family situation.

One of my boater friends, who lives on her boat with her dog, insisted I should interview Alex for my research, and she introduced him to me when we were all in a stretch of the canal just outside Ware. Alex has outstanding credentials and he is well known among boaters as being very nice, exceptionally clean and polite, and discrete enough not to get involved in canal gossip. Alex is divorced, and before buying his boat had never thought of living on the canal. He is a 58-year-old musician from Wolverhampton. However, he initially introduced himself to me as a gardener, which I had no reason to disbelieve (although I never introduce myself as an anthropologist unless I have to). After getting to know him and his boat, I saw a set of drums in the corner and I learnt that he regularly goes to France, where he records music. He sees himself as an outdoor person who likes nature and, in particular, the woods (he says, probably more than the river), but as it turned out he is by profession a musician who has lived all around London throughout his life. When he got divorced, the realisation came to him that he could not afford to live as he wished. Moreover, he has two young children and he was determined somehow to be with them as much as possible while they are growing up. He managed to get joint custody of the children with his former wife, but he still needed to be able to support a living situation that would comfortably accommodate him and the children.

He said that he sat down with a friend of his, looking at all the options on the table and going over various ideas. Following his divorce, he found himself in an unexpectedly dire financial situation. In the end, the most outrageous solution was also the most feasible one: to live on a boat. Most people I've talked to who live on a boat have had some experience of canal life. They either had friends or family live on a boat, so there was some familiarity with the canal before they themselves decided to take the plunge. Or perhaps they visited people on boats and spent time with them, found out that they liked it or were intrigued enough to decide to go for it themselves. For Alex, he said, it was a total new discovery. Starting life from the beginning, from scratch, without any preconceptions, just in order to be able to both break and not to break with the past. He wanted a divorce, but he also wanted to be with his children after he got joint custody with his former wife. Alex's children and creating rather than renouncing a family life became pivotal in his decision-making. The children loved the boat, although don't love the new one as much, Alex says. Alex has managed to upgrade himself to a newer, bigger, more polished narrowboat, which he bought with all interior fittings and complete with towels. An ex hire boat. The children were more fond of the old, smaller, wobblier and slightly smelling-of-diesel boat. Perhaps it was the novelty. No other children in their school live on a boat.

Alex keeps his boat in immaculate condition. It was certainly the most clinical boat I ever visited, almost as if it had never left the showroom. Alex shows me every detail of it over a cup of tea. But the way he describes his memories of his earlier boat are all in terms of the many senses they evoke: the smell of diesel that never left the children's clothes; the constant movement and the difficulty to keep the boat still; the warmth in the winter, as it was small and easy to heat, and the cramped cosy spaces that kept them together. And, paradoxically, by living in a small place, he has much more easy access to the large open spaces that he really likes, and a sense of freedom by being closer to the rural landscape, the woods, the forests and the animals and their peculiar smells and sounds. Alex is philosophical about the many changes in his life; for him, the new situation – of more comfort, order and space – is much more desirable and certainly intentional. Freedom comes up again in conversation – it is the financial freedom that affords him the mobility to enjoy nature – the woods, the water, the animals. Mobility and freedom are interlinked, and Alex references his children as a source of knowledge about his sentiments regarding his own situation.

> They really liked it when we were on the other boat. They talk fondly about the other boat… it was a very basic boat. They like this boat as well, but the other boat was more of a new experience for them, and they were younger as well. They like the freedom of the boat and that we move to a different place… they like being out in the wild… and I think if I had known I would have done it years ago. I wouldn't live in a house again. They are not what they are cracked up to be. They are cold, they are expensive, and you just exist to pay for your mortgage. But in a boat, it's great. You can move, you can go anywhere, you have that freedom… I don't really like going down to London. I've been down to London – to Limehouse. But I like it when it's remote and rural. I really like the River Stort. That has some lovely places. I'd really like to do what other people do in the summer. They wave goodbye in the spring and they say see you in the winter, and they go off and travel around the system, don't they?

It is not the extraordinary mobility across continents and peoples that breaks with the everyday that's most desirable for Alex. It is an everyday humble mobility of the linear canal setting, mooring up in different locations and getting on with work and leisure in this context – ideally, getting to do new things and experience new places within the constraints of the linear village. The small boat was described as affording more freedom. Constrained interior living spaces do not limit the sense of freedom and enjoyment, which is enhanced because of the ability to experience more of the outside and the ability to move across other spaces.

But for some boaters, central London is not the place of great geographical connection, the opportunity to sample all the amazing places otherwise denied, nor the place that remotely keeps changing and passing by while cruising through it. London is the place that encroaches antagonistically into the boater's life and physical and mental wellbeing, and the boat is the thing that keeps that person safe from it. Being on a boat means an individual can keep away while being close and be able to avoid people's intrusiveness while remaining relatively on public view. Living on a boat mediates not just a fully immersed life in the metropolis but also a life abstracted from it. The materiality of the linear village in its watery reality, and the social conditions associated with it, allows it to be but an illusion that an individual can go in and out. Alex is not very much interested in central London: 'I wouldn't want to take the kids to London. It's too many people, and it's rough, sadly… I tend to live in my own little bubble. In my own reality. I don't live in the real world.'

But the linear village can also simply be a through space. A location where someone can be a constant tourist. Literally passing through and not relating with anything. Place or people. A fleeting passer-by over and over in a repetitive manner. From Alex, I met Kenneth and Clara, who I often find moored near our boat, especially in the winter. They live on a wide-beam that is fully fitted in the style of a penthouse flat, and everything in it is catalogue-perfect. The boat is Kenneth's personal project. He has been working on his boat for about eight years. For five years, Kenneth and Clara have lived together. He is in his 60s and she is in her 50s – they are both retired. And while Kenneth's family is rooted around Essex and Hertford, Clara has family, friends and a home in Scotland. They are some of 'those people' who Alex says wave goodbye in the summer.

Both divorced and with children from previous marriages, Kenneth and Clara know exactly what they want. They want a boat (that is, a mobile space) and a flat (that is, comfortable place) all in one, somewhere pleasant in their own image and aesthetic criteria – a space where they do not need to renounce any home luxuries but that can be mobile and remote if need be. They claim to want to keep away from their large families, while at the same time having somewhere for them to visit. They like spending winters outside London on the Lee. In the spring, they travel very slowly through London from the Lee Navigation to Regent's Canal, do some sightseeing, some shopping, and some leisurely visits to the city for food and entertainment, before ending up cruising on the Thames for the summer. They use their boat as transportation in some ways too, when they moor in various locations in order to visit locally; this can be for special occasions like birthdays and anniversaries, or in order to keep a medical appointment or an appointment at the hairdresser's, etc. I interview them jointly, and this brings a completely new dynamic to the discussion, as the roles change progressively during our time chatting. 'We go to London all the time. We go through London once or twice a year. Normally we spend four or five months on the River Thames. We've been on quite a few rivers.'

But it is not so much the magnificent scenery or extraordinary adventure on the boat which matters. Talking about living on a boat, Kenneth says:

> How do I describe it? It's just a way of life. What governs your house existence it's because I was brought up in a house, I went to school, and then back to my home, and then I went from home to work, and you're on a treadmill. Aren't you? You're on a treadmill to earn money just to pay for your house.

Being liberated from certain conventional constraints, having the freedom boaters talk about – whether in work or not, any gender or age – comes down to very simple things in the end. It is the freedom to enjoy an everyday life. It comes from mobility and the water. Kenneth and Clara (just as with other boaters) have a regular itinerary. It comprises specific distances covered in the winter, enough to fulfil the two-week constant cruising requirement by the Canal & River Trust, but without venturing too far out, and the same for the summer, although covering a different part of the river. The fact that life is lived on water changes everything; the starting point for every day is somewhere else, and the perspective on town life comes from the outside (or inside water, out towards land).

> We don't like to moor up in towns. We're normally a bit out of town. We never moor up in Stanstead Abbotts… and when we go up to Ware [Hertfordshire], we are just in between Ware and Hertford, in the middle. So we have a lot of walking distance, and the reason is because we like the lifestyle. We like peace and quiet. If someone comes and moors next to you, it's easier to chat and get along with them. That, and that relations can't visit us so often.

With a decisive swipe, Kenneth has also described the benefits of being in a 'pod'-like condition. Cruising on the canal while not being connected, people struggling to locate you, friends losing interest and relatives alienated, can actually be a bonus. Water mediates a different kind of sociability. He talks about mooring outside Ware or Stanstead Abbotts. But the River Lee cuts through both places, and wherever people moor, their experience is marked by an outside perspective looking in, a non-fixed location, repetitive movement, limited access to amenities, disruption between the self and others, a set of possessions that travel with self, an immediate contact with nature and a dominance by the elements.

The encased state of being in a boat that moves, floats, cruises, slides on water, is so personal that is difficult to draw conclusions as to what the boundaries are. Douglas is a continuous cruiser who also has a flat in London. He is a 52-year-old manager working for alcohol dependency services in Tower Hamlets. Originally from north-west England but brought up in North Wales, he has lived all his adult life in London. For him, the boat is like camping on water. Unlike all other interviewees, he craved having a boat for ages before taking the decision to buy one. He had also fixated on his specific boat, which was on sale for a year before he bought it, and which, daily, he saw moored on the Regent's Canal on his way back and forth from work. He owns the oldest and most rundown boat (by far) of all interviewees.

The smell of diesel is strong. But so is the smell coming from the *macchinetta*, the moka pot, in action. The boat's interior is packed tight with cushions, pillows and duvets, and a fireplace, which is obviously a later addition to the boat and too big for the space, keeps it warm and dry. With most of its original features intact, it retains an authentic sense of being, dating from the canal-cruising days in the early to mid 1960s. Talking to the owner, an interesting and complex profile of the boat emerges in terms of the affective qualities that the boat has on the owner. He bought the boat from the previous owner for the same price as the earlier owner did 10 years ago, and both felt that they did well out of the sale. Now he has embarked on an adventure to make his boat even better than it ever was, and for him to live as a part-time boater, a better and more realised life. For Douglas, continuous cruising as practice is continuous holidays. It is also a project that offers a more physical involvement to survive than his management job, which is mentally fatiguing and people-focused. The logistics are no less complex, but the desire for the boat is upped by having the constant comparison between life on water and life on land. Douglas notes that:

> There's less demarcation between the rest of the world and yourself when you're on a boat. It may well all be in the mind, because of course you're on a boat in a navigation canal so are almost as imprisoned as you are in a flat. I suppose there's a kind of romantic idea that you can go anywhere, 'cause of course you can quite easily jump off the boat and go walking places around – and it's true in a

sense that I explored much more of London and Hertfordshire and Lee Valley than I would have done without a boat. So yes. There's the space thing… And there's the movement thing. Flats don't move anywhere. And if they do it's bad news, whereas boats move all the time which is good. It's more natural. Maybe it reminds us of our more primordial selves… But there's something nice about that. I think this is one of the extraordinary things about the boat, that it's a very different place. It doesn't seem to be entirely of the modern world. Perhaps that's because I don't have a TV and I don't have all those kinds of things on the boat. So even if you come from the centre of town and you come in the boat it feels as if you are somewhere else. It's an escape from the more extreme elements of urban living… Yes, I don't want to make it sound like having a TV is urban living but… Hustle and bustle, and traffic, and noise, and the anxiety, stresses of doing a job, commuting, being with people, public transport, the road systems, supermarkets, blocks of flats, car parks.

And so, in fact, all the material aspects that comprise the world of boating – the enclosed space and lack of comfort, movement when static and slow when moving – and everything that makes it difficult, is all that makes it extraordinary. Of course, Douglas, as a part-time boater, represents a group that is not very clearly defined. For a lot with lived-in-boats, the boat is not the only home. Douglas and others like him can split their time between being on water and being on land. And so the sense of leisure, holidays, staycation, break, whatever one calls it, is always there. It brings the current canal system back to the ideals of those post-war boaters and the establishment of the British Waterways Board, when the values of leisure and cruising overtook the need for function and labour, transportation and commerce.

To go back to Alicia, she is a boater who knows how to use her boat as transportation and as a home. So far, the boat as a mode of transport hasn't been in evidence, despite it being the most obvious use. The origin and whole purpose of the boat was to transport goods effectively. Where has that gone? For all the nostalgia and romanticism of canal heritage, it might have gone undercover, become implicit. Alicia likes the River Stort for the summer and Regent's Canal, Hertford Union and the River Lee around Hackney for the winter.

I loved Roydon, and I loved Sawbridgeworth. I love the whole of the Stort, it is amazing. When I am in London, actually, I go to Hackney

Wick quite a lot, because I've got a season ticket at West Ham, and now I can just bring the boat outside the stadium for when we've got a home game. So, during the winter, I was either on the Hertford Union, or I was up the River Lee. I'd go down the stadium on a Saturday and go back on a Sunday night. Do the water and toilet at the same time. There's an Elsan in Hackney Wick.

So, we are back where we started from at the beginning of this chapter. Predictably, for boaters, London is not just about opportunities and good living. It is also about water points and Elsans. They become, possibly, the biggest landmark of the capital in terms of importance. Without those bits of place, nothing is possible. And, therefore, a visit to the stadium makes more sense if it's accompanied by a visit to the water point. That's how the logistics are upped, and what action and materiality look like in everyday life on the water (figs 5.17–5.19).

Fig. 5.17 The River Stort is much loved by boaters, but only gets busy in the summer. River Stort, Roydon, Essex. Source: author

Fig. 5.18 My neighbour's early breakfast on the water. Lee Navigation, Clapton, north-east London. Source: author

Fig. 5.19 In January 2017 the Lee had frozen in certain parts, and continuous cruising was suspended. Stanstead Abbotts, east Hertfordshire. Source: author

The materiality of the water has its own agency, which is acted upon us as we take action and control in our daily lives. And, therefore, it is no surprise that I met Cecily through my own boat. She has become my most trusted boater friend exactly because of the link we have through the boat. In many ways, my respect for my boat is mirrored onto Cecily as her previous owner. In her early 40s and by far the most experienced boater out of all the people I've met on the canal, Cecily has been on a boat on the canal and the River Thames for over 10 years, most of the time as a continuous cruiser. She has always lived with her partner. Now she paints and she works part-time, and lives on a newly acquired boat permanently moored on Regent's Canal. She recounts her experiences with fondness but, no less, frankness regarding the rougher aspects of being a boater in London and also the marvel of an alternative way of the everyday. Just like all others I spoke to, she wasn't brought up on a boat but adopted the boater life as an adult. We have had lots of meetings, dinners, formal and informal interviews, some more successful than others, some more focused than others, and I have recorded a lot of her and her partner's experiences on the canal. Some days I just see her and wave across the towpath, as she is busy with boater activities.

> There's also hard work. There's a sense of freedom to it. On land, you're so connected to other people. You're inevitably stuck next to other people, you have other flats below you or above you. The amazing sense of freedom and movement, you can be liberated by being on the thing that is your home… There's a limit to what you can do. There's only so much time and space. The funny thing is you're more part of the world, you're sort of more observed by the world in more of a way, you're slightly more, you hear everybody's conversations when they walk down the towpath, everybody sees you, you can't leave the boat and go into the public sort of thoroughfare, you feel you are slightly more part of the world – which is nice, is not a bad thing – but wherever you moor up you instantly meet up with people, which is magic. You instantly know your neighbours for two weeks.

Cecily is one of those rare boaters who used to cruise along the whole length of the London canal system. But the canal has become significantly busier, and in her experience London neighbourhoods have changed remarkably since the earlier days of continuous cruising. West London, according to older boaters, was friendlier, and the Springfield area, out in the wilds, totally deserted. Boaters now feel less safe in west

London and generally avoid it, while they scrabble for space and double-moor around the Springfield area. But pubs, and markets, and shops are always landmarks. Cecily tells me:

> You would remember certain favourites, but I suppose they would only be favourites because they were near to your mooring. They are your favourite shop – and I would go there more, or I would cycle up. If I was in Victoria Park, I'd go up to Dalston 'cause my favourite Turkish supermarket there is on Ridley Road. I used to always make a track when I was near there. Or when I was in Ladbrook Grove, I would always make sure to go across to Portobello Road, 'cause there's all those lovely Spanish shops. Borough Market, when we were on the river. We were by Tower Bridge, but eventually we had to move, sadly. Before that, even the engine wouldn't run. It's terrible isn't it? But that was different. 'Cause the river is an entirely different thing again. It's so magical having that thing – every day going with the tide. You hear the water coming in, it marked your day. Whenever high tide was, it even affected your television channels, your cooking; I always remember the triangular cakes. It was irresistible.

Cecily's experience of London tells us that every locality can be local when living on the waterways, because places are connected by water. With the local came habits and routines that are not too dissimilar to living on land, except for the fact that they are mobile and changing, mostly in a repetitive and circular way. But Patrick is more critical about his life on the canal. Like everyone else, he exults in the value of feeling unbounded and free despite all the complaining that relates to a sense of isolation through cruising. And so, movement is in the context of everyday action. It is made special by being ordinary boater routine.

> The thing I like most about boating is the cruising, is the independence, is the movement, that I am not stuck in one area, and also is a chance to find a nice place, a new place where is quiet and peaceful. But also the river is changing, so I wouldn't want to be stuck in one place. So I go back next year, and, it's horrible, they have built a racetrack. It's a way of moving with the river and not being trapped.

Action and movement on the river is not a constant in a trivial sense. It doesn't designate a frantic state of being. There's tranquillity, and change is mostly to do with immersion in an environment which – urban or rural – forms part of the human being-in-the-world experience.

Conclusion

Cutting through London's urban landscape runs a historic canal system that flows and connects London to the rest of the country, and which is very much in use today. Linking distinct and seemingly unconnected parts of London, which look like a series of villages, it is described as a 'linear village' with its own dynamic, unmistakable character. It is notable for its non-fixity, the non-static aspect of those dwelling on it, and its being bounded and unbounded by its element: water. This character has gone through many changes, most dramatically after World War 2. The waterways carrying coal, milk, malt and sand became the rivers and canals of holidays and self-discovery, making them the places to get away to, places of social activity, physical engagement with landscape and peaceful relaxation. More than a mode of transport, commerce or industry, the waterways offer a connection to the past in order to construct a more meaningful present and a vision of a healthy future.

And ultimately, the canals transformed into homes and an integral part of the mundane, less sensational everyday life of the city. The London canals are still a working space and a private place. In many ways, the canal has a history of life that merges the public with the private and this is carried through to today, first within commerce and transport, then a combination of leisure and heritage, and as a form of dwelling: tourists, travellers, visitors, holidaymakers, people playing sports games, people out and about, mix with the private world of a personal life of washing, cooking, toilets, rubbish, watching TV or listening to music – all sorts of daily activities. Continuous cruising, although a political decision by the British government, became a lifestyle on water with particular implications for London and urbanism that added another layer of complexity to the lives of those for whom the canal is their home. In this way, the canal is still characterised by movement. Some of its romanticism is alive, as is the feeling of lack of comfort and feeling of being marginalised even when in the centre of cultural and urban action. The attachment to the boat framing the outside world never ceases to offer an alternative sense of being-in-the-world – a perspective that is physical, poetic and metaphoric, and an affective quality that involves all the senses.

> Past experiences feed into the present, anticipating the future. Our temporal experience 'colours' the manner in which we understand the present from the lived perspective of the body. This is always limited, ambiguous, shifting and changing: some aspects of landscape become foregrounded at one temporal moment and fall into the background at another. Embodied perception shifts and changes, is always in flux and is related to our interactions with sentient others, human or nonhuman. (Tilley and Cameron-Daum 2017:9)

As such, landscape and the built environment does not and cannot exist apart from the events and activities with which it is implicated. It is physically and socially produced (Tilley 1994:10). Heidegger and Merleau-Ponty stressed important ontological characteristics of the relationship between inhabited space and social being-in-the-world. Spaces receive their essential being from locations and not from 'space' (Heidegger 1972:332). If 'dwelling', in Heideggerian terms, forms a primordial part of that which is to be human, this necessarily requires a consideration of the body as a privileged vantage point from which the world is apprehended. 'The experiential landscape is always limited, ambiguous, shifting and changing; some aspects of landscape become foregrounded at one temporal moment and fall into the background at another' (Tilley and Cameron-Daum 2017:9). In Lefebvre's imaginary survey of the everyday, the point is to discover not just how we live but also how we imagine we live lives up to the reality of it, and what does it mean for the 'art of living'. Concerned about what makes life meaningful, Lefebvre wrote rather emphatically, 'No! our lives are still unrealized, and our consciousness is false.' And in pursuit of meaning, he suggested a survey of the everyday, because 'nowadays, we do not know how we live' (Lefebvre 2008:195), to find out what happens in the life of an individual and how the trivial when taken socially is not trivial at all. Somewhat melodramatic in that remark, but forceful enough, it is a reminder that the everyday – and how we live it – is the source of everything in doing and thinking that is special, highly individual and meaningful. Some decades later, the proposal has been taken up on an ever-increasing scale and is currently becoming all the more diverse, especially when dealing with questions of place, heritage, social identity and urbanism (Billig 1995; Bourdieu 1977; Massey 2005; Sheller 2017; Swyndedouw 2004; Urry 2002 [1990]). It challenges the idea that space is a container for action and brings in a dynamic production of space that has to do with spatial processes and relational thinking about spatial experiences. The study of an ongoing production of space into social theory is an embodied approach to mobility that involves the visual by paying a closer attention to all the senses (Adey et al. 2014; Sheller 2017; Sheller and Urry 2006). Through a materialist approach and a stress on materiality of landscape there is an emphasis on being there, observing and interacting. The London waterways, canal system or the 'linear village' as urban landscape, both historical and as a lived experience, are involved in action rather than separate from it, hidden and invisible in many parts of the city until they suddenly appear, are marked by the water's own movement and that of those who dwell on it.

As Sheller states: 'all the world seems to be on the move' (Sheller 2017:627). Mobility is a key practice and value of our time. But it's wrong to identify mobility with freedom, because not only are attempts made to control and restrict – a characteristic theme of the everyday life on London waterways – but the way mobility is experienced is contradictory, contingent and often antagonistic to the built environment, because what is described as a linear village can mean a more integrated experience of the city by bypassing all the elements that would make London prohibitive for a vast group of people. The constraints of limited finances are less repressive on the water. Moreover, the real and physical proximity to desired spaces makes London more accessible, more friendly, more enjoyable. This can lead to a more profound sense of belonging in the city and identifying with it. It is often experienced as material freedom. And yet for many boaters, there is an almost nostalgic sense of leaving London behind while slowly cruising ahead: the boaters distant, surrounded by their own possessions and moving with them, in some cases in a contradictory relationship with the city.

The boater's neighbourhood is not a fixed place, but it alternates every two weeks, so the real reference to his or her dwelling is the towpath and the shops and parks that line the waterways. The same with the people the boater connects with as neighbours. They too alternate as new people moor up or move away, or as the boater continues with cruising. The name of the boat and the boat itself is a calling card. The boater can recognise who is moored nearby, and relationships can themselves be fleeting; they go with the flow. But the sense of belonging is rooted in the route of travel and is as solid as it is distinctive. While London looms big with its many complexities, boaters can feel overwhelmed by the unfamiliarity of the new places, mixed emotions about the move, and resentful of the sheer numbers of people. As an antidote, continuous cruisers choose to follow a routine in their movement on the canal.

Mooring in a repetitive pattern, returning to favourite spots along the cut, and following a seasonal plan that means some familiarity and a routine is preserved in the everyday, reverses an impersonal relationship with London into an intimate canal-based one that is transformed into a series of villages contained in an all-encompassing linear village, much of it experienced through the confines of the boat. In this way, the outside becomes the inside and the inside is outside in public view and within public engagement as a boat cruises the canal, goes through a lock, or is moored up by the bank. The linear village of London, and its traffic, change dramatically from urban areas to the more rural parts and the outskirts of the city. The constant materiality of the boat not only changes the environment in which it is found and which it moves through, but it is itself changed by the environment as parks change into private houses or council estates, houses change into clubs, bars and restaurants, fields into meadows, and car parks into industrial spaces. But much more needs to be known and understood about the peculiarity of life lived on the canals and rivers of London that give the city a special profile historically and in the present. As the linear village changes, there is a sense of flow, but most significantly a pervasive feeling of not being bound down by one's circumstances, and that a good mooring spot, and a good opportunity, will be nailed even if provisory.

Methodological note

Within anthropology and phenomenology, a number of studies are arguing for an embodied knowledge of the natural landscape and of the built environment through people's different perspectives and the sensuous experience (Ingold 2013; Lund 2005, Rhys-Taylor 2013; Tilley and Cameron-Daum 2017). The body becomes the primary research tool in studying how meaning is ascribed to things and experiences. Embodiment is a consideration of spatio-temporal relationships; space and time are not outside social relations (Tilley and Cameron-Daum 2017). With participant observation, the emphasis is knowing from the inside (Ingold 2013; Tilley and Cameron-Daum 2017). It's about how being 'there' relates to being-in-the-world as not an abstraction. In particular, urbanism is increasingly understood as a complex emergent global system of networked connections, dominant mobility regimes and critical counter practices (Dudley et al. 2012; Newman and Kenworthy 2015). Traffic congestion, air pollution, demographic explosion and inequality underlie an urban condition that shifts our understanding of what cities are and how they are lived in. It calls for an urgent new approach and a reconceptualisation of the study of dwelling and movement within the urban landscape.

Ethnographically, the research is based on participant observation over a two-year period and on 20 formally structured interviews. During this period, I travelled up and down the whole of the Lee Navigation throughout the year and the River Stort in summer, the Hertford Union Canal several times and through to the east end of the Regent's Canal in spring, summer and autumn but not in winter. The boaters I interviewed were fairly evenly representative of all ages, and equally of both sexes, in couples and single, working full-time, part-time, students, self-employed, retired, unemployed, in volunteering, in commerce, engineering, the arts and crafts, humanities or just cruising, and mostly middle and lower middle class white British. Their names have been changed. None were Asian, African or minority ethnic (i.e. BAME) or foreign (except for myself). A small number of interviewees were LGBTQ.

Predictably, I started the research with several false ideas. The first was that, by taking continuous cruising at face value, if everyone and everything is moving and continuously cruising, then I don't need to move very much myself. Initially, and very naively, I thought that surely by next year I should be in Birmingham or at least maybe Oxford. This is a misconception I shall examine here and try to unpack how it comes about and what it means for its wider implications regarding motility and the sense of freedom associated with living on water. Two years later, I was still on the Regent's Canal and the Lee Navigation. Being a continuous cruiser – though not full-time – I had, unknowingly, already acquired the relevant habits. At that stage, my thinking was: I'll get on with my continuous cruising regardless, and I'll catch everyone as they go by. They will also tell me about all the exciting things they have been up to in all other parts of the navigation. The inland waterways offer so many opportunities, as the river stretches from east to west and west to east. It is going north to the Midlands from the west, and Hertfordshire and Essex to the east. As it happened, I often encountered the same cluster of boaters at their specific locations.

The boaters I have chatted to were either introduced to me by other boaters, so they may be loosely related through friendship or family ties, or are boaters I approached walking along the towpath. Some of our conversations are included in detail in this chapter. This random way of approach is a very good system. Some I subsequently met again purely by chance or river destiny, others I totally lost touch with (though no doubt I'll meet them again if they are on the river), and a couple of boaters who

I kept bumping into I became friendly with. And sometimes, the same boats would have different owners. Some interviews were unexpected and others that were planned failed or took longer to materialise than was useful. That's the nature of the canal. Bowles (2015) discusses at length the very specific problems that he encountered as an anthropologist researching the London canals through participant observation and interviews, theoretically – in reference to anthropological literature – and how it worked out for him in practice. He questions how you pitch a tent on the water. Everything and everyone is mobile. Which anthropological literature can be adapted to analyse life on the country's canals and rivers?

Moreover, the research was conducted during the winter months (and written up in the summer and autumn), which makes it extremely difficult to meet boaters and formally arrange interviews. Boaters are either closed in with the curtains drawn and sleeping by 8 o'clock (or so it seems, and they say so themselves), or out working, shopping or visiting friends in town (in order to have showers or do their washing). Because the towpath is dark by 5 o'clock in the evening, there is hardly anyone about. If there is anyone, they most likely are concerned with boater tasks, making a fire, cooking or attending to daily chores, rather than talking to anthropologists about their daily life. For those who find themselves with a broken engine in a marina, life is slightly more sociable but rather more stressful, as the boat is home, transport and identity all rolled into one.

References

Adey, P. and Bissell, D. (2010). 'Mobilities, Meetings and Futures: An Interview with John Urry'. In *Environment and Planning D.: Society and Space* 28: 1–16.

Adey, P., Bissell, D., Hannam, K., Merriman, P. and Sheller, M. (eds). 2014. *The Routledge Handbook of Mobilities*. London: Routledge.

Beck, U. and Sznaider, N. 2006. 'Unpacking Cosmopolitanism for the Humanities and Social Sciences: A Research Agenda'. In *British Journal of Sociology* 57(1):1–23.

Bialski, P. and Otto, B. 2015. 'Collective Low-Budget Organising and Low Carbon Futures: A Interview with John Urry', *Ephemera: Theory and Politics in Organisation* 15(1):221–8.

Billig, M. 1995. *Banal Nationalism*. London: Sage.

Bourdieu, P. 1977. *Outline of a Theory of Practice*. Cambridge: Cambridge University Press.

Bowles, B. 2015. *Waterways: Becoming an Itinerant Boat-Dweller on the Canals and Rivers of South East England*. PhD thesis, Division of Anthropology, Brunel University.

Burton, A. 1995 [1989]. *The Great Days of the Canals*. Twickenham: Tiger Books.

Canal & River Trust 2017a) 'Enjoy the Waterways'. http://canalrivertrust.org.uk/enjoy-the-waterways

Canal & River Trust 2017b) 'National Consultations'. http://canalrivertrust.org.uk/national-consultations

Cresswell, T. 2006. *On the Move: Mobility in the Modern Western World*. London and New York: Routledge, Taylor & Francis.

Dudley, G., Geels, F., Kemp, R., Dudley, G. and Lyons, G. 2012. *Automobility in Transition? A Socio-Technical Analysis of Sustainable Transport*. London: Routledge.

Featherstone, M. 1993. 'Global and Local Cultures'. In *Mapping the Futures: Local Cultures, Global Change*, edited by J. Bird, B. Curtis, T. Putnam, G. Robertson and L. Tickner. London: Sage, pp 169.

Hadfield, C. 1981 [1968]. *The Canal Age*. Newton Abbot: David and Charles Publishing.

Hannerz, U. 1990. 'Cosmopolitans and Locals in World Culture'. In M. Featherstone *Global Culture: Nationalism, Globalisation and Modernity*. London: Sage.

Harvey, D. 1989. *The Condition of Post Modernity: An Enquiry into the Origins of Cultural Change*. London: Keith Woodward and John Paul Jones III.

Harvey, D. 1993. 'From Space to Place and Back Again'. In Bird, J. et all (eds) *Mapping the Futures: Local Cultures, Global Change*. 3–29. London: Routledge.

Heidegger, M. 1972 [1927]) *Being and Time*. London: SCM Press.

Hewison, R. 1987) *The Heritage Industry: Britain in a Climate of Decline*. London: Methuen Publishing.

Ingold, T. 2013. *Making: Anthropology, Archaeology, Art and Architecture*. Abingdon: Routledge.

Jerome, J.K. 1953 [1989]. *Three Men in a Boat. To Say Nothing of the Dog*. London: J.M. Dent and Sons Ltd.

Jonas, A. 2015. 'Rethinking Mobility at the Urban–Transportation–Geography Nexus'. In *Transportation and Mobility in the Production of Urban Space*, edited by J. Cidell and D. Prytherch, 281–93. London: Routledge.

Larsen, J. and Urry, J. 2011. 'Gazing and Performing'. *Environment and Planning D: Society and Space 2011* 29:1110–25.

Lefebvre, H. 2008 [1947]. *Critique of Everyday Life*. London: Verso.

Lowenthal, D. 1985. *The Past is a Foreign Country*. Cambridge: Cambridge University Press.

Lund, K. 2005. 'Seeing in Motion and the Touching Eye: Walking over Scotland's Mountains', *Etnofoor: Anthropological Journal* 18:85–110.

Lynch, K. 1972. *What time is this place?* Cambridge, Massachusetts: MIT Press.

MacCannell, D. 1999. *The Tourist: A New Theory of the Leisure Class*. Berkeley: University of California Press.

Marx, K. 1975 [1833–4]. 'Economic and Philosophical Manuscripts'. In *Early Writings*. Harmondsworth: Penguin.

Massey, D. 1991. 'A Global Sense of Place'. *Marxism Today*. 35(6): 24–29.

Massey, D. 2005. *For Space*. London: Sage.

Meyrowitz, J. 1985. *No Sense of Place: The Impact of Electronic Media on Social Behaviour*. New York: Oxford University Press.

Newman P. and Kenworthy, J. 2015. *The End of Automobile Dependency: How Cities are Moving Beyond Car-Based Planning*. Washington DC: Island Press.

Rhys-Taylor, A. 2013. 'The Essences of Multiculture: A Sensory Exploration of an Inner-City Street Market'. *Global Studies in Culture and Power*. 20(4), Ethnography, Diversity and Urban Space. London: Taylor-Francis, pp 393–406.

Press Association, 2011. 'Tesco Threatens Legal Action Over OFT Dairy Price-Fixing Fine', *The Guardian* 10 August.

Rolt, L.T.C. 1999 [1944]. *Narrowboat*. Stroud: Sutton Publishing

Sheller, M. and Urry, J. 2006. 'The New Mobilities Paradigm', *Environment and Planning A* 38(2):207–26.

Sheller, M. 2017. 'From Spatial Turn to Mobilities Turn'. In *Current Sociology Monograph* 65(4): 623–39.

Stiglitz, J. 2004. *The Roaring Nineties: A New History of the World's Most Prosperous Decade*. New York, London: Norton

Swyndedouw, E. 2004. *Social Power and the Urbanisation of Water – Flows of Power*. Oxford: Oxford University Press.

Szerszynski, B. and Urry, J. 2006. 'Visuality, Mobility and the Cosmopolitan', *The British Journal of Sociology* 57(1):113–31.

Tilley, C. 1994. *A Phenomenology of Landscape: Places, Paths and Monuments*. Oxford: Berg.

Tilley, C. 2002. 'Metaphor, materiality and interpretation.' In Buchli, V (ed) *The Material Culture Reader*. Oxford: Berg, 23–6.
Tilley, C. 2004. *The Materiality of Stone*. Oxford: Berg.
Tilley, C. and Cameron-Daum, K. 2017. *An Anthropology of Landscape: The Extraordinary in the Ordinary*. London: UCL Press.
Urry, J. 2002 [1990]. *The Tourist Gaze*. London: Sage.
Urry, J. 2007. *Mobilities*. Cambridge: Polity.
Urry, J. 2011. *Climate Change and Society*. Cambridge: Polity.

Part II
The public sphere

6
'We're all mad down here.'
Liminality and the carnivalesque in Smithfield Meat Market

Caroline Wilson

The cutting room is a hanging forest of carcasses: rose-pink and off-white; violet rumps hung before white panels. Against the urgent trill of fridges and the cold sound of rushing air, the hard metal surfaces resound with the rattle of overhead rails, the dull thumps of cleavers, with whistling and song, in raucous call-and-answer.

In the frenzy of busy nights, a lamb is undone in three minutes, from strung-up carcass to bits of body in bins. The cutters know all the bones, how the curves of flesh conceal them. The knife barely needs to seek them. Unhook the lamb from behind you, cold and stiff, and slam it onto the scored wooden chopping board with a bone-shuddering thud. Hold it against you, knife downwards and flowing along the shoulder-blade, hack the sinews, sling it into the metal bin with a cold gong-peal sound. Around, rotate, hacksaw to ribcage with a dry rasp, slap-slap, bin. Toss the trailing sinews and kidneys to the floor, cleaver to spine, count the ribs down, with thumps growing louder and sharper until the spine is severed, repeat through the night.

Introduction

It is the bone-white towers of Smithfield that first catch your eye. From afar they promise something grander or more holy, echoing with their neoclassical style the nearby domes of the Central Criminal Court and St Paul's Cathedral. Drawing nearer, onto Charterhouse Street or West Smithfield (fig. 6.1), there is some edge of sadness to the towers, barely

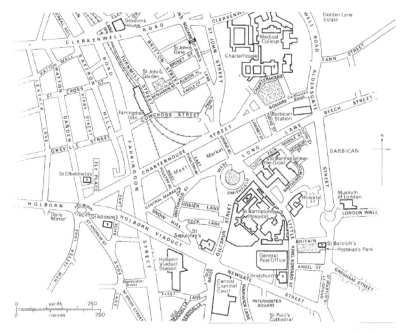

Fig. 6.1 Smithfield and its surroundings. Source: adapted from Forshaw (1990)

discernible: streaks of dirt, rust, crumbling stone. Their boast of splendour rings hollow, they preside over a building that was once grand but is now grubby and battered, a jumbled mismatch of buildings. Modern parts are clumsily affixed to the Victorian main market (MM) building: huge numbered metal doors for loading, a filthy glass awning obscuring decorative stone arches overhead. Downhill, concrete arches join the older building to Poultry Market (PM), with its strange, dark, looming beehive windows in black brick and greying concrete (fig. 6.2).

In Cowcross Street, it's all pristine stone pavements, perfect, smooth brick and the glib language of commerce and advertising enticing wealthy customers into expensive cafes for spiced chai lattes and superfood salads. As you cross the street to MM, the city fabric changes. The pavements have a dark, tarry gleam, streaked with dirt, the gutter filled with polystyrene cups and cigarette ends. It's haunted with an uneasy smell, uncannily familiar, that lingers in corners and hits you through open doors in gulps of cold air: the pale smell of raw meat. Between windows blank and blind with dust, with bright-painted cast iron gratings, the red-brick walls are worn, the Portland stone dark and grubby (fig. 6.3). The walls are plastered with warning signs speaking

Fig. 6.2 The entire market as seen from west Charterhouse Street. General Market (GM) is in the foreground, followed by Poultry Market (PM), then Main Market (MM) in the background. Source: author

Fig. 6.3 Main market building, daytime, from Charterhouse Street. Source: author

a different language to those in Cowcross Street: a language of brute functionality, ringing with absent threat: 'Do not reverse without an authorised banksman!' 'Caution! Forklift trucks operating!' The anxiety reaches a pitch of greater urgency around the loading bays, their metal doors guarded by a regiment of battered yellow bollards. 'LOOK LEFT' the road markings cry, criss-crossing in alarming yellow, inverting: 'LOOK RIGHT'. Moving along, the walls are marked with traces of another world. Names are carved into the brick, the stone smeared with handprints, cigarette ends inserted into the building's seams. The building is charged with a feeling of absent presence.

Empty and silent by day, the building comes alive at night. Approaching the building at 2a.m., its busiest time, beyond the sleepy yellow streetlights there's a harsher light – fluorescent, with a steely purity – a cold vitality that's underlined by the sounds: a chorus of reversing sounds, a drumroll of trundling engines. Closer still, you can see that the building is encircled by rows of white vans; you can hear a clatter and shiver of metal trolleys, and the leitmotif of Smithfield: a resounding slam of metal on metal, wood on concrete, echoed by a yell: 'OI!'

Anthropological studies of markets in large urban contexts often treat markets as paradigmatic of something in wider society. Geertz, Geertz and Rosen's 1978 study *Suq: The Bazaar Economy in Sefrou* treats the bazaar like a magnifying glass through which ethnicity, class and various dynamics underpinning Moroccan society are highlighted and intensified by high-stake situations of buying and selling. Likewise, Bestor's (2004) study *Tsukiji: The Fish Market at the Centre of the World* explores how economic institutions are shaped by socio-cultural forces in wider Japanese society, and how the market in turn shapes Japanese food culture. The study shifts dynamically between intensely local details of Tsukiji and much broader values surrounding food, drawing connections between both (see the introduction to this book). A similar study of Smithfield would certainly be possible. Yet market workers (MWs) do not see Smithfield as the centre of the world, or as microcosmic of anything in wider society; indeed, they pride themselves on Smithfield's contrast with its surroundings, describing it as 'a different world' and 'a time warp', where outside rules do not apply. Following in this spirit, this study will explore Smithfield in all its local, specific detail, to examine what makes Smithfield unique in itself rather than representative of other socio-cultural dynamics.

A night in Smithfield

The night begins at around 10p.m. Shop men arrive to unload deliveries and load orders for larger customers. During the busiest times, lorries and vans are blocking the roads, and the pavements are teeming with life, meat is moving inwards and outwards, loading andunloading, boxes piled onto pallets, speared by forklift trucks and spun away.

Lorries from slaughterhouses reverse onto the loading bays (fig. 6.4). Up on a red platform, surrounded by a crazy complex of buttons and machinery (fig. 6.5), the drivers help MWs sling bundles of carcasses onto a slow-moving conveyor belt of hook rails, which lowers them into the dim grey-metal service corridors (fig. 6.6). Here, Davey the rail man guides them to their respective shops, sending them swaying and rattling along a dense network of overhead rails with a shove of his metal shepherd's crook.

From around midnight, the cutters are ready in their cutting room (fig. 6.7), a refrigerated box of white panels scattered with exclamatory warning signs, with a cold that cuts to your toes, and a low ceiling with hooks and rails. During busy times, it's noisy and crowded; duck to avoid a line of carcasses trundling towards you on rails; keep your wits about you, ready to answer the abuse flying your way ('Get back in the ugly shop, you ugly bastard!'). People wander in and out with trolleys, appear framed in the doorway briefly, exchange yells, disappear. Some are old friends, others unknown ('Right, who are you, and what do you want?'). On busy nights, the tempo is ramped up to an incredible speed: Rob rampages about the tiny room, slinging bags of meat, batting carcasses out of his way, hauling them about in a lumbering dance, organising orders, arguing with customers ('No, you're all done mate!' 'You've had four, and that was it.' 'No, you're the one that's fucking about, not me.'). He joins in with banter, cackling heartily, scolds inexperienced workers: 'OI! ANTON! USE A FUCKING GLOVE!'

The shop men scrabble about in the bins, bent double as the cutters throw meat at them, groping bare-handed at cold, soft lamb shoulders, dripping trailing bleeding adhesive bits of flesh, hands saturated with the homely smell of lamb fat, gripping greasy forelegs below the elbow, tumbling them together into plastic-smelling bags.

With your back to the service corridor, pick your way across the cutting room, around carcasses, past quarters of beef and hatstands of smiling pigs' heads, through a glass door and you're into the shop front (fig. 6.8). The shops are boxed off from each other with white and stainless-steel panels that gleam in the harsh white tube-lights. At some stalls, the

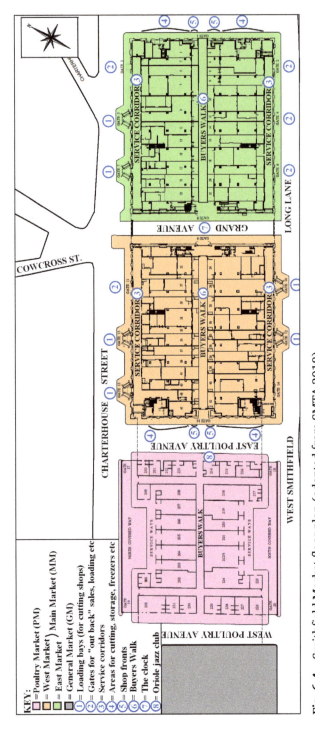

Fig. 6.4 Smithfield Market floor plan (adapted from SMTA 2018)

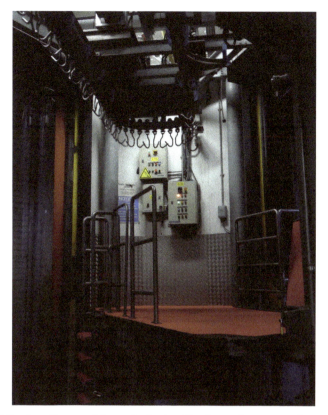

Fig. 6.5 Loading machinery in the loading bays. Source: author

Fig. 6.6 Service corridor. Source: author

Fig. 6.7 A cutting room. Source: author

Fig. 6.8 Shop fronts. The purple pillars of the original building are still visible on the right. Source: author

white is broken with bucolic backdrops, images of cows grazing green pastures, cooked meat artfully presented. The salesmen arrive at 2a.m. and arrange the displays in glass cabinets: trays of pale-smelling chicken legs, lamb breasts marbled pink and white. Gleaming plucks and hearts, burgundy-brown or the deepest red, tripe with its earthy stench, piles of sheep's heads: skin-off, red and madly grinning through dull blue eyes; skin on, hard and yellowish, tongues twisted in agony.

Although bright labels boast special offers, pitching is unheard of among salesmen. Most hard-sell activity is limited to mobile phone conversations and text-message exchanges with large customers; salesmen remain reserved with the customers in Buyers Walk, serving them in an almost pointedly unhurried fashion ('I like to make 'em wait. Makes us look popular,' a salesman winked at me as he refused my help in serving the gathering queue). Still, it's a bustle even out here, with thin tinny music, yells and swearing across the fridge sounds.

And out, past the glass cabinets, you're in Buyers Walk, with customers sauntering and shuffling, MWs rattling and trundling past with trolleys and pump-trucks, salesmen dancing in the aisles. Downhill towards the market's centre, you'll come out in Grand Avenue, underneath the clock that stands as synecdoche for the whole market, the market's heart. Grand Avenue is lined with elaborate cast iron grating, lorry height, bold in green and lilac-blue, vaulting overhead in star-studded arches. Most striking are the iron gates to Buyers Walk, thrust open now: blue, purple, green, gold. Lions with tongues protruding, sea shells, a leafy twisting burst of gaudy colour (fig. 6.9).

A constable (security guard) gave me a tactile tour of these gates. Running his hands along them, he showed me the workmanship, where they were joined, where they were broken. 'Try to push it. See how heavy it is.' I felt the immense, cold resistance against my own force. 'Ya see?' he beamed, triumphantly. He summoned me to a room behind the office, where parts of the gate were lovingly kept while waiting to be re-affixed. He handled each one tenderly, passed it to me to show me the weight.

From under the clock, looking back along Buyers Walk, above the rows of stalls in white and metal, you can see the original structure again: lilac-blue and magenta pillars and arches holding aloft the wooden slatted ceiling, 'Like the upside-down hull of a ship,' said a shop man. It's painted a different kind of white to the white below, with skylight windows that let in the pale light of dawn when the night comes to an end and everyone is exhausted, tempers are frayed, the avenues are lined with rubbish, and everyone wants to go home. And at the furthest point

Fig. 6.9 The gate at the entrance to Buyer's Walk, seen from Grand Avenue. Source: author

at each end, plaques commemorate the market's completion, echoing the gates in twisting leaves: 'Completed 1868' (fig. 6.10).

People would often gesture to this date when telling me the building's history or when joking about a fellow MW's age ('He remembers when this was built!'). But for most MWs, Smithfield's story begins hundreds of years before this date. Davey dreams of making a film about Smithfield. It would open with the excesses of Bartholomew Fair, with people being burned, before fading to modern times: a Smithfield cutter (and professional boxer) receives a blow to the chin from his friend and collapses to the floor. He regains consciousness, laughs. 'What the fuck you do that for?' This sense of seamless continuity between past and present violence and laughter is widely shared among MWs; for them, Smithfield today continues this tradition of lawlessness and wild abandon.

History

Attested in 1174 as 'a smooth field,' where livestock was sold, the market was originally situated outside the city walls, sharing its site with other institutions, industries and activities that could not be tolerated inside

Fig. 6.10 The top part of the building, seen from East Market looking downwards towards West Market. Source: author

the walls: St Bartholomew's Hospital, Newgate Prison, slaughtering, tanning and prostitution. As MWs are keen to relate, Smithfield was the site of numerous executions, most notably the gruesome death of William Wallace and, later, the burning of heretics, with some 200 being burned at Smithfield during the reign of Mary I (Forshaw 1990:39). Smithfield continued as a site for society's unwanted even after the city overspilled its original walls and absorbed Smithfield into its heart. Smithfield was notorious for its slums (or 'rookeries'), which were eventually cleared in the 1840s (Forshaw 1990:163).

Smithfield continued to trade in live meat until the mid-nineteenth century, until it was deemed a place of such 'cruelty, filth, effluvia, pestilence, impiety, horrid language, danger, disgusting and shuddering sights' (Maslen 1843:16) that it could no longer be tolerated in such a central position. Eventually, the live market was moved to Islington and the current building was built in 1868 to house a carcass market. Designed by Sir Horace Jones, its open ironwork allowed for the circulation of air, which kept the building cool and was ideal for keeping meat fresh (Forshaw 1990:79). General Market (GM), now abandoned, was added in 1899 (Forshaw 1990:83), and the brutalist Poultry Market

(PM) was completed in 1963, after the original PM was destroyed by fire. Some MWs remember: 'They said it was only a little fire. We come back the next day and the building was gone!'

The most significant event in living memory is the 1990s refurbishment. The market's interior, once open, was divided into boxed-off shops; the number of shops was significantly reduced to make way for refrigerated storage rooms and freezers. The loading process was mechanised, making pullabacks and pitchers redundant (see table 6.1). The market was made accessible to forklift trucks, so that bummarees (meat carriers), already dwindling in number since meat started arriving precut or boxed, and therefore easier to carry, became a 'dying breed' (see Kerridge 1988; Forshaw 1990).

Although there is some tension between 'guv'nors' and other workers, all MWs are united against a common enemy. Central to the market's sense of identity and place in the world is the age-old rivalry with the City of London (CoL), which owns and rents the land and sets down regulations which are largely ignored. The CoL wryly acknowledges this struggle: 'Smithfield has its own code of conduct quite apart from that laid down by regulations' (Metcalf 1991:159). The threat of being closed and moved out of town has always overshadowed the market; the CoL is clear that 'closing the markets and thereby releasing the area for development would produce a vast influx of funds to City's cash' (Metcalf 1991:161). Older MWs remember being discouraged from working at Smithfield years ago: 'They said it would be gone soon.' This constant sense of impending doom, of being out of place and unwanted, is crucial to MWs sense of identity, as will be explored throughout this chapter.

Smithfield: workers and trade

The typical 'old boy' MW is male, white, working class, based in Essex or Kent, and originates from London, able to boast of his cockney credentials: 'This is a little pocket of the old East London!' However, there has always been more diversity at Smithfield than some would like to admit. Billy, a cutter, frequently remarked that 'It was all whites up here. No blacks, no foreigners...' but as others point out, there have always been well-established foreign-born or non-white MWs ('Well, he was more English than black,' says Billy of one such well-known figure). 'I'm still out on my own though,' admits one MW of south Asian heritage. 'They try to fire me, I just pull the race card!' Now, several workers in

Table 6.1 Smithfield market workers

Employer	Job title	Role	Hours (approx.)	Notes
individual shops	'guv'nor'	managing director, senior salesman	undefined	viewed with ambivalence; considered a category apart from other MWs; earn a lot (upwards of £50,000 p.a.)
	salesman: shop front	take payments, serve customers, write receipts, take orders	2a.m.–8a.m.	most senior of shop employees
	salesmen: out back	as above, but work with larger orders at the back door of shops; also manage shop men in loading and unloading	2a.m.–8a.m.	
	cashiers	take payments; handle cash	2a.m.–8a.m.	many are female
	shop men	load, unload, transport, various odd jobs	11p.m.–8a.m.	more junior, worse paid
	cutters	cut whole carcasses into smaller pieces	11p.m.–6a.m.	
	butchers	cut meat as required	11p.m.–6a.m.	
self-employed	bummarees	gather large orders from across the market into one place for collection by customers	2a.m.–8a.m.	remembered with affection; now only approximately eight on the market
City of London	railmen/ hookmen	guide carcasses into appropriate stalls using overhead rails; ensure shops have enough meat hooks	9p.m.–2a.m.	

(Continued table 6.1)

(Continued table 6.1)

Employer	Job title	Role	Hours (approx.)	Notes
	cleaners		various shifts over 24 hours	many are from Nigeria; most have little relationship with market workers
	constabulary	security guards	various shifts over 24 hours	now have limited powers; mostly well liked by market workers
self-employed/ individual shops	pullabacks	brought carcasses from backs of lorries to front of lorries for unloading		redundant since refurbishment
self-employed/ individual shops	pitchers	brought carcasses from lorries to respective shops		redundant since refurbishment

various occupational divisions are foreign born. Many are from southern and eastern Europe; other nationalities include Brazilian, Vietnamese, South Korean and Kurdish-Cypriot. Many are accepted and loved, others less so.

Most women on the shop floor are cashiers, with about four female salesmen (MWs never use the term saleswoman) and one woman constable. No women work in other occupational divisions; indeed, the 2012 BBC documentary *The Meat Market: Inside Smithfield* notoriously documents the plight of the only-ever female shop man, who left complaining of sexism.

Customers who carry out transactions 'out back' are businesses collecting large orders: kebab shops and some well-known restaurant chains. Customers in Buyers Walk are generally of two types: high-street butchers, generally from a similar background to MWs and well-versed in Smithfield banter, and members of the public, with whom relations are notably strained. They argue over prices, complain the salesmen; they lack basic manners. '*Gimme* this. *Gimme* that,' complains Jonny. 'Honestly!' MWs attribute such problems to cultural differences: very few of these customers are white British, the most commonly cited origins being Turkish and Kurdish. Any rudeness is met with equal doses of rudeness: 'Because they know the way you are… I can be as rude as I want. And if someone upsets you, you can tell them where to go, basically.'

Despite this apparent disregard for customer service, and despite frequent complaints from MWs that business is declining ('Two for one in Tesco's!' a bummaree liked to complain. 'Can't get two for one here!'), some shops are said to make a tidy profit. One shop apparently claims to have made a turnover of 7 million one Christmas, although some suspect that this may be an exaggeration. Still, many guv'nors and senior salesmen are comfortably off, as other MWs like to point out. 'Oh yeah, they all drive the big flash cars and all, don't worry about that,' says a shop man with heavy irony. 'They've got plenty of money… they'll tell you they haven't, but they don't do too bad.'

The meat itself keeps up with modern consumer demands, coming from all corners of the world, bearing various labels certifying itself as a certain breed, fed on a certain diet, free-range, organic or halal. Few MWs showed much respect for such labels. 'Is the chicken corn-fed?' asks a customer. 'Nah, we feed 'em on Weetabix!' comes the reply, to hearty laughter from other salesmen.

Part 1. Inside the market: embodied labour and kinship

The market consists of 42 shops. I was told that no one knows the total number of MWs, but estimates range between 500 and 750. Occupational categories are as shown in table 6.1.

'I've been here 30 years... and my father, 50 years before me. And my grandfather, 80 years before that...' Smithfield is a place of family; MWs count lyrically backwards through the generations, listing their ancestors at Smithfield. Most MWs find work through family ties; several generations still work side by side. A young saleswoman remarked that she loved coming to work, 'to spend a bit of quality time with my dad'.

Beyond blood relations, people frequently remark that the entire market is one family, even one single body: 'We're family here. And we look after family. Have a go at one of us, you have a go at 2000 of us!' People had known each other their whole lives, seen people die. Plaques commemorate MWs who have died; their ghosts haunt the building. Billy's late friend appeared to him in the changing rooms upstairs. 'Then he left, didn't say a word. It broke my heart.'

Indeed, for some, Smithfield's family-like ties are more valuable than real kinship ties: many remarked that they had spent more time with each other than with their families. Some continue to work long past retirement age, confessing that Smithfield offers an escape from the monotony of home life: 'You just sit around, wait for the wife to finish the ironing....' MWs contrast to Marx's alienated worker, feeling more at home while working (Marx 1992:326).

In the 'Tail Piece' of the market's quarterly newsletter the *Smithfield Gazette*, 'Fred' – the pen name taken by the group of senior MWs who contribute this piece – declares: 'We are together because Smithfield is our home' (SMTA 2015:8).

A violent initiation ritual, 'getting married' (sometimes called 'your birthday'), marks MWs as 'part of their little family', as one recent initiate puts it, producing local bodies (Appadurai 1996). Though now only performed occasionally, is it often talked about, described with excitement and amusement. The initiate is always a male MW – someone new to Smithfield or celebrating some kinship-related milestone such as a marriage, 21st birthday or any birthday. He is rendered passive – wrapped in box-wrapping, tied to something – stripped naked and violently pelted with the most defiling of produce. Pig's blood is essential;

rotten eggs, offal, rotten product, ice water. Although violent, it is attended with raucous laughter, a sense of anarchic, riotous joy, as further explored below.

Likewise, kinship-like relations are forged through apprenticeship relations. Just as MWs count through the generations of their family, so too can they trace their apprenticeship genealogy ('I taught the bloke who taught him how to cut'), a phenomenon that Bestor labels 'fictive kinship' (Bestor 2004:240). Fiddes claims that cutting ('dismemberment', he calls it) is an act of domination (Fiddes 1991:82). Yet cutting under the gentle guidance of Charlie, who learned the skill as a schoolboy from his grandfather and passes it down the generations, and who receives an affectionate pat on the shoulder from one of his students ('very good teacher'), seems less an act of brutal domination, more a skill that forms parental ties.

These ties go beyond mere fictive kinship, finding material realisation. They are sedimented in the flesh, inscribed in the body. As you learn to cut from your elders, it sculpts your arm muscles, marks you with scars, inhabits your body and mind. 'I was cutting again, last night,' complains a cutter, savouring his fag-break outside. 'Can't get away from it.' He demonstrates on a box-pile how the motions flow, how part of him cannot ever stop.

For some, the tools (always yours and yours only) become an extension of the body. 'You look a bit fucking dangerous with that knife!' a female salesman yells after a butcher wandering about with a vague yet fierce air to him, still clutching his knife. 'It's stuck to me,' he replies. Body and environment are mutually constitutive; like Wacquant's boxer, the MW 'is inhabited by the game he inhabits' (Wacquant 1995:88). The work and environment as a whole marks everyone in its physical and sensual intensity. You are daubed in blood, your hands saturated with grease. The cold seeps into your body (some are convinced that the sharp temperature changes explain Billy's frequent blackouts while driving), the fatigue makes your body ache. The strange rhythm of days turns the most intimate cycles of the body on their head: a saleswoman confided that when she started working at Smithfield, she stopped menstruating.

Pressing on through the long nights, in the dark outside and the bright cold inside, there is a certain emotional way of being in Smithfield. 'I love the job, but I hate it at the same time. It's weird, man,' a shop man confesses. Smithfield is a place of love and hate, pain and laughter, the humour as merciless as the cold and the harsh lights. Davey's father's memories still ring true today: 'Everyone had the hump like, you know… lots of people getting up early and working hard and maybe for not much money… so yeah, a lot of people were very aggressive. But my dad said to me […] you could get up in the morning with the hump, he said you'd get to Smithfield and someone would say something make you laugh, like. He said it was brilliant – he said it was so full of people laughing and joking.'

The environment marks them aggressively, and MWs respond with equal aggression, with a cheerful disregard for safety and for the building. Walls are smeared with handprints, chipped away; salesmen laugh as they try to piece together bits of battered and broken stalls; a CoL engineer lives in constant despair, spending long nights trying to piece together the destruction MWs leave in their wake. Davey can trace memories of his childhood across the surface of the stone; he used to come as a child with his father, a bummaree; he shows me where the wheels of the old bummarees' barrows chipped away the walls. The bodily engagement with building is so intense that social relations become sedimented in the building with engraved names, initials and jokes; in PM, whole conversations are registered on the walls (fig. 6.11).

Body, work and building are co-constitutive, each element sustaining the other in a relationship that is aggressive yet organic and vital. Older MWs are regarded as part of the architecture: 'They built this place "round him, back in 16-whatever!" In a striking description

Fig. 6.11 'Where's Danny?' 'Round ya mum's.' Banter via graffiti on the walls of PM. Source: author

of Smithfield in the old days, when the stalls were divided not by white panels but rows of carcasses, a young salesman told me that 'the stalls used to be made of meat'. Smithfield comes alive in an architecture of flesh; 'This is a living, breathing market!' Davey would exclaim. The trade is seen as living, sustained by the embodied skill of elderly MWs: 'When these people die, the trade'll die with them,' said a shop man. And many remark that the place in turn keeps elderly MWs alive, those who work long past retirement age. 'When people leave this place, they die. Dunno why.'

Part 2. The market and the other: liminal identity and carnivalesque performance

'I strolled in the dark early hours through the City, place of enormous wealth. The silence gave a sense of comfort and a feeling of power over the banking giants.' – 'Fred' (SMTA 2016a:4).

When the city around is asleep, it's the liminal figures that take centre stage. The pavements heave with drunken revellers: one staggers down Buyers Walk; as MWs around him blithely ignore him, he steadies himself with both hands flat on a display cabinet, staring at the raw meat as if trying to cling to it as the stable core of a spinning universe. A homeless man finds his way behind a stall and collapses asleep. 'Ever seen *The Walking Dead?*' Keith, a salesman, shouts to me. 'Well, now you don't need to'; he nods to a regular customer inching down the aisle, hunched and ancient, grinning blindly. MWs tell me of people dressing as clowns to frighten co-workers, of the shady figures, gangsters, criminals and madmen who frequent the market, of prostitutes, drunkards and clowns who stumble into their domain, as if all are part of an ensemble cast of the marginalised, and Smithfield their stage.

Keith's *The Walking Dead* reference implies a strange continuity between these liminal figures and the dead who come alive in MWs' imaginings of the market. MWs often speak of all the bones in Smithfield, unearthed by construction work, the ghosts, the screams people hear at night. They would tell me of the executions, lingering on gruesome details of bodies pulled apart; 'William Wallace, he was hung, drawn and quartered up here. Put his head up on the bridge, his legs…' Its historically liminal position, by the hospital, threshold between life and death, where violent criminals met gruesome ends – all these were prominent in MWs' imaginings of Smithfield. It is a topsy-turvy world, a world on the fringes of the civilised, sane, living, waking world.

With the pale dawn, the market fades and the silent sweep of commuters through Grand Avenue begins. They appear almost flimsy, in suits, heels and skirts, their firm, brisk stride contrasting to the MWs' proud swagger. In my blood-smeared whites one morning I notice the looks they give; a woman walking hurriedly with a grim expression eyes me with disgust. When I return her gaze, she quickly diverts hers to the floor without altering her pace. In interviews, office workers describe with unease and disgust the spectacle of bits of bodies left behind in the mornings: an eyeball, a head, a trail of blood. Butchery, raw meat and blood are widely associated with lack of civilisation, and with barbarity and violence (Fiddes 1991:89). Likewise, many modern consumers view meat and animal as strictly distinct, bounded categories, eschewing products too reminiscent of their living, animal origins (Fiddes 1991:230). A BBC documentary, *Kill it, Cook it, Eat it,* follows people's horror as they observe, for example, 'How chickens are turned into nuggets' (BBC 2010). MWs work with a substance that disrupts these categories in a way unsettling for many – a substance half way between animal and meat, recognisable as both. As Douglas explains, disruption of bounded categories is profoundly disturbing, threatening the project of civilisation itself (see e.g. Douglas 1978:55).

MWs are aware of this, aware of their appearance in their blood-stained overalls. A *Smithfield Gazette* article reveals the MWs' gratitude to cafes that accept them in their bloodied whites (Smithfield Market Tenant's Association (SMTA) 2016a:3). They return the disdainful gaze with pride and defiance, chin up, chest out, but in private they confess to feeling unwanted. Some are humorous about their feelings of rejection: 'We're all naughty boys here,' laughs Jonny, a salesman. 'No one else would have us!' Others are less cheerful. 'People are wary of you,' says Frank, a butcher. 'They see your white coat and they know you chop up animals; they think you're gonna chop them up.'

All this is intensified by the constant threat of closure, the knowledge that the CoL does not want them there, that locals and office workers in the increasingly gentrified surroundings complain about the smell, mess and noise. And, as the daily furore around the EU referendum made clear, many MWs feel ignored and despised in society at large, worried that their children face an uncertain future. A constable voted leave with a heavy heart: 'They say the EU is supposed to protect workers' rights, but we weren't seeing any of it. We felt left behind.'

Epitomising the EU and the CoL's opposition to their way of being are the health and safety signs covering the building, the omnipresent voice of authority. Human images in the signs 'Hard hats must be worn' and 'pedestrian route' are faceless, the figures abstracted to dead symbols. These are the texts of non-place: 'addressed simultaneously and indiscriminately to each and any of us: they fabricate the "average man"' (Augé 1995:100). It was in the service corridors, where these signs reach a particular pitch of anxiety, that Davey told me: 'It's not just the market. It was faces, people, boxers, gangsters...' Smithfield's community cherishes its members for their quirks and eccentricities, yet these signs represent 'a power that is not individualising, but... massifying' (Foucault 2004:243).

Yet the voice is undermined by other voices, co-present with them in a single utterance. Several signs have been graffitied (fig. 6.12). In their bold lettering and absolute commands, the voice presents itself as absolute, monoglot; the graffiti challenges this, playing with the space between word and object, speaking subject and word (Bakhtin 1981:276). The original words remain yet are shot through with the obscene words of Smithfield's social world, with a contradictory orientation to the same objects: health and safety, hygiene and danger. The signs become heteroglot; MWs' voices are heard even in the words of authority. Additionally, they have turned the dead symbols back into their friends. A faceless hard-hat head is given glasses resembling the salesman at his desk nearby. A forklift driver is given an impossibly large belly and labelled 'Teggy'; the letters sprout limbs and smiling faces, labelled with names.

Fig. 6.12 Graffitied signs. Source: author

MWs must continually fight to maintain locality against these forces that invade and threaten to undermine their very sense of humanity. Yet MWs ultimately must submit; their locality could not exist without this hostile authority. The building is as much the CoL's as it is theirs; its very existence is due to these inimical outside forces, built to replace the old live meat market. Unable to create their own protected enclave of locality that is theirs alone, they must co-opt the projects of the other, co-exist with them in constant, aggressively humorous struggle. As further discussed below, the most developed idioms in Smithfield are of resistance: sadness, anger and opposition. MWs' identity is dialectic, with opposition to outside forces at its heart.

Humour is essential in the MWs' subversive identity, their struggle against authority. Smithfield sees its humour as the 'popular corrective of laughter applied to the narrow-minded seriousness of the spiritual pretence', of the dominant order (or of anyone who thinks too much of themselves) (Bakhtin 1984:22). One anecdote demonstrates this corrective in action: 'I recall a right old snob coming down, being shown 'round the place. A Labour MP, I think. He was ignoring all the staff, so somebody got hold of a sheep's eye and chucked it at him. Got him right on the back of the neck. The place was in uproar' (Usborne 2015). All through the night, the air rings with the sounds of fridges, engines, trolleys and the shouts and laughter of the people as they yell in abusive exchange. It makes the ungodly hours bearable: 'banter up here – fantastic'. Humour is considered an essential life force that keeps the world alive and continually revitalised. Commenting on the decline of the market, the economy, and society in general, Jonny would explain: 'It's 'cos people are too serious these days.' In the old days, Kevin, a bummaree, said, 'There was more life. You had a laugh.'

In the anecdote above, the use of a body part to bring the high-and-mighty down to earth is significant. Smithfield is marked by a celebration, through humour and ritual, of the earthiness of existence. Jokes revolve around sexuality, defecation, the phallus, the buttocks, parts of the body 'through which the world enters the body or emerges from it, or through which the body itself goes out to world' (Bakhtin 1984:26). Penises are scrawled everywhere; people's backsides are common property ('I need a sign on here saying "do not touch – do not enter",' jokes a shop man). Billy's hands are endowed with healing powers; but such apparently mystic powers are degraded, brought down to earth, made flesh (Bakhtin 1984:20): his powers mostly cure constipation, mystic-utopian powers of the carnivalesque that open the body to the world through defecation. "Ere, what happened to Steve when I put my hands on his stomach?' He asks Jonny for proof. 'He was shitting for weeks.'

'Getting married' is an intensified celebration of human/animal flesh as one, all one with the market family and one with the world. The use of rotten product is most striking. Anxiety about contaminated produce lies at the heart of most regulations that plague MWs' lives. The disposal of rotten material is intensely regulated. The most severely contaminated produce is kept at the sad end of PM, behind a series of doors in a white-bright cold room with a smell that clasps my temples and stomach with the memory of it. In that room, trembling with fatigue and sickness, I remember how desperately I wanted to leave. For Kristeva (1982), abjection is part of our ordering of self against non-self, part of our project of maintaining bodily integrity. Yet the initiate is rendered passive, stripped naked (this requirement is heavily emphasised: 'They tie you to a table, yeah, naked, with all your private parts hanging out…'); his agency, his barriers to the outside world are undermined in a gory spectacle as he is covered in blood, bits of bodies, abject matter that should be kept apart from the self. 'Getting married' dramatises 'the fragile border (borderline cases) where identities (subject/object, etc.) do not exist or only barely so – double, fuzzy, heterogeneous, animal, metamorphosed, altered, abject' (Kristeva 1982:207). He is absorbed into one body, that of the market family and the animal bodies he works with. Through imagery of slaughter, death and dismemberment, he is painfully reborn (indeed, an alternative name for 'Getting married' is 'Your birthday').

Among the violence, there is a riotous joy in the transgression of ordered demarcation, of separation, a *jouissance*. 'One does not know it, one does not desire it, one joys in it [*on en jouit*]. Violently and painfully' (Kristeva 1982:9). One does not know it. Indeed, the ceremony is riddled with uncertainty and contradiction. Commentary on the ritual was limited, questions answered with a shrug and a laugh. 'It's just what they do.' Showing me a video, Jonny explained simply, 'He's getting married.' 'But… when? To whom?' I replied, confused. 'No one knows. He doesn't know.' Not knowing, knowing only the pain and *jouissance*, the smell and the cold shock of abject matter, the hard pavement to your face. 'Getting married' is a raucous, joyous celebration and dramatisation of MWs' contradictory position in the universe.

Indeed, the whole culture of Smithfield celebrates disorder and contradiction. 'It's all wind-ups down here,' was a common catchphrase. A wind-up is simply a story that isn't true, nonsense told with wide-eyed sincerity. The guv'nors were notorious bank robbers; Billy used to be an assassin; I was working undercover for Smith, Chairman of All Markets, conspiring to close the market. One salesman laughed: 'There's no truth up here!' A great source of humour was chaos, things out of place, illogical, impossible happenings. Old characters are fondly remembered for amusing, nonsensical behaviour: the 'Mad major', 'who went to work in a bowler hat, cashmere coat, bright yellow gloves and went home on the bus in his bloodstained smock'. Billy the Fib, in distinctly carnivalesque fashion, 'once went into a pub dressed as a priest, ordered brandies for his mates and then walked out' (SMTA 2016a:2). In Smithfield, laughter 'frees human consciousness, thought, and imagination for new potentialities' (Bakhtin 1984:49).

For Douglas (1978), dirt is what is swept to the edges as part of the ordering project of culture – just as Smithfield was swept to the edges of the city centuries ago, just as MWs feel they are matter out of place now. Thus, dirt and contamination are inherently linked with disorder, unreason and madness. MWs go straight to the heart of what marks them as liminal, into that contradictory space of dirt and unreason, between life and death, self and other, animal and meat, between life-sustaining food and potentially fatal contaminating substance, where the dead come to life and madmen reign, and they embrace it as the heart of Smithfield's world. Smithfield is a world between real and ideal: it is a community like any other, but also a lived performance of an ideal, utopian order. Smithfield is a carnivalesque world, a space where conventional order, reality and reason are suspended, a 'bodily participation in the potentiality of another world' (Bakhtin 1984:48).

Fiddes argues that meat exemplifies 'the masculine world view that ubiquitously perceives, values, and legitimates hierarchical domination of nature, of women, and of other men' (Fiddes 1991:210). MWs' attitudes are more ambivalent, marked by celebration of the cycles of life and death that unite all living things; by identification, even empathy. An MW contemplates the idea of killing a cow. 'That cow looking you in the eyes […] It's like shooting someone, innit? I dunno if I'd be able to sleep.' Performing a popular joke, a salesman holds a skinned sheep's head next to his own: 'Who's the best looking here?' A common prank involves producing a pig's trotter protruding from one's sleeve as a hand: a human–animal metamorphosis, a lived grotesque form. The contradiction in attitudes – sadness and laughter – is resolved through that fearless humour that Bakhtin describes, that can laugh in the face of death – one's own death, or the grisly reminder that an animal has died: its dull-blue eyes and skeleton-grin. In one Tail Piece, 'Fred' humorously

Table 6.2 Oppositions between meat eating and vegetarianism

Meat eating	Vegetarianism
Smithfield Market	outside
real hunger for food	sterile hunger for money
life-giving healthy diet	life-draining diet
real world (local?)	(fantasy world? nightmare world?) impossibly vast, endless
common people	land-grabbing elite
(brick, marble and stone?)	concrete
vitality	listlessness
abundant life	mass annihilation
natural	unnatural
care and love	(indifference?)
(laughter? noise? chatter?)	silence

prophesises his death, encouraging his friends to drink merrily 'as the ashes return to the earth' (SMTA 2015:8).

Indeed, meat, like laughter, is believed to sustain the vitality of the world. Violence, death and domination are associated with the opposite: vegetarianism. Table 6.2 demonstrates the oppositions as conceived in the texts below. Text A is the *Smithfield Gazette*'s July 2016 'Tail Piece' (SMTA 2016b:8). Text B is a comment, written by a prominent MW, on a YouTube video posted by a lorry driver, documenting the torments of parking at Smithfield, entitled *Smithfield: The Parking Challange* [sic] (Martinelli 2016).

Text A – *Smithfield Gazette* 'Tail Piece'
Dreams are mysteries most probably prompted by factual events. What happens when daytime awareness stops and night time dreams lead to weird, sometimes frightening situations? After being locked into a world of reality, are we drifting into a vision of the consequence of an act of supreme selfishness?

In this nightmare I dreamt of walking almost forever throughout the world in every hemisphere. Around me were dead bulls, cows, steers, calves, pigs, sheep, lambs, goats, turkeys, and their devastated owners.

Tip-toe through the vegans, you'll know who they are, they are the ones with the celery sticks in their mouths looking like they need more substantial fillings. Move quietly through the vegetarians, pale but still eating fish; advance into the real world where we stewards raise meat and poultry, the natural food provided.

Stop now; hear the 'starve the world' fantasists; 'let's kill off billions of cows and bulls, let everyone else eat whatever they can get to survive'. The greatest terrorist act of all time has begun. Ask those who lay you to rest to preserve your teeth to use on your premature gravestones to help those who survive to wonder what sort of ancestors we inherited.

If you wish to stop eating fish, as vegans do, you can speed up the total decline of our world and help to achieve the total extinction of the human race. And, by the way, these animals vegans claim to protect are now extinct; nobody it seems wants a pet cow!

Millions of humans die slowly from disease and injury. Those who rear life-supporting animals do not allow them to suffer such agony or 'caring homes'. Their parents and family will never need to mourn. Our animals will not grow old, anymore than a butterfly, they are God's gift to all, created to give health and life.

Yours as ever,
'Fred'

Text B – comment on YouTube video
Absolute nonsense – are Vegans running the show? For your guidance it is NOT 'Smithfield' markets' which itself shows you lack of knowledge and even minimal appreciation of the. GREATEST and only Market actually within the City. This is 'Smithfield Market' protected by the laws of the land and still providing a superb barrier against the huge Supermarkets from squeezing the common people into a meatless and killing diet.

Smithfield does more than any such self promoting supermarket to provide Parkin g than anyone of them.

Smithfield is an absolute icon to show how those who love and believe in its family, can snub the noses of the wicked, greedy, selfish land- grabbers. Do you really want a city of concrete and no heart? If not support the long term of Smithfield Meat Market.

Although still opposing earthy vitality to the sterility of the dominant order, these texts move beyond the carnivalesque. The latter subverts a power with a clear hierarchical structure (e.g. king on top) and easily locatable textual or material manifestations (the crown, the prayer, etc.); anti-structure, madness, freedom, superabundance, counter-posed to structure, order, repression and containment. Breaking rules, defacing signs, subverting hierarchy, 'Getting married', are all in this spirit. But in an age of decentralised, multiform power (the EU, the CoL, bankers, supermarkets, politicians), the operations of such power have no obvious tangible manifestations. Indeed, they are perceived as deliberately opaque; even I was semi-seriously accused of working undercover for the CoL, conspiring to close the market. It is a power that no longer restricts but positively creates discourses and moulds subjects (Mitchell 1990:564). Thus, humour cedes to anger and fear. The new power can only be represented in terms that spill over into garish, semi-abstracted imaginings of the piling up of bodies, 'fantasies of sheer catastrophe and inexplicable cataclysm' (Jameson 1991:46).

Carnivalesque mockery, subversion and excess are the most common idioms of opposition in Smithfield. But sometimes resistance takes other forms: wild rumours and, darker still, when Smithfield's signature aggression won't suffice, rage. This rage was effectively channelled by the Vote Leave campaign. Fresh from berating an inexperienced foreign-born worker, a cutter stormed into the cutting room, kicked a meat bin in an exaggerated performance of hyper-masculine bad-temper. But there was real, hard anger in his voice when he spun around and pointed at me: 'Vote leave, Caroline! Vote leave! Leave. Get them all fucking out, love!'

Part 3. The dying market: loss and lament

The market dies as you move downhill. Beyond MM is PM, a 'ghost town', said Keith. Beneath its skull-like dome (fig. 6.13), the fridges sound with a higher pitch of urgency, drowning out the voices below. At the far end, the stalls are empty; a tour guide told me that this emptiness worried the SMTA, that they feared it could creep upwards into the market and 'nibble it away, bit by bit'. Out into West Poultry Avenue, beyond the discarded concrete blocks and the ground that shudders with passing trains in the void below, the smell of vomit and piss, GM stands desolate. Rumours circulate that the CoL deliberately let it go to ruin, as an excuse to demolish and redevelop it. The emptiness is dangerous: it has agency and appetite; it could creep into the market itself and finally destroy it.

On an empty day, at the edge of West Market, an elderly salesman stands idle and silent, framed against the plastic curtains that blur the

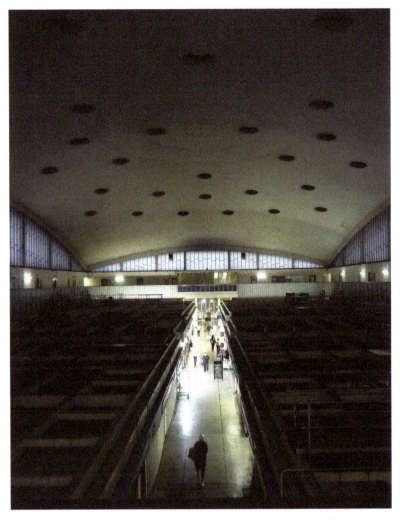

Fig. 6.13 A ghost town: inside Poultry Market. Source: author

lamplit night outside. He snaps into life when I ask him how the market once was. 'Now *that* was a market!' he beams. His gestures become animated: 'If you imagine, 400 sides of beef, it looked just incredible!' And up to the present again, the excitement fades. 'Not like this. This is a mickey-mouse market.'

In quieter moments, when the laughter fades and the aggression is calmed, there is another idiom central to Smithfield life: reminiscing about a cherished past, expressions of love, loss and lament. People delighted in describing the old market. 'You'd a loved it. There used to be all meat hanging up.' 'It looked lovely!' an elderly salesman says with a smile. Their descriptions convey a strong visual aesthetic, deeply embedded in Smithfield's social world, one initially alien to me, borne as it is from intense communion between body and environment (see Charlesworth 1999).

There is also a tactile aesthetic of tangibility and immanence. 'It was all sawdust!' says the elderly salesman brightly, spreading out his hands to trace an organic, earthy memory. The meat wasn't screened behind glass, people said. Transporting it used to be a full bodily engagement, the celebrated 'Smithfield shuffle': 'one arm swinging free, eyes fixed doggedly ahead, blasphemy to anyone in the way!' (Forshaw 1990:88). Now you stack identical blocks of cardboard, as many complain: 'It's all in boxes now.'

'It was all open,' everyone would say. Several drew me diagrams to demonstrate intersecting avenues, tracing paths, emphasising the possibility of movement through. The spatiality, the way of moving around the market, has an aesthetic and social charge, discussed by Bachelard as 'the poetics of space' (e.g. Bachelard 1969; Stasch 2013:561). The openness was a togetherness: 'You've taken the humour out of the market,' someone complains. 'You used to go down there and it was all open with shouting and balling' (Usborne 2015). Cutters could throw meat across at their friends, Charlie nostalgically recalls. Indeed, people move in a way that still resists the market's new spatiality, wandering freely between each other's shops and cutting rooms as if the divisions never existed.

Indeed, people sometimes talked as though the dividing steel, glass and white panels weren't really there: 'If you imagine all this gone', 'You could take all this away.' 'Mickey-mouse', flimsy and transient, a parasite upon the real market building underneath. 'This is original,' people told me, slapping the bold purple iron pillars that descend, an anchor to the past among alienating white (see fig. 6.8).

The old market was brick and sawdust, blue and magenta cast iron, gas lighting, a warm golden glow on sides of beef, swirls and strokes of all shades of red, coral, pale pink through crimson to dark purple. There's a new colour now. Red, blue and yellow are the health and safety signs, the absent voice issuing orders, plastic block-colours, abstracted and purified from the earthy, organic colours of the old-time market, and its feeling of identity and history.

And most of all, the new market is whiteness, steely bright. Whiteness is the refurbishment, the death of the old ways. Whiteness is refrigeration, the ruthless cold and hard blank panels of the lonely sealed-off storage rooms that replaced the lived, open space of the old shops. Leaning on the stainless-steel counter, I can feel it drawing the warmth out of my hands, the cold core in the gleam of metal; the sound ricochets off its surfaces, hard and hollow. MWs would often grumble, 'It's all refrigerated now,' and widespread mistreatment of fridges had the refrigeration engineer in constant exasperation. White is the material effect of biopolitics, new discourses of hygiene imposed by outside power, anxious about a diseased, weak, inefficient population, constructing new relations between people and their environment. Whiteness is the omnipresence of death as 'something permanent [that] slips into life, perpetually gnaws at it' (Foucault 2004:244). For MWs, the old market was simultaneously dirtier and 'cleaner', meat everywhere on the floor, but 'No one died, there weren't these diseases back then. All this hygiene....' Now it is 'too clinical': for MWs, the new discourse on hygiene has invented a new kind of dirtiness and cleanliness, has invented death and diseases.

The refurbishment, with its mechanisation and rationalisation of labour, resulted in mass redundancies. Workers were replaced by those mute blank towers of identical white boxes, fluorescent pink piggy cartoons, and all that machinery in the loading bays where Davey works alone. In operation, the machines hiss and click, the noise drowns out conversation, sending dangling bunches of carcasses slowly down the rail, animating them in agitated movement with its hydraulic clicks and shudders. This is what Jameson describes as 'That enormous properly human and anti-natural power of dead human labour stored up in our machinery – an alienated power [...] which turns back on and against us in unrecognisable forms' (Jameson 1991:35). And it continues even after the loading is done, the lorries have gone and the carcasses are in their shops, and people pass, alone, through the white corridors and all those signs, past the red empty stage, the hiss and click and dull metallic gleam of the dead labour of their lost companions.

'Gone, but not forgotten', as a memorial to a recently deceased MW on Grand Avenue declares. On quieter mornings, older MWs gather to reminisce about the old days, recounting anecdotes about old friends (see SMTA 2016a:2), reciting litanies of fallen comrades 'You remember X?' 'Aw yeah! He was a nutter, X!' 'And you had the pitchers and pullbacks, shunters…' 'You remember the bummarees, how they all used to go round in pairs?' Like the aggressive humour, imaginings of cataclysm, and rage, lament and loss are paradoxically a vital force at the heart of Smithfield life. While the empty rooms ring with silence, Smithfield is kept alive in the warmth and eloquence of MWs' reminiscences.

And like this mechanisation, like the devastation and ruin that creeps up the hill from GM, a new aesthetic of commerce and advertising, a new kind of post-modern, standardised space, non-place is pressing in on the market. The surroundings used to be a continuation of the market, full of spin-off trades: sausage-skin makers, pie makers, butchers' equipment shops (Forshaw 1990:90). All have gone now, replaced with office blocks and expensive cafes where MWs never go. 'That road there,' says Keith of Charterhouse Street, 'is like the divide between two civilisations.' Only a few greasy spoon cafes hold fast against the tide of gentrification.

In their narratives about Smithfield and its history, MWs would trace detailed maps orientated around the church, the hospital, the bones in the earth and execution sites, sometimes speaking of them as if they were part of the market. MWs clearly considered themselves as belonging to Smithfield, not just the market. Indeed, one MW merged PM's history with that of St Bartholomew the Great Church, telling me PM was one of the oldest buildings in London, the only one to have survived the Great Fire of London. Most of all, it was Smithfield's clock that orientated narratives: important events were often said to have happened 'under the clock', even if this wasn't strictly true; references to the market as a whole were often accompanied with a gesture at the clock. All these places serve as monuments for MWs, holding together the fabric of place and time as lived by its people, allowing them to orientate themselves in a meaningful environment, giving them a sense of history and temporality (see Augé 1995, Lynch 1960).

But Smithfield's newer surroundings are increasingly strange to MWs. Billy grew up in Smithfield, worked there his whole life, and has a lot to say about it, but some places are a blank in his mental map of Smithfield. When I ask him if he knows that Amazon's headquarters are just by Smithfield, I draw a blank. '... No.' 'Well, you know that huge office block right by GM?' '... No.' It is strange, following the market along the grubby pavement as it sinks into desolation down the hill, to come up against those pure depthless panes of glass that loom in two-dimensional grids against the sky (fig. 6.14). In MWs' minds, the new office block is not part of the surrounding city; indeed, its glass repels it, shattering the ruins of GM into a dark jumble of fragmented images of itself.

Smithfield's night-time world is equally strange to the people who work in these offices; none I interviewed had ever seen it. They pass in the mornings, dart glances at the piles of boxes, the debris being cleared, with dim and fleeting curiosity stifled under the press to get to work.

Fig. 6.14 General market against the office block, seen from West Smithfield. Source: author

Many frequent visitors to the area are totally unaware of the market. 'To them, this place doesn't even exist,' said Tony the bummaree, as revellers spilled onto the street nearby, 'and to us, it's the centre of the universe.'

And, on the dirty pavement by PM, between metal bins and battered orange-painted metal-grate doors in dark brick, construction workers cleared away the remains of Smithfield's beloved Cock Tavern to make way for a high-end jazz club. I asked a young man, sweeping debris under its grubby concrete arches, 'What is this place?' He contemplated me sullenly before asking his companion: 'What *is* this place?' I asked the workers about the area. Huddled on the pavement for a coffee break, they mostly answered with shrugs. 'We're not from round here.' The market? 'A bit of a dump.' Would they visit the club once it's done? The response was a bitter laugh. Like the place they inhabit, the object of their labour stands opposed to them as something utterly alien (Marx 1992:324). 'They wouldn't even let us through the door! The rich and that!'

The jazz club's website speaks of a different experience of detachment, boasting that guests can 'enjoy a glorious sense of disconnection from the outside world' (Oriole 2015). Yet with this thrill of disassociation comes a sense of loss, a desire for authenticity, one that is

Fig. 6.15 An image from the collection *Bummaree* in the reception area of offices along East Poultry Avenue. The bummaree can be seen pulling his barrow behind him; bummarees no longer work like this. Source: author

enthusiastically catered for by the club and other surrounding businesses. Its cocktails are each named after a locality, marketed as capturing its essential *couleur locale*. A tour guide told me many of her clients were office workers who had never seen Smithfield at night. Workers in the offices above Smithfield (the same who complain about the mess and the smell) are greeted with a life-sized black and white piece from the photographic collection *Bummaree* hanging in the reception area (fig. 6.15). Pulling his barrow behind him, yelling some blasphemy with a broad grin. The black and white image of a grinning rosy-cheeked cockney is readier for consumption; the fleshy, fatty, bloody reality is less appealing.

None of the office workers know the man's name, but Davey does. 'Yeah, the geezer with the barra. He was a bit loud apparently, my dad said.' For Davey it's a shallow fragment, a Platonic shadow of Smithfield's lived reality, of a real place that has an immediacy in his mind, where he can place himself exactly.

> That's just a... a still, of... one person, like, you know? Pulling his barra through the market, but you'd have to dodge him. [...] What

> you're looking at there is where we were standing, like, say we came in off the pavement, and walked into the market… what you'd see would be people buying meat, butchers, barras, all that, *that,* that was what it was like…

From urban space densely and intimately lived to non-place, without history or sociability (Augé 1995:77), from building, work and workers as one body to isolated, alienated and lost individuals – Smithfield's surroundings stand in marked contrast to the market at its heart. The non-place threatens to creep into the market's empty spaces, like the jazz club, the offices upstairs that have nothing in the world to do with Smithfield; could it finally swallow it whole? Shatter it into shallow, fragmented images of itself? Move the market out of town, reducing the building to a 'stupid facade,' as Davey puts it 'with all like boutique-y shops and that'?

Conclusion: in this valley of tears

There are murmurings that this is indeed Smithfield's fate. With the congestion charge, expensive rents and parking chaos, it would make economic sense to move the market elsewhere, as some younger, more hard-nosed and business-savvy salesmen will quietly admit. But the loudest, most prevalent sentiments are of three types: outright denial, noisy opposition and loud, angry prophesies of doom, like Kevin's favourite phrase, pronounced with a booming voice, chin-up proud: 'This market will be gone in three years!'

But, as should now be clear, the threat of closure has always hung over Smithfield. The market has suffered so many blows, each marked by speculation that this was the end: the congestion charge, several threats from the CoL (see, e.g., Metcalf 1991:174), right back to the removal of the live meat market.

A poem was published in the *Illustrated London News* to mark this latter event. Although a journalist's parody of a MW, the poem rings remarkably familiar with contemporary MW narratives. It shows that a vivid, developed genre of lament, a sense of loss and impending cataclysm is not new to Smithfield; in fact, the market today was born in a moment of sorrow.

> Don't speak to me, Nat – I can't bear it! I'm fifty-four year old come tomorrow;

And of course in my time, in this walley of tears, I've had my 'lowance of sorrow.

I've burned three wives, but that's nothink- I mean nothink at all in comparasin-

To the high-pressure-burster of biler-like feelings that now is my bosom a harassin'. (Forshaw 1990:58)

The poem ends with a speculation that sounds remarkably familiar: 'But I've heard – The Wedgetarians has bought Smiffield and intend to conwert it into a Kitchen Garden.'

Smithfield's identity is built on a raucous celebration of liminality, on a sense of constant struggle against the oppressive powers that be. It is sustained and given its life and energy through humorous subversion, through rage and through that bitter and indignant sorrow at what has been lost.

Smithfield's nonsense world is a performance of a utopia and is also built on a mythology of fading utopia: those better days, that *real* market, the openness, all the old characters and the laughter. A fading utopia that is still fighting proud, even if MWs are ultimately doomed to lose that fight. Their position is key in that fight: once outside the city walls, Smithfield is a noisy, smelly, rude enclave at the heart of the CoL, a 'time-warp' back to the good old times, a little pocket of the old east London, a last bastion for the 'common man' against the supermarkets, the banks, the EU, the greedy city, still holding fast against the sweeping tide of commercialisation. MWs weave their history together with the history of the church and hospital; they see themselves as belonging to Smithfield, as a continuation of its traditions of excess and violence.

And all this is rooted in the material: from the clock, which orientates memories, the cast iron structure, the *real* market that is theirs and that they fight to defend, to the walls they engrave and graffiti, that are marked with physical traces of memory, the signs they humorously undermine, the parts of the building that they constantly break, to the imagined material: the bones in the earth, the underground passageways and rivers, the bodies that were torn apart centuries ago. The materiality of the building, as mentioned above, is even thought to sustain some MWs' lives. If it were moved, even if the social structure remained intact, there is a sense that something fundamental would be lost. Moving would be the end for some. 'I wouldn't follow it. I wouldn't go on,' said Kevin, speaking in a gentler, sadder tone, for the first time since I'd met him.

So many pieces written about Smithfield end on a note of doom and uncertainty about how long Smithfield will last. I will end with words of defiance from 'Fred': 'Smithfield is forever! When will we leave? NEVER' (SMTA 2015:8).

Methodological note

Smithfield is an intensely sensual and emotional world. As such, the phenomenological method, with its close attention to sensory and affective experience, is key to exploring Smithfield. As Charlesworth notes, 'It is the *socialised*, phenomenal body that inhabits, because it is inhabited by, a world full of resonances, of fear and anxiety and pleasure' (Charlesworth 1999:21). As a middle-class female student among mostly working-class men who had spent most of their lives in Smithfield, I am differently socialised from MWs. Thus, for a full understanding of the resonances of their world, extensive ethnographic work was necessary.

I visited the market between midnight and 8a.m. every weekday for two months. My initial apprehension about carrying out ethnography in a place of work proved unfounded: two shop men quickly took me under their wing and arranged for me to observe the goings-on in their shop. I combined this with wandering up and down the market, catching people in idle moments for a chat. This proved an effective method, giving me access to a great number and diversity of MWs. Once MWs were satisfied that I was not a CoL inspector, I was received with great warmth, provided with a generous supply of tea and conversation. Most MWs appreciated my interest; they loved the market and enjoyed talking about its history, sharing their memories and concerns. Even the one figure who was markedly hostile enjoyed complaining to me at length: there was no health and safety, everyone was crooked, too many immigrants: 'You put that in your report!'

The butchers and cutters were spatially removed from the main walkways as they worked in specialist cutting rooms. Fortunately, one group of cutters found great amusement in having a female presence in an otherwise exclusively male part of the market, and frequently invited me to observe 'how the real men work'. I occasionally helped gather cuts into bags (some cutters were amused, others mortified at the prospect of me helping with such work). On one occasion, I cut lamb carcasses under the careful, patient guidance of an experienced cutter.

Local office workers were questioned in brief unstructured interviews; CoL authorities were contacted for interview, but refused. Other local workers, passers-by and customers were briefly quizzed; I frequently relied on a soft opening question such as: 'What is this place?'

Many MWs felt betrayed by previous attempts by outsiders to represent the market – most notably the BBC documentary, widely resented as an unfair portrayal. Some complained to me of the documentary's portrayal of MWs as racist; yet others criticised the same documentary for not including enough of their complaints about immigrants. The biggest grievance was with the documentary's focus on the female shop man and her complaints of sexism.

Class and gender offered additional obstacles. 'It's 'cos they think you're posh; they're testing you,' chuckled a salesman when I told him about another MW offering me lewd pictures of himself. We were quantifiable others to each other, each aware of the stereotypes the other had of us. MWs would play with stereotyped images of themselves, and I was sometimes unable to distinguish truth from playful fiction. One MW, who frequently made provocative racist remarks, claimed membership of the National Front while another laughed away his assertion as a ridiculous lie, leaving me unsure who to believe. Another MW boasted about all the East End gangsters he knew; others dropped hints about 'all the sex and violence that goes on here'. 'This is my manor,' a bummaree joked, in a lowered, aggressive tone, exaggerating his Estuary English vowels, aware his accent is culturally salient, sometimes seen to index aggression and criminality (see Eckert 2008 for discussion of indexicality). During moments like these, I often caught those around watching for my reaction with amused anticipation.

Previous ethnographic work has explored how informants negotiate power imbalance by confronting ethnographers with a stereotyped performance of themselves (e.g. Rampton 2005:96). There were additional complexities in our relationship dynamics that informed my methodology. As a young woman alone in a male-dominated environment, I also inhabited something of a satirical persona of a naïve and delicate young lady. For example, my standard response to provocative or lewd banter was to feign mortification. My ethnographic work never entirely lost this element of performance and play. This approach was entirely appropriate, as the spirit of performance and playful antagonism of outsiders lies at the heart of Smithfield life.

References

Appadurai, A. 1996. *Modernity at Large: Cultural Dimensions of Globalization*. Minneapolis: University of Minnesota Press.
Augé, M. 1995. *Non-Places: Introduction to an Anthropology of Supermodernity*. London and New York: Verso.
Bachelard, G. 1969. *The Poetics of Space*. Boston: Beacon Press.
Bakhtin, M. 1981. *The Dialogic Imagination*. Austin and London: University of Texas Press.
Bakhtin, M. 1984. *Rabelais and his World*. Bloomington: Indiana University Press.
BBC. 2010. *Kill it, Cook it, Eat it* [television programme]. London, 7 January.
BBC. 2012. *The Meat Market: Inside Smithfield* [television programme]. London, 31 May.
Bestor, T. 2004. *Tsukiji: The Fish Market at the Center of the World*. Berkeley and London: University of California Press.
Charlesworth, S. 1999. *A Phenomenology of Working Class Experience*. Cambridge: Cambridge University Press.
Douglas, M. 1978. *Purity and Danger: An Analysis of Concepts of Pollution and Taboo*. London: Routledge and Kegan Paul.
Eckert, P. 2008. 'Variation and the Indexical Field', *Journal of Sociolinguistics* 12(4):453–76.
Fiddes, N. 1991. *Meat: A Natural Symbol*. London: Routledge.
Forshaw, A. 1990. *Smithfield Past and Present*. London: Heineman.
Foucault, M. 2004. *Society Must be Defended*. London: Penguin.
Geertz, C., Geertz, H. and Rosen, L. 1978. *Meaning and Order in Moroccan Society: Three Essays in Cultural Analysis*. Cambridge: Cambridge University Press.
Jameson, F. 1991. *Postmodernism, or, The Cultural Logic of Late Capitalism*. Durham, NC: Duke University Press.
Kerridge, R. 1988. 'Among the Bummarees', *The Spectator*, 15 July: 18. http://archive.spectator.co.uk/article/16th-july-1988/18/among-the-bummarees (accessed 15 October 2018).
Kristeva, J. 1982. *Powers of Horror: An Essay on Abjection*. New York and Chichester: Columbia University Press.
Lynch, K. 1960. *The Image of the City*. Publication of the Joint Center for Urban Studies, Cambridge, Massachusetts. London: MIT Press.
Martinelli, P. 2016. Re: 'Smithfield Markets, The Parking Challange'. https://www.youtube.com/watch?v=KJoTYJcYb4U (accessed 9 January 2019).
Marx, K. 1992. *Early Writings*. London: Penguin.
Maslen, T. 1843. *Suggestions for the Improvement of our Towns and Houses*. London: Smith, Elder & Co.
Metcalf, D. 1991. 'Smithfield Meat Market: The Ultimate Pre-Entry Closed Shop', *Work, Employment and Society* 5(2):159–79.
Mitchell, T. 1990. 'Everyday Metaphors of Power', *Theory and Society* 19(5):545–77.
Oriole. 2015. Oriole. http://www.oriolebar.com (accessed 15 October 2018).
Rampton, B. 2005. *Crossing: Language & Ethnicity among Adolescents*. Manchester: St Jerome.
Smithfield Market Tenants' Association (SMTA). 2015. *Smithfield Gazette* 154, October.
Smithfield Market Tenants' Association (SMTA). 2016a. *Smithfield Gazette* 155, January.
Smithfield Market Tenants' Association (SMTA). 2016b. *Smithfield Gazette* 157, July.
Smithfield Market Tenants' Association (SMTA). 2018. 'FAQs'. https://www.smithfieldmarket.com/faqs (accessed 15 October 2018).
Stasch, R. 2013. 'The Poetics of Village Space When Villages Are New: Settlement Form as History Making in Papua, Indonesia', *American Ethnologist* 40(3):555–70.
Usborne, S. 2015. 'Smithfield: London's Centuries-Old Meat Market where your 8am Fry-up Comes with a Pint of Stout', *The Independent*. http://www.independent.co.uk/life-style/food-and-drink/features/smithfield-londons-centuries-old-meat-market-where-your-8am-fry-up-comes-with-a-pint-of-stout-10342318.html (accessed 15 October 2018).
Wacquant, L. 1995. 'Pugs at Work: Bodily Capital and Bodily Labour among Professional Boxers', *Body and Society* 1:65–93.

7
Observation and selection: Objects and meaning in the Bermondsey Antiques Market

Dave Yates

Although early morning, it is London, so the streets are far from empty, but at 2a.m. they feel quiet at least. The start of the market's day is signalled by the end of the day for the surrounding hotels – revellers stand outside the bars smoking, some wrapped up and heading home. It is a liminal time between the two cities, and the market crosses the border between the two just as the recently rescinded status as a 'marché ouverte' would have crossed the line between legal and illegal. Much of the market's trade still takes place by torchlight in these small hours, but this is more so stock can be bought before the dealers must open their shops, rather than to avoid the attention of the authorities.

The market square is lit from suspended cables between hotel and apartments, and the space no longer supports the 200 stalls that it once did. Instead, the light falls on paved stone and heavy wooden blocks – an architect's concept of public space defined through seating. Pushed from building site to car park during the surrounding renovations, the market struggled on through the sheer ongoing traction of performance – people doing what they do. Yet before dawn, before the traders and even before the stalls, the market space is empty, waiting for life to emerge.

Unfolding from a van emerges the hunched but proud figure of the matriarch of the market. Chairwoman of the association, she arrives first to check the facilities and perform the roles she has created for herself. On cue, a man emerges from a previously invisible door,

Fig. 7.1 Bermondsey Antiques Market around 2a.m. Source: author

spilling light into the paved square. The lady's goods are wrapped, boxed and stowed onto trolleys; they move easily with practised efficiency. The lady takes a folding chair and props it behind what instantly becomes 'her' stall. Discussion is loud and strained: the man is nearly completely deaf and towers over her by at least a foot. But understanding is reached and news updates are circulated, with just a nod towards the unobtrusive presence of the researcher. Students are known to seek out the market, and such things have become an accepted part of the market's performance. With a positive reference from the matriarch, the researcher is henceforth, thankfully, ignored.

Discussion reaches an end with mutual agreement, established links are maintained and the work continues. The elderly man is now joined by a younger; he is late and, with grumbles, they get to work. Two carts, piled high with heavy folded wooden stalls are rolled out to the market space. They are over 60 years old and were hand made. Until recently, they were cared for by a third-generation stall maker. Now the youngest son has sold up and become a midwife. The old stalls are a bane to the council: they are neither bright nor light, but they are dearly loved by the traders. Although change is always underway, the market traders hold on to the stalls with the great affection that solid wood brings in windy weather.

With a few hand signals and even fewer words, the stalls are laid out across the square. The locations are the same each week, and each is placed carefully at invisible markers. Each table is set with steel poles and wooden slats that can be built up into the stall by the traders when they arrive. Together with tarpaulin covers, rain-shielded areas are constructed for the display of goods. Such methods are avoided unless completely necessary due to the sail-like nature of the covered stalls; 'When it rains: put on the covers, when it is windy: leave them off – if it is both: HOLD ON!' Since the enclosing redevelopment all but surrounded the site, the area has become renowned for its treacherous wind tunnel microclimate.

Although still not yet light, traders begin to appear; one emerges from a car parked a long while ago having driven up the night before. This habit lingers from times when stall pitches were as prized as the goods, and often traders would be woken with a tap at the window from a keen buyer. Still staggering from sleep, the trader guides a runner to various desired items for show on his stall. As more vehicles, traders and stock arrive, the stalls begin to be adapted to display the variety of goods. Each stall emerges as a little ecosystem of meaning evolving from the empty petri dish of the square. Some are covered with felt, some adorned with fold-out shelving for extra space, while others have glass cabinets laid down to securely display smaller items. The chairwoman lays down homemade velvet-covered pads onto a sheet-covered stall. Each pad displays a selection of brooches, pins, rings or another set of items. They are collated together aesthetically or historically – groups of items from a period or design. The pads are functional – crafted to be quickly moved and displayed, a technology of stalling-out often, making the process systematic and easily returned at the end of the day. Further, each categorises the items into groups so that instead of having to manage singular items, the trader manages collections and groups. Later, when the customers arrive, the pads become display units, allowing whole groups to be moved around and offered for closer inspection. As the items are laid out onto the stall, routine patterns and connections are drawn and redrawn. The pads have regular places that they occupy on the stall, but these often change depending on what else has been brought. They are not simply placed either: each pad is roughly positioned before being re-placed in the exact, required spot – thus allowing checking and rechecking each time the pads are touched.

Thick-rimmed glasses perch on the end of this trader's nose, but her sight is keen and the movements of the hands are quick with practised expertise. Each item is touched, sometimes only for a moment, and squared towards an aesthetically pleasing position. Items that have come loose from their display are refastened, and loose gems are collected while the search continues for their lost brothers and sisters. Pads are selected and laid out gently, and as each is touched histories are remembered, prices noted, and somewhere a tick is lodged as part of an ongoing stock-take. The performance is called a 'drudgery and chore' – more 'finding space' than artistic creation, but it is also important to the trader's life and as such is done with great aptitude. Some items come out of boxes, are assessed and then returned without display. Sometimes they are in want of allure, others have been displayed without gaining interest once too often. This aspect of stalling-out is a constant process and even after the market is in full swing the traders continue to touch, rearrange and change their display.

It is a constant process of selection and adaptation to the customers, the weather, the stock and the day. It is also pragmatic – some items are found broken and those that are deemed wanting are placed to one side awaiting menders who come and visit the stall. Always this process is one of security – protecting the goods through

Fig. 7.2 'Edna' stalling-out at Bermondsey Antiques Market: each item touched, each history remembered. Source: author

constant reaffirmation and spatial design where a gap on the table would quickly signify a theft. The more expensive items are constantly checked, and each space is known, each angle and set is remembered, just in case, when the back is turned, one should go missing

Each technique of stalling-out is different, each type of stock as unique as its temporary owner. The selection of stock is a reflection of history and of chance, of finance and of love. Some traders will come to stall-out in vans full of furniture, others come only with a suitcase of rings and chains. Some stalls easily envelop their stock, others spill out covering two or three stalls spreading out over the floor – spilling meaning onto the pavements like brambles across a garden path. Some trade silver, some jewellery; some specialise in ivory and canes; some have a hankering for wooden boxes, and others have expertise in pre-war pornography. Even when one stall holder appears less 'selective', choosing items more suitable for a boot fair, this remains a selection – this trader's approach is accepted, if only to highlight the boundary and difference in quality of stock. He or she makes a living, just like everyone, and is loved and accepted, but the stock is not of the quality that others choose. While some sit comfortably on a wealth of knowledge and respect for their trade, others are perched on the edge of opportunity – but they are all trading, stalling-out and part of the market's operation. The market emerges through these detailed sets of performance and of selection. Each systemic process, from the individuals directly involved in the stalls and the stories of the items, becomes part of the market.

The sun has yet to arrive, but the market has come to life. Many coated huddles of traders gather around early sellers, torches clasped under chins, magnifying glasses clamped in eyes. Items are inspected, appreciated and discussed. At one stall, quite a crowd gathers – but these are not early buyers or tourists, these are traders. This stall sits bathed in light as buyers who have yet to stall-out their own goods search for interest and for profit. Worth emerges from discussions and there is much openness and support between the traders themselves. Many trade between each other, each managing to make a small profit on the last purchase. These selections between traders are important to the balancing of the trading day, and items will pass between traders several times before being sold 'out' of the market. This early exchange is important to both the market's cohesion and its character.

Beneath the surface of the market stalls are the depths of selection that go into the goods on sale. Items are rarely bought in perfect *condition, and instead a wealth of goods build up at their homes, cluttering stairs and spare rooms awaiting cleaning or repair. Each market represents a selection of goods: what could be bought, what is ready to be sold, what is new, and what was found. Bermondsey Antiques Market's stock-in-trade is obvious by its title, but only for a given definition of the word 'antique'.*

What is sold and what was once sold at this location changes as global trends for demand in antiques and availability of goods shift in response to external pressures. Key players in the market have a small role in keeping the character as close as possible to what they remember as the thriving market of yesteryear. Landscaped changes to the area are forcing diversification and change, and although this is met with resignation by some, others see it as a natural progression, a time to evolve or perish. The performances that go on to bring the market into place are constantly changing events of communication, each performing that decision of what will be at the market and what will not. As the market emerges into place, its communicative acts of presence appear to other people as part of their environment – something to select from, to build meaning of self and of place, and each performed together – in place.

(Author's field notes and images, Bermondsey Antiques Market)

Bermondsey Antiques Market

Bermondsey Antiques Market (BAM) has a long and complicated history, and yet has remained resilient; it has continued to function as an antiques market throughout the changes. Since 1949 it has been located just south-west of Tower Bridge Road in the London Borough of Southwark (fig. 7.3). Although the previous name, New Caledonian Market, is now out of date to some, local bus stops still use this designation on their signs. Historically, the market has shifted location three times and changed name four times, but is constantly referred to as the same market. This notion of change is important, as it highlights how social forms can change many parts, location and even name, yet remain functionally the same.

In the past 15 years, the market has gone through a drastic change. Until 1995, BAM was primarily a traders' market, with up to 75 per cent of sales being with other traders as opposed to the general public. However, changes in buying practices and a significant redevelopment of the location have both had a large impact on trade. In March 2013,

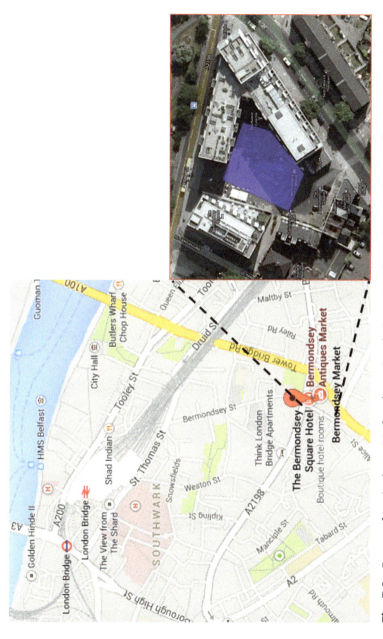

Fig. 7.3 Bermondsey Antiques Market shown in relation to London Bridge Station. Satellite image with shaded area showing the market space. Source: author

Fig. 7.4 A very quiet early start for the traders at Bermondsey Antiques Market, around 4a.m. Source: author

Southwark Council selected London-based Sherman & Waterman to take over management of the market. The company, and specifically director Michael Collins, run several other markets in London and the South East, notably Old Spitalfields Market on its most successful day. The image in fig. 7.4 was taken at around 4a.m.; prior to redevelopment, this time was key to the trader's day; now only a couple of traders start this early.

Markets provide wonderful access to the social construction of meaning through things. As researchers, we are able to observe people as they pass through a market and engage with their surroundings, as we engage with our own. We watch as they take on the everyday sensory experiences that form their awareness of the world around them. They observe the market and parts of the market, what they can see and categorise and what they buy or do not buy. We can say they *always select*. Selections are processed observations of what is familiar, what might be new or interesting, or simply what might be seen as significant. This chapter explores the role of material objects and their agency in such selections and interactions. It argues that while the market becomes part of an observer's social world, the observer also becomes part of the market. This relationship between place and identity has been understood in the following main ways: as a 'social-spatial dialectic' (Soja 1980); perhaps more abstractly as 'People make places and places make people' (Borden 2002); and finally, more poetically, as 'As place is sensed, senses are placed; as places make sense, sense make places' (Feld and Basso 1996:19). All three theorists describe the relationship as co-constructive, non-linear and dynamic in nature.

Here, such dynamic acts of communication are analysed through a focus on the material culture of the market, traced along the network of interactions. The data is presented in phenomenological descriptions and long quotes from interviewees. It explores multiple scales of analysis: from the entire market, as an ontological entity itself, to the processes of individual parts. Such multiple perspectives demonstrate how singular acts of an individual make up the larger processes, but further how such shifting of comparable analytical perspectives provide anthropological insight.

After a brief look at previous work on contemporary Western markets, this paper discusses the many levels of selection and interaction between people and objects. The first section looks at the selection of traders by the manager. It then goes on to describe acts of selection as stall holders select items for stock. We see how traders select stock and what activities go into selection. Also, we see how many of the selections are reported as constructions of the self: the stall holders' choices reflect their own perceptions of their identity. We see how stock, identity, display and social choices are all intertwined in the construction of meaning and of identity. Currently available texts lack such a descriptive analysis of markets, one that facilitates an understanding of the processes behind the form yet immerses the reader into the physical *place*. This article works to address this gap.

Through phenomenological description, we see how divergent cultural sets of people use the same place to understand the world and structure their own identity. Also, we follow a particular item as it is passed from one person to another, across a network. This section indicates how the item's agency becomes translated as it passes through each system, along a network. Such analysis draws on actor–network theory (Callon 1986; Latour 2005; Latour and Porter 1996; Latour and Woolgar 1979; Law 1999) with a focus on the distributed agency of an object through a network. The paper concludes that acts of observation, selection and communication through and between observable social forms are both constructive and constructed by those same observations, and, furthermore, that observation is, itself, a social act.

Material culture and markets

Marketplaces sometimes have long histories that involve numerous changes in location, trading goods and even name. They can appear suddenly over just a matter of hours; where once there was a quiet street or plaza, a market emerges into the social world. Markets are able to organise through small disparate flexible structures (Smith 1999) (stalls) into higher-level (large, more complicated) structures, yet direct control of markets is often convivial. Markets remain, if nothing else, social spaces. Prices, values and social ties can be seen to play out in a very particular location that may, in just a few short hours, disappear.

> Markets can offer possibilities not just for local economic growth but also for people to mingle with each other and become accustomed to each other's differences in a public space – thereby acting as a potential focal point for local communities that could revitalise public space.
>
> (Watson and Studdert 2006:vii)

Watson (2009) focuses on the 'difference' of markets, not just in their locations but in their use by many different types of people. Watson describes the sort of social interaction at public places as forming 'weak social ties', but suggests that these ties have the potential to develop into stronger bonds. Markets, for Watson, are places to be 'rubbing along', as if 'rubbing-up' against difference, a form of social encounter where the social framework is more flexible (Watson, 2009). Such frameworks could be seen as encouraging adaptability in places. Markets, therefore, are places where someone can see and do different things – a testing ground for social norms and values and interactions. Suggestively, then, markets are places for more than establishment of mere value of goods.

Markets, like any social gathering, are arenas for the sharing, construction and adaptation of meaning. As such, they are formed through the distribution of agency across heterogeneous networks of people and things, mediated by the meaning that they construct. It should be noted that while the abstract notion of markets has been studied (Lesourne 1995), and in particular the notion of self-organisation has been applied to financial markets (Lesourne 1995; Plattner 1989; Stauffer and Sornette 1999), rather this work focuses on manifestations of distributed agency and how this agency helps form social groups, structures and ultimately the market itself.

Markets are often seen as very particular types of place. Many texts uniquely describe markets as self-organising systems: they form social-spatial structures that are predominately constructed through bottom-up interrelations (Lesourne 1995). This is never more present than in the discussion of markets in the creation of value. To the economist, a market's raison d'être is the generation, qualification and communication of value (Beckert 2009; Berndt 2009; Elder-Vass 2009; Vanberg 1997). The production of value in markets is the most commonly discussed area. In particular, Beckert argues that various social, economic and political problems are solvable through the interaction of people (and things), based on the social-structural embeddedness of markets. In other words, people gather and share goods, they decide on value, and the market allows them to do this as it is an established area of trade and mediation.

It should not be under question that the value of goods is manifested through trade, and that spaces for such trade are typified by 'markets' in general. That said, such processes do not find some reified price – some abstract yet inherent character of the item in question. Indeed, one only has to open a newspaper to realise that the global economic market has not reached stable prices on a single item. While value is generated in markets, it should not be assumed that this value is anything more than a fleeting set of interactions across the network of the product's own biography. Once exchanged, the value is, in all senses of the word, history. Value remains constructed only through the process of exchange, and, I argue, so do features of meaning or identity.

Harking back to discussions of markets as systems that drive towards equilibrium, Beckert's analysis focuses on how markets are driven by a demand for order. This suggests either that: a) people are all 'good' down deep and they want things to be orderly, or b) the 'invisible hand' of the libertarian economy drives all exchange towards rational action and, therefore, towards order. In some respects, Beckert's analysis is accurate, in that an acceptable pairing of value and goods is required for trade. Yet while exchange value is important information for the goods, the value is not inherently tied to the object – only to the moment of interaction. It would seem just as possible that exchange in goods offers a constructive moment of agency and meaning for all parties concerned, and, therefore, value is not seen as a problem to overcome (balanced by economics of rational action) but a creative act. Further, it is possible that the construction of meaning of the world directly affects the world.

The focus of this paper is on this process of formation of place and identity through a study of Bermondsey Antiques Market. Bermondsey is hardly an 'informal' market (Deener 2009); there are organised groups and individuals taking strong leads on market decisions alongside many people making smaller decisions that lead to personal profit.

Observing selection

The use of the term 'selection' here is done to understand the process of observation, awareness and processing of one's environment. When we observe a person, place or event, we compartmentalise the phenomena in order to understand them. We select from our understanding of the world a suitable match with the sensory experience. Further, what we select from the world and what we ignore, or simply do not perceive, we leave behind. Here then, observation is creation of meaning – an act of differentiation between one part of the world and another. Multiple selections, and selections from selections, form patterns of behaviour at different levels.

We can see such selection at different levels in the market: from the individual trader, the stall, then the customer and the market itself in Bermondsey. These different scales are understood as comparable phenomena. The manager selects traders for the market; the traders select objects to trade; the buyers select objects to sell. Rather than a linear, or hierarchical, model, these are nested processes that, despite a difference in physical size, operate in directly comparable ways. By tracing the path of individual items across many different layers we are able to describe how each act influences the market as a whole. These multiple levels of operation of the market all work together to form the market's very identity – a sense of place.

Selection of traders by the manager

The manager makes weekly decisions about which of the traders can have a pitch at the market. The traders are at the whim of the manager (or the quality of stock they are able to bring), but for the manager the capacity to curate the market they wish to see is facilitated or constrained by the availability and quality of the traders he or she can select. The free will of the trader affects the market, as does the free will of the manager. Rather than assume the manager's choice of trader is more important or powerful than other selections, the approach here moves the focus to functional shifts in agency that have dual causation up and down the scale of the network.

The text below is taken from an interview with Michael Collins in his capacity as manager. During the interview, Michael confirmed regulars, moved stalls based on their stock, invited new people and extended others across more stalls; in short, he constructed the market through a series of selections.

> *DY: 'How many "new" people do you have each week?'*
> *MC: 'Probably about 10 or 15. Every week… Because I flyer with my name and email on every stall in BAM and Spits. Or they come through from Town and Country, who run the Covent Garden space where I have a sub-lease, and they put them onto me like that.* **Then I will talk to them and if what they sell fits and if their personality fits then I let them in. But it has to be both. It is not just your stock that gets you in. Your personality has to fit.** *Invariably, 9 out of 10 will do it and they will want to come back… When they do come, they will want to stay, and that is the sad thing actually because I cannot give them a permanent pitch.* **I want the dynamics to change.** *So you get this guy coming in with some incredible stuff… And when he comes back AGAIN… it is manic and everyone is all over him. And he comes to me and says… 'Why can't I come every week?'… But I know it would not be like that every week for him. I do say to them… you cannot have it every week… but it depends what is available at the time. Who is away, or not.*
>
> (Field audio: interview with Michael Collins, BAM manager (author's emphasis))

Michael manages his selections so that they can be both dynamic and also a good social fit. Visual and social integration are both key, as the market benefits from incorporating traders who are interconnected (friendly) and who bring a certain quality to the market. If they fit, they will drive connectivity and, also, the traders will sell more.

Arguably, we could say that the manager's choices are more powerful as no single trader has the influence to deselect another trader. However, such an analysis makes arbitrary distinctions between agents rather than perceiving the processes of the interactions between these agents. Further, it assumes stable states of agency within the network – it suggests that a position of power through one connection is confirmation of power through all networks, regardless of constitution. Agency, being the power to act or to impact the world, is fundamentally dependent on the constitution and passage through the network of interaction. By observing the market through a focus on the network, we understand how a fleeting set of interactions work. We can draw comparisons between Michael's selection of traders and a trader's selection of stock.

Selection of items by a trader

The choice of stock, or, more precisely, the acquisition of stock, is not simple. At times it involves relationships with long histories that require careful balancing. At other times, faster, impulsive decisions are required. Such decisions, if made in error, can lead to having stock that the trader is unable to sell. At other times, traders can simply buy too much and sell too little. When a trader first starts out dealing, it takes a long time to find the right kind of goods that can be sold on to make a profit. Those lucky enough to make it through the early stages of a career in trading build up sufficient connections that the amount of time needed finding stock is reduced. Those able and lucky enough to make the right selections are the ones who go on to trade for many years. 'Right' in this sense is a misnomer, as such things are not right or wrong, but about whether they work, or not, in the moment. A completely random selection of items brought to a market might still gain a certain level of profit for a trader. In this sense it would be impossible, or possibly just pointless, to suggest that this selection (being random) was 'right', rather the agency of the items found themselves having value in the market space. Placed in an empty street in the middle of the night, such items might appear to have no value at all.

Regardless, when one passes along the aisles of the market there is a strong feeling that the items have popped into existence, almost as the market does, overnight. Even when suitable items are found by traders, they often require cleaning, repair or research before they can be priced and displayed.

> *When we used to buy things in auctions, we used to get things and they were really filthy... if they were damaged they would go to the silversmith. But if they weren't, inevitably they would be filthy so they had to be cleaned. When you're buying from people, people want to make sure it looks nice. And I tell them 'Make sure it looks nice, and I'll be generous.' [laughs]*
>
> (Field diary: interview with 'Donald', BAM trader)

'Donald' makes it clear that when items are brought to his stall and offered to him for sale, they need to be in a good condition for him to buy, and indeed if the item is in optimum condition it will benefit the seller.

So, in the biography of an object, 'Donald' and his partner Pam work in the field of restoration as much as they do in sales. Pam shows how this specificity of performance behind the final stock offered for sale on the stall is key both to the display of stock and the knowledge of the customers' expectations.

> *… everybody has slightly different customers. We, for example, put everything in perfect order. We have… [hesitates] sources who just buy it, and they have dents in and they might have holes in them, and they don't want to be bothered to take them to be repaired. So they are taking less money, while we take the time and effort to take them to the silversmith and have it all done there.* **Our customers know that what they are getting is in perfect order.** *So they pay that little bit more…*
>
> (Field diary: interview with 'Pam', BAM trader (author's emphasis))

As Pam states above, their customers choose their stall because they know they will get clean items in good repair. Their stock, their stall and the work they do is systematically performed at many levels.

The level of the meaning and value held within each item at the market is of such complexity that it requires a certain level of involvement to feel confident about a purchase. Knowing an item's provenance, without having to rely on the seller, is of great value to dealers, but not every sale is made this way. Indeed, most of the sales, even between dealers, take place because of the connection to the particular trader who is selling. As we shall see below, 'people buy from people' and this is because they are unable to *know* enough about an item to independently confirm its likely value. Instead, they build connections of trust with individual traders; they select the identity of the individuals rather than selecting the truth of a singular statement (value). It is for this reason that selective acts of items for display are also statements of the self.

Selections for sale and of self

Acts of selection are part construction of meaning and, therefore, of identity. Such construction of meaning is comparable to the translation of agency in the network. In the passage below, we see how one trader communicates statements of identity and meaning. These selections become materialised not only in his choice of stock and his style of dress, but in his choice of friends and their choice of him.

I amble along the market corridors taking pictures and muttering to myself: just another odd character surrounded by many. But this observation feels inaccurate as I pass by one particular stall. I first notice the man and then the stall, yet both appear to have come from the same distressed, shabby and quite dark world. The man is tall, thin, and is adorned – rather than dressed – in torn clothing that neither looks old enough nor worn enough to be so frayed. It feels to me that each item of apparel has been specifically selected – not in a broad style, but as a direct statement. It is not simply that he has worn the items to the point of ripping, although that remains a possibility; this man is wearing the torn clothing as a symbol, a sign of distress. The tears are not symmetrical yet remain balanced, and although large areas of skin show on his torso and legs his clothing remains attached – functioning still. Those areas of skin showing are liberally covered in tattoos; they cover much of his neck and arms, all the way down to the hands – which are the most striking, the most interesting. Small diamond-shaped tattoos in close tessellation cover over half of his hands – they are unusual. Bracelets and bangles, necklaces and earrings sit under long limp hair that is not exactly dirty, but far from styled or cared for. He is gaunt and it seems to me that he is familiar with drug abuse, although perhaps in the past as there is little evidence of it now; he looks healthy, if pale. Crucially, he, like his clothes, match his stock: they are tattered belongings... but interestingly they are put into relief by his shoes. Sitting at the end of the skinny grey jeans are a pair of shiny, clean black boots. They are heavily styled with black and white faux animal markings and worn in a particular fashion, untied with the tongue sticking out.

He is often, but not always, at the market. Just as often I have seen him, he appears with an entourage of like-minded, like-styled people, who sit comfortably on the floor nearby smoking, creating small piles of dog-ends on the floor. This comfort for the pavement gives the impression that they exist somewhere beyond PAYE payslips. And this idea is echoed in the tattooed hands that would render the owner ineligible for employment at the nearby financial companies. They are statements of differentiation – separation from what they observe as their environment.

Often this man is accompanied by – or he accompanies, it is not clear – a beautiful and equally gaunt woman. Dressed to match, she carries the same pattern of tattoos on her hands, yet slightly fewer in number. I begin to wonder whether each is a way of keeping count – a tally, a record of something bigger. A technology of sorts, something to remind them as they reach with their bare hands through the world. The signs and symbols between the two are so similar – their signs blend and grow together like moss covering different surfaces in a garden. Often this trader appears with a tatty top hat, standing, unusually, in front of his stall rather than the more conventional position of behind.

To him this place is neither style nor is it work, but it is money and opportunity – a place where such things are still available to one distressed by the street. This distinction, this statement of darkness, is made most clear in his choice of adornment for his stall. Here, I realise that his place in the market is made real. His stall, much like himself, symbolises darkness and decay. Old plastic dolls' heads pulled from a skip perch next to one another in rows. Black feathers sit on dark velvet headdresses beside images of children with forlorn faces smothered in dirt. Shrunken monkey heads, sculls and complete sets of human teeth are displayed against green velvet and framed in dark wood. They are macabre – often 'found' items, sometimes crafted with skill and vision.

Dark and decaying, they are like the trader and his partner: beautiful in their reclamation of death. Another joins him at the stall, and this newcomer confirms the style choices, matching the stallholder in his tattered shirt, earrings and scruffy hair. Yet perhaps he has yet to join the inner circle, as his hands remain bereft of tattoos, and while they are clearly friends, this younger newcomer is an acolyte. It is nearing lunch on a weekday and he sits, not working, just passing time, helping to make the pile of dog-ends on the floor bigger. As he sits, I note his torn short and holey jeans – but his shoes are new shiny brown leather boots and tied loosely on his feet, tongue hanging out.

(Field diary and field audio, BAM)

There are several acts of individual selection described above, but what is particularly illuminating in this passage is how different individuals select from each other and are bound together through this process. The trader himself is defined by his approach to style, both in the cultivation of the distressed nature of his clothing and his selection of distressed stock. This is also represented in his choice of social connections and their own selections. The material forms he chooses to reflect aspects of his personality are aesthetic, but also they hold a particular type of agency: they act as an extension of his proposed self – neither accurate nor complete, but part of a process of construction of the self.

The reasons behind such selections of death and decay could be sought in interview, but in trying to search for a linear cause of this, the interplay behind the selection and meaning would be missed. Additionally, what would be recalled by the informant would change depending on how well the informant knew who was asking the question. This trader, his stall, the items on his stall and even his friends all display the same interrelated nexus of meaning. They share values and norms, and they bring these to the market, giving the market further character while gaining some additional 'flavour' themselves. While it is likely that some of these shared values would be appreciated by the people themselves, their reasons for such values would likely be highly personal/unique. There is communication of style and of lifestyle between this trader and the items that he sells, and in this way he signifies a particular set of messages.

The message strength – the unification and volume of it – means that it more likely to be selected for or against. The materiality of the messages, when combined together in a culturally communicative way, facilitates adoption by another – you see them more clearly, understand their 'otherness' in a more distinct way. This is not to suggest that such things define an identity better, only that there is an identity there – a signification of presence. The more integrated the identity, the more defined a selection for or against may be. People interested in the stock of the seller described in the field diary passage above need not have tattoos, but they might select the macabre identity as signifying something for their own need. An image of a Victorian boy with plucked-out eyes may be selected by a perfectly happy mother of two from Kent, yet this same image solves a puzzle, unlocks part of some discussion, within.

What is more, the narrative behind a purchase raises the significance of this exchange, as the distinct character adds to the 'moment'. The man described in the passage above represents a very clear statement – the exact nature of the statement is debatable, and accuracy of which an illusion anyway, but the impact is palpable. The message is clear in magnitude but not quite in direction: it is scalar and non-reductive in nature. To put this another way, if we were to focus on the exact nature of one part of the message, we would know less about the wider possible sets of interactions. The message is not created by a single thing or choice by the individual, but through a process of selection that spreads agency across a network from the stall, to the material forms, to the trader taking that sense of identity from one to the other. Even if that identity could not be clearly defined, it has agency. Arguably, the network of shared identifiers could act to amplify the message, even if the message content remains vague.

Selection between people: 'People buy from people'

'Real buyers' – as the traders call those who routinely purchase goods from the market – buy because of the people in the market rather than because of the goods themselves. This may seem counter-intuitive; however, these 'real buyers' purchase goods to make a living selling elsewhere. The items themselves are fleeting; the connections between people remain. Traders, dealers and buyers often repeated the common phrase that 'people buy from people'. Those who come regularly to buy at BAM do so because of the connection they have with the traders; they select the market and they select the traders, long before they may select an item. The repeated selections of items from the traders are repeated, reinforced selections of the traders themselves, so that they become part of the performance of the market itself. The relationship facilitates exchange with trust that the transaction will benefit both sides. We see this when a buyer from the US stops and chats during an annual visit.

> **DY**: 'When you say to your customers, "I am going to London to buy," do you tell them which markets?'
> **US buyer**: 'No. Are you kidding me?!'
> **DY**: 'Would that be giving something away…?'
> **US buyer**: 'YES!! It would. Honestly, I have really good steady customers and if they knew they would fly over themselves and that would be the end of that.'
> **DY**: 'So you are not buying for other traders?'
> **US buyer**: 'No no… They are individual collectors. But what you don't understand is that when I am coming over here, I am paying $1,400 airline… $300 a night for my hotel room and it is cold! Don't get me wrong – I am enjoying this, but it is cold. So, when I put a markup on my pieces, it has to cover these costs and then pay me back for my time. It does get really expensive. So, what happens is that my customers then see this stuff on eBay and they see how much cheaper it is, and it is hard for me! I cannot do those prices… But my customers are willing to do it because **people buy from people**. You see there are a couple of pieces on that stall over there that I want, so bad, but that dealer is so snotty to me I'm like: you are not getting my money. **I would rather work with someone that I would come back and see in a couple of years and that I want to talk to.** It is not all about the money. It is like that owner or manager or organiser just came around and he seemed really friendly and that

makes a difference. You know... even when you are just going around. People buy from people [...] but there are great bargains here.'
(Field diary: US buyer in conversation,
BAM (author's emphasis))

Above, economic exchange and profit is made through a network of communication, and if the link were direct, bypassing the US buyer, then she would miss out on the profit. This trader from the US has been coming for many years, and her own performance of 'scouring the London markets for bargains' is being troubled by that apparent ease offered by internet auction sites. Interestingly, she cloaks her finds in a shroud of secrecy, keeping the name of her sources a secret from her own customers. When I asked the question, I predicted that the buyer would use the name of the market, its own narrative and history, to weave into the narrative of the item. Instead, she leaves the exact nature of the market secret, its own aspect of the story, and she uses the simple fact that it comes from London instead – the market, the item's and the city's identity becoming communicated through the transaction of a single item.

Through exchange the value of an item is constructed, and, likewise, through communication meaning is constructed. Each complex set of exchanges hold reaffirmation of old and new sets of meaning, yet they are only manifest in the articulation, the performance, of the moment. The US buyer above uses the practicality of business to rule who she makes deals with and echoes the convention that 'you buy from people' – it is the social connection that one builds, not the money or even the item. The interconnectivity of trading is supported on the basis of trust; people want to trust in the selections the trader has made, and this enables them to make their own selections. Although on an individual level the selections are functional, their shared properties develop into multiply shared cultural norms. At one level these selections are about quality and future profit, but at another level the selections are from other people's selections. Selection takes place across a network as well.

Selection across a network

This section analyses the passage of a single item between people and details how agency and identity change as the item changes hands. It tracks an item as it becomes part of the performance of the market.

Activity at BAM often begins around 2a.m. One member of the market's cohort arrives pulling a small trolley laden with bags and boxes. He is a 'runner', but that is no longer a suitable description for his role.

'Rob' does cash-in-hand work helping traders stall-out, and although he rarely buys, he has a history of working at antiques markets. Today he has brought some items for show.

> *I found these in a skip on the way to the market this morning. Quite interesting... 1986 – charcoal drawings – that's Greenwich Tunnel. I have actually walked through there. It was in a skip... sad in a way because people throw things away. Quite nice really. I have a few other bits here....*
>
> (Field diary: conversation with 'Rob', BAM worker)

Rob pulls items from red-and-white plastic bags, showing them to anyone who appears interested. In conversation it transpires that Rob often brings items into the markets from skips or house clearances and sometimes from other, more general, markets. The drawing is an unframed charcoal sketch on heavy drawing paper. At one point this item was either lost or purposefully discarded; now the item's narrative continues.

'Chris', another trader at BAM, buys artwork either in bulk or one piece at a time and mounts/frames them, selling them on from his stall. On a later visit to the market, I see an item on his stall that looks familiar: a charcoal drawing of a tunnel scene.

This single item has been traced through the market and then back out again, selected, re-selected, re-presented and then sold again. We can trace what we know of this item through a network that forms the item's meaning and value – from rubbish to antique. Fig. 7.5 illustrates this as a linear set of differentiations through time.

From the artist to the end buyer, each stage is a selection from one system to another – communication across worlds. The item is discarded as rubbish (thrown, literally, into the environment) and re-selected by another whose connection with a different set of cultural values gives the item more value. This is part of the biographies of things explored elsewhere, but in a different way, by Kopytoff (1986) and Hoskins (1998, 2006).

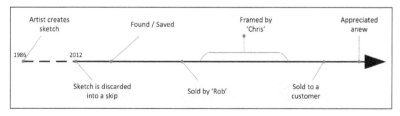

Fig. 7.5 The timeline of an object – 'from rubbish to antique in a week'. Source: author

We might suggest that Rob, being part of the market, selected the item. Therefore, the market's agency was articulated through Rob; without the market (and without Chris), the item might not have appeared valuable. Framing and shielded behind glass raises the item from a mere sketch to something that 'deserves to be protected'. The final stage of the item (that we observe) is when a customer passes and sees the item and buys the drawing. The item was 'brought back to life' and now likely exists on a wall, holding with it the narrative plot of being 'discovered' at BAM.

Conclusion

Here we have explored BAM through different, yet not divergent, scales of the market. Such scales demonstrate how singular acts of individuals, their agency, are distributed through exchange and, importantly, through observation of such selections. Here then, objects are technologies not only of communication, but of identity and meaning. The objects, as highlighted so clearly by Latour (2005), allow multiple, complex and inherently incommensurable meanings and emotions to be communicated through the operation of one system selecting from another.

Markets, rather than being simply a place to construct value in objects, are places to exchange all meaning – of which monetary value is but one expression. Indeed, meaning is not so much created or held in the construction/transaction moment, but rather it is an emergent and arbitrary product of the exchange. Exchange with value is exchange of value – or, indeed, exchange of meaning. Instead of politicalising the concept of value and therefore of exchange, we can elevate ourselves from such a discussion completely by realising the separation of 'exact', or monetary, value, from either people or object. Regardless of the importance of transaction, value is the emergent property of the interaction and the attempt of human consciousness to bring exact 'meaning' to said interaction – a ratification of an abstract moment. Objects act to mediate between one state and another – the bridge between the 'here' and the 'there', between place and space.

Methodological note

This chapter has been drawn from research undertaken during my doctorate (2011–14). It is primarily ethnographic in methodology, with photographic images either taken by me or as part of autho-photographic sessions which were used as an elicitation tool during in-depth, iterative interviews. The research focuses on one 'place', which happened to be a market. Unlike other such research on markets, it was not focused on topics of price, exchange, commodification or economies of any kind. Rather, it aimed to understand the complex relationship between identity and place – namely that place and identity co-construct each other.

Initial contact with the informants was made through Southwark Council, whose permission and authorisation were gained. Initially, I attended trading association meetings to meet and greet key players in the market's organisation. Specifically, this focused around a 'matriarch' and stalwart of the market who, with her kind assistance, provided not only strong introductions to traders and buyers, but help and thoughtful analysis on observations. Her position within the market afforded her a particular position and extra space behind her stall. Much of the research findings and all of the conclusions both delivered here and as part of the larger thesis are delivered with thanks for the conversation, tea and offer of a seat at very early hours of the morning.

The market only opened between 4a.m. and 2p.m. on a Friday, which made observation of the coming and goings of traders discrete in nature, in that the sessions of observation were bounded within this time. On many occasions, research commenced long before any stalls or individuals had arrived at the market, at around 2a.m. – although this conclusion was faulted on the first of many days when, after I had been standing for 45 minutes in the cold, wet and darkness of Bermondsey Square, a key informant appeared from her car, which she had parked, and in which she had slept, from the night before.

Traders at the market were largely welcoming, having been used to some attention, but in some instances there was refusal to engage. Over the many months of engagement, it became apparent that this was due to security reasons surrounding the value of the antiques on sale. As part of the research process, auto-photographic sessions were attempted – with mixed success. After initial discussions and a follow-up in-depth semi-structured interview, informants were offered a disposable camera and asked to take images to reflect the nature, identity and characteristics of the market that they felt were most important. The intention was then to feed these images back to them at a later date to elicit responses and explore topics. Of those interviewed, almost half rejected the idea of taking pictures. Of those who did take photos, many of the images returned were of fingers or unusable in discussion. Where images were returned, the majority of these were of other people in the market. Discussions surrounding these images were always interesting and often aided exploration in unexpected directions, yet there was not enough complete data to do a visual analysis of it.

References

Beckert, J. 2009. 'The Social Order of Markets'. *Theory and Society*, 38(3):245–69.
Berndt, C. and Boeckler, M. 2009. 'Geographies of Circulation and Exchange: Constructions of Markets. *Progress in Human Geography*, 33(4):535–51.
Borden, I. 2002. *The Unknown City: Contesting Architecture and Social Space*. Cambridge, MA: MIT Press.
Callon, M. 1986. 'Some Elements of a Sociology of Translation: Domestication of the Scallops and the Fishermen of St Brieuc Bay'. In *Power, Action and Belief: A New Sociology of Knowledge?* edited by J. Law, 196–223. London: Routledge.
Deener, A. 2009. 'Forging Distinct Paths Towards Authentic Identity: Outsider Art, Public Interaction, and Identity Transition in an Informal Market Context'. *Journal of Contemporary Ethnography* 38(2):169–200.
Elder-Vass, D. (2009). 'Towards a Social Ontology of Market Systems'. Working Paper 2009–06. Colchester, UK: University of Essex.
Feld, S. and Basso, K.H. 1996. *Senses of Place*. School of American Research Advanced Seminar Series. Santa Fe, USA: School of American Research Press.
Hoskins, J. 1998. *Biographical: How Things Tell the Stories of People's Lives*. London: Routledge.
Hoskins, J. 2006 'Agency, Biography and Objects'. In *Handbook of Material Culture*, edited by C. Tilley, W. Keane, S. Küchler, M. Rowlands and P. Spyer, 74–84. London: Sage.
Kopytoff, I. 1986. 'The Cultural Biography of Things: Commoditization as a Process'. In *The Social Life of Things: Commodities in Cultural Perspective*, edited by A. Appadurai. Cambridge: Cambridge University Press.
Latour, B. 2005. *Reassembling the Social: An Introduction to Actor-network-theory*. USA: Oxford University Press.
Latour, B. and Porter, C. 1996. *Aramis, or the Love of Technology*. Cambridge, MA: Harvard University Press.
Latour, B. and Woolgar, S. 1979. *Laboratory Life: The Social Construction of Scientific Facts*. Princeton University Press.
Law, J. 1999. 'After ANT: Complexity, Naming and Topology', *Actor Network Theory and After* 46(S):1–14.
Lesourne, J. 1995. 'Self-Organizing Markets'. In *Markets, Risk and Money*, edited by Bertrand Munier, 59–89. Springer.
Plattner, S. 1989. 'Markets and Marketplaces'. In *Economic Anthropology*, 171–208. Palo Alto: Stanford University Press.
Smith, C.S. 1999. *The Market Place and the Market's Place in London, c. 1660–1840*. PhD thesis, University College London.
Soja, E.W. 1980. 'The Socio-spatial Dialectic', *Annals of the Association of American Geographers* 70(2):207–25.
Stauffer, D. and Sornette, D. 1999. 'Self-organized Percolation Model for Stock Market Fluctuations', *Physica A: Statistical Mechanics and its Applications* 271(3):496–506.
Vanberg, V. 1997. 'Markets: Anthropological Aspects'. In *Society*.
Watson, S. 2009. 'The Magic of the Marketplace: Sociality in a Neglected Public Space', *Urban Studies* 46(8):1577–91.
Watson, S. and Studdert, D. 2006. *Markets as Sites for Social Interaction: Spaces of Diversity*. Bristol, UK: The Policy Press.

8
Rank and file on Harrington Road. Rhythmanalysis: Stories of place and the place of stories

Alex Young

Introduction

The pale hues of The Ampersand Hotel, with its frilly iron railings and Regency columns, unfurl onto the pavement in three neat steps before me. Quivering on its pole is the Union Jack, its free rein governed by a leash, for one certainly would not care for exuberance, as this street must appear a sombre affair. Stationed in South Kensington, west from Earl's Court, east from Sloane Square, the hotel has endured since the eighteenth century. Alongside the hotel – between the files of cars, lorries, buses, pedestrians and intermittent bicycles, each observing its own rhythm – is a rank of hackney carriages. Their territory is an island drawn out in the centre of the street by a hem of dashed yellow lines.

The eager panting of the cabs' idling engines performs the ticking bassline; this hum is for humdrum as The Ampersand's Union Jack is for wind. Weekdays, at 5 or 6 o'clock as those who work in the neighbourhood leave for home or the pub, the hum quietens. As one cab glides out of the rank, another glides in the rear. But at midday, the rank is at capacity, seven cabs within the borders of the hemmed island and another three whose drivers flout the advocated rhythm and perch behind the rank. As the cabs multiply, the panting intensifies; as they depart, it quietens. Forever undulating, the rank listens attentively to the street; a metronome, it mirrors its rhythm. The wearily bitter odour of exhaust fumes from the chugging cabs responds too, in time, broken by little else than the dustbin lorry and its sweet pungent wake. Rarely, the rank empties – generally in the early hours of the morning, before the tube opens and after the last stragglers lurch and maunder outside nightclubs. During this time, the nagging hum ceases and a tension dissipates. The linear rhythm of the metronome relinquishes its grip on the tempo of the street. Drivers dare to turn volte-face across the rank, buses turn sharply out of the stop transgressing their established territory, private hires and delivery drivers pause on the side of the road to drop their loads. When there is no cab in sight, occasionally a fare will hover atop the central reservation on the pedestrian crossing. Files of vehicles shuttle past either side.

This rhythmic scene continues to unfold around me as I fidget once again on my off-kilter chair, teetering on the faux marble tiling distinguishing the terrace of Cafe Floris with its happy orange facade (fig. 8.1) from the grey gum-peppered pavement of Harrington Road. Between my rickety vantage point and The Ampersand Hotel are the black cabs, stranded on their hemmed island, files of traffic passing on either side (fig. 8.2). This scene can be described in ways as infinite in number as those who play roles within it. From one hundred dispositions would spring one hundred stories. Though this may be, it is from a rather specific disposition, a disposition learned in part, that I hope to tell just one story. The implications of this story travel far further than this short stretch of Harrington Road.

Fig. 8.1 Two women exchanging goodbyes as they leave Cafe Floris. Source: author

Fig. 8.2 The Ampersand Hotel at dusk, towering over a full rank on Harrington Road. An Uber driver is waiting for their passenger on the double yellow lines opposite. Source: author

Henri Lefebvre, the twentieth-century French philosopher and sociologist, is well known for his work on everyday life and the social production of space that expanded the reach of Marxism and influenced a generation of urban theorists. Lefebvre's work is unreservedly human in spirit and, though often deeply theoretical, it always comes back to the lived experience of place and everyday life. A key tenet in Lefebvre's work is the idea that space is a social construct, that we organise our cities, and space more generally, jointly, based on shared values and in such a way that it shapes our day-to-day movements, activities and perception of the world. Lefebvre's work also sought to pluralise Marxism's notion of time and emphasised the importance of thinking through (social) time and (social) space together, and what their roles are in creating the conditions for the survival of capitalism. It was with his last work, published after his death, *Elements of Rhythmanalysis* (Lefebvre 2004), a text arguably best appreciated as the fourth volume of his *Critique of Everyday Life* series (Lefebvre 1947, 1961, 1981), where Lefebvre most comprehensively examined the importance of thinking through urban realities and everyday life, as well as the social production of space and time – the four key focuses of his work – together. The book intricately stitches together these themes to form an interpretive manual for perceiving and understanding, a way of not only seeing, but hearing and feeling, experiencing experience holistically – a disposition, in short. *Elements of Rhythmanalysis* teases out from diversity general traits, finds order in disorder, the extraordinary in the ordinary, reunites the quantitative and the qualitative, 'does not isolate an object, or subject, or a relation. It seeks to grasp a moving but determinate complexity (determination not entailing determinism)' (Lefebvre 2004:12). As Highmore (2005:69) elaborates, 'rhythmanalysis is an attitude, an orientation, a proclivity; it is not "analytic" in any positivistic or scientific sense of the term. It falls on the side of impressionism and description, rather than systematic data collection.'

Although a disposition, something that is considered primarily a property of the mind, the body is necessarily at the centre of any rhythmanalysis. For Lefebvre, '[the] human body is the locus and centre of interaction between the biological, physiological (nature), and the social (or what is often called the "cultural"), with each of these levels or dimensions having its own specificity and therefore its own time and space or, if you will, its own rhythm' (Lefebvre, Régulier and Zayani 1999:11). Elden (2004) notes that the body is not only an object of analysis, but also a tool of analysis. Rhythmanalysis requires us to reflexively engage with the continually unfolding and evolving relationships our bodies have with surrounding bodies, materials and spaces, attuning to these entities and developing an insight into their capacities for action, or alternatively, what capacities they have to enable or prohibit action. Paying such close attention to the body results in any analysis being multisensorial in nature, so the rhythmanalyst must not '[privilege] any one of [his] senses, raised by him in the perception of rhythms, to the detriment of any other. He thinks with his body not in the abstract, but in the lived temporality' (Lefebvre 2004:31).

In order to satisfactorily grasp urban experience, Lefebvre advocated an embodied and multisensorial sensitivity to rhythms, a method that closely interrelates both time and space while being centred around the concrete experience of everyday life and its malleability at the hands of the capitalist process. As an analytical disposition, rhythmanalysis seeks to reveal the multiplicity of ways in which society organises the everyday lives of individuals through examining complex entanglements of differing temporalities, their structure and functions. It seeks to understand how a city's movements, flows and rhythms – from the traffic during rush hour to the crowds of revellers on a Saturday night – are structured not only through the built environment but also through the ephemeral, through rituals, what is repeated, what is not, and the resultant cycles. Through such analyses, the entangled objectives of multiple agents – human and non-human, material and immaterial, physical and digital – that simultaneously have the propensity to facilitate and restrict one another can be explored through examining their ever-evolving composition in relationship to their ever-changing environment and its various spaces, bodies and technologies. As Hetherington (2013:23) proposes, 'attention to the rhythms of the built environment is one that challenges a Cartesian outlook on its spatiality as something fixed and plan/grid-like and alongside this to call into question overly dominant understandings of time as something linear and chronological'.

Rhythmanalytical or not, the stories we tell matter. With their narrative magic, places we will never step foot in are conjured before us and become our world, freeing us from the confines of our own travels. Without this mediation, we cannot experience what is not immediately surrounding us. It is only with stories, in all their forms, that we can transcend our bodily cage and achieve a certain omnipresence, over space and through time. Although it is true that we experience some of the world for ourselves, it is but an infinitesimally small fraction of the whole and, moreover, it is no less mediated an experience, one that is seen through a lens – our dispositions – shaped, coloured and curved by stories not our own. So, stories help us make sense of our shared condition of being in the world, putting pen to the contours of our reality and shading the voids in between. Here, 'story' should be taken in the very broadest sense: a representation of a perceived reality. If it is possible with stories to change how we see through what we see, and what we see through how we see, to reshape the lens through which all things must pass, then the stories we tell and are told find new meaning, modifying our perceptions and conceptions of the world.

The rhythmanalytical project seeks to change the world through the act of observation itself. As Lefebvre writes, '[the rhythmanalyst] changes that which he observes: he sets it in motion, he recognises its power' (Lefebvre 2004:35). Lefebvre appears to take inspiration from Heidegger and Manheim (1987), who describe poïesis as an activity that brings about a threshold occasion where one thing becomes another, similar to the blooming of blossom or a butterfly metamorphosing from a cocoon, but instead of the transformation occurring in the physical world, the bringing-forth occurs within the artist, poet, philosopher or, in this case, the rhythmanalyst.

Lefebvre acknowledges that in some aspects the rhythmanalyst is similar to a poet or a person of the theatre, both concerned with the act of telling. He goes further and comments on the contributions of art and music as well as poetry and theatre to the everyday – again, storytelling disciplines. Where then does rhythmanalysis, both the act and product, differ from these established fields? How does rhythmanalysis differ from pliant storytelling? To Lefebvre it begins in how they lack a deep reflection on the everyday and instead most often become a passive constituent of the everyday. For Lefebvre, the act of rhythmanalysis means that, 'works [that] might return to and intervene in the everyday. Without claiming to *change life*, but by fully reinstating the sensible in consciousnesses and in *thought*, [the rhythmanalyst] would accomplish a tiny part of the *revolutionary* transformation of this world and this society in decline' (Lefebvre 2004:36). So, the work of the rhythmanalyst is more than simply a passive telling of place, but seeks to change place and everyday life through the very act of telling itself. The rhythmanalyst takes the everydayness (mundanity) of the everyday and transforms it, metamorphoses it through poïesis, changing it by doing nothing more than perceiving and conceptualising it differently. Through internalising the lessons of rhythmanalysis, they become part of our consciousness, our dispositions; we start to perceive the world differently, and so the world is different. But the influence of rhythmanalysis is not limited to our internal selves. The stories we tell, the way we go about our everyday lives, the way we interact with our cities, they all change as we change. Through learning to perceive the world differently, through embracing a rhythmanalytical disposition, all that we create changes as we change, and so others – those who listen, read and experience that which we tell, those who we interact with in our everyday lives – they change too. With rhythmanalysis, we can take a small step towards revolutionising our world.

We have discussed the potential of rhythmanalysis to take a small step towards transforming our everyday life and outlined the nature of rhythmanalysis itself, but not why Lefebvre felt it necessary to do so. Arguing that capitalism in the twentieth century had increased in scope, Lefebvre recounted how capital dominated cultural and social spheres as well as the economic, distorting the rhythms of everyday life. Lefebvre understood the knotted nature of everyday life and capitalism, observing that everyday life provides a critical medium for capitalism's survival.

Stories of place

Harrington Road, like most urban roads, is neatly apportioned into several parallel thoroughfares. On either side, bracketing these five thoroughfares, are two colossal five-storey buildings. These are not vast mansions, however. From the browns of the bricks, the stylistic flourishes, the subtle disparities in architectures, we know these buildings are not two but many. The colourful branding of the resident businesses – Cafe Floris, Khan's Indian Restaurant, Librairie La Page, to name only a few – means they compete for the attention of passers-by, who pause to eye their offerings through wall-to-wall ceiling-to-floor glass windows. The grandeur of The Ampersand Hotel – itself sharing a wall with NatWest Bank, the most contemporary building in the immediate vicinity – looms over the street. Its ruffled late-Victorian ostentatiousness is not tempered by its understated grey tones. The hotel is comfortable standing among its opulent west London neighbours, a Lamborghini dealership around one corner and the Victoria and Albert Museum around the other. Step out from Khan's or The Ampersand and you find yourself on paving slabs, raised from the tarmac, heralding their pedestrian usage. Further towards the centre is the roadway; vehicles travel east by The Ampersand and west by Floris and then, finally, between the flows of traffic, the black cabs hum idly on their yellow-hemmed island.

When approaching a cab in the rank, almost without exception, the fare will stand on one side of the pedestrian crossing waiting for the little green man to light the way. On the man's signal, the vehicles halt, the fare marches on in anticipatory silence and approaches the window of the first cab in the rank to begin negotiations (fig. 8.3). This is the correct

Fig. 8.3 A potential passenger shows a cab driver a piece of paper with the address of his destination written on it before getting into the back of the taxi. Source: author

etiquette. If a fare appears at the wrong cab, they'll be shooed to the front of the rank by the driver. A hurried businessman bypasses the ritual negotiation at the cab window and reaches straight for the door, the driver visibly dissatisfied. Sometimes involving a smartphone or, much more rarely, a map, the negotiation takes only a brief moment.

By law, hackney carriages are required to accept all fares, presumably making pre-journey negotiations redundant, although this is not the case. The drivers subvert the prescribed rhythm. Albeit an increasingly scarce event, after a brief to and fro, some drivers will shake their head and make a sharp gesture towards the cabs behind. The fare walks on. This practice, known as brooming, is frowned upon by the trade. The issue is a regular talking point in the digital enclaves of cab drivers, where the community is pained to consider what actions can be collectively taken to combat their falling revenues due to increased competition from loosely regulated Uber, the Silicon Valley firm that facilitates hailing taxis with a few taps on an app. There are several reasons why jobs are broomed; perhaps the driver will consider the proposed trip too short, hence not justifying the length of time waiting on the rank, or until very recently the driver may not have had a credit card machine. As of November 2016, however, hackney carriages have been required to carry a card machine at all times; however, this represents another prescribed rhythm that drivers subvert, by claiming the machine is not functioning when a passenger asks to use it.

Brooming is billed as a practice the profession can no longer afford since the unwelcome arrival of Uber. It is through interactions on Facebook pages rather than in union meeting rooms that drivers are taking collective action to counter this onslaught. The trade's consensus is that its unions have become toothless, dogged by infighting and ineffective management. One measure taken is photographing the licence plates of fellow cabbies who engage in practices deemed harmful to the profession, before posting the details of the supposed misdemeanour along with a photograph and the registration number to private Facebook groups used by the trade. This name-and-shame approach is employed to discourage others engaging in acts deemed as self-serving and collectively harmful. One instance where social pressure has achieved its objective is found in how the trade has boycotted the use of the Uber app as a way of plying for fares. Uber had added the option to hail a black cab, resulting in a significant number of cabbies signing up and offering their services on the app, but through a spontaneous campaign on the streets and online, chastising those who participated, it soon became impossible to hail a black cab using the app. These are digital interventions with physical repercussions, changing rhythms and changing place itself.

Once complete, negotiations are consecrated by the sharp clink of the opening door and the subsequent wholesome clunk of it slamming shut. The rhythms of the driver and fare acquiesce. The cab fidgets as passengers shift their weight, its indicator flashing, still panting naggingly. Indicate right, three-point turn. Indicate left, edge into traffic. The cab pulls away and after a cursory splutter it catches its breath and begins to purr. The driver swiftly salutes the driver who beckons the cab to join the flow of vehicles, and meanwhile cabs in the rank shuffle forwards, promptly filling the vacuum – a cycle that is repeated again and again, each time the same yet different. Rarely, drivers will tap their smartphones and break rank, foregoing their position in the queue, the negotiation digital rather than physical (fig. 8.4).

Fig. 8.4 A driver breaks away mid-rank. Mostly this happens when the driver has accepted a fare on one of the ride-hailing apps that the profession uses, such as Hailo or Gett. Source: author

Fig. 8.5 A cab driver sits on the bonnet of his cab while smoking a cigarette between jobs. Source: author

After catching a fare, cab drivers often return within hours, sometimes mere minutes, then again the next day and perhaps the next. There are many regulars. Faces are familiar. Waiting for fares, drivers congregate in the small pockets of relative safety between the cabs, normally in no more than threes. Alone for a cigarette (fig. 8.5) or chatting in a group, their utterances confined to their hemmed island, murmurs that become lost in the hum. 'You can go where you like, but drivers tend to come to the same places,' Kevin tells me between fares, 'it's just force of habit now.' Our conversation is disjointed, its measure set by the repeated shuffling of the cabs. 'Had my hips fixed a couple of years ago, couldn't walk before then, but now every time I stop…,' the door of the cab slams shut, 'I'm out. Can't sit in here for five seconds!' Reflexively leaning one arm on the cab door, Kevin surveys the rank before looking away; 'A lot of them have gone now, I mean, they've left the trade. A lot of people are leaving the trade at the moment.' After Kevin waves to a passing cab driver for what must be the third time in the same number of minutes, I comment that there must still be some friendly faces. 'Yeah!' – my observation was met with unchecked enthusiasm followed immediately by silence – 'There used to be…' Kevin's voice fades with his words barely audible over the threatening hum of the metallic masses throttling past either side. 'I'm talking about contemporaries my age – I'm nearly 60, I've been driving for 20 years. My first day was

Diana's funeral, I didn't want to go out to work. Every road was closed. My wife made me go. "You've been studying for three years, get out there and make some bloody money!" she said, "Stop making excuses!"'

There was a sense of loss that saturated our discussions that day. A loss of community, friends, of pride, a financial loss too and, in sum, the loss of a way of life. Our conversation soon returned to Harrington Road and the years Kevin has spent coming here. 'But yeah, Floris,' says Kevin, gesturing at the cafe I have so often frequented during my time here, 'I go there regularly. They give me change, they've got toilets. If I buy one coffee there every day, it's like £700 in the year.' For Kevin, the road is saturated with meaning, with relationships past and present.

> There used to be a Welsh driver who would come along here. A fiery Welshman, Graham, lovely bloke. He sometimes comes around now, but he's stopped working here, gone other places. Anyway, a bus driver came round here and clipped him, he shouts and the bus driver put his finger! So Graham goes up the road. Obviously, the bus has to stop but the driver wouldn't open the doors. So Graham was booting it – and this was before I'd had my operation. By the time we were all up there, of course the police arrive and the bus driver says, "I'm being attacked! I'm being attacked!" And we say, "No, he hit him and gave him the big finger!" Anyway, someone on the bus turned around and was a witness against the driver…

We are interrupted, as our conversations always are. 'Hello there!' says Kevin, followed by a clink. His greeting is dutifully reciprocated by the passenger, before the door clunks shut. As Kevin winds down the window of the cab to shake my hand, I ask whether he will return to the rank today; 'I probably will! I probably will. You never know.'

All interactions are inevitably declared and consummated by the familiar clink-clunk. Rhythm meets rhythm and anoints anew. Inside the cabs, each their own aluminium islet amidst a sea of traffic, drivers fleetingly indulge in their own private rhythms. Newspapers, mobile phones, a snack, coffee (figs 8.7 and 8.8). During these transitory interludes, proud drivers will frequently use the time to speedily clean their cabs, vigorously polishing and every so often raising their head in anticipation of the inevitable shuffle. Exceptionally, the street will be startled by a horn. A reminder to shuffle forward or a notification that lights are green.

'Well that didn't take long?' I say as Kevin returns with the customary clink-clunk. 'No, never does these days… you asked me why I come here,

Fig. 8.6 Besides the rank on Harrington Road, waiting for the traffic lights to turn green, two drivers express different views on the author. Source: author

Fig. 8.7 A cab driver reading a book on her Kindle between jobs. Source: author

Fig. 8.8 A cab driver resting his head on his hand and looking at a photograph of a woman while inching towards the front of the rank. Source: author

it's because no one puts their hand out and stops me!' Coming up to rush hour, the shuffle hastens. 'You know, my first year as a cabbie I cleared gross £42,000, 20 years ago. All right, I was young guns and eager, but last year I worked January to January, 269 days, and I averaged £142 a day gross. There's no benefits from that, pensions, bank holidays, and by the time I put diesel in here, the running of it, it comes to £36/37,000. Take 10 grand off for running the cab, insurance and all that, it's £26,000. That's paper-round money! That's how it is.' We shuffle forwards. 'At the moment, it's always like this; no one's being paid. This is a rush hour. Where's the fares?' This is a story told on cab journeys, posted on trade Facebook groups and in conversations on ranks around the city. The explanations the drivers provide for their predicament are wide-ranging, complex and multifaceted, but the whims of capitalism unify them all. Although Uber drivers often provide a convenient and ever-visible lightning rod for criticism, protecting and obscuring the socio-economic structures that Uber stemmed from, the reality is understood by drivers to be much more nuanced. 'Well, look around the houses here at night; you won't see any lights! There's no one home; they're owned by overseas investors! To me, this is one of the richest areas in the world. When you think that an apartment here –you can check in the estate agent windows down the road – it's about three and a half million! A two-bed apartment!

Three and a half million in Hollywood and you can buy a ranch! People say, "Oh, Hollywood is richer." No!'

After yet another obligatory shuffle, Kevin's ire turns to Uber: 'The problem we have at the moment is that Uber are so heavily subsidised. They're doing it to get rid of us! And Uber are really big investors in driverless technologies – get rid of the driver, get rid of us, and mop up! I talk to other cab drivers and they don't get it… "Oh, you know, driverless technology, won't happen for years and years!" And you say, "It's here now!"' After a thoughtful silence, Kevin turns back to me; 'I don't think big business has a very compassionate attitude.' Courtesy of speculative investing, Uber can raise billions of dollars of cash from investors, allowing it to run at a loss in the short term since it, and its investors, expect to be able to operate as a monopoly in the future once they have forced individual cabbies out of the trade by making their work economically unviable. Many conversations concern the notion that faceless powers govern much of the drivers' everyday lives, whether these powers be big business, the advancement of technology, regulatory agencies, the relentless onward march of capitalism or, as it most often is, a combination of them all. The rank on Harrington Road, as a place and feature of the urban environment, is itself faced with obsolescence due to such forces. With the proliferation of smartphones, and with businesses like Uber combined with a loose regulatory system, the rank is rendered increasingly superfluous as more people unlock their phones to hail a taxi, normally arriving anywhere in London within a couple of minutes, from the comfort of their living rooms. 'This is how the world works now. It's habit, they do it everywhere they go. People like to think their driver is outside.' With a plummy accent, Kevin pulls back his shoulders and makes a buoyant hand gesture; 'They say, "Oh! There's my driver!"'

The cabbies, their relationships, politics, digital doings – they're all but a small fraction of the unfathomable totality of Harrington Road that they exist within and without. The fluid and responsive rhythms of the rank contrast with the strictly timetabled buses, the bus stop's arrivals board forever counting down to the next approach (fig. 8.9). Never more than 10 minutes to wait, the buses' rhythms are both diurnal and nocturnal. The jellyfish crowd waiting for the bus repeatedly swells and billows after school and contracts in the early hours, pulsating in perpetuity. The latest rendition of the Routemaster nods at times past with its patriotic red and appropriation of the iconic design of its predecessors, except now, being part electronic, it gleefully whistles to a standstill. Inevitably a figure will raise a hand, signalling the bus to stop – an enduring relic of a rhythm supposedly confined to the past; today,

Fig. 8.9 People wait as the digital timetable counts down to the arrival of the next buses. Source: author

regulations demand buses to come to a standstill regardless of a raised hand, although both driver and passengers eagerly collude to defy another prescribed rhythm. Back door opens, passengers file out. Front door opens, passengers pile in. As the bus, at a standstill, fills, it obliges the oncoming vehicles motoring towards the junction to flow around its red mass. The traffic lights at the junction conduct the next move. On red, the little green man shines and pedestrians walk freely over the crossing; barely a head turns to survey the traffic, people placing their faith in others' respect of the persuasive charm of these few colour-coded lamps. Red, amber, green. With a buzz and a whistle, the bus sets off with staccato mopeds and treble vans joining the cacophony. While the traffic light is green, the columns of oncoming traffic cease, as do pedestrians at the crossing, each awaiting their respective cue from their respective conductor.

Owing to the locality, with its wealthy francophone residents, the Lycée Français, the Institut Français and the French bookstore across the road from The Ampersand, the rambling chit-chat is perfumed with notes of French. French is, of course, only one of many languages to be heard, given the many huddles of tourists with their wide eyes dashing between Google Maps and the road, as well as the diverse nationalities of the city's inhabitants. Tourists experience Harrington Road, and the city, from a disposition not like that of others. Time moves more slowly for these transient peoples, who take a pace unfamiliar to those for whom the street's presences are but a daily afterthought; for the commuter the street is but a route to a destination, for the tourist the street is both route and destination. A pause to admire the hotel's grand architecture, the curiosity to take to Wikipedia and seek local histories, a slowed walk to compare ratings of local restaurants. These interludes of interludes often clot the pedestrian flow – particularly at peak hours, before and after school or work. Come rain or snow, those walking Harrington Road find their priorities suddenly individually disordered but collectively cohered. Commuters, residents, shoppers, students and tourists scramble for shelter. The street hastens, pedestrians scurry and jostle, crowds gather under the welcome refuge of the bus shelter; then there is relative quiet once shelter is sought. Drivers return to their aluminium islets, and prospective passengers, with little patience for the little green man, dart towards the cabs at paces hardly seen in kinder weather, many foregoing Uber for what, in an inversion of circumstances, is now the most desirable option. Concealed and closely observing the events of the road, no matter the weather, is the hotel's doorman (fig. 8.11), dormant until the hesitance of a taxi before the steps or the sound of a suitcase being dragged along the pavement alerts him to an arrival.

Though seldom so, buses are late, betraying their timetabled decree. If this coincides with the school bell, just before 4 o'clock most

Fig. 8.10 A woman staying at one of the luxury serviced apartments opposite The Ampersand Hotel stands and watches as her luggage is loaded into the Middle East Cargo Services freight van. Source: author

Fig. 8.11 The doorman of The Ampersand Hotel holds the door open for a guest. Source: author

weekdays, the crowds will spill out from the bus stop into its surroundings. Children, not yet submissive to the dictated codes of a prim London street, will sit on the hotel's steps, and passers-by will jostle impatiently through the throng. Pairs and small groups cease their chatting while manoeuvring through the crowd, and lone walkers momentarily sheathe their phones and submit full attention to what is physically before them. Nearby, the single-file queues at the cashpoints wait in devout silence, leaving a respectful distance while customers are paid their respects. A larger crowd; more anxious glances over shoulders.

Whether a guest at The Ampersand relaxing in the hotel lounge, the waiter finishing up at the cafe opposite, or the student sitting in an apartment down the road, anyone can digitally meld the rhythms of the street. The tired waiter, arm outstretched, phone in hand, opens the Uber app. 'Where to?' A few taps, the destination entered. A moment to calculate, every turn of the journey mapped. Small cars icons populate the map and float sheepishly along the grid representing the surrounding roads. Confirm pickup. 'Optimizing pickup', 'Finding your ride', 'Meet

Fig. 8.12 An Uber driver in a Toyota Prius waits at the side of the road with their hazard lights flashing, the rank can be seen in the distance. Source: author

outside 15 Harrington Road', '2 MIN AWAY', '1 MIN AWAY'. 'Arriving now'. The passenger, eyes darting between the phone and the oncoming traffic, finally matches number plates and signals to the driver by waving the phone screen in the car's direction. The driver pulls up in near silence. Only an electric whir dissonant to the choking hums of the black cabs separates the car from the soundscape of the street. The driver pauses nervously on the double yellows (fig. 8.12). Some passing drivers swerve with exaggerated motions, others sound their horns; cabbies look on from the rank, not hiding their contempt. And then as silently as they come, they go, leaving the rank all but a relic in their rear-view mirror (fig. 8.15). No option to pay cash.

A cab stops beneath The Ampersand's Union Jack (fig. 8.13). The concierge flutters down the flight of stone steps, promptly opening the cab door to greet the guests while simultaneously relieving them of their luggage. The flight of steps sets the rhythm for the guests. Stride by stride, a pedagogic drumroll, an introduction to the novel rhythms of the hotel. On a guest's departure, a flitter towards the rank will follow the flutter. Another of the street's denizens who has no time for the little green man, the concierge waits expectantly for a gap in the traffic. A brief survey of the traffic, a dash, negotiation, clink-clunk, cab fidgeting, three-point turn, salute, swing toward hotel, clink, concierge out, guest

Fig. 8.13 A black cab driver smiles as he drops off a family arriving at The Ampersand Hotel. Source: author

in, clunk, swing, drive. And then concealed once more, again dormant until conducted once more to play conductor (fig. 8.14).

Conclusion: Stories of place and the place of stories

Harrington Road and its surroundings are read and written by its denizens, consciously or not, as a script allowing for certain actions and disallowing others, possibilities communicated through a complex system of signs – not only road signs, of course, important though they are. This is a symphony with not one conductor, but many. The arc of the road, the yellow lines painted on the road's surface, the sound of horns, little green men, people's gestures and motions – all conducted conducting conductors. So, this is not a script by a solitary author written to be passively read as immortal and immutable by a solitary reader – it is a script that has been both read and written over the passage of histories by innumerable authors, some known, others not, and continues to be simultaneously reread and rewritten by innumerable more in a state of constant barely fathomable flux. A palimpsest penned in a myriad of languages, its totality understood by no one, fragments understood by all. Every tourist, every driver, the concierge, Uber, the government – they are all authored and authors through their very

Fig. 8.14 The doorman stands alone waiting in the lobby of The Ampersand Hotel. Source: author

Fig. 8.15 Harrington Road seen through the rear windscreen of a hackney carriage. Source: author

presence, physical, cultural or digital. Chaos that by some marvel presents itself as coherence. A script where each line exists to be championed or chided, and adhered to, ignored or changed. All actors have their role, their script, but improvise they do.

The script for the drivers of hackney carriages was first set out hundreds of years ago, and many of the drivers' rhythms apparent today are but whispers of yesterday's. Cabbies speak proudly of their profession being the oldest regulated public transport system in the world; the first regulated black cabs took to London's streets in 1654 when Oliver Cromwell passed an act of parliament setting up the Fellowship of Master Hackney Carriages. It is almost idle to note that society and its technologies – a relationship that should concurrently be inversely formulated as technology and its societies – has undergone immense change since the hackney carriage's inception, and the rhythms that would resemble Lefebvre's conception of the meta-stable equilibrium then would not now. It is, in part, these rhythms that have traversed the intermediate centuries from then until now that result in the present discordance, the arrhythmia, in today's symphony. Without doubt these rhythms have transformed, to some extent, over the course of time. They will have mingled with some rhythms, clashed and coalesced with some more, since they are, as already propositioned, not immortal and immutable. That said, remnants of archaic rhythms are certainly discernible to the rhythmanalyst of today.

The act of hailing a cab with a raised hand from a street corner, the inherited materiality of the rank alongside the rituals and etiquettes coupled to it, the driver's encyclopaedic knowledge of the city's streets. Compare these rituals associated with the hackney carriage to what is made possible through the advent, and adoption of, digital technology. Through the Uber app, without raising a hand or searching for a rank, a passenger can, with a few taps, hail a car that will arrive within a few minutes – wherever he or she is in London and at whatever time. Riders need not open their wallets; payment is taken automatically from a stored credit or debit card, and a fare estimate is provided prior to departure. For the driver, there is little barrier to entry. Drivers are not required to commit to undertaking a costly and intensive three- to four-year training course (the equivalent duration of an undergraduate degree in the UK), memorising over 25,000 streets and learning to, on command, verbally recite the most efficient turn-by-turn route between any two while at the same time being able to note whether junctions or roundabouts are crossed and what points of interest may be alongside the chosen route, or, for that matter, undergoing a minimum of 13 periodical examinations. This laborious process, a process that contributes to the great pride felt among black cab drivers for their profession and its history, is replaced by a few cursory checks: a criminal background check, a medical and a simple topographic test. Before the advent of satellite navigation systems and their ilk – so the vast majority of the hackney carriage's history – there was an obvious necessity to be able to navigate the city's streets without assistance. Today, however, the destination is input by Uber passengers before the car has arrived, the most efficient route calculated, and turn-by-turn instructions provided; as Kevin comments, 'The world has changed, you've got it on your phone now. When I did [the knowledge], there wasn't sat navs.' Apps such as Waze go a step further by tracking their millions of users' speeds and locations and combining that data with user-submitted reports of incidents, closures and other relevant information, to continually calculate and update these step-by-step directions over the course of the journey to ensure the fastest route is always taken – something that no matter how many years of training black cab drivers submit to, they cannot alone replicate. It is worth noting that something Uber will never replicate is the prestige associated with driving the iconic black cab and the pride the drivers feel for their historical profession. 'The pride is immense,' says Colin, a cabbie I met at the rank on Harrington Road who had only in the last few years 'passed out', the trade's term for passing the knowledge of London and receiving a hackney carriage licence (a term, incidentally, also used for referring to completion of the first stage of British Army training), 'that's one reason why I've never entertained the idea of becoming an Uber driver. It's about prestige. It's kind of elitist but in a good way, not in an arrogant way, you know….' And with the prestige comes quality, as Steve attests, using the discount clothing retailer Primark as a metaphor for Uber, another example of a race-to-the-bottom capitalist entity, 'It's like I just said to Greg, the thing is if you go to Primark – and first of all you come out with 32 bags, because it's cheap and nasty – but after you've washed it and it's gone out of shape, you'll go back to where you started from: Ralph Lauren!'

The rhythms that emanate from the weight of rituals designed so many years ago – ranks, hailing by hand, the knowledge – for a society of different demands and technological capabilities, grate against those of the 'modernisers' who embrace the dictums of global capitalism and technological change. Hetherington (2013:21) – referencing Sheringham's (2010) conceptualisation of the city as an archive 'where the past is conveyed through the everyday materiality and lived practice that shapes their composition' – talks of the 'evocative power of the past to engage active subjects' and how material traces of the past remain part of the urban fabric. The resultant state is one of arrhythmia. It is as ordinary to observe a nondescript black electric car whizzing to a halt by the pavement next to the rank on Harrington Road – dithering on the double yellows, hazards on, waiting for the phone-waving passenger to approach – as it is to observe a fare walking over to the window of a black cab, anything but nondescript, engine ticking and chugging, idling on the rank. With the rank being an artefact from another era, and the trade so intimately connected to it, both physically and economically, it could be seen as the ultimate symbol of the grim power of capital to render obsolete. As tempting as this explanation is, it is also careless. Capitalism and its artifices are too often seen as a natural force – something that pre-exists and has its own complex internal organisation that is uncontrollable and destined to never be fully understood; something that transcends, and is external to, humanity – but this is a well told lie, and Harrington Road provides an exemplary flashpoint.

This is arrhythmia by design. An important author of the script that sets out the role for a black cab driver on Harrington Road, one that constructs the structure of the chamber that a driver's everyday rhythms rumble through, and certainly the author that receives the most condemnation from drivers for their current predicament, is Transport for London (TfL). TfL sets out and enforces the policies with respect to the usage of ranks, the right to ply for fares on the street (as opposed to booking over the phone or via an app, as is mandated by TfL for private hires), the legislation related to the taking of payment and what training is required to acquire a hackney carriage licence (pass 'the knowledge'). Regulators such as TfL are formations within the capitalist system that are purportedly designed to curb the effects on people of the worst excesses of capitalism, or to limit negative externalities, in economic textbook terms. In this instance, the laissez-faire approach taken, an approach that is wholly ideological insofar as it does not subject drivers working with (or for, depending who you ask) huge monopolies like Uber to the same requirements as for individual black cab drivers, or at least approximations of them, has directly resulted in the present discordance, or arrhythmia. It should then too be interrogated for to whom these so-called 'negative externalities' are limited, if not the cabbies. It is easier to refer to people as 'negative externalities'; it strips away their humanity and leaves in its place a simplified but hollow calculation. To the cabbies of Harrington Road, whose careers are threatened by 'modernisation', the only people who see their 'negative externalities' curbed are 'Travis and his £50 billion mates', to quote Steve, another Harrington Road regular Kevin introduced me to, who is here referring to Travis Kalanick, Uber's billionaire CEO and co-founder. Like all drivers I spoke to, Kevin too has strong feelings on the matter: 'Regulators don't take pride in us. We get voted the best cab service in the world, year in, year out, and you would think TfL would have pride in that, but it don't seem to mean anything to 'em. They're the ones that will ultimately put the boot in us', Kevin had told me resolutely, punctuating his assessment with an abrupt sip of a coffee he had just bought from Cafe Floris. As long as capitalism is allowed to drive on untamed, the hackney carriage will continue to be but a black blur in Uber's rear-view mirror. Steve had arrived while Kevin was mid-sentence; 'I mean, I think we have a lot of advantages, but I don't think people in power are giving us any help…'.

The arrhythmia that reigns on the rank of Harrington Road is not isolated. By this I do not mean, merely, that this discordance (or disruption, to take a buzz-word from the Silicon Valley lexicon) extends to all London's, Britain's or even the world's ranks and roads, although this is no doubt true. By this I mean that arrhythmia is the default state of capitalism. What we have here on Harrington Road is a concrete instantiation of an abstract ideological battle, a battle between the further entrenchment of untamed neoliberal capitalism and the call for more government intervention to protect workers through regulations or other means. Is Uber not the ultimate embodiment of all that neoliberalism represents? Inbuilt into the structure of its service are the ideals inherent in neoliberalism (profit over people): price gauging (or as a feature using algorithms, such that prices quoted to passengers increase instantly when there is increased demand from passengers or a decrease in the supply of drivers), the obsolescence of their own employees (Uber is investing billions of dollars in self-driving technology with the express purpose of replacing drivers) and the minimisation of drivers' rights and wages (Uber treats its drivers as being self-employed rather than employees of the company, meaning it does not have to guarantee a minimum wage; Uber is currently appealing an employment tribunal ruling that drivers must be treated as workers).

It is an unfortunate irony that Uber and black cab drivers are actually, as noted, in an unremarkably similar predicament: both are struggling with precarity, low wages, long hours, and share similar socio-economic backgrounds; it is typical of capitalism, with its simultaneous destructively creative power to divide and conquer the working classes. It should not be surprising – although given the present tensions it may be – that black cab drivers and Uber drivers have a lot in common. It is a miserable quirk of capitalism that specialist labour is replaced by generic and unqualified labour for the sake of economic efficacy, irrespective of substance. The animosity among taxis drivers provides an everyday instance of this with traces of conflict seen on a daily basis – cabbies not letting Uber drivers out at junctions, for instance, or a Toyota Prius pulling up beside a rank. This inevitably leads to a situation where capitalism has institutionalised distinctions between the working classes. Of course this serves capitalism well, splintering and creating conflict between socio-economically similar groups while simultaneously providing a convenient distraction from injustices inherent in capitalism and rendering any possibility of cohesive collective action between these groups unlikely. A much-lauded characteristic of driving a taxi, whether black cab or Uber, is the sense of freedom it provides; 'You can work unlimited hours, where you want, when you want,' says Kevin. But of course, this freedom is really the freedom to act in a certain way within strict prescribed boundaries that Kevin has no direct control over – a fictive freedom. The prisoners are free to act more or less how they wish within their cell. As Greg, another of the Harrington Road regulars mused, 'At the end of the day, I have to come out for work whether I have Uber here or not, and that's the case for most drivers.'

We see that the materialities, technologies and ideologies of the present, and the remnants of those inherited from our past, have a distinct and very real effect on everyday rhythms and place. We see that the structures of daily lives are deeply affected by government regulations, advances in technology, economic ideals and the weight of history, the one-time necessity for cabs to be easily accessible at a rank, and for their drivers to memorise how thousands of roads connect to one another, for instance. Impersonal forces, with origins far removed from the denizens of Harrington Road, govern every aspect of daily life down to the most intimate bodily movements, the raising of a hand to hail a cab or the tapping of a phone screen to do the same. We see rhythms are not confined to a discrete segment of time and space but reverberate through history and resonate around a globalised world, often with consequences most damaging for those already most exploited. It is for these reasons that rhythmanalysis as a way of perceiving and telling finds purpose. Through an actively reflective engagement with place and everyday life we can hope to disentangle and hence revolutionise our incumbent relationships – material, social, digital, ideological, bodily – that provide the structure for capitalist society. The stories we then tell must not be passive reproductions of the world, devoid of poetry, critique and reflection, and instead must carefully embrace another way of telling which grasps their inherent power to create and recreate, to revolutionise, and instil life into everydayness. This is the place of stories.

Methodological note

My exploration into the rhythms of Harrington Road began in the spring of 2015 and continued intermittently, often with long gaps in between, until January 2017. There was the opportunity – over the course of days, nights, seasons and years – to immerse and re-immerse myself in the rhythms of the road and capture an understanding of place that was far longer term than I had originally anticipated, although, at the same time, this stop-start approach led to complications. There was no timetabled or structured approach to my visits; instead they were sporadic and planned at the last minute, with the one exception being during initial fieldwork in mid-April 2015 when I stood witness to three consecutive dawns turn to dusk on Harrington Road. Other than this singular exception, my visits so many months later would take place when time would allow, most often compressed between other research commitments.

So, although over the course of what was almost two years I visited Harrington Road several times across seasons, there were long hiatuses between trips and threads of thought became hard to hold onto. As a consequence of this structural vacuity, I repeatedly found myself, upon studying my fragmented notes, to be making the same observations ad nauseam, albeit each time perceived and formulated somewhat differently but with the overall character generally remaining the same. Both impulsively and uncritically, my response was to problematise this, seek a solution and organise my fieldwork and note-taking such that this would no longer continue.

After rereading Lefebvre, the serendipity of this supposed complication became clear. What I stood to gain from my chaotic approach, in which the same observations were made again and again, was a valuable insight into the repetitions of the road. Through the chaos came clarity, cycles became transparent, the measure of the street apparent – the rhythm palpable, and with the right words life was created out of chaos. What was perhaps the most productive outcome was how in each noted repetition, difference was there to be found – not only in the observed event itself but in the ways in which it was perceived. This difference within repetition is crucial to Lefebvre's approximation of rhythmanalysis. As Hetherington notes, '[rhythms] are made up, [Lefebvre] suggests, not only of the built environment and infrastructures through which people move but through repetitions of activity that also produced ripples of difference that mean that any one time in the city is never quite the same as another' (Hetherington 2013:23). As is so often the case, structure seems to manifest itself virtually autonomously from the unstructured, or at least from what is perceived as such. From this point on, allowing whims to grasp me, I succumbed to a structurally unstructured approach, not to lead rhythms but to be led by them.

Contingency, ever apparent, played a further role in the choice of locale. For the original research I was interested, quite specifically, in cabbies and their relationship with place. My requirements were straightforward: I sought a well-used taxi rank with somewhere nearby convenient for me to sit for long durations. This led me to Harrington Road, which happened to be ideally situated in that there was Cafe Floris, with its outdoor seating and cheap coffee, which happened to provide an ideal vantage point across from the rank. Lefebvre in his famed rhythmanalysis of Rue Rambuteau in Paris sits on his balcony overlooking the road below in order to achieve a 'certain exteriority' so as to discern how 'noises distinguish themselves, flows separate out, rhythms respond to one another' (Lefebvre 2004:38). But of course, as Lefebvre notes 'to grasp a rhythm it is necessary to have been grasped by it' (Lefebvre 2004:37), and therefore it is also necessary to find this elusive balance between exteriority and interiority. It is a well-used trope that when deeply immersed within a culture, society or just a general way of being, it can be arduous achieving the distance required to attain valuable insights. Then, inversely, it is needless to say that being too far outside of something will likely not be fruitful. Instead, 'In **order to grasp** and **analyse rhythms**, it is **necessary** to get **outside them, but not completely... A certain exteriority enables** the **analytic intellect** to **function**' (Lefebvre 2004:27). Cafe Floris, with a terrace cordoned off from the road, provided me with the right balance of exteriority and interiority.

Mostly the rhythms carried me. Notably, though, for a day in early 2017, around two years after first setting foot on Harrington Road, this dynamic was deferred when discussing the rank, the road and the trade with any driver on the rank willing to chat. Although not a structured interview – there were no comprehensively premeditated questions or anything written in preparation – to describe this as something as informal as a chat is perhaps misleading. Before arriving that day, I had already constructed an identity for myself on Harrington Road as well as in relation to the trade. In short, there were topics that would inevitably be at the forefront of my mind when approaching drivers. This combined with the imposed asymmetries that are incidental when openly recording the conversation make this a relatively less spontaneous affair. With few exceptions, cabbies were generally glad to have someone listen to them speak passionately about their concerns about the precarity of their centuries-old profession. One of the most prevalent concerns voiced was how they felt sidelined; that the powers that be, notably TfL, were unhearing.

References

Elden, S. 2004. 'Rhythmanalysis: An Introduction'. In *Rhythmanalysis: Space, Time and Everyday Life*, edited by H. Lefebvre. London: Routledge.
Heidegger, M. and Manheim, R. 1987. *An Introduction to Metaphysics*. First edition. New Haven: Yale University Press.
Hetherington, K. 2013. 'Rhythm and Noise: The City. Memory and the Archive'. In *Urban Rhythms: Mobilities, Space and Interaction in the Contemporary City*, edited by R. J. Smith and K. Hetherington, 17–33. Oxford: Wiley-Blackwell.
Highmore, B. 2005. *Cityscapes*. Basingstoke, Hampshire: Palgrave Macmillan.
Lefebvre, H. 1947. *Critique De La Vie Quotidienne*. First edition. Paris: B. Grasset.
Lefebvre, H. 1961. *Critique De La Vie Quotidienne*. First edition. Paris: L'Arche.
Lefebvre, H. 1981. *Critique De La Vie Quotidienne*. First edition. Paris: L'Arche.
Lefebvre, H. 2004. 'Rhythmanalysis: An Introduction'. In *Rhythmanalysis: Space, Time and Everyday Life*. London: Routledge.
Lefebvre, H., Régulier, C. and Zayani, M. 1999. 'The Rhythmanalytical Project', *Rethinking Marxism* 11(1):5–13.
Sheringham, M. 2010. 'Archiving'. In *Restless Cities*, edited by M. Beaumont and G. Dart, 1–17. London Verso.

9
Holland Park: An elite London landscape
Christopher Tilley

Introduction

London is never silent. The roar of traffic pervades the places of the city. In an angular landscape of brick and concrete, glass and steel, the built environment dominates in its overwhelming and overarching solidity and hardness. The smell of diesel permeates the air. In the streets, in the city centre, the termite-like masses ebb and flow in accordance with diurnal rhythms. One is never alone in a city that seems, because of its teeming humanity, indifferent to its populace: anonymous, replaceable, expendable, mobile, transient. Collectively, any notion of community here remains just a distant dream in a nightmare world of transnational flows that global capitalism reproduces day by day and year by year. People become the digits of the city in a digital age in which any sense of a natural world, something existing outside of the cultural domain of people and their doings, seems irrevocably lost, a world that once was, or may have been, but is definitely gone for good.

 I am walking in central London, going west down a gentle slope. The ground is wonderfully soft under my feet. I am walking on light brown wood chippings. A subtle rotting odour of woodland vegetation and the fragrantly scented white flowers of cow parsley fills the air. This is Chestnut Walk. Stately mature trees line it on either side. It is early on a summer morning. Sunlight filters through the leaf canopy above, creating soft patches of dappled light (fig. 9.1). The dominant sound is bird song – many different birds. I can distinguish a chorus of their distinctive voices greeting the new day. There is dense woodland on either side of the path, and I can't see the birds within it. Although I can

Fig. 9.1 Looking west down Chestnut Walk. Source: author

see a long distance down the slope in front of me, not a single built structure is visible. Perhaps even more remarkably, I cannot see a single person. I am entirely on my own, in a natural environment, within an area, that all the statistics show, has by far the densest population in the city. What kind of place could this be: might I be daydreaming that I am somewhere else – perhaps remote west Wales or the Forest of Dean? I am walking through Holland Park (fig. 9.2).

My momentary solitude is brief. As I continue my walk, a young male jogger comes into view, pounding up the slope, panting, in shorts, trainers and T shirt, headphones on, health tracker strapped to wrist, seemingly oblivious to the surroundings. He has brought the city with him. Beyond there are two dog walkers chatting. No doubt the conversation concerns their canine companions and their quirks and idiosyncrasies. All the dogs here are honorary humans.

It is possible to walk through but not enter the woodland. Pathways criss-cross it in seemingly bewildering complexity, and it is bounded off by low fences with spiky scrub beyond. Small notices at regular intervals inform the visitor of BYELAW No. 4: 'Do not climb over this fence. It is an offence to enter this enclosure.'

Going further towards the centre of the park, I pass a small pond with a wooden bridge over it. The pond is covered with duckweed. On a small island, moorhens with bright red bills are nesting. A statue of a seated third Lord Holland looking south, cane in hand, is in the middle

Finding your way around

Fig. 9.2 Map of Holland Park (Courtesy of the Friends of Holland Park)

of the pond. A pigeon sits on his head, and shit runs down his bronze face (fig. 9.3). A schoolboy passes by, giggles, and takes a picture on his iPhone. Beyond, I encounter a stone wall of large granite blocks with shrubs above screening the view beyond. Outside there is a bamboo water pipe that periodically crashes down, emitting a sonorous booming sound. Beyond the pipe, steps lead upwards to a bamboo screen with

Fig. 9.3 A pigeon on Lord Holland's head. Source: author

Fig. 9.4 The entrance to the Japanese Garden. Source: author

dwarf pines (fig. 9.4). A small sign announces that this is the Kyoto Japanese Garden, a place for quiet and contemplation. Inside, there is a beautiful pond filled by a gushing waterfall (fig. 9.5).

The sound of running water is now all-pervasive in this area of the park. Had I come here in the evening it would have mingled with that

Fig. 9.5 Inside the Kyoto Garden. Source: author

of Italian arias carried on the breeze from the nearby opera pavilion. In the pond, huge carp swim lazily around passing by a pebble beach, stones set in grass, stone lanterns and acer trees. An elderly Indian lady with grey hair is sitting on a mat opposite the waterfall meditating. Below the waterfall, sitting on a low granite bridge across the pond, a young Asian man is feeding the fish with breadcrumbs, despite the numerous signs telling you not to do so. As the fish rise to the surface, he photographs them on his phone. On the far south side of the garden there is a bench. Below it there is a wide crack in the otherwise immaculate concrete and pebble-dash surface painted bright red (fig. 9.6). Beyond is the simple and austere Fukushima Garden of Remembrance fringed with bamboo.

Going out of this area of the park I pass a very tall walking man. I have to look at him several times before I realise that this is not a man (fig. 9.7). To the south, the formal Dutch Garden contains a mass of brightly coloured bedding plants – red, white and blue – set within neatly clipped low box hedges. It is bounded off by a brick wall from the northern wooded area of the park (fig. 9.8). Only a few of its 40-odd memorial benches are occupied. One elderly gentleman smoking a cigar is reading the *Financial Times*, a lady beyond him *The Daily Telegraph*. The memorial on one bench reads: 'In loving memory of mother Stanislava Engel 12.12.01–8.01.90 who loved flowers, Wieslaw'. Another reads 'In memory of Mrs Edie Langley Born 12.10.13. Died 5.1.98. A true

Fig. 9.6 The crack under the bench in the Kyoto Garden. Source: author

Fig. 9.7 Walking man. Sculpture by Sean Henry. Source: author

Kensington lady'. Trailing along the wall behind her bench, wisteria is beginning to flower; in front there are pure white exquisite alliums.

Next to the Dutch Garden there is a small lawned enclosure bounded by well-clipped yew hedges. In the centre stands a golden contemporary sculpture (fig. 9.9). A plaque states that it is *Meridiana*

Fig. 9.8 View of the Dutch Garden, opera tents beyond. Source: author

Fig. 9.9 *Meridiana* by Helaine Blumenfeld. Source: author

by Helaine Blumenfeld OBE FRBS: 'The inspiration came from spending the long late summer afternoons here seeing children chasing their own shadows… It was the ephemeral, ungraspable beauty of passing time and changing light that the artist captures… *Meridiana* meaning sundial in Italian.'

Fig. 9.10 The chess set. Source: author

Beyond *Meridiana*, concealed behind another elegant and perfectly clipped dark yew hedge, there is a giant chess set (fig. 9.10). A man and a boy are moving the chess pieces around. A well-dressed woman, mid to late 30s, stands nearby photographing them on her iPhone: foreign tourists. In the Iris Garden, a member of the Parks Police is speaking on his mobile. A peacock struts slowly in front of him. A squirrel, eating something, is perched on the top of a rubbish bin looking quizzically towards the peacock. The irises in the formal beds surrounding a round stone-clad pond are in full bloom, resplendent in reds, yellows and blues. A couple of people, standing on the lawn, are painting on easels by the distinctive Ice House with its elegantly tiled domed red-brown roof.

I peer through one of the windows of the Belvedere restaurant (fig. 9.11). It is elegantly furnished; chandeliers hang down from the ceilings of the former summer ballroom of Holland House. The menu outside the entrance displays a mixture of French, Italian and English cuisines. Dinner for two with a bottle of house wine costs between £120 and £140. Outside, the Napoleon Garden, with a large central modern sculpture and picnic benches, is shaded by mature trees. Three young children are climbing the sculpture watched by two women speaking Italian. A white female couple speaking Spanish pass by and someone speaking Russian (?) on her mobile. Gardeners arrive in an electric cart and start emptying the rubbish bins and cleaning the paths.

Fig. 9.11 Outside the Belvedere restaurant. Source: author

In an arcade leading to the Orangery, the wall is decorated with a series of striking murals. A sign reads that these were commissioned by the Friends of Holland Park and were painted by Mao Wen Biao between April 1994 and May 1995. They depict an imaginary garden party held by the Earl of Ilchester in the grounds of Holland House in the 1870s. Ladies in elaborate trussed dresses, some carrying ornamental umbrellas, and men in dark suits and black top hats stand socialising on a lawn, with the backdrop of a grand Jacobean house behind them. There are elaborate white-tented pavilions in the formal gardens with knot box hedges. In one scene, a maid dressed in grey uniform bends down to serve a young child of the upper classes (fig. 9.12). In another, a peacock is strutting around in the midst of the lavish garden party. None have been defaced.

There are a few people sitting outside the park cafe in the morning sunlight drinking coffee. A young woman walking very quickly past, speaking French and pushing a very large expensive-looking pram, narrowly misses hitting both a dog and a child who is chasing a pigeon. She is unlikely to be the mother; rather an au pair or a nanny.

To the east of the cafe there is a grand staircase with pillars on either side surmounted with griffins. These are the remains of the ruins of the mansion house that now form the entrance to the summer opera. The gates are closed. The top of the opera pavilion is emblazoned with 'INVESTEC OPERA HOLLAND PARK'. Smaller notices read 'Investec: wealth and investment'. I cannot see anything of the ruins or surviving

Fig. 9.12 Mural in the arcade leading to the Orangery by Mao Wen Biao. Source: author

Fig. 9.13 The opera pavilion. Source: author

east wing of the grand house. They have been obliterated by the huge pavilion and a sea of surrounding white tents (fig. 9.13).

As I am walking down to the Ilchester Place entrance, a couple of dogs and their walkers go past as I pass two prominently positioned parks police cars. Just inside the gate entrance, there is a 'no cycling' sign in the middle of the tarmac road leading up to the cafe and the opera. A woman cycles past on one of the Santander bank sponsored hire bicycles. The bikes' stands are incongruously situated just outside the park gates. On the gates, I read a large blue and white sign, 'The DOG CONTROL ORDERS (offences and penalties) Regulations 2006', from which I learn that dog fouling incurs a maximum penalty of £1,000, that I may be directed to put my dog on a lead which is no longer than 1.22 metres or 48 inches long, and that I am not allowed to have more than two dogs on leads.

A man walks into the park with a dog on a retractable lead that soon extends, I estimate, to at least four times the length specified on the notice. Looking up towards the park cafe, I spot a woman exercising no less than five dogs of all different shapes and sizes, a professional dog walker. A black fitness trainer is instructing a white woman doing step-ups on a bench. An elderly and overweight female jogger struggles by.

Looking to the south of the opera, one can see across an extensive flat sports field, at this time empty apart from a few crows, down towards Kensington High Street (fig. 9.14). In the south-west corner of the field, next to tennis courts, there are cricket nets, golf nets and fitness

Fig. 9.14 View south across the sports field to the high-rise flats on Kensington High Street. Source: author

equipment. Only the tennis courts are currently being used. A sign posted on the golf nets reads: 'Members of the public are reminded not to urinate in this area and should use the public toilets. Anyone found doing this will be asked to leave the park and possibly banned by the park'.

Behind the tennis courts, a high brick wall separates the park from newly constructed white high-rise luxury flats on Kensington High Street with balconies overlooking the park (fig. 9.14). This is almost the only place where buildings visually intrude into the park interior. Such flats fetch about £5 million and appear to be empty. On the wall, a series of signs posted at regular intervals read: 'Warning Anti-climb paint' (fig. 9.15). Several have been defaced to read 'climb paint'.

Holland Park

Holland Park is the name given to an urban park in the Royal Borough of Kensington and Chelsea (RBKC) and a residential area of west London in its vicinity. The RBKC is an inner London borough (local administrative area) just to the west of the centre. It is the second smallest and the most densely populated in the UK, with an estimated population of 158,000 and a population density of 13,000 per km sq. According to the 2011 census, 71 per cent of the residents are white, of which 39 per cent are white British. A further 10 per cent are Asian, 5 per cent of multiple ethnic groups, 4 per cent black African and 3 per cent black Caribbean. The RBKC is the richest borough in the UK.

Fig. 9.15 Defaced anti-climb paint sign. Source: author

The RBKC currently spends £3 million annually on parks and green spaces, of which £1.2 million, or 40 per cent of the entire budget, is on Holland Park. All other parks in the borough that are staffed employ a maximum of two gardeners/park keepers compared with up to 18 in Holland Park.

The park itself is a small remnant of a grand country estate dating back to 1606 bought by Sir Walter Cope, who built a mansion house here, known as Cope's Castle, later as Kensington House and then Holland House. A royal courtier, Cope was one of the richest men in England. The original estate, comprising the four manors of Kensington, was huge, stretching almost as far south as the River Thames (Miller 2012). The Jacobean mansion and its surroundings were remodelled on a number of occasions. The mansion was fire-bombed during World War 2 and only the east wing (now forming part of a youth hostel) and the first storey of the southern facade (forming a backdrop for a temporary summer opera pavilion) and terrace now survive, together with outbuildings comprising a stable block (occupied by a park office and the Parks Police), the Orangery (used for weddings and a whole series of other events such as talks and Christmas carols), the Ice House (used for a summer art exhibition), the ballroom (now a restaurant) and associated walled formal garden areas.

The house and what is now the park was the private residence and pleasure grounds of a succession of aristocratic families. The owners effectively prevented the entire area being built over. The area was sold to London County Council in 1952 for use as a public park, and after the abolishment of the latter passed into the management of RBKC in 1986.

The park itself covers 22.5 hectares and is roughly rectangular in shape. It is topographically varied, with the land gently rising from the south to the north, with the highest point being in the far north-east corner and dipping markedly to the west. Holland Park is by far the largest park/green space in RBKC, but small and relatively less well known when compared with the much larger royal parks of central London (Kensington Gardens, Hyde Park and Regent's Park). It takes about 10 minutes to walk from north to south through the entire park, and 5 minutes from west to east.

The park consists of three distinct areas (see fig. 9.2). In the almost flat southern end of the park there is a large sports field with four tennis courts, exercise machines, and cricket and golf nets in the south-west corner. An area centred around the remains of Holland House contains formal gardens bounded by walls and clipped hedges, toilets, the park nursery with staff offices, a car park, toddlers' playground, two more tennis courts, a park cafe with indoor and outdoor seating, a giant chess set, and other facilities mentioned above. The northern half of the park is dominated by woodland enclosures, with two formal gardens at its northern end (the D Garden and Sun Trap area). A new ecology centre (an RBKC educational facility) is located on the western side, together with an adjacent children's adventure playground and preschool. Apart from woodland, there are some open lawned areas nearest to the house and above the Sun Trap in the far north.

The wooded areas are criss-crossed by two long walks from west to east across the park (Chestnut Walk and Lime Tree Walk). There are a large number of smaller paths that, to a visitor unfamiliar to the park, can appear to be bewilderingly complex; some are straight and formal, others meandering – remnants of both formal and informal woodland estate designs that changed over time.

Today, from the pond containing the statue of the third Lord Holland, five paths forming a rough star shape radiate out in different directions, part of an original 'wilderness' historic landscaping feature originally featuring eight *allées* and affording formal vistas through the trees to countryside beyond (Miller 2012:8). In the northern part of the woodland today, there is a wildlife enclosure and a wildlife pond (see fig. 9.2).

Besides these features, there are a large number of contemporary modern sculptures found in the area around the house and in the D Garden and Sun Trap area, some by well-known and respected artists. Even from this minimalist description it can be appreciated that this is a very diverse and complex park indeed. A massive amount has been packed into a small space. One can be constantly surprised and delighted during a walk through the park by the sheer diversity of what is to be found and encountered here. The RBKC justly regard it as the jewel in their crown.

Park use

This section is based on participant observation and structured interviews with 75 park users (see methodological note). People of all ages use the park in roughly equal numbers; there is also a roughly equal split in terms of sex (table 9.1). There is great diversity in terms of the nationality and ethnic heritage of park users, roughly 50 per cent being white British (table 9.2). The vast majority of regular park users who use the park all year round live in the immediate vicinity of the park (within a 10- to 15-minute walk) and walk there, generally for no longer than 10 or 15 minutes. However, there are substantial numbers of people who

Table 9.1 The ages of 75 park users interviewed

Age:	18–25	26–40	41–60	>60
Number (percentage):	11 (15%)	20 (26%)	19 (25%)	25 (33%)

Table 9.2 The nationality/ethnic heritage of the 75 park users interviewed

Nationality	Number	Percentage (%)
White British	36	48
Black British	2	2.5
White European	26	35
Asian	4	5
Black African	2	2.5
White USA	4	5
White Australian	1	1

Table 9.3 Places where the 75 park users interviewed came from

Local/in vicinity of park	Another part of London	Elsewhere in UK	Foreign tourist
49 (65%)	14 (19%)	2 (2.5%)	10 (13%)

also visit from other areas of London at weekends, and substantial numbers of tourists during the summer months (table 9.3). Most spend between one or two hours in the park. Regular users may visit two to five times a week and generally for shorter periods than occasional or infrequent visitors (table 9.4). The occupations of regular park users and many occasional users are predominantly professional in character, with a high proportion in the banking/finance sectors (table 9.5). The main reasons for visiting the park are walking and relaxing, dog walking, looking after children, jogging or fitness training, socialising and an interest in nature (table 9.6). The principal attractions for tourists are the Japanese Kyoto Garden and, for a minority, the summer opera. Of the main park facilities, the park cafe, which has both indoor and outdoor seating, is the most regularly used and popular facility (table 9.7).

Table 9.4 Time spent in and frequency of visits to Holland Park by the 75 park users interviewed

Time spent				
Up to 30 mins	Up to 1 hour	1–2 hours	2–3 hours	Over 3 hours
9 (12%)	34 (45%)	18 (24%)	10 (13%)	4 (5%)
Frequency				
first time	once a week	two to four times a week	five times or more per week	occasionally (from twice a month to six times a year)
11 (14.5%)	7 (9%)	12 (16%)	14 (18.5%)	31 (41%)

Table 9.5 The occupations of the 75 park users interviewed

Occupation	Number
banking/finance/accountancy/consultancy	15
housewife	8
other professional	8
student	7
higher education/teaching	7
IT	5
retired	5
manager of own company	4
work in park	4
shop worker in locality	4
chauffeur	1
doctor	1
architect	1
senior civil servant	1
artistic director	1
film maker	1
interior designer	1
fashion photographer	1

Table 9.6 Principal reasons why the 75 interviewees visited the park

Principal reason for visiting park	Number	Percentage (%)
walking/relaxing/looking at people	18	24
dog walking	12	19
children	11	14.5
sightseeing (Kyoto Garden)	6	8
jogging/exercise/fitness training	5	6.5
socialising	5	6.5

(Continued table 9.6)

(Continued table 9.6)

Principal reason for visiting park	Number	Percentage (%)
flowers/trees/nature/greenery	5	6.5
work	4	5
playing Pokémon Go	2	2.5
yoga	2	2.5
lunch	2	2.5
stayed at youth hostel	1	1
on way to work	1	1

Table 9.7 Use of park facilities by 75 park users interviewed

Facility	Number	Percentage (%)
park cafe	57	76
Belvedere restaurant	11	15
opera	13	17
Ecology Centre	14	19

The social rhythms of the park

The park has a number of distinct social rhythms that vary according to the time of the day, the seasons, the weather and the day of the week. It is thus an ever-changing place. If it is raining, even in the summer, there will be few people. During the colder months when the days are shorter, the park is relatively deserted at most times, with perhaps only 50 or so users in total in any 30-minute period, except on a Sunday afternoon.

On a typical summer weekday morning between 7.30a.m. and 10a.m. there are relatively few visitors. The park's gardeners and maintenance staff mainly spend their time emptying bins, removing rubbish and litter picking, cutting grass, sweeping up paths, tidying up along the alcoves around the Orangery and the park cafe, tidying up the children's playgrounds and cleaning the toilets. The park is being prepared to look its best for the day ahead. If it has been a fine, sunny Sunday, Monday is the worst-possible morning for the staff. The litter bins will be overflowing, and the wear and tear on the park will show.

At this time of day, mainly joggers, fitness trainers and their clients, and dog walkers occupy the park. Most are to be found to the south of the house. This pattern of early morning park use is replicated every weekday. The park is distinctly *white*. The majority of the trainers and joggers are in their 20s and 30s, the dog walkers are of all ages. Men and women are present in equal numbers, and almost all are local residents.

From 10a.m. the park staff are engaged in other tasks: hedge and grass cutting, leaf sweeping, maintaining borders, weeding and planting in small groups. Delivery lorries pass through the park at this time to service the cafe and restaurant and the youth hostel and, during June and July, the opera. There are noticeably fewer joggers and fitness trainers at this time. A new group of users begin to occupy the park, younger women pushing prams, usually singly, sometimes in pairs. Others are with toddlers or young children. The children's play areas begin to fill up.

Individuals and couples and small groups stroll through the park. Some occupy the benches in the Dutch Garden, others those outside the Belvedere restaurant, in the Rose Garden and around the sports field, or sit inside or outside the park cafe. Many are elderly, some, a minority, are obviously tourists. Overhearing them talk to each other or, as frequently, on their phones, English is only being spoken by about half of them; there is a cacophony of voices in different languages, although the park is still overwhelmingly white. Those sitting on the benches either look at the park and watch other users, read or, more commonly, talk on or play with their phones.

The Kyoto Garden now has up to 60 visitors, who come and go on a constant basis. They usually spend about 10 minutes here, as there are few benches and nowhere else to sit. There are fewer dog walkers than earlier in the morning, but they still maintain a strong presence, mainly around the house. The sports field is now being used by organised school groups playing football and cricket and athletics; all the tennis courts are full.

A few people now occupy the D Garden and the Sun Trap area in the north of the park. Youth groups from the hostel pulling their bags walk south towards Kensington High Street. Tourists come and stroll through the formal gardens and visit the Kyoto Garden. School groups occupy the Ecology Centre and wooded wildlife enclosure. Some people – individuals, couples or small groups – walk through the wooded areas in the north of the park, but this area remains quiet and relatively depopulated compared with the rest of the park.

Between 12.30p.m. and 2p.m. other people who work locally come and sit in the park to eat. Some are shop and office workers; others in high visibility gear are construction workers from developments in the vicinity. Most remain for only about half an hour. Some just sit and smoke. Others come to visit the cafe for lunch; the cafe is usually full.

After 2p.m. the park now largely returns to its pre-lunch rhythm of social use. If it is sunny, there are many women with prams and children, individual strollers and sitters, or couples and more tourists. After 3p.m. schoolchildren walk back home through the park. They spend longer in it now, playing, and sometimes there are groups of 20 or more, a favourite spot being the area outside the Belvedere restaurant.

After 5p.m. local residents walk through the park either from east to west or north to south on their way home. Most are gone by 6.30p.m. Almost all the gardening and parks staff have left. More joggers and fitness trainers appear, and increased numbers of dog walkers. The restaurant receives its first early-evening clientele. Groups of dog walkers chat or stroll through the park around the house. Picnickers sit on the North Lawn and around the edges of the sports field if it is warm and sunny. The evening brings out drinkers – usually older single men, sometimes small groups of younger men. Occasionally they occupy a bench in the wooded area, more usually discretely placed benches to the west of the restaurant and near to the tennis courts. The park remains predominantly white. After 9.30p.m. in summer (or 4p.m. in winter), the park completely empties out and becomes a dead social place. The gates are locked, and the only occupants are late diners in the restaurant, who exit through the car park entrance on the west side, and people staying overnight in the youth hostel, who have no access to the rest of the park and enter from the east down a narrow iron-gated unlit tunnel.

On Saturdays, the social rhythms of the park are similar to those on weekdays, except there are more people walking through and occupying the benches in the area around the house, and people are not passing through going to work or school. Youth groups playing football or cricket or doing athletics with their trainers in organised groups in the mornings heavily occupy the sports field. The tennis courts are usually full all day if it is good weather. In the afternoons and evenings, sports activities here are informal and unstructured, and people not engaged in these sit in groups on the grass around the edges. There are the normal streams of dog walkers and joggers, women with prams and children walking through or occupying the play areas. Fitness trainers and their clientele can be found until the early evening. People come to enjoy the planting arrangements in the formal areas.

From mid June until early August, up to 1,000 people attend the opera in the evening, both during the week and at weekends. Some dine in the Belvedere restaurant and along its roof terrace; others frequent the cafe. The hostel is usually full, and people using it spill out into the park. The Kyoto Garden may be temporarily occupied by a hundred or more people and is crowded, and many tourists visit. The wooded area, as always, remains comparatively quiet and serene. Ethnically the park is much more mixed, much less of a white place, and it remains very crowded until well into the evening.

On a warm sunny Sunday afternoon between 2p.m. and 7p.m., the park reaches its peak capacity. Streams of people enter it both from the south and the north. Flows of people into it from the western and eastern entrances are noticeably less, mainly locals. Every bench will be occupied, both in the wooded area and everywhere else. The narrow paths around the Kyoto Garden now resemble the London Underground at rush hour. The North Lawn and adjacent areas, margins of the sports field, lawned areas around the tennis courts on the western side, the D Garden and Sun Trap area are fully occupied and crowded. The children's play areas are full. People are sunbathing and picnicking in groups. These areas now resemble a green beach. There are many larger families with people of different generations, grandmothers and grandfathers, mothers and daughters, smaller family groups, groups of friends of the same age strolling, and tourists both from other parts of Britain and around the world. The park's staff are driving around frantically emptying the bins, with rubbish spilling out around them into their motorised carts. Towards the end of the afternoon, it becomes a losing battle that will continue on a Monday morning when the park becomes quiet once more.

It is usually only on a Saturday, and more commonly on a Sunday, when men can be seen pushing prams, or holding children by the hand, or playing ball games in areas where they are permitted outside the sports field. This is when there are also big groups of family and friends. Sometimes there are children's birthday parties with balloons and games, with up to 30 adults and children. All of London in its ethnic and linguistic diversity appears to be here, and those visiting the park become truly representative of the city as a whole rather than largely those who live in its vicinity. Some come from the more socially deprived and distant part of the RBKC in North Kensington, others from the rest of London and the surrounding suburbs; a substantial number are tourists. There may be up to 5,000 visitors or more in the park at this peak time, and many stay for two to three hours or more.

During the weekend, many of the local people who use the park regularly during the week do not visit. Thus, socially, there is a self-segregating rhythm, with a huge influx of outsiders accompanied by a relative absence of park use by local residents who stay away from what has become a crowded and noisy place that they no longer find congenial.

The social structure of park use

We can represent the social composition of the park in terms of five concentric circles. At the inner core are those who work in the park all year round. These include the RBKC parks management team, the gardeners and park keepers, the Parks Police, those who work in the youth hostel, cafe and restaurant and the Ecology Centre, and members of the Friends of Holland Park, who voluntarily give up their time on a regular basis to foster the wellbeing of the park.

Almost all of these people who work in the park live considerable distances away in other parts of London. Thus the inner core dwell away from the park, with the exception of the majority of the Friends, who live in its vicinity. For most, it is simply a place of work. So those employed in the restaurant and cafe and hostel spend most of their time here working inside and mainly just pass through the park on their way to work. Only the park location makes the work different from any other low-paid service job in a hotel or restaurant or in an office in the city.

Those employed in managing and maintaining the park, together with the Friends, have an altogether different, more intimate and knowledgeable, relationship with it. All these people – managers, gardeners, the teachers and staff who work in the Ecology Centre – know each other to a greater or lesser extent and interact on a regular basis. But even these people who do work in the park may only do so for shorter or longer periods of time during part of their working life.

The Friends, by comparison, are a permanent and local presence. Their role was described to me as being 'a mixture between a watchdog and a fairy godmother'. No substantial changes to the character of any aspect of the park can be made without prior consultation with the Friends, from a major alteration such as the recent construction and design of the Ecology Centre, or the current plan to hard landscape the terrace in front of Holland House, down to the colour schemes and planting arrangements of the flower borders. The Friends are highly influential and are kept very well informed by the RBKC about all aspects of the park. They are not only informed by those who manage the park, but are very proactive in informing themselves and talking to all involved. They have no formal power to do anything, and cannot make any decisions, but informally they constitute a parallel and unpaid management team that monitors what is done, how it is done and whether agreed official management decisions are actually carried out in a timely fashion. They also actively promote future policies and practices desirable to them.

The Friends publish a glossy colour quarterly magazine, distributed to all members. They organise and take nature walks on the first Saturday of every month in the park. They also organise tree and moss walks in the park led by botanical specialists, and sponsor other walks such as an autumn fungi foray run by the Ecology Centre and given by a specialist from the Natural History Museum and talks about the birdlife of the park by noted ornithologists. They also sponsor and publish books and leaflets about the history of the park and its house, the Kyoto Japanese Garden and notable trees in the park, and even publish Christmas cards for sale. All these activities are designed to encourage an interest in the park by others and thus a desire to preserve it.

Subscriptions, donations, fund-raising events, including an annual art exhibition held in the Orangery, and publications all contribute revenue. The Friends provide substantial additional funds for the enhancement of the park. They have no intention of ameliorating RBKC funding cutbacks or providing substitute funding for the park budget, which might be assumed, or hoped for, by some RBKC councillors; 'watchdog and fairy godmother' are entirely apt terms to describe the Friends' role.

Most Friends live in the vicinity of the park, but others live in other areas of London, some abroad. The vast majority are normally sleeping or inactive members, but can get very vociferous and strongly express their views if they are unhappy with future plans for the park. Most of the active Friends are retired white British, and a majority are female. The chairperson and the secretary invest an enormous amount of time and personal effort in the park, amounting to almost a full-time job. In effect, it is their own extended landscape garden. Always there, the Friends can be regarded as the emotional life and soul of the park, symbolically residing at its innermost core. They deeply care about the park because their own biographies are bound up with it and the park is an important part of their own lives. Those who actually do the work in the park rather than talk about it may feel sometimes that they have a little too much influence.

The second circle consists of local residents who live in the immediate vicinity of the park and use it on a regular basis. They come here to use the park for a wide variety of reasons (see table 9.6), and in many ways regard it as *their* local park. A number told me that they had chosen to live in this part of London because of the presence of *this* park.

The third circle consists of less regular visitors who live further away in other parts of the RBKC, including the socially deprived area of North Kensington. This has its own much smaller park, Kensington Memorial Park. In all respects Kensington Memorial Park and Holland park are as different as chalk from cheese; Kensington Memorial Park has no grand buildings and walled gardens, few facilities other than a sports field, tennis courts and a children's play area, no sculptures, only a few planted borders, no mature trees, no woods, no peacocks, no ponds, only few benches to sit on. It has a shabby seasonally open kiosk rather than an indoor cafe for refreshments. Much more prone to vandalism and anti-social behaviour, it lacks an influential Friends association. There are no full-time gardeners and only a mobile police presence. The relative poverty of the park directly mirrors that of the local residents who use it. People living in this area of RBKC are only likely to visit Holland Park at weekends and almost exclusively during the summer months.

The majority of residents who live in the vicinity of Holland Park are very wealthy indeed, with a higher proportion of high earners (over £60,000 per annum) than anywhere else in the UK, with the highest proportion of people working in the financial sector. This is reflected in the occupations of park users listed in table 9.5. Sociologically, RBKC has been described as the borough of London's super rich or as being the territory of the 'alpha rich' (Savage et al. 2015; Webber and Burrows 2015), although many long-term residents may be asset rich with the sky-high rocketing of house prices since the 1990s, while having a relatively modest disposable income. 'Some of the richest people on the planet, on *the planet*, live around here' (Julian, gardener, emphasis in original).

Gardening and maintenance of the park and all the other parks in RBKC has long been outsourced to private companies that the RBKC appoints. Quadron has had the contract since 2003. The gardeners are therefore not directly employed by the RBKC. The current contractor is Idverde, which merged with Quadron, through its acquisition, in the summer of 2016. Idverde is a Paris-based multinational conglomerate specialising in local authority contracts for landscaping and park maintenance in the UK in London, Birmingham and other big cities. It has an annual turnover in the UK of £90 million and employs 1,600 staff (http://www.idverde.com/en/). Idverde/Quadron aims to provide both an efficient service and high standards of maintenance to RBKC and profits for its shareholders. Most of the gardeners are on the minimum wage.

> I'd be happier if I were employed by the Royal Borough rather than Quadron, because you'd have more job security and more importantly you'd have better money. The rates of pay here for gardeners, agreed upon by Quadron and the Royal Borough, is shocking. Gardeners get £15,000 a year, which to me is poverty wages. Absolutely atrocious. We've had a couple of per cent pay rise since I've been here. It's a labour of love, but it is very difficult. You've got to be either living at home with your parents or you can be lucky enough maybe to have a council flat, where you can pay the rent, or sharing a flat with five or six people in a little box room. And it's difficult. We are the richest borough in the land as far as I'm aware. (Edward, park gardener)

Meanwhile, it is highly probable that some park users have either private or institutional shareholdings, such as pension plans, in the outsourced management company. Thus, Holland Park faithfully reflects the stark economic realities of the class-divided and grossly inegalitarian character of London as a global financial and investment capital dominated by corporate services (see table 9.8).

The gardeners I spoke to loved the park and their work. They invested their lives in it, found great satisfaction in their standards of care, felt that the management company generally treated them well by giving them good opportunities to advance their horticultural skills

Table 9.8 Some generalised contrasts between park workers and regular park users

Park workers	Park users
live elsewhere	live in vicinity
long and arduous work hours in gardens and park facilities	short visits for pleasure and relaxation
all weathers and seasons	fine weather, particularly in the summer
low income	high income
silent in relation to park management decisions	vocal in relation to park management decisions
serve and facilitate	served and facilitated

and obtain qualifications on day-release schemes at colleges, and so on. They also felt that park users widely appreciated what they did. What demoralised them was the wages. While park users can and do complain if they think things are going wrong with park management and inadequate resources in the context of central government imposed cutbacks in local authority spending, park workers felt intimidated and unable to complain about their own situation.

The fourth circle consists of people from a much wider area of Greater London, and their visits are occasional, perhaps as infrequently as once or twice a year and again largely during the summer. The fifth, outermost, circle consists of British and international tourists and visitors. This may also include those who own investment property in the vicinity of the park but only use it on an occasional basis. They generally visit the park on only one or a few occasions a year, or in some cases more regularly, but only for a few weeks.

Views of park users and visitors

We have seen that there are a wide variety of specific reasons why individuals come to the park. In this section, I discuss their thoughts about the park as a place and the various areas within it. Park users were asked if they had a favourite area of the park. Twenty per cent liked all of it rather than any particular area, and what they liked in particular was the contrast and variety that was to be found (table 9.10). It was the park as a whole that was meaningful to them. Beyond this, 58 per cent appreciated in particular the unique wooded areas or the 'world class' Japanese Garden. It was the latter rather than the presence of the woodlands that drew the majority of tourists and occasional visitors to the park. Another favourite area was the Dutch Garden and formal gardens. A minority were interested primarily in those areas related to their own park usage, for example those who wanted to exercise their dogs off leads.

Table 9.9 lists those features interviewees liked best and least about the park. The tranquil and relaxing park environment and the quietness of the park compared with the rest of London was most important, and again the variety of places in the park was highly valued. A substantial number had nothing negative to say about the park, but for over 20 per cent the worst thing about it was that it was too noisy and crowded during the summer months in particular. Frequently, the same person would say that they loved the quiet while also stating that the park was a noisy place. These contradictory statements relate very

Table 9.9 The likes and dislikes of 75 park users

Like best about Holland Park	Number	Percentage (%)
tranquillity/relaxing environment/quietness	24	32
variety in park/different spaces	15	20
natural feel/like the countryside	14	19
wildlife/trees/gardens/flowers/greenery	12	16
sociable and friendly people	8	10.5
small and compact size	6	8
Kyoto Garden	5	7
well maintained	4	5
different from other London parks	3	4
dogs-off-leads area	2	2.5
sports field	1	1
Like least about Holland Park	**Number**	**Percentage (%)**
nothing	28	37
too noisy/too many people	16	21
too little space for dogs off lead	4	5
not enough signage	3	4
too many restrictions	3	4
too many loud and noisy tourists	3	4
too many dogs and unruly dogs	3	4
too much woodland/shade	3	4
cycling ban in park	2	2.5
the opera	2	2.5
children/youths	2	2.5
not open all the time	1	1
Pokémon GO players	1	1
too far away from where I live	1	1

strongly to the social rhythms of the park discussed above and were reflected by regular park users avoiding the park at weekends in particular. When asked to describe what they felt about the park in words or phrases, there were a great variety of responses (table 9.11). The sheer strength of affection for the park is clear, as were contrasts and contradictions in the responses, for example 'quiet day – lovely; busy day – hell'.

Table 9.10 Named favourite areas given by 75 park users

Favourite place/area in park	Number	Percentage (%)
Kyoto Garden	23	31
Wooded areas	20	26.5
all of it	15	20
Dutch Garden and formal gardens	6	8
cafe	2	2.5
dogs-off-lead area	2	2.5
North Lawn/daffodil lawn	2	2.5
by Earl's Court entrance	1	1
D Garden	1	1
sports field	1	1
historic house	1	1
Lord Holland's Pond	1	1

Table 9.11 Analysis of the words and phrases used by 75 park users to describe Holland Park

A: general evaluative words used to describe Holland Park	Number of respondents
beautiful	24
pleasant	8
wild	6
pretty	5
lovely	5
natural	5
clean	3
good	2
wonderful	2
haven	2
gem	1
serene	1
source of interest and meaning	1
precious	1
imaginative	1

A: general evaluative words used to describe Holland Park	Number of respondents
picturesque	1
quirky	1
charming	1
interesting	1
inviting	1
amazing	1
nostalgic	1
delightful	1
B: Experiential emotional and embodied effects of Holland Park	**Number of respondents**
peaceful	21
quiet	16
tranquil	10
safe	5
not so quiet/noisy	4
somewhere nice to explore	3
relaxing	3
calm	3
therapeutic	2
enjoyable	2
quiet in winter	1
noisy at weekends	1
not too loud	1
restful	1
invigorating	1
fresh air/not polluted	3
cold	2
sound of water in the Kyoto Garden	1
C: social characteristics of Holland Park	**Number of respondents**
sociable	4
nice/friendly people	3
too many people	2

(Continued table 9.11)

(Continued table 9.11)

C: social characteristics of Holland Park	Number of respondents
cultural	2
grey socially	1
musical	1
alive	1
rich	1
elite	1
ethnically mixed	1
good for all ages	1
caters for different groups	1
family orientated	1
accessible to all	1
busy at weekends	1
overused	1
quiet day lovely; busy day hell	1
not institutional	1
uncontroversial	1
D: Comments on general physical characteristics and environment of Holland Park	**Number of respondents**
varied/variety/diverse/different places	22
well kept/managed/maintained/tended	10
seasonal interest/change	8
small/intimate/not too big	5
informal	3
hidden/secluded/secret	3
historical	3
accessible/convenient	3
cosy	2
feels like not being in London/escape from the city/like countryside	4
good mix formal/informal	2
good location/close to central London	2
private	1
hidden	1
away from people	1

D: Comments on general physical characteristics and environment of Holland Park	Number of respondents
away from busy streets	1
separated well	1
good use of space	1
enclosed	1
arty	1
rustic	1
spacious	1
stylish	1
looks different from different perspectives	1
architecturally interesting	1
E: Comments on physical and natural features of Holland Park	**Number of respondents**
green	19
flowers/superb flowers/gorgeous flowers	5
open	3
forest	3
mature trees	2
colourful	2
peacocks	2
gardens and trees	1
woodsy	1
shady	1
natural woods	1
botanically interesting	1
lots of plants	1
topographically varied	1
F: Comments on or mention of park facilities	**Number of respondents**
good facilities	3
nice cafe/good coffee	3
good for kids/enjoyable for children	3
wildlife friendly	2
nice playgrounds/play areas	1

(Continued table 9.11)

(Continued table 9.11)

F: Comments on or mention of park facilities	Number of respondents
good bathrooms	1
environmental	1
good for sports	1
good to exercise	1
dog friendly	1
local place to walk	1
good tennis courts	1
dominated by sports field	1
Kyoto Garden	1
G: Comparisons with other London Parks	**Number of respondents**
out of the ordinary/atypical/different	4
less like a park/like a city park	2
H: General evaluative comments on the park	**Number of respondents**
love it/makes me happy	5
horrible on rainy day	1
place to while away the time	1
grateful it's here!	1
without it living would be impossible	1
essential city facility	1
too much fencing	1
too small	1
favourite park	1
restrictive	1
too small	1

The vast majority felt that it was an extremely well-managed and kept park that successfully catered for the different interests of individuals and groups, was safe, a good place to come and socialise with others, and friendly and welcoming. The intimacy or relative smallness of the park was an important element in its appeal. A number of people contrasted it positively with other much larger and less varied London parks, and the nearby royal park of Kensington Gardens in particular, which was considered to be far more uniform and less interesting in character. Park facilities were highly valued. Being in the park was therapeutic to many, ameliorating the deleterious effects of city life.

From the overwhelmingly positive nature of the words and comments used, it is evident that Holland Park might be understood as being a kind of model park that many others in the city might want to emulate. The manner in which local people value their park, or particular places in it, is materially objectified in numerous unobtrusive ways. Some go and sit on the same bench on a regular basis and look at the park from 'their' place. Regulars visit the cafe frequently, and it is effectively a social hub for them. Some go back again and again and meditate under particular trees or in their own special places. Regular dog walkers meet and chat, exchange pleasantries and discuss the foibles of their pets. Members of the Parks Police on patrol stop and chat with locals, some of whom they know by name.

There are over 180 memorial benches in the park. Their presence and the touching inscriptions on some indicate how much the park is valued and treasured. Gardeners say that while they are at work, they sometimes find piles of ashes; whether these are of human or animal origin, they are unsure. Children delight in the 'forest school', in which they are taken out to experience being in the woods. Most have no gardens or other green spaces to explore in this part of the city. Adults can pretend they are not in London at all and find peace and quiet away from the alienating city streets. Those with a botanical interest can marvel at the mature and rare exotic trees in the park or delight in the presence of the tree ferns and other tropical plants in the Sun Trap area, or the borders and shrubberies elsewhere. Many appreciate the opera and the sculptures and summer art exhibitions. Everyone said they felt safe anywhere in the park. This is undoubtedly because of the permanent presence of the police in the park, who, while patrolling all the other parks and green spaces in RBKC and the neighbouring Borough of Hammersmith and Fulham, have their offices there.

Who is a park for and what should a park do?

There was one mantra that everyone I talked to could agree about: a park is an open public space and is there for everyone. It should cater for a variety of interests and users and 'tastes'. In accordance with this, people without children felt that the provision of play areas was important, and those without dogs supported the rights of dog owners

Table 9.12 The responses of 69 park users in relation to the hypothetical question: 'If you should decide the park budget what would you spend the most and least money on?'

Rank order	Sports	Plants and lawns	Children's facilities	Wildlife and Ecology Centre	Opera	Sculptures
1	2	31	7	28		
2	11	24	12	19	2	2
3	17	9	21	8	2	6
4	13	4	17	9	5	21
5	19	1	4	3	12	30
6	7		2	2	48	10

to exercise their pets in the park. People who had no interest in sports felt a sports field was needed, while those who didn't like formal gardens and planting arrangements were happy that they were there for those who appreciated them.

Table 9.12 shows the responses of informants when asked to rank spending priorities in relation to the park. Spending on the park gardens and the woodland areas and the Ecology Centre were ranked highest, that on the opera and sculptures lowest, with sports and children's facilities, already well provided for, given mid-range rankings. Most people deliberated over this, and quite a few commented that they were not just thinking about themselves and their own particular interests.

The RBKC park managers try their best to strike an equitable balance between the interests and values of different users, in a largely successful manner, but in the limited space of a relatively small and very diverse public park, some users will always remain dissatisfied in one way or another and want more of it for themselves. Some of the main social tensions in the current usage of Holland Park are the following.

- Between specific user groups and others: dog walkers, people who want to cycle through the park fitness trainers, those interested in wildlife conservation and the botanical history of the park and those who are not.
- Between those who value and wish to preserve and enhance remains of the historic house and those who value its current use as a venue for the summer opera.

- Between those who regard the aesthetic and environmental qualities of the park environment as paramount and those who would like the park to have a more direct educational and cultural role and significance.
- Between regular local users and outsiders, principally tourists, and whether this is, or should be, primarily, a park for locals.
- Between those of a broadly 'libertarian' persuasion who think that people should be able to go anywhere and do pretty much whatever they like in the park, and those who think regulations and restrictions are both necessary and beneficial. The majority of park users fall into the latter category.
- Between RBKC, park management, the Friends and other park users. The very existence of the Friends suggests a distrust of the park management as a potential 'enemy'. Some park users felt strongly that this was their park, a people's park, while suggesting the RBKC thought *it* owned the park and made decisions in relation to what RBKC councillors rather than park users wanted.

Only three of these issues will be briefly discussed below, through lack of space, although all of them are interrelated and overlap with each other.

Social tensions in park usage

Dog walkers make up about 20 per cent of park visitors in the survey and go there on a regular basis, some as many as three or four times a day (table 9.6). A persistent complaint from dog walkers was that there was only a small area of the park where they were allowed to exercise their dogs off the lead, along the eastern side of the sports field and to its north in front of the remains of the historic house and the park cafe. This is always the busiest part of the park. Throughout the rest, there is a strict dogs-on-leads policy designed to restrict disturbance to wildlife and prevent dogs entering the wooded enclosures, which are all fenced anyway (see below).

As the wooded area is the quietest area of the park, many dog walkers feel this would be the best place to exercise dogs and would be potentially far less disruptive to other park users. A few feel actively discriminated against. One chauffeur who came to exercise his female boss's dog every day said, 'There are all these children's play areas with facilities, but nowhere where we can go and play with our dogs.'

Some park users without dogs would clearly prefer dogs not to be there at all, pointing out that they can be frightening bounding up to women and children and generally disturb other park users by begging for food, and so on (table 9.9). They were anyway pleased that almost everyone was assiduously careful about removing dog mess. The Parks Police enforce the dog-lead policy, but have more persistent trouble with dog owners flagrantly breaking the rules than with any other user group. Almost every time I have been in the park, there have been dogs off leads in areas where this is forbidden, and especially in the wooded areas, where their owners think they will not be seen.

There is also a strict no cycling/skate-boarding/roller-blading policy in the park. This is enforced to prevent accidents in relation to both people and dogs. Again, some local residents would like to be able to cycle through the park on an east to west route (there is a north to south route immediately outside the park on the eastern side): 'There's a pressure group, well a self-interest group [referring to the Friends]. They may come across that they want to maintain the character of the park, but they tend to sort of have very enclosed views. And one of my bugbears is there is no cycle path east to west, and I really think that is a social responsibility' (Ian, regular park user).

A few locals, together with more tourists, occasionally do cycle and are stopped by the police. Somewhat ironically, hire bike stands are provided immediately outside some of the park entrances. This is part of an official scheme promoted by the London Major to increase cycle use in the city. As part of this policy, people can cycle freely through other parks in the city.

Fitness trainers use the park as a place of work with their clients, and attempts were made to register and control what they do by park management in 2016 to reduce pressure on and erosion of the park and its facilities, such as when using benches for step-up exercises. One view is that they and their wealthy clients exploit the park for their own convenience while giving nothing back.

Some park users feel corralled and controlled in the wooded conservation areas of the park. They wish to wander and explore these unique and beautiful woodlands in central London. But all the paths through the woods are fenced. There is very limited access, except on a few open days each year in just one area, which is termed the 'wildlife enclosure', in the northern part of the park (see fig. 9.2). The Ecology Centre organises these visits. The other wooded enclosures are permanently out of bounds for everybody. The argument, strongly supported by the Friends, is that if the public were allowed to freely use these areas, they would become rapidly degraded. The preservation of the woodlands is indeed one of the primary aspects of the constitution of the Friends. There is good empirical evidence to support their view. Where small woodland areas have been opened, ground vegetation rapidly disappears and the densely wooded spaces open out.

The presence of the woodlands is why so many people feel that the park is like the countryside, has a 'natural feel' and is very different from other London parks – less manicured and more wild and 'rustic' in character. A minority of park users, on the other hand, feel there is just too much woodland in such a small park. It would be better if it were opened out a bit with more open green spaces in between: 'Too dark, too many trees'; 'They're OK but it's much better around the house'; 'Too densely wooded, inaccessible. Too much woodland in a small park'; 'They are forbidden, so they have no interest for me'; 'The wild doesn't seem to be there really. I don't think you need that much. There's no point if you can't see anything and the trees aren't labelled so you don't learn anything' (visitors' comments).

In relation to these wildlife and conservation issues, it is pertinent to ask: is an urban park primarily for the benefit of the people who use it, a social space, or is it there for nature conservation rather than people? Is it possible to resolve the contradiction? What kind of wildlife and what kind of nature is being preserved, and for whom anyway?

The bird population, consisting of about 60 breeding species, is quite high for London, including woodcock, sparrowhawk and tawny owl. There are also bats, and many boxes are provided for them and for the birds. Because of the woodland, there is a higher proportion of woodland species than in other London parks. The lack of water means there are rather few water species compared with other parks. None of the birds is rare or endangered.

With the park being a very small green island in an extraordinarily dense built urban environment cut off from other green spaces in London, there are very few species of mammal. Those that live in the park are basically grey squirrels, rats, various species of mice, and a few foxes. As regards plant life, there is also nothing nationally rare, but there are a fair number of different species of wild flowers, mosses and lichens.

The wooded area of the park was originally the arboretum of the grand Jacobean house. There are many mature trees in it from all corners of the world. There was a large planting programme towards the end of the nineteenth century, including probably many of the different exotic oak trees to be found in the park, a selection of less common trees and horse chestnuts, ashes, poplars, limes and beeches, some of which are coming to the end of their natural life or are increasingly susceptible to disease. The number of different tree species present is around 555, of which 240 are different species or cultivars. There are still 'lost' trees to be found in the woodland enclosures. So, in this sense, the wooded areas are very far removed indeed from being an English woodland. What is being preserved here is essentially unnatural nature. This, it should be noted, is by no means an atypical example in terms of environmental policy and nature conservation objectives in the UK (see Tilley and Cameron-Daum 2017: Chapter 2).

One particular issue for the Friends is the loss of a substantial number of mature and rare trees. The chairwoman and the secretary of the Friends are both deeply versed in botany and share a profound knowledge of this aspect of the park. They can readily recite the names, characteristics and origins of the notable trees and plants within it. A book and a booklet have been published about the rare notable trees of the park (Kettlewell and Wood 2016; Patwardhan 2009). The Friends are currently actively instigating a tree management plan and the purchase of replacement trees following the loss of many old trees in recent years (20 per cent of the notable trees recorded in a tree guide and survey in 2007 have been lost as a result of old age, storm damage and disease) (The Friends of Holland Park 2016:13).

The only plant species in the park that might be considered to be rare and endangered are the exotic trees, global imports from the nineteenth century, arising from British colonialism and exploration of the globe, the exploits of Victorian and later plant collectors (see e.g. Musgrave, Gardener and Musgrave 1998). The issue here, then, is the survival of botanical history, quite literally living on, in the present. But most park users, while liking trees in general, are unaware that there are so many unusual and interesting species in the park, and only a minority have either any botanical knowledge or much interest in them.

Some of the Friends think that the numerous school groups in the wildlife area, used as a 'forest school' by the Ecology Centre to teach pre-school and primary school children, are themselves creating too much disturbance. In this sense, learning about nature, while being positive, may also have detrimental consequences in the long term. The Ecology Centre has made an attempt to stop adverse impacts, by placing logs on either side of the paths to deter the children straying from off them. Another measure has been to rotate the areas being used. However, with young children playing in the woodland, this is, of course, difficult. Too much control over their movement would directly contradict their freedom to explore, enjoy and learn.

Part of the perceived overuse of the wildlife area is, itself, stimulated by the requirement imposed on the Ecology Centre by RBKC to retain financial viability. Members of the centre themselves acknowledge this and try as best they can to mitigate against their own impacts on the woodland ecology

> There is a bit of a conflict: we do have to generate an income, and the forest school gets children coming all year round, but before we did forest school – maybe, five, six years ago – we peaked and troughed in the spring, and no one used to come in the winter, so there was a natural time for regeneration, but now we are there all year round so there is a lot more pressure. (Member of the Ecology Centre team)

A contested event: benefits and problems of the opera

A summer theatre of sorts has existed in Holland Park since the late 1950s. In 1964, the Holland Park Court Theatre was opened. Since then, the events have always been staged in the same location: on the south terrace of the Jacobean house using the remaining first storey of the original house as a spectacular stage backdrop. Summer performances in the 1960s included works by the Royal Ballet, Gilbert and Sullivan productions and Flamenco dances staged in the open air on a temporary wooden stage. From 1987, after RBKC assumed management of the park in 1986, a tented pavilion was erected and semi-professional opera began, together with theatre and dance. Performances have, therefore, now been going on for well over 50 years on the same site. Michael, the current opera director, began managing and staging events in 1989 that grew and grew. By 1996, opera events dominated with the establishment of Opera Holland Park, and by 2000 they were exclusively opera. The company now stages 36 evening performances a year under a much grander canopy and pavilion seating 1,000 people.

The opera since its inception has been funded by RBKC as a public service, but has never paid for itself through ticket sales and fundraising. The loss amounted to £762,000 in the 2014–15 financial year, and £864,000 in 2015–16. This sum amounts to 72 per cent of the entire budget spent on maintaining Holland Park for a year (RBKC 2016). Opera Holland Park was given a golden handshake of £5 million pounds by RBKC in October 2015 (equivalent to the entire park budget for four years), was transferred out of the council and became a private charity with the hope that through corporate sponsorship and ticket sales it would break even in the future. Opera Holland Park has a 25-year lease on the site and has become a permanent feature of Holland Park.

The opera audience is mainly London based, including many people who live locally in the vicinity of the park. The audience is also nationwide and international, partly because of the lesser-known works that the opera stages as part of the repertoire. Opera Holland Park has a lot of local support and over 2,000 Friends. Some of the Friends of Holland Park are also Friends of the opera.

I rhetorically asked Michael, the opera director, why opera is staged in Holland Park rather than in other less affluent areas of London. He maintained that this was the result of a narrow-minded British cultural attitude in which opera is perceived as being for 'them' (a rich cultural elite) rather than 'us' (ordinary people), despite the fact that tickets cost considerably less than for a rock concert or premiership football match that nobody calls elitist, and that 1,500 opera tickets are given away for free. Opera would simply not work elsewhere in an ordinary London park. It is thus an entirely appropriate cultural event for Holland Park with suitably refined and low-key acoustics without amplification. A rock concert is unthinkable here and would be vigorously opposed by local residents. However, a substantial number of park users want something different: 'a jazz festival or something like that' (park gardener); 'a variety of different events like it used to be not just damned opera, opera and more opera' (long-term local resident).

One obvious way one might conceive of the opera is that it has always been a vanity project of RBKC. Politically, the reason it exists is because it contributes to the image the borough wishes to project of itself in relation to London, the nation state and the world beyond. This is certainly the view of the local Kensington Labour Party. A headline in its newsletter reporting the decision to give the opera a £5 million golden handshake as a final settlement reads: 'Tories "insult to struggling families": council prioritises opera over vulnerable and homeless' (Kensington Labour Party 2014). However, without state or corporate sponsorship, opera is unlikely to survive anywhere. It should not, of course, be necessary to help the poor and deprived by getting rid of the cultural arts in a rich borough and a rich country.

Michael, the opera director, regards the opera as contributing tremendously to the social life of the park. Parks are for people and their enjoyment, and a fundamental part of this since Victorian times has been putting on public events and performances. He has himself known the park since his childhood and reckons that back in those days he probably climbed most of the trees (nobody is permitted to do this today) and ran around on the sports field with his friends and went to some of the performances in front of the house. The park has enormous personal significance for him.

> I always loved the park back then and I think now it's London's best park. I think it is the most interesting sort of Londony park. It feels like a bit of a country estate. It's got those interesting formal elements like the Dutch Garden, the Rose Garden, the Japanese Kyoto Garden, and the house in the middle sort of gives it a uniqueness. There's something about the scale of Holland Park that I really like. In fact, I have just planted a tree on the North Lawn in the park, one that they needed, and put my mum's ashes underneath it, so it has a relevance, it's important to me. My view of the park, now I've been doing there what I've been doing for 28 years, is that parks in London, and certainly the Victorian ideal of a park, is that you go there to do things; that's the old bandstand concept or the boating lake or the fetes and the fairs, all those things quite apart from having an open space and running around and doing sports. I consider them as primarily cultural spaces.' (Michael, Opera Director)

Michael's favourite part of the park is where most people go, the most intensively used social space of the park: the formal gardens and the cafe, Orangery and Belvedere restaurant areas. The opera brings up to 1,000 people a night into this area and increases its intense vitality.

> It's a massive thing. If you are a tourist and walking through Holland Park one afternoon and there is a 70-piece orchestra and a 60-piece chorus on stage, and you can hear it like it's in your front room, that's an amazing gift for us to give to London. (Michael, Opera Director)

Furthermore, the opera goes on without preventing anyone else from walking through or enjoying the park: 'We're an opera company, and people stand right outside our gate making noise, and we are generous.'

The opera in this view encapsulates what the essence of a park should be: it's for people and socialising, pleasure and entertainment for all, and not therefore for wildlife or nature conservation. But the 'generosity' of the opera in relation to other park users is obviously tempered by the fear that the noise some of them will make will destroy the operatic performance, particularly people getting rowdy and drunk in the vicinity. This is why there has been strong opposition to the application by the youth hostel situated next door to serve alcohol and have an events licence. Similarly, the Parks Police will soon move on people picnicking on the sports field directly in front of the opera pavilion if they create too much noise. The opera, therefore, to survive, has to defend itself against these aural threats to its artistic integrity and existence. For the other 320 days of the year, this does not matter.

One huge area of concern to some is the relationship of the opera to the remains of Holland House. A consistent complaint on the part of some local residents and Friends is that the presence of the opera pavilion seriously detracts from the ambience of the house in particular and the wider park in general. This is because even though the opera performance season is relatively short, it takes up to five months each year to put the pavilion and stage up and take them down again. This conceals a view of the house and access to it.

> Half of our members love it, half hate it. The Friends are neutral, not trying to promote it, not trying to stop it. But since we have it, our role is to think about it and what impact it has on the park. We think all these white tents are inappropriate, and both we and Opera Holland Park would prefer a better solution. You sit in the Dutch Garden and it's a different experience because you can't see the house, and you come in from the North Lawn and you don't get a sense of the house. We would like to see the front terrace of the Grade I listed building open to the public for longer each year. To our surprise, we found that Opera Holland Park had a similar view. (Chairperson of the Friends)

Another issue is that the opera does not just consist of a large pavilion, but also of a series of surrounding tents and marquees, to the west and north of the main opera pavilion. Three hundred or so tables in these tents are hired by opera-goers for private dining. They bring their own food and drink with them. This supplements opera income from ticket sales. A final issue is unwanted vehicular traffic in the park – lorries delivering tents and equipment, and, before performances, people arriving in taxis and cars bringing their heavy picnic hampers with them.

> During the summer when you could wander around and enjoy the gardens, it is now overwhelmed with tents, the numbers of people bringing their picnics, including us sometimes. They take over. You really begin to feel the opera has taken over Holland Park. And I think that is the biggest change, some of which we enjoy but there

is a loss, a decline in the quality of the sense of being in a London park, a slightly lower-priced Glyndebourne. (Jack: long-term local resident)

There's no problem with the opera, but seven or eight years ago they decided to stick up all these nasty tacky little tents and charge people to eat their sandwiches, so they all queue up with Waitrose bags and chiller boxes along here [by the park cafe], and there was a lot of traffic coming and going delivering them. They charge between £20 and £60, depending on what tent you have, and in the opera programme they should be promoting all the restaurants in the borough for the prosperity of the borough, not just trying to make a few quid for themselves. There were big vehicles coming here all the time. Now they can't come after 11a.m. They were coming all day long. That's the worst thing that has happened… it's all these bloody tents. You used to be able to see the facade of the house before you had the opera. That was part of its charm. Holland Park, Holland Park House. I was talking to this lady who had been coming since the beginning [of the opera], and she said it has become quite pretentious and it's lost its charm. It's money grubbing… This was an oasis to be treasured, and peace and harmony is what we must protect at all costs. (Paula: long-term local resident)

A partial solution might be to have a permanent roof structure, but this has been vigorously resisted by the Friends and RBKC management, as has the idea of having a permanent opera structure elsewhere in the park: 'I wouldn't mind, and I've said that, but they'd never let me, building a concealed opera house in those woods. I think that would be beautiful, and we could do it with greened roofs and be very much part of the environment and hardly visible, but that will never happen' (Michael, Opera Director).

It is interesting to comment in this respect that when I asked visitors what they liked most about the park, not a single person except the youth hostel manager mentioned the historic house (and the youth hostel is part of the house). The house is a fundamental structural element of the park, primarily now in relation to its ancillary outbuildings and formal gardens on the western side. However, it remains a largely absent material presence, taken for granted, its significance unrecognised by the majority of park users. During the opera season, the full attention of the audience is directed to the house facade as a permanent stage set, appreciated by many.

When I did specifically ask about it, some regular park visitors and all the tourists I spoke to said they did not realise the house was even there! Partly, this is because the remaining eastern wing of the house cannot be visited by the public, as it forms part of the youth hostel. Another factor is the seasonal presence of the opera, and a third the complete absence of interpretation boards or information about it. The area in front of the house had been permanently closed to the public for about 30 years. The RBKC, Friends and the opera have together worked to provide public access outside the opera season during the past few years.

In terms of standards of landscaping and maintenance and design, the area occupied by the opera has been the worst part of the park when arguably it might be the best, restored in accordance with how it might have appeared in its grandeur in the mid nineteenth century. At present, there is a scruffy area of artificial grass in front of the house and no planting arrangements or other features such as the circular basin and fountain and ornamental shrubs and trees that used to exist. The area is effectively a no-go area for the park gardeners, who can do nothing about it, since the opera covers the entire area for so long. At present, plans are under consultation to hard-landscape this area in a more sympathetic and attractive manner that will also benefit the opera by providing a permanent base, including underground electric cabling and so on, and reducing the time to set everything up and take it down again. The opera also means that the south terrace in front of the house cannot ever be properly landscaped in harmony with the architecture of the building.

Local park or tourist destination?

'The only question we get asked is: where's the Japanese Garden?' (Gardener's comment).

Since the 1990s, the park has become increasingly a London visitor destination, with a substantial increase in visitor numbers and foreign tourists. When I asked long-term residents and park users what were the most important changes they had noticed in the park during the last 30 years, the answers were always the same: the construction and subsequent impact of the Kyoto Garden and the arrival of the opera. The park is no longer just a local park for local people. This is in part due to its central location and easy access by public transport links. The historic house, outbuildings and formal gardens, the opening of the

Kyoto Garden in 1991 and the summer opera in 1996 have, together, made it somewhat equivalent to other major London visitor attractions.

During the summer months, as discussed above, many locals feel that their beautiful and beloved park has effectively been taken away from them. The Kyoto Garden has become a big draw; this was unforeseen by long-term residents, who initially thought it was a good idea and supported its establishment, but now somewhat regret it. Japanese tourists are regularly bussed in from London hotels. Holland Park is advertised on the RBKC website, in guide books and on various internet platforms such as TripAdvisor as a place to see. The fact that the opera similarly attracts many more people and some non-local London residents and tourists to the park is similarly problematic for some locals, and they deeply regret the perceived negative effects.

The youth hostel has always brought in outsiders and tourists to the park since it was opened in 1959, long before the Japanese Kyoto Garden and the opera. Victoria, the current manager, says the old YHA youth hostel is now more like a hotel under its new Safestay (since 2015) commercial management. She does not like the term 'hostel', because it has negative connotations for some: 'It's you, your wife, your children, groups of school children from the UK visiting London and from all over the world. It's a great mixture of different types of people and accessible to all.' The reception is open 24 hours a day, but access to the park itself from the hostel is closed when the park gates are locked. So, for much of the time, particularly during the winter months, the hostel may be in the park but is physically cut off from it.

Victoria, the youth hostel manager, is proud of the fact that the youth hostel occupies such a beautiful Grade I listed building of great historic importance, and is also appreciative of the new buildings: 'It's here for people to come and see how beautiful the park is, the best park in London, and London itself.' She says that she would like to open up the house and the hostel grounds so that it could be seen and appreciated not only by people staying there but by other park users. She regards the hostel as being socially inclusive in a neighbourhood that is socially exclusive, with people living in the immediate vicinity of the park complaining about noisy guests at night, and who don't like laundry and other delivery vans coming and going, people moving in and out, pulling their roller bags, and generally 'lowering the tone' of the place.

She has no knowledge of or relationship with the Friends, and characterises the relationship between the hostel and the park management and the opera as an uneasy one: 'There are definitely barriers within the park. There is a snobbery against the hostel… they don't have much to do with us. It's them and us, the police, the park management, the opera and us. They have never befriended us or helped us in any way.'

The opening of a new Design Museum in the old iconic refurbished Commonwealth Centre building next to the park in November 2016, estimated to attract upwards of 900,000 visitors per annum (see Wilson 2016), is likely to significantly increase the numbers of tourists visiting the park in the future, and is of enormous concern and dismay to many local residents who simply don't want the park further publicised and visitor pressure increased.

Concerns about increasing visitor numbers in the park expressed by the Friends and local users are in considerable tension with wider RBKC objectives. The RBKC has its own public relations department and wants to promote the borough, spread its 'fame', bring people in who will contribute further to the local economy. The opera has now become an internationally significant event with highly praised productions on, compared with the Royal Opera House, a tiny budget. It needs people to come and appreciate it, corporate sponsors, and publicity in order to survive, and it does bring substantial additional spend into the borough in addition to its own dining tents.

Conclusions: the park as free space or social cage?

This chapter is a small part of a much broader study of Holland Park and other London parks. London parks, together with London's numerous garden squares, are one of those great Victorian and Edwardian social institutions that make life tolerable for many in the city (see discussion and references in the introduction to this book). Ideally, they are a mixing place for all people and classes, a democratic leveller of social distinctions. Arguably, green spaces form the very heart of London, all too often taken for granted and overlooked in terms of public spending priorities. Parks are currently under threat, with an overall budget cut across London of 8 per cent, with 22 per cent of local authorities regarding their parks as being in decline (National Heritage Lottery Fund 2016). In Holland Park, the cuts are just beginning to bite, because park maintenance has always been relatively high profile within RBKC. To neglect parks, and to neglect Holland Park in particular, would reflect very badly on the borough's high standards and reputation.

Holland park is the preeminent material objectification of the borough itself, whose managerial concern for its residents, manifested primarily in standards of maintenance, is made visible on a day-to-day basis. Many residents have long-term memories of what the park used to be like and can compare the past and present state. The park is there to be seen and experienced by the public, in a manner that is entirely different from other hidden council services (such as the quality of day-care and support services for the elderly) that are not visible to residents on a daily basis, out of sight and therefore out of mind. Both local residents and those from elsewhere in London and beyond need this free space. Their response to it as an escape from the pressures of the city is overwhelmingly positive.

One of the jobs of the Parks Police is to move rough sleepers on and out of the park. There are only a few rough sleepers, and only a small amount of vandalism, drug and alcohol abuse takes place because 'those kinds of people don't live around here'. In this sense, the park is almost self-policing. Those locals who do complain about tourists and opera-goers in their park, or rowdy people in the hostel, will of course be tourists themselves elsewhere in places in which their presence might also not be welcome to local people.

From this point of view, we can regard Holland Park and other London parks as cages for 'suitable' social activities and 'suitable' people: regulated and self-regulated, restricted, limited, proscribed, enforced, in which human freedom is illusory. At the beginning of this study, I went around the park and counted the number of disciplinary notices (e.g. no dogs, no ball games, no climbing, no cycling, keep off the grass). There were no less than 109 of various kinds and sizes throughout the park. Many have subsequently been taken away in the hope, as one of the Friends told me, that people would behave with a sense of civic responsibility and discipline themselves. The cage of Holland Park, catering primarily to the tastes and desires of what may be described as a new kind of local London modern aristocracy, manifests the hidden hand and nightmare of history in a kind of collective amnesia to continuing social injustice. But the sheer variety of the individual views of park users, rich or otherwise, is enormous. They neither think nor talk in the same voice.

> There isn't a funfair here. It's always going to be on Shepherd's Bush Common. There's a lot of nannies that come here, because it is a very wealthy area. It's difficult for a single man to come here; that's what I found with my kid on my own. A male with a child is very much an outsider. (Park user)

> The Kyoto Garden doesn't really interest me. I don't like the sense of how you are supposed to behave in there. It's rather formalistic. You have to keep moving, you are supposed to go round in a certain way. It doesn't ring true with our national characteristic, keeping off the grass and being told. I don't like that controlling nature, that very tight pruning. (Park user)
>
> There is a large part of the park that is completely inaccessible to anyone. If I was a rough sleeper I'd come here. It's a good place. You'd maybe get some scraps from the Belvedere, pick a few quid out of the Japanese pond [used by many tourists as a wishing well]. (Park gardener)

The park has always been an elite landscape to be enjoyed by the wealthy, influential and powerful. It remains so today, not so much by design or desire, but by default. The park reflects and refracts issues of class, power, domination and resistance in wider society in so many ways that are not immediately transparent or obvious. These are to be found among the flower borders, in the woodlands, in the Kyoto Garden, blowing in the wind in the sophisticated musical soundscape of Italian arias. Holland Park: a flawed place of wonder and delight.

Methodological note

This chapter is a brief discussion based on an ongoing research project. The research discussed here took place in Holland Park between March and December 2016. It involved participant observation in the park over this period, structured to take place at different times and on different days throughout the park. In-depth unstructured interviews were conducted with 20 different informants, either in the park or elsewhere. The 75 structured interviews were all conducted in the park between Monday 30 May 2016 (a spring bank holiday) and Friday 17 November. Some of them, if the interviewee was prepared to spend the time, continued as much longer non-structured interviews. The structured interviews with park users were undertaken to take place in different areas of the park, at different times of the day and on different days of the week. Part of this work involved collecting some basic information about use of the park itself by the public, since even basic statistical information is non-existent. This is summarised in the tables in the text. Different park user groups were targeted in order to obtain as representative a sample of the views of visitors to the park as possible, in particular those of local residents who know it best and whose responses would therefore be much more informative than those of a casual first-time visitor. Of course, a fair number of people refused to be interviewed or said they had no time, for example: 'eating me lunch, mate' (construction worker sitting on bench on eastern side of park); 'I don't speak no good English' (Asian nanny pushing pram through Sun Trap area); 'Sorry, I'm working with these dogs. Some other time' (professional female dog walker in front of park cafe); 'Noooo' (old white lady sitting on bench in Dutch Garden); 'I'm late. Sorry. Good on you anyway' (middle-aged white female walking two dogs past Ecology Centre); 'Can't you see we're working?' (fitness trainer on North Lawn).

Had these interviews been confined to the summer months, the sample would have been inevitably biased towards tourists and occasional visitors. Schoolchildren were not interviewed, nor were children's play areas entered. The names of park users and gardeners used in the account are fictional. The names of other people are their real names, as their identities are impossible to conceal; their permission has been sought and kindly given.

The research was conducted before the Grenfell Tower disaster which highlighted the gross inequalities within RBKC and more widely within London, discussed in the chapter.

Acknowledgements

I would like to express my enormous debt to all those who talked to me and answered my questions about the park and made me feel so welcome in it. Without the help, time and patience of so many people, this account would have been impossible.

References

Kensington Labour Party. 2014. 'Tories "Insult to Struggling Families"'. November. https://kensingtonlabour.com/2014/11/ (accessed February 2019).
Kettlewell, J. and Wood, R. 2016. *Notable Trees in Holland Park*. London: Friends of Holland Park.
Miller, S. 2012. *The Pleasure Grounds of Holland House*. London: Friends of Holland Park.
Musgrave, T., Gardner, C. and Musgrave, W. 1998. *The Plant Hunters*. London: Ward Lock.
National Heritage Lottery Fund. 2016. 'State of UK Public Parks 2016'. https://www.heritagefund.org.uk/publications/state-uk-public-parks-2016 (accessed February 2019).
Patwardhan, P. 2009. *Trees from Two Continents*. Mumbai: Tanya Publications.
RBKC. 2016. 'Environmental and Leisure and Residents' Services Budget Summary'. https://www.rbkc.gov.uk/sites/default/files/.../Revenue%20Budget%202016_17.pdf

Savage, M., Laurison, D., McKenzie, L., Miles, A., Snee, H., Taylor. M. and Wakeling, P. 2015. *Social Class in the 21st Century*. London: Pelican.

The Friends of Holland Park. 2016. 'Notable Trees Guide'. *The Friends of Holland Park Magazine*, winter.

Tilley, C. and Cameron-Daum, K. 2017. *An Anthropology of Landscape: The Extraordinary in the Ordinary*. London: UCL Press.

Webber, R. and Burrows, R. 2015. 'Life in an Alpha Territory: Discontinuity and Conflict in an Elite London "Village"', *Urban Studies* 53(15):3139–54.

Wilson, T. 2016. *The Story of the Design Museum*. London: Phaidon.

10
From pollution to purity: The transformation of graffiti and street art in London (2005–17)

Rafael Schacter

Author's field notes, 14 March 2017

I've changed, but the city has changed too. This is clear. Indisputable.

I've become exhausted of the image. Of its reduction and contamination. I've become exhausted of having to explain that this is not that, that not this.

Yet it's clearly not just me. The city, my home, has transformed too. Of course it always does, it was ever thus etc., etc. And I wouldn't simply say 'beyond recognition', as the fact is that it's all too recognisable. It's just shifted in subtle but often deleterious ways. It's reshaped in an often invisible yet injurious manner. Yet these sometimes indiscernible, sometimes incontrovertible transformations are all too visible, clarified within the images the city churns out, the images it enforces, it affords. They become all too clear in the way the image is treated, in the way it is produced and consumed, circulated and erased.

Walking through parts of the city today, I must admit I get a slightly queasy, uneasy feeling in my stomach. It's horrid to say that, and I feel somewhat like an old man shouting at the clouds (shouting at the chemtrails), yet it's impossible to deny. Things just feel… well, surreal, insincere. Of course, it's hard to escape this in Shoreditch, where I now sit (drinking a flat white of course… if you can't beat them!), to deny the incredible way that things have changed here over the last 10 (not to say 20 or 30) years. But it's happening in Camden town too. It's happening in Brixton. It's even happening in Croydon!

Fig. 10.1 A Shoreditch canvas: a plethora of tags, posters, stickers and paste-ups. Source: author

Here the image becomes part of the requisite backdrop, the mise en scène. *Here it becomes complicit. It becomes part of rather than apart; it becomes the disordered order.*

'Yeah it was smoked mutton. It tasted… old.' (Shoreditch, 2016)

A white Porsche speeds by, revving its engine as it heads up the street. The soft-top is down and some insipid (and thus even more offensive) electronic muzak leaks out, dying away as the vehicle takes a corner. I continue walking down the street. Once the petrol fumes dissipate, the aroma of fine coffee beans and even 'finer perfumery' comes into play. It fills the air up until I reach a group of rubbish sacks awaiting collection. I dodge them, sliding off the pavement and into the road as a snaking line of tourists filters past. 20? 25 of them, perhaps? All wielding cameras and backpacks, all following a pied piper of a tour guide as he narrates a post-modern story. It's Jack the Ripper intertwined with Banksy. A grisly combination. I listen for a while, before noting my indifference.

I wander on, past the non-stop corporate chains. J Crew. APC and Nudie. Club Monaco and Versus Versace (I am genuinely stunned). I wander past the Pure Gym and the purebred pooches. Past the pavement cafes with their PR brunches. Past a plethora of eager Ubers and a street-style Sunday magazine fashion advertorial. Past the

Fig. 10.2 Shoreditch beach: artificial turf, deckchairs and wide-screen TV. Source: author

hipsters on fixies (stereotype, I know, but true!) and the sneaker boutiques. Past the AstroTurf-ed sun deck (sponsored by broadband provider EE) with large- (in fact, mammoth-) screen TV. Past the sun deck with the deckchairs and the people all sitting facing the screen. Almost comical but… but really not.

The images are everywhere. Huge murals and small tags. Stickers and posters. Wild-style pieces and monochrome stencils. Yet the absolute omnipresence of them is just a bit odd. Not some work, but ALL the work. Not here and there, but <u>everywhere</u>. As if there is an invisible marker, a hidden eruv from where the images begin. On the left prohibited. On the right, expected… Here thou shall paint. There thou shalt not. Its ubiquity points, of course, to its acceptability. Not only in the more legal manifestation of the image, the corporate street art, the neo-muralism, the sanitised, institutionalised mural as trophy art (which features on pretty much every street), but so too in the work that is passively avowed, the graffiti that exists in such a strangely agreeable way. The admissible dissidence. The sanctioned sedition.

The prevalence also seems to allude to their all-too-easy status. A lack of true commitment? A lack of true risk? Artists are thus here, right now, openly painting in the bright light of the day. Painting openly. During lunchtime! Painting what is, what must be actively desired. Bestowing the site with its 'individuality' (in contrast to the city's other shopping districts). Providing it with its 'raw urban cool'

Fig. 10.3 The images everywhere: tags, stickers, and admissible dissidence. Note the small red sticker placed over the nose of the pasted-up 'one love' kid. Kitsch resistance. Source: author

(thanks to Tripadvisor for that). The perfect decorative backdrop. For fashion shoots ('yes! that's sexy! hold that'), for the mass of amateur photographers (perhaps I saw 15 or 20 each hour), for the constant walking tours pounding the pavements (and blocking the traffic in amusing ways). The images saturating the area were thus being consumed by a quite distinct group. Of tourists, for the most part. Of shoppers, for the other. And they were being produced, so it seemed, pretty much <u>for</u> that group. Produced to be Instagrammed. Produced for the 'likes'. Produced with website links so as to ensure the smooth delivery from the physical to the digital. Produced for what seemed like instrumental reasons, reasons other than in and of themselves. As a friend said to me earlier that same day, 'If you're working there, you're just being lazy.'

There are old works mixing with new, little or no sign of erasure. The familiar cycle of production–circulation–destruction replaced with a more static temporality. Even with the apparent griminess, everything thus feels more or less official. Like it was here to stay. Like it was fit for purpose, showing, revealing how the space works. That it was the space marked out for 'creativity'. That it was the space marked out for painting. That it was the space marked out for rebellion. Of course, there are conversations happening too. There are graffiti artists painting on top of street artists, implicitly and explicitly disagreeing with their vision. The nature of the graffiti artist's body so discernible in their human-sized pieces (you can see the flow of their arm, the height of their body at full stretch) working over the mechanically assisted street art, the cherry picker, scaffold assisted, three-storey-high murals (those works that cannot exist but for technological/institutional abetment). For the most part though, and on both sides of the aesthetic coin, the work is pretty traditional. The most basic, cut-it-by-numbers of stencils. The most kitschy, trite of imagery. The most radiant, colourful of murals – the pleasant, acquiescent modality of street art. But so too the most conventional of graffiti styles. Those functioning within the framework of that which has always been produced and that which always will be. Within the 'subway art' paradigm, wild-style as the utmost edge of the possible (graffiti as utter orthodoxy). The images are thus entirely what are to be expected. And this, it feels, is key. Both the street art and the graffiti visible here are almost quaint in their flawlessness. In their status as perfectly imagined. Graffiti as archetype. Street art as stereotype. Not the plethora of different forms and styles, different approaches and methodologies. But a very restricted palette, an edgy form of Sunday painting.

Fig. 10.4 Graffiti as archetype/street art as stereotype: a street art mural 'dogged' by a series of silver and black 'throw-ups'. Source: author

It feels bad to be so critical. And, I must admit, I am very conscious of that fact. More to the point, could I not have said all this 10 years ago? Was it really all so different then? Is it me or it that has changed? I am very aware of the waves that Shoreditch has gone through. The initial post-industrial ingress in the 80s; the influx of the YBAs in the 90s; the inundation of hipsters in the 2000s; the invasion of property developers of today. Yet my own forays into Shoreditch started over 20 years ago now (it scares me to say that). They started in the mid-90s (1995 to be precise) when I first stepped into Hoxton Square to go to the legendary Blue Note. Entering another universe (spatially and sonically). Entering into what then seemed like a different world, a type of London I had never encountered. I thus saw the developments first hand; I am not and I was not unaware of the changes that were taking place. Yet what seemed, at the time of my research in 2005, as a place that for all its faults still contained some possibility, a place in which things still seemed undefined, today just feels so entirely set. Maybe it's the high-rises that have made the big difference, the physical, architectural transformation, the knocking down and building up that has begun to occur. The new squares with their twee names. The creative place-making creating the perfect non-places (the same-same unique). The luxury flats and extravagant boutiques. Maybe it's that everything now seems so thoroughly cleansed of difference. That it's now purely about profit. Now just about accumulation... Argh, there I go again! As I sit here, I battle with it. Is it me or it that has truly changed! I know things are different, but really?

Yet the way the images work, what they do, how they function, this does not lie. For all my angst, this is the incontrovertible truth. The differing ways they are utilised, allowed. The ways they worked then and the ways they work now. What was once a practice containing an urge towards insurgency now seems today to have settled for the comfort of the consensual. What once seemed to contain an implicit and explicit critique of the city, now seems to merely uphold and sustain it. Of course, I see very clearly that this may simply sound like a classic (and perhaps boring) story of avant-garde to passé, a story of the life and death of every once-radical art practice. And I do not claim that this is for everything, that this is for all aspects of the image. It's the authorised practice, the desired image. I have always thought that the images a city enables can act as barometers for the changing nature of its landscape, indicators of its possibilities. And the transformations these images have gone through can hence be something of importance not merely for those interested in its status as art, but rather for those interested in the life of the city itself. It's changing, they're changing. We change, it changes. But what does this really tell us? What does it reveal?

Fig. 10.5 From avant-garde to passé: street art as the ultimate in kitsch. Source: author

Fig. 10.6 Passé by OX, Paris, 2017: street art through the looking glass and back (to a space of actual innovation). Image courtesy of OX

In diametric opposition

In the summer of 2005, as part of my thesis for an MA in Material and Visual Culture at University College London, I conducted a small ethnographic project investigating graffiti and street art in the capital. Latterly published as *An Ethnography of Iconoclash* (Schacter 2008), the article explored the production, consumption, circulation and erasure of these illicit artefacts, the cycle of 'fascination, repulsion, destruction, atonement' (Latour et al. 2002:15) generated by these highly efficacious, highly problematic images. Working with London-based graffiti artists and graffiti erasers, with pro-graffiti supporters and anti-graffiti authorities, *An Ethnography of Iconoclash* attempted to surpass the traditional focus on subcultures and gangs, on criminality and masculinity that studies of graffiti then (as now) so often elicited, and to focus, instead, on the specific material qualities, the particular performative features that these images incorporated.

As may not be entirely surprising, the research I undertook entirely transformed my understanding of this image world. What had initially appeared to me as a decorative disarray (albeit a strangely alluring one) came to be appreciated as a complex aesthetic language with a very rational order: the frenzy of the insurgent hieroglyphics came to not only be materially disentangled, but recognised as a practice containing a very clear correspondence to traditional calligraphy (only location and legality, in fact, distinguishing them). What had initially seemed like a deeply *anti*-social act (even if a strangely seductive one) came to be comprehended as an act of the highest civility: the practice was not only a deeply communitarian one, the direct opposite of the habitual trope of the lone, disaffected, graffiti-spraying vandal, but equally contained an utter fidelity, a total commitment to the city. Yet more than solely transforming my understanding of the *image*, An Ethnography of Iconoclash came also to entirely reconstruct my comprehension of the contemporary city – my comprehension of London, the city of my birth. What had formerly appeared as an environment saturated with restrictions and constraints, came to reveal itself as one in which possibilities were endless – as if through a worm hole (or a looking glass), the space of the city seemed to radically expand, its backstage secrets wrenched open, its hidden depths forcibly revealed. What had previously seemed to be a domain regulated by those with the financial or political capital to dominate it suddenly became one in which 'their' space could be hijacked, 'their' communicative tools commandeered; it became a site in which one's inter-subjective reach could be radically expanded, in which restrictive media forms could be re-appropriated, a critical publicity generated through force of will alone.

Yet as can be noted, I hope, from the introductory field-note section to this essay, in the years since I undertook this original research, from then in 2005 to now in 2017, much had changed. In fact, I would argue that in almost every manner, from production to consumption, circulation to destruction, street art and graffiti in London today functions in an entirely divergent manner to the independent public art of just over a decade ago. While in 2005 street art was quite clearly a *post*-graffiti practice, a form whose practitioners were grounded in the ethical and conceptual prerequisites of graffiti, by a set of procedural and technical qualities that were a clear extension *of* and yet implicitly emergent *from* this antecedent form, by 2015 street art had metamorphosed into something radically other, into a clearly capitalised, institutionalised 'Street Art', a form set in diametric opposition to its progenitor. As I have explored in depth (in Schacter 2017), the early street artists' explicit desire for a more open, inclusive visuality, a more integrative aesthetic approach, set alongside their trenchant independence and tactical understanding of urban space, produced a form of art that was contagiously, intentionally accessible (in both visual and physical terms) – a quite compelling, irresistible visual trap. Yet the perfect mix of seemingly oppositional qualities they created (both innovative and approachable, both loaded and yet legible) not only made street art irresistible to a now huge constituency of potential viewers, but equally so to the (ever-ready) forces of capital. While the mere witnessing of graffiti was a profound hazard and thus something impossible for the market to co-opt or contain, the potent combination of accessibility and subversivity that street art contained sidestepped the feeling of dread that graffiti implied while retaining the innovative thrill it comprised. It felt edgy yet was perfectly safe. It felt rebellious while being entirely secure. Unlike graffiti, then, these images could be securely appropriated (by the advertising industry, the art industry, the media). They could be appropriated in order to entice people to consume almost anything, anything that was (illusorily) related to these symbols of the new. They could be utilised to sell products as diverse as soft drinks and cars. They could be used to sell the notion of a bohemian cool, perfect for the emergent creative enclaves that cities such as London were desperate to develop. Advertising companies would thus not only *follow* artists (as real-estate agents were previously known to do) – agencies putting up hoardings and adverts in previously utilised graffiti sites, piggy-backing the artists' site-specific knowledge and eye for space – but they would often directly employ artists to activate their campaigns with street-art-friendly designs. Moreover, the active deployment of street art became a cheap way to give a shop, a restaurant, even an entire district the aroma of cool, the veneer of creativity that the burgeoning Creative City discourse of Richard Florida (2004) proposed. While London had by no means been a key global destination for graffiti then, nor been particularly renowned for innovations within the emerging post-graffiti discourse, it came to play a pivotal role in this transformation, in the movement from the diffuseness of street art to the specificity of its capitalised successor. It had a vast amount of accessible capital as well as an already ingrained status as a global media and advertisement centre. It had the violent brawn of capital and the resourceful, canny brain of the culture industry. It had, it's hard to ignore, Banksy and the media-savvy stunts that he cleverly deployed. And while Barcelona and Berlin can thus be seen to have provided the space for stylistic and aesthetic innovations, New York providing origins and Paris heritage, by 2008 London had become the new-found commercial hub, the industrial capital of global street art.

Active solicitation and passive affirmation

Coming from the top-down perspective of city authorities, the first clear change we can see today is a quite obvious alteration: an inversion of public policy. What was once absolutely illicit has now become set in a curiously liminal position, a position in which council authorities have become arbiters of taste, in which judicial authorities are now providing aesthetic rather than purely legal judgements. While in 2005 the terminological distinctions between graffiti and street art were thus still somewhat fluid (as can be seen in the interchangeable usages of the term in my original article of 2008), today there is a clearly defined separation. Not only has street art become capitalised and delimited, moving from a term denoting a multitude of techniques to one denoting just a few – that being colourful, often kitschy, stencils and large-scale murals (as I discuss in Schacter 2014a) – but it has equally come to act as a corrective, a solution to the always and already negative status of graffiti. Graffiti will always be a dirty word, ingrained as it is with over 20 years of hegemonic castigation, but 'street art' (now officially demarcated and fixed) has now come to act in direct contradistinction to this contaminant; it is the 'acceptable', the 'likeable', the societally tolerable revolutionary image, the term preventing the cognitive dissonance and 'logical' impossibility of 'good' graffiti. As such, whereas graffiti is for the most part appreciated purely as dirt, the classic matter out of place that necessitates isolation and removal before contaminating its surroundings (Douglas 1966), street art has become, quite contrarily, a substance set perfectly *in* its place. Its ability to hold implicit and explicit value (able to be torn off the street and sent directly to auction, able to call forth tourists through the creation of a 'subcultural cool'), its ability to be contained within the normative frameworks of contemporary art (to be art rather than non-art, to work within the sphere of the market, the sphere of the instrumental), its ability to be contained within the normative frameworks of contemporary *city* (to be appropriately framed and correctly ordered, to work with and not against), has led to a state in which its apparent subversion is hegemonically avowed and restrained, in which it provides the *necessary* subversion the city requires, the necessary subversion not only contained but both established and enabled by the power it appears to threaten (Greenblatt 2004[1995]). It has led to a state in which street art functions to provide a service, a benefit to its surroundings, in which it works to establish a distinct order not *dis*order for the city.

This move from pollution to purity has been enabled through a dual system of acceptance, through what I term *active solicitation* and *passive affirmation*. The former process, active solicitation, functions in a quite straightforward manner. This is street art as a sanctioned form of contemporary 'urban' muralism, street art as a licensed public art. This is street art as a practice overtly commissioned and actively engaged by local councils, by arts funding bodies, galleries, private businesses, advertising and design agencies. This is street art as a quick method to an innovative, subversive 'look', as a (relatively) cheap form of urban renewal, a 'creative city' art. Shoreditch, of course, is full of this actively solicited 'street art', this neo-muralism – huge colourful displays on every other street, pointing towards an idea of innovation while being firmly stuck in the plop-art mud. But many other parts of London are becoming more and more suffused with it too. Simply follow the path of 'regeneration', to Camden Town and Brixton, to Croydon and Bethnal Green. If you paint it, they will come (or so the creative city mantra goes). Yet the latter process, street art's passive affirmation, occurs through a more subtle technique, a more understated mode of authorisation. This is acceptance through inaction, endorsement through acquiescence. This is a form of approval that emerges through the *suspension* of removal, the blurring of legitimation. Whereas all aspects of independent public art were previously ripe for removal, any unsanctioned image disavowed, today street art has become a *semi*-legal practice (if not completely so). In the London Borough of Hackney, for example, an area which has clearly benefited (in economic terms) from the presence of street art (from the tourism it engenders, the gentrification it enables, the creativity it implies), the local council in fact now *explicitly* separates its handling of graffiti and street art. As outlined in the recent graffiti policy document (anon 2016), the council 'recognises' that:

> ... some public opinion on what constitutes graffiti has changed and that some 'Graffiti' is now considered to be 'Street art' and that some members of the community now consider that 'Street Art' actually makes a positive contribution to the urban environment. In recognition of this the Council accepts that properly authorised and appropriate street art may be recognised and supported subject to appropriate permissions being sought and granted and subject to that art not being a detriment to local environmental quality [sic].

Wrap your head around that one. If authorised and appropriate, it may be recognised and supported. If positive, it is street art, if detrimental, graffiti. Let's not even step into the question of what defines propriety, of what a positive contribution truly is. Yet, what's more, we also learn that what was previously considered graffiti can transform into street art, if, that is, it is not harmful to 'environmental quality', not inimical to the 'enjoyment of the location by users' (anon 2016). Not only is the question of which 'users' neatly sidestepped (and that's ignoring the profoundly unsettling use of the term itself: once 'citizens', now 'users'), a privileged 'community' implicitly declared, but so too a semantic hierarchy is made crystal clear. Graffiti can never be allowed, it is always a danger. Yet street art contains the ever-present possibility of utility, of value, the ever-present possibility of admission by a community of like-minded citizens. The city thus passively marks out the good from the bad through choosing what *not* to mark out, choosing what *not* to remove. It passively separates the functional from the (literally) irredeemable through an archetypal process of bowdlerisation, an excision of what is (at the time) considered the 'improper', the 'offensive', yet an effacement that serves only to weaken that which remains. The process of erasure that was so intrinsic to street art, so key to its life cycle, thus occurs through a radically different mode of attribution today: street art is saved, graffiti erased. Street art protected, graffiti redacted.

Circulation to stasis

Today, street art images in particular work in a fundamentally different manner to previously adjudged. While they formerly functioned through constant circulation, through a constant cycle of production, consumption and destruction, which led to an ever-increasing cascade of images, today these objects can no longer flow in the same manner. The 'iconoclash' they were set within, the con/destructive clash which led to the inevitable creation of 'new images, fresh icons, rejuvenated mediators' (Latour et al. 2002:16–17), which inevitably led to the increasing cycle of practice, has today halted, the cycle abated, circulation suspended. The strange hesitation of the iconoclash has been replaced by a bland acceptance, the feeling of uncertainty by certitude: these objects cause no harm (they are legible, legal, suffused with no dirt). They function correctly (to indicate innovation, to indicate 'cool'). They legitimise the city (the permissive subversion upholding the norm). They are thus reclaimed, or rather *reprieved*, from the systematic erasure they were previously subject to, given amnesty while graffiti is, for the most part, condemned. The continual escalation of images, the cycle of defacement and refacement so key to the iconoclash, is thus stymied through street art's adherence to the normative codes of public space. And the concomitant power that destruction brings, the proliferation it encourages, the 'gesture of reverence' that it reveals (Gamboni 2002:88) is impoverished by these images' 'success'. Destruction alludes to the power of graffiti, insinuates its efficacy. Destruction enables the production of ever more works, enables the ceaseless cycle of incompleteness to proceed. Acceptance shows that these artefacts create no heat, that they glide all too smoothly. The latent ephemerality of the graffiti and street art image is thus replaced by the new-found monumentality of street art, the monumentality that functions as a 'representation of an affirmation of the actually existing order of things', the monumentality that contains no critique but which reinforces the 'seemingly unchangeable status quo' (Buchloh 2003:123). The ephemerality that was part of the very process of street art and graffiti, a temporality completely at odds with the practices of the contemporary art world, at odds with its traditions of maintenance and conservation, is thus traded for the brute materialism of the monument, the amnesic oppression of our bronze men on horseback, the static stability of the permanent. The power of the ephemeral to generate disappearance from sight but not from memory (Young 1992) is replaced by the finitude of the living art object, its status as completely effortlessly forgetful. The power of destruction to enable us to in fact *remember* (Kuchler 2001) is replaced by the digital apprehension of *all*, by the indifference and neglect that the preservation of the infinite allows. The work of (street) art in the age of technological reproducibility thus creates an enormously extended reach yet a concomitant diminishment of its efficacy.

Yet while this solicitation and affirmation, this stasis and monumentality remain so key for street art, in Shoreditch, as we saw earlier, this reversal of temporality has begun to pervade the graffiti regime as well. Graffiti may not be actively solicited, but it is passively affirmed; it may not be directly co-opted, but it is not removed. It pervades the site; it is, as we have seen, *everywhere*. This presents us with a conundrum. In particular, as corresponding quite perfectly with the increasing acceptability of street art, we have seen a radical increase in the punishment for graffiti in the UK. In London in particular, artists have continued to receive ever-harsher custodial sentences in an escalating cycle of injudiciousness, a cycle in which the financial implication of damage caused (which has increased over 20-fold since trains have become privatised) has led directly to increasing jail time: two to three years, in category A prisons, for placing pigment on a surface, being today not uncommon. So what is, in fact, actually happening? How can these two realities simultaneously exist? Well, it would seem to me that the only explanation can be that Shoreditch is not real. Perhaps this sounds ridiculous, but I feel it may actually be true. It is not what it seems, it is not what it portends. It doesn't do what it says on the tin; it is, it seems, a myth. The only explanation is that Shoreditch is *Shoreditch-land*, a theme park, a recreational simulacrum, a corporate spectacle. And as we know, down the rabbit hole weird things can happen. Through the looking-glass, even graffiti becomes acceptable, even graffiti, the arch pollutant, can come to be something that an area can *actively desire*. Here, graffiti bestows an idea of rebelliousness, an idea of urbanity (in both senses) that helps to increase footfall, increase profits. Here it adds to the frisson. Here it adds to the very notion of 'real'. Yet what it lacks, however, is what is in fact key to the practice of graffiti itself. What it lacks is the heightened performance, the ritual *doing* of graffiti. It forms an image of graffiti with no sticky residue, an image with no depth.

The movement to art

While the new-found semi-permanence and semi-legality of these images still contains the distributed personhood and agency of their makers (Gell 1998) – albeit one now mixed with other mediators, such as the city council's removal teams or the works' commissioning bodies – the performative power they once contained, the visceral, visible remnant of their formation, becomes dulled by their processual ease. The all-too-comfortable exercise of construction generated by the increasing acceptability of street art (and of graffiti *in Shoreditch only*), the absence of the innate danger and risk so intrinsic to the traditional graffiti and street art image (the fact that dedication is visually revealed through the consistent endangerment of liberty), has turned street art into a purely representative rather than mediatic image. It places total focus on the secondary artefact rather than the primary, the processual performance, on final product over anterior act. The ritual charge of the unsanctioned image, the marked, heightened, framed modality of practice (Bauman 1992), the ritual charge emergent from their status as 'not just something material but [as] a performance', as 'not so much a static object' but a 'dynamic set of relations' (Elsner 2007:43), hence dissipates with its reduction to image alone. Street art becomes purely about beauty, aesthetics, *surface*. It becomes purely about art historical issues such as 'style and form', such as 'mimesis and aesthetics', rather than more complex and immersive 'ritual concerns' (Elsner 2007:29). The *corporeal illicitness* so present to graffiti, the works' ability to visually transmit the tension and euphoria encountered by the artist to spectators who latterly share this experience, is no longer generated once their performative genesis is entirely equivalent to the safe, stable, sedate nature of studio practice. The radical difference between fine art and graffiti art is hence subdued, the status of graffiti as performance art, as an action, as *happening*, exchanged for its status as image alone. As 'mediators of activity' rather than basic vehicles of meaning (Tilley 1999:265), these works simply no longer carry the intensity, the pressure, the fervour, the *commitment* so crucial to the graffiti and street art; they no longer carry the performative aspect of spectatorship, the interactive process between image and viewer. Street art is now *just* that image on the wall (the heads without the hunting), no longer a residue of a heightened ritual action, no longer containing the aura of its intensely heightened performance. It is a cult object turned into an art object, an 'instrument of magic' reduced to a 'work of art' (Benjamin and Arendt 1999: 218).

This movement towards art, towards its equally auratic and economic values, towards its modalities of conservation and permanence, also begins to hint towards the larger museological turn that street art has now become set within. It is not simply that these artefacts have come to move from street to museum, however, the fact that street art has become an equally oxymoronic and omnipresent part of the private sphere, but rather that street art has further engendered the transplantation of the museum to the street itself, the modalities of correct practice, the rituals intrinsic to the museum (Duncan 1995), relocated to the exterior realm of the public sphere. Here, the mode of the image's consumption radically changes. The transformation of street art into art, into pure image, something no longer tactile but instead abstracted, no longer sacred but profane, no longer ephemeral but perpetual, has thus caused the treatment and apprehension of these artefacts to become couched within the formal values of the museological realm, that of connoisseurship and conservation, of validation and theatricality. Official guided tours, for example, are thus today a habitual part of the street art ecology (available throughout London, although centring on Shoreditch), tours that serve to generate a curatorial authority and narrative fixity so coherent with the traditions of the museum yet so at odds to that of graffiti culture. Active restoration and protection is now a common practice (from the famous works of Banksy trapped within plexiglass to the local conservationist collectives such as the UK Reactivation Team actively maintaining and refurbishing street art works), methodologies upholding the conventions of stasis and preservation so present within the museological tradition and so conflicting with its illicit counterpart. Works are now publicly commissioned and professionally installed (using teams of volunteers and heavy plant equipment), even artificially illuminated in a manner normally only seen within the institutional realm (as can be seen in a recent large-scale mural by the popularly acclaimed artist Stik, again in Shoreditch, lit up each evening by enormous floodlights). The street hence becomes a space of preservation rather than participation, dispassionate contemplation over bodily engagement. It becomes a place of exhibition rather than encounter, of things observed but not felt. As such, and just like the objects incorporated within the classical museum, these artworks lose the unrestrained vivacity they once contained. They are complete (rather than always in the *process* of completion). They are not liable to the changes and dangers of a life truly lived. These images come to function as ethnographic objects devoid of all their previous cultural implications, detached from their use value, severed from their life worlds. They become only half living (if not dead), abstracted, neutered, tamed.

While the oft-described connection between the museum and mausoleum first made by Adorno (1955) can today be seen to have been somewhat disrupted through the more reflexive status of the contemporary institution – the museum as a space of respite from the mass media, the museum as the site that carries all history within it and thus enables the production of the new (Groys 2010) – the museification of the *street* remains held within the most traditional, most conservative of Enlightenment-era approaches. This is the museum, in Agamben's terms (2007), as a space in which 'what was once – but is no longer – felt as true and decisive has moved' (Agamben 2007:84), the 'museum' as that symptomatic space (any space in fact, including that of an 'entire city') that presents the 'exhibition of an impossibility of using, of dwelling, of experiencing' (Agamben 2007: 84). The trope of street art enabling the largest museum in the world thus, in fact, becomes a profound danger. The city as museum it creates serves merely to heritagise this space, to cleave it from everyday life. It becomes a site of the tourist gaze not of critical interrogation. It becomes a site of the selfie, the selfie with the requisite edgy urban backdrop. It becomes a site in which street art is specifically produced *for* this mode of consumption – in which site specificity is abandoned, in which embedding one's work within the intricacies of space is instead superseded by the desire for virality, by hashtags and likes, by a street art produced *explicitly* to be circulated on a smartphone. The city, like the museum, is hence turned into a site of visitation rather than habitation, a city to be seen but not touched.

And the increasing heritagisation of street art (Merrill 2015) thus goes hand in hand with the increasing heritagisation of the city, the spectacularisation of street art and the spectacularisation of the metropolis, the aestheticisation of street art and the aestheticisation of the street, working together to unite sites through a modality of display and extravaganza, through a base reduction of space and place. Shoreditch, our offender in chief, thus becomes ever more sanitised and Disneyfied, more real than the original (Baudrillard 1994). It becomes a site ensuring that only 'safe and selected images will be preserved', a site 'based on superficialities', based on the 'desire to consume the spectacle' (Walsh 2002:139). It becomes a site in which street art functions through 'flooding the senses', through creating a 'sensory distraction', street art as 'phantasmagoria' (Buck-Morss 1992:22). And it provides the perfect exemplar of what Cameron and Coafee term gentrification's third wave (Cameron and Coafee 2005), gentrification not solely as the creation of an artistic milieu for the 'production of art' (the 'first wave'), not solely as the 'commodification [...] of this artistic milieu' (the 'second wave'), but rather that of an 'explicit public-policy engagement' that focuses on the 'public consumption of art' (Cameron and Coafee 2005:46), an explicit public policy of active solicitation and passive acceptance. Street art becomes entirely dependent on the mode of the tourist city and the needs of the creative city, dependent on a cultural policy in which the arts are employed to mainline a notion of authenticity into a site. Street art becomes the affected authenticity, the feigned fantasy that the tourist experience requires. Artificially stimulated to provide the veneer of edginess, the charade of rebellion, the affectation of innovation that the creative and tourist cities so desire, street art creates a sanitised heritage, a literal facade, a distant relative (by marriage) of its graffiti ancestors.

Conclusion

At the start of this paper, I wanted to reflect back on the changes that have occurred within this image world over the last decade, to see what has changed since I wrote *An Ethnography of Iconoclash* back in 2005. I wanted to see how these objects worked now compared with how they worked then, to see how their mode of production, consumption, circulation and destruction measured up today, to see what, if anything, had shifted. As we can now see, it doesn't make for pretty reading. Street art's journey into capitalisation, into today's authorised, canonised Street Art, has left it in a truly sorry state. What was once still an idealistic, experimental practice, a practice working very much within the radical purview of graffiti, had by 2015 become fully detached from its forebear. And what emerged was a form that embraced the 'attractive' over the interrogative, the superficially beautiful over the difficult yet critical. What had once thus implicitly and explicitly critiqued the commercialisation of the public sphere was now part and parcel of its very commercialisation. Capitalised street art simply failed to integrate within its site (rather coming to either dominate it through the maximalist modality of neo-muralism or to use the city as a medium towards an end of digitisation); capitalised street art failed to follow its non-instrumental urge (rather, acting strategically); capitalised street art failed to contain its independent values (yet problematically acting as if autonomous); capitalised street art failed to act consensually (and rather embraced the mendaciousness of the kitsch or the 'cool'). The various ways that these images were produced, consumed, circulated and destroyed has, as we have seen, thus radically altered. Much of today's street art is produced without risk, without commitment, produced so as to be circulated online, not experienced in person. It is consumed within the modality of the tourist city, consumed in the thinnest, most reductive of ways. It is monumentalised, protected. It is on life support rather than being allowed to let nature take its course. What has come to dominate is thus an aesthetic devoid of its prior ethic, an image devoid of its content. Street art imitated post-graffiti while turning it into a purely decorative facade. It was its sanctioned, uncommitted, commercial other.

Graffiti is still present and is still, for the most part, other. It still functions to work against, antagonistically, agonistically. Outside the bubble of Shoreditch it still retains its explosive edge, its urgency. Yet so much of it has now moved even further inward, attempting to evade the surveillance city, attempting to evade the self-surveillance of social media. So much of it has got even more intransigent, the need to produce ever faster, ever harder, increasingly intensified. It always seems, I feel, that a city gets the graffiti it deserves. The city creates its graffiti as much as its graffiti creates it. The explosive colours and extravagance of Barcelona. The death-defying pixação of São Paolo. The vivid muralism of Valparaíso and the hyper-innovation of Paris. The hardcore graffiti and conservative street art of London: its condensed, unsparing, brutal graf (in which it is speed and damage, urgency and insanity that act as formal measurements of distinction), its twee, tacky, tawdry street art (in which success is measured through Instagram likes and social media appearances, commercial licences and gallery purchases). Of course, I recognise it is hyperbolic to define such a black-and-white cleavage.

Fig. 10.7 Still antagonistic: standing out amidst a wealth of other tags, OKER and OFSKE remain proudly antagonistic. OKER's tag is in the centre of the top doorway. OFSKE's moves downwards from the middle section. Both appear to have been using the same writing implement (same colour, same width). We can thus surmise they wrote these at the same time. Source: author

Fig. 10.8 Still other: again, OKER and OFSKE make their presence felt. OKER is here written as OK (with a face depicted in the O). OFSKE is written as OE (also with a smiley face in the O). Source: author

Of course there are exceptions. Of course things are more complicated than I suggest. But the feeling that it engenders is just so radically dispiriting. That this is what this most vivacious of practices has become. Stable, fixed, clear. Consensual, safe, profitable. What used to excite me were the constant changes, the looseness and ebullience, the irreducible difference that they displayed. The fact you never knew how long a work would survive, the fact that you knew it had been produced through such a charged event. The fact that it was so outside of what was seen as 'rational' – a waste of time, a waste of effort, a waste of paint. The feeling that seized you when seeing some works was just unforgettable. A work by the artist Goldpeg, for example, a work up on the highest part of the highest building in the very centre of London's King's Cross. A work that forced you to imagine her crawling up drainpipes, clambering over ledges. A work that forced you to imagine her standing there in absolute plain sight (!), reaching up to her maximum extent, stretching out to her maximum reach while she painted her iconic design. How did she get there? How did she do it? How did she achieve such magic? Perhaps she had waited a few seconds when finished, admiring the view from the most perfect of crow's nests, from the most privileged of views… or perhaps she left without even looking back. It's the performance, stupid! Seeing that piece was so much more than witnessing an image. It was witnessing an entire complex of actions, a whole lifetime of thoughts. It was witnessing a practice outside the norms of the city, outside the norms of art. It was witnessing an image that would shine and disappear, resonating long after it had vanished from sight. And the monumental and domineering murals that stand in their place? These are static images, only skin deep. These are adverts not actions. They are *just* art. The *merest* of mere ornament.

This is depressing, I know, I'm sorry. But much of the street art in London today is just another failed public art (in terms of an art for the public good). It is plop art for the noughties, site-specific art that is entirely un-site-specific. And where does this take us? A good question. As publicly owned private spaces (POPS) come to multiply in London, as they so perniciously present us with these false commons, many of the images in question let them glide past to easily. They don't critique them, but allow them. And they must in themselves be questioned and critiqued. This too is happening of course, there are other voices, there are other strategies. I have presented a very worst-case scenario, a very negative tale. But if Shoreditch can tell us anything, it can provide a warning for the future. All of London will end up like this if we sit back and let it. It will become an island of Disneyland within an ocean of exploitation. It will become a city as fantasy, a city without public, a city without commons.

Methodological note

This chapter is based on information garnered from approximately 15 years of research within the field of independent public art, data emerging from my work in scholarly, curatorial and professional capacities. This has included over 22 months of multi-sited field work with a group of street and graffiti artists as part of my doctoral studies (and a continuing partnership with the numerous collaborators that emerged out of this engagement), the authorship of several articles, essays and books on different aspects of this aesthetic field (see Schacter 2013 and 2014b, among others) as well as the curation of a number of international exhibitions exploring both the conceptual ideas and creative evolutions that unfold from these equally material and cultural practices. Having spent the last 15 years deeply immersed within the territory of this aesthetic arena then, acting as both witness to and often unwitting participant in the huge developments and transformations this field has undergone, I take a wide view in this chapter in order to explore how the theories proposed in my first research project from 2005, published as *An Ethnography of Iconoclash* in 2008, stand today. The chapter is thus based on hundreds if not thousands of conversations over the last 10 years with individuals from all possible sectors of this art milieu – from artists and activists to gallerists and dealers, from council authorities to anti-graffiti vigilantes, from supporters to erasers of these potent material forms.

References

Adorno, T. 1955. 'Valéry Proust Museum'. In *On the Museum's Ruins* by D. Crimp, 1993. MIT Press: London.
Agamben, G. 2007. *Profanations*. New York: Zone Books.
Baudrillard, J. 1994. *Simulacra and Simulation*. Ann Arbor: University of Michigan Press.
anon. 2016. *Hackney Graffiti Policy Document*. https://hackney.gov.uk/media/2653/Hackney-graffiti-policy/pdf/Hackney-graffiti-policy.pdf?m=636486758376870000 (accessed 11 January 2019).
Bauman, R. 1992. *Folklore, Cultural Performances, and Popular Entertainments: A Communications-Centered Handbook*. New York: Oxford University Press.
Benjamin, W. and Arendt, H. 1999. *Illuminations*. London: Pimlico.
Buchloh, B.H.D. 2003. *Neo-Avantgarde and Culture Industry: Essays on European and American Art from 1955 to 1975*. Cambridge, MA: MIT Press.
Buck-Morss, S. 1992. 'Aesthetics and Anaesthetics: Walter Benjamin's Artwork Essay Reconsidered', *October* 62:3–41.
Cameron, S. and Coaffee, J. 2005. 'Art, Gentrification and Regeneration – From Artist as Pioneer to Public Arts' *International Journal of Housing Policy* 5(1):39–58.
Douglas, M. 1966. *Purity and Danger: An Analysis of Concepts of Pollution and Taboo*. New York: Praeger.
Duncan, C. 1995. *Civilizing Rituals: Inside Public Art Museums*. London: Routledge.
Elsner, J. 2007. *Roman Eyes: Visuality and Subjectivity in Art and Text*. Princeton, NJ: Princeton University Press.
Florida, R. 2004. *Cities and the Creative Class*. London: Routledge
Gamboni, D. 2002. 'Image to Destroy, Indestructible Image'. In *Iconoclash: Beyond the Image Wars in Science, Religion and Art*, edited by Bruno Latour and Peter Weibel, 88–135.
Gell, A. 1998. *Art and Agency: An Anthropological Theory*. Oxford: Clarendon Press.
Greenblatt, S. 2004[1985]. 'Invisible Bullets'. In *Shakespeare: An Anthology of Criticism and Theory 1945–2000*, edited by R. McDonald. Malden, MA: Blackwell Publishing.
Groys, B. 2010. *Going Public*. Berlin: Sternberg Press.
Kuchler, S. 2001. 'The Place of Memory'. In *The Art of Forgetting*, edited by A. Forty and S. Küchler. Oxford: Berg Publishers.
Latour, B., Weibel, P., Boltanski, L., Gamboni, D., Ristelhueber, S., Mondzain, M.-J., Sloterdijk, P., Belting H. and Obrist, H. 2002. 'Iconoclash: Beyond the Image Wars in Science, Religion, and Art'. Exposition, ZKM, Center for Art and Media, Karlsruhe, 4 May-4 August. Karlsruhe: ZKM.
Merrill, S. 2015. 'Keeping it Real? Subcultural Graffiti, Street Art, Heritage and Authenticity', *International Journal of Heritage Studies* 21(4):369–89.
Schacter, R. 2008. 'An Ethnography of Iconoclash', *Journal of Material Culture* 13(1):35–61.
Schacter, R. 2013. *A World Atlas of Street Art and Graffiti*. Yale University Press.
Schacter, R. 2014a. 'The Ugly Truth: Street Art, Graffiti and the Creative City', *Art & the Public Sphere* 3(2):161–76.
Schacter, R. 2014b. *Ornament and Order: Graffiti, Street Art and the Parergon*, Farnham: Ashgate.
Schacter, R. 2017. 'Street Art is a Period. Period!'. In *Graffiti and Street Art: Reading, Writing and Representing the City*, edited by Konstantinos Avramidis and Myrto Tsilimpounidi. London and New York: Routledge.
Tilley, C. Y. 1999. *Metaphor and Material Culture*. Oxford, UK: Blackwell.
Walsh, K. 2002. *The Representation of the Past: Museums and Heritage in the Postmodern World*. London: Routledge.
Young, J. E. 1992. *The Counter-Monument: Memory against Itself in Germany Today*. Chicago: University of Chicago.

Index

Page numbers in italics are figures; with 't' are tables.

The 32 Stops (Dorling) 2–3

Abram, David 134, 145
acceptance 415, 416
Ackroyd, Peter 180
ACORN clusters 7
active solicitation 413–14
actor–network theory 309
Adorno, Theodor 419
aestheticisation 420
aesthetics 35
affect 200
affirmation, passive 414
Agamben, G. 419
agency 309, 310, 312, 320, 322
Aickman, Robert 213
airplanes 72
'alpha territories' 74, 81
Amin, A. 5–6, 34–5
The Ampersand Hotel 325, *327*, 331, 340, 342–3
    doorman *341*, *344*
Anchor and Hope pub *226*
Anderson, B. 98
apartment building 140
apartments 79–80, 92–3
    see also flats
apotheosisation 125–6
Appadurai, A. 21, 39
apprenticeship 279
Arendt, Hannah 418
Armenians 109
Aron, Raymond 1
arrhythmia 347, 348
Augé, M. 18, 22, 23, 283
aura 35

Bachelard, G. 291
Back, L. 32, 97
Bagnall, G. 35
Bakhtin, M. 284, 286
Banksy 412
Barnsbury 7–8, 9
Basdas, B. 200–1
Basso, K.H. 309
Bauman, Z. 34
beating the bounds 195

Beauvoir, Simone de 1
Beavers Estate 20, 151, 153–77, *153*, *154*, *155*
    Shopping area at 'the bottom' 168, *168*
    tunnel *158*
Beckert, S. 311
bedrooms, 17 Cheniston Gardens *77*
bedsits 76, 79, 89, 90, 92–3, 106, 111–12
'beginning ladies' 153, 176
belonging 38, 174, 199
Belvedere restaurant 360, *361*
benches, memorial 385
Benjamin, W. 26–7, 418
Bergson, H. 33
Bermondsey Antiques Market 301–24, *302*, *307*, *308*
    stalling out *304*
Bestor, T. 49, 51, 266, 279
biographies 18
birds 389
bison frame 154–5, 160, 176
black cab drivers 52, 332, *334*, *337*, *343*, 345, 346–8, 349
Bloch, Maurice 127–8
Blokland, T. 36–8
Blumenfeld, Helaine 359
boarding houses 86, 88–9, 90, 106
boats 204–57
Booth, C. 88
Borden, I. 309
Bourdieu, P. 6–7, 10, 11–12, 35, 127
Bourne, L. 178, 180
Bow, Old Ford Lock No 19 *208*
bowdlerisation 415
Bowles, B. 213–14, 257
'the boys' 166, 171–3, 176
British Waterways Act 1995 222
brooming 332
Brown, Michael 160–1
Brunswick Centre 117–47
    interior view looking across the precinct from O'Donnell Court *132*
    shopping precinct *123*
    view of winter gardens *120*
Brunswick Square *119*
Buchli, Victor 129
Buchloh, Benjamin 416
Buck-Morss, Susan 420

426 LONDON'S URBAN LANDSCAPE

building, and thinking and dwelling 14
built environment 28, 55, 134, 201, 253, 254
  Beavers Estate 156, 173
  Cheniston Gardens 75, 82, 108
Bummaree 295, *295*
buses 338–9, 340–1
bustop, people waiting *339*
Butler, T. 6, 7–8, 9–10, 35
buyers 319–20
Buyers Walk 271, *272*

cabs 325–6, *327*, 331–8, *331*, *333*, *336*, 342, 345, 346–9, 350
  black cab driver *334*, *337*, *343*
Cafe Floris 326, *326*, 335, 351, 352
Cameron, S. 420
Cameron-Daum, K. 215, 253
Canal & River Trust 221–2, 223, 226–7
canals 204–57
capital 6, 7, 16, 35
capitalised street art 421
capitalism 330, 347, 348, 349
Cardiff 31
carnivalesque world 286
Carsten, Janet 127
Certeau, P. de 15, 19
Charlesworth, S. 298
Chen, Y. 31
Cheniston Gardens (CG) 67–112, *68*, *70*, *85*
  aerial view of rear extensions *91*
  Maid on the front door of a townhouse *88*
  studios, entrance *84*
  view towards the central corner of the street with the birch trees from a top-floor flat *102*
chess set 360, *360*
Chestnut Walk 353, *354*
circulation 415
City of London (CoL) 274, 282, 289, 296
Clapson, M. 180, 181
Clapton *249*
class 6, 7, 127, 135, 187, 197, 377
  and boaters 256
  and Butler and Robson 9, 10
  and gentrification 55
  and neighbourhood 35
  'old boys' 274
  and parks 54
  and Rhys-Taylor 26
  super-rich 42
  upper class 86, 89
  white working class 50
Clifford, J. 119
Coafee, Jon 420
Collins, Michael 313
commercialisation 421
communities 34–41
  Beavers Estate 174
  Cheniston Gardens 106
  see also Surbiton
commuting 188, 232
'concrete jungle' 135
conservation areas 75–6
conservationists 107
'Considerate constructors' panelling *210*

contestation 19–20
continuous cruising 222, 224, 227, 228, 235, 241, 252, 256
Cope, Sir Walter 365
Le Corbusier, Charles Edouard Jeanneret 130–1
corporeal illicitness 417
'cosmopolitan belonging' 36, 110
council houses 92
council tenants 142–3
country of origin 95–7
Creative City discourse 412
Critique of Everyday Life (Lefebvre) 217
cruising 204–57
cultural capital 6, 7
cutters 263, 267, 291, 298
cutting 279
cycling 388
Czordas, Thomas 128, 134

Daily Telegraph 132
Deane, Edna 92
de Beauvoir, Simone 1
de Certeau, P. 15, 19
Degen, M. 200–1
Design Museum 398
destruction 415, 416
Distinction (Bourdieu) 7, 10
DOCOMOMO-UK 129
dogs 363
dog walkers 53, 371, 372, 385–6, 387–8
doorbells 71, *71*
Dorling, Danny 2–3, 8–9
Douglas, M. 282, 286
la duree 33
Dutch barges 236, *238*
Dutch Garden 357, 358, *359*, 378
dwelling 14–15, 16, 19, 34, 133, 253
dwelling inequalities 94
Dyos, Harold James 180

East Market *273*
Ecology Centre 366, 371, 374, 375, 386, 388, 390–1
economic capital 6, 7
Edensor, Tim 200
Elden, Stuart 328
elderly 141
elite, London 74, 86, 89, 105
Elsans 216, 248
Elsner, Jas 417
embodiment 13, 255
ephemerality 416
erasure 415
Eriksen, T. 21
The Ethics (de Spinoza) 200
ethnicity 95, 149–50, 364, 367, 371, 372
ethnography 75
An Ethnography of Iconoclash (Schacter) 410–11
everyday life 16–17, 253, 329
exchange 48, 127, 305, 318, 319
  and value 51, 311, 320, 322
existentialism 130
exteriority 351, 352

family accommodation 140–1
family and Smithfield Market 278
A Far Cry from Kensington (Spark) 92
Favero, P. 50
Featherstone, M. 217
Feld, S. 309
fictive freedom 349
fictive kinship 279
Fiddes, N. 279, 282, 286
filter beds 186–7, 198–9
    and the busy Portsmouth Road *184*
financial freedom 228, 243
fireplaces 80–1
First Church of Christ Scientists 73
Fish Island *210*
fish symbol 197–8, 200
fitness trainers 388
flanerie 75
flâneur 27
flats 76, 79–81, 89, 90, 92–3, 111–12, 364, *364*
    see also Brunswick Centre
Florida, Richard 412
Forshaw, A. 291
Foucault, M. 283, 292
Foundling Court 121, *122*, *138*, *139*
freedom 225, 228, 233, 239, 243, 245, 254, 349
French language 339
Freshwater Sardine Festival 192, *194*, 198
Friends of Holland Park 374–5, 387, 390, 392
Fukushima Garden of Remembrance 357

Galicians 79, 93, 94, 109, 110
Gamboni, Dario 416
gardening 376–8
gardens
    Beavers Estate 159, 168, 169
    Brunswick Centre 120, 131
    Iverna Court 109
    parks 52
    Surbiton 188
    see also Holland Park
Geertz, C. 43, 44, 266
Geertz, H. 266
General Market (GM) *265*, 273
    against the office block *294*
gentrification 9, 55–7, 74, 420
'getting married' 278, 285
Gibb, Robin 94
Giddens, Anthony 34, 127
globalisation 5, 21
Goldpeg 423–4
graffiti 131, 283, 403–25, *406*
    and banter 280
graffitied signs *283*
Grand Avenue, Smithfield 271
Grand Union Canal 220
'Great Sunday Squat' 92
Grenfell Tower fire 38–9, 112
Griffiths et al. 181

habitus 6–7, 9, 10, 11–12
Hackney 43–4, 53, 414
hackney carriages 332, 345, *345*, 346, 348
    see also cabs

Hackney Marshes *238*
Hadfield, Charles 213
Hall, S. 21–2
Hall, T. 31
Halper, T. 179
Hannerz, U. 21, 36
harmony 29
Harrington Road 325–52, *327*, *340*
Harvey, David 4, 105
Heathrow 72, 151, 157, 170
Heidegger, M. 14, 20, 133, 253, 329
heritagisation 420
Hertford Union Canal 206, *207*, 220, *220*, *222*, *223*, *231*
Hetherington, K. 329, 347, 351
Hewison, R. 212
Heyerdahl, Thor 189
hierarchy, spatial 135–44
Highmore, Ben 328
High Street Kensington (HSK) 67
Hillesluis, Rotterdam 36–7, 38
Hodgkinson, Patrick 119, 130, 131
Holland, Lord 354–5, *356*
Holland House 365–6, 394, 395–6
Holland Park 54, 101, 353–401, *355*
Holland Park Court Theatre 391
homeless 141–2
Hoskins, J. 321
Hounslow, borough 149, 155
Hounslow West 149, 150–77
houseboats 204–57
housekeeper 88
Houseman, M. 195
housing estate 151, 153–77
the 'Hub' 169–70, *169*
Hugh-Jones, Steven 127
humour 284, 286, 289
hypermodernity 22

iconoclash 415
identity 13, 15, 144, 315, 318, 320, 322
    on Beavers Estate 174
    liminal 281, 297
    and place 21, 308–9, 323
Idverde 376–7
illicitness, corporeal 417
Illustrated London News 296
Inclosure (Consolidation) Act 184–5
India 50
inequalities 94, 112
Ingold, Tim 201
initiation ritual 278–9
Inland Waterways Association (IWA) 213
Intentions in Architecture (Norberg-Schulz) 134
interiority 351, 352
Irish residents 85
isolation 156–71, 173–4, 176, 251
Iverna Court 109

Jackson, E. 36
Jameson, F. 289, 292
Japan 49–50, 51
Japanese Kyoto Garden 356, *356*, *357*, *358*, 368, 371, 373, 378, 396, 397
Japath street market 50

Jenks, C. 27
Jerome, J.K. 204
Jonas, A. 216
Jones, H. 36
Jones, Sir Horace 273

Kabyle 11
Keane, Web 200
Kensington 67–112
Kensington and Chelsea, borough 42, 81, 364–5, 376, 398
Kensington Gardens 101, 384–5
Kensington High Street, view from Holland Park *364*
Kensington Labour Party 392
Kensington Memorial Park 376
Kilburn 21, 22
Kingston 181, *182*, 185
kinship 278–9
kitchens, 17 Cheniston Gardens *78*
Kopytoff, I. 321
Kristeva, J. 285
Kyoto Garden 356, *356*, *357*, *358*, 368, 371, 373, 378, 396, 397

Labour Party 392
lament 290–1, 292, 296–7
landscape 195–6, 199, 201, 253, 254
Larsen, J. 214, 215
Latour, B. 322
Latour et al. 410, 415
Lee, river 208, *238*
Lee Navigation 205–6, *207*, 210, 216, 220–1, *221*, *226*, *231*, *249*
  Tottenham *236*
Lee Valley Marina, Springfield *233*
Lefebvre, Henri 29–30, 52, 214–17, 327–8, 345, 351, 352
  and the everyday 253, 329–30
Lefi parade 190, *191*, 192
The Legends of Sething *193*
library 169–70
lifts 137–8
liminal identity 281, 297
linear village 213, 214, 252, 255
London Calling (Butler and Robson) 6
Longhurst, B. 35
loss 290–1, 292, 296–7
Low, S. 53
Lowenthal, D. 212
LSOA 155, 173
Lund, K. 217

MacCannell, D. 212–13
Main Market (MM) 264, *265*
maisonettes 90, 92
Manheim, Ralph 329
Mao Wen Biao 361
Marcus, Sharon 138, 140, 142
markets 48–51, 263–99, 301–24
market workers (MWs) 266, 267, 271, 274–81, 283–7, 289–91, 297, 298, 301–24
  and history of Smithfield 272, 293
  reminiscences of 292
  stereotypes 299

Marx, K. 215, 216, 278
Maslen, T. 273
Massey, D. 4, 21, 22
materiality 201, 250, 254, 255
material world 12, 13
mausoleum 419
Mayol, P. 15, 16–17, 20
McClellan, Jim 178
McKie, David 178
McLeod, Mary 129
Meadows Estate 157, 174
meat 267, 271, 273, 274, 277, 288, 291
  and Fiddes 282, 286–7
The Meat Market: Inside Smithfield 277
megastructure 129
melody 29
memorial benches 385
memories 18, 32–3, 195, 200, 297, 416
Meridiana 358–9
Merleau-Ponty, Maurice 43, 128, 131, 133, 134, 145, 253
Metcalf, D. 274
Metro, Paris 18
migrants, long-established 110
Miller, Daniel 41, 47, 97–8, 126
Mintz, S. 48
mobility 108–11, 218–19, 225, 228, 243, 245, 254
modernism 126–8
Monty Python 189
monumentality 416
Moore, Rowen 179
mooring 222, 223, 224, 245–6, 255
The Muffin Man 67, 69, *69*, 72, 98, 110
multiculturalism 107
murals 361, 414
  in the arcade leading to the Orangery, Holland Park *362*
museum 418, 419
Muzzio, D. 179
Myrtle 144

Narrow Boat (Rolt) 211–12
Narrowboat Cafe 240
narrowboats, cost 235–6
National Park City 53
'negative externalities' 348
neighbourhood 15, 16–17, 35, 97–8, 104
neoliberalism 348–9
networks and selections 320–2
New Caledonian Market 306
New Delhi 50
noise 158
non-places 22–3, 293, 296
Norberg-Schulz, Christian 132–4
North Kensington 376
nostalgia 211, 212

O'Donnell Court *132*
OKER and OFSKE *422*, *423*
'old boys' 274
Olwig, Kenneth 195
Olympic Park 215, 216
One Way Street (Benjamin) 26–7
opera 368, 372, 385, 386, 391–6, 397, 398
opera pavilion, Holland Park 361, 363, *363*

the Orangery, Holland Park 361, *362*
'other place' 109–11

paint sign, defaced anti-climb *365*
Pallasmaa, Juhani 134
Paris 26–7, 30
    Metro 18
parks 52–4, 197, *220*, 221, *222*, 353–401
Passé by OX *410*
passive affirmation 414
the past 32, 33–4, 108, 211, 252, 290, 349
    and Benjamin 26, 27
    and Blokland 37
    and Sheringham 347
    and Sinclair 44
peer groups 37
the personal 14
phenomenological walk 28
phenomenology 1, 13–15, 133–5
place 14–15, 17–18, 19–26, 39–41, 308–9, 323
    Beavers Estate 174
    Surbiton 196, 201
Place de la Concorde, Paris 26–7
planes 151
play areas 240, 371, 372, 373, 376
play park, Beavers Estate *161*, 162
poïesis 329, 330
Pooley, Thomas 185–6
population, in Cheniston Gardens 94–5
postmodernism 219
Poultry Market (PM) 264, *265*, 273–4, *280*, *290*
Pound, Ezra 67, 73
poverty 3, *87*, 376
power 109, 218, 288–9, 299, 313, 349
    and street art 413, 416, 417
preservation 419
Priestly, J.B. 181
protection 418
publicly owned private spaces (POPS) 424

Quadron 376–7

rage 289
railway station 31
rationalism 130
Rebel Cities (Harvey) 4
rebelliousness 417
Regent's Canal 220, *231*
Relph, E. 40
renovation 107–8
repetition and difference 351
residents' association 105
resilience 174
restoration 418
Revill, G. 31
Rhys-Taylor, A. 25–6, 32
rhythmanalysis 75, 328–30, 350
rhythms 29–31, 67, 72–3, 345, 370–4
river bank, Bow *209*
River Stort *231*
Robson, G. 6, 7–8, 9–10
Rolt, L.T.C. 211–12, 213
Rose, G. 200–1
Roseberry, W. 48

Rosemary Avenue, Hounslow West *150*
Rosen, L. 266
Rotterdam 36–7, 38
rough sleepers 399
Royal Borough of Kensington and Chelsea (RBKC) 42, 81, 364–5, 376, 398
Royal Society for the Encouragement of Arts, Manufacture and Commerce (RSA) 155

Samuel, R. 107
Sartre, Jean-Paul 1
Savage, M. 35
Scheld, S. 53
Schlör, J. 31
Seamon, D. 134
Seething Freshwater Sardine Festival 198
Seething parade *191*
Seething Villagers 189–99
selections 308, 309, 312–22
self 13–14, 21, 131, 174, 246
    and Kristeva 285
    and MacCannell 212
    and Rolt 211
    and selections 309, 315, 317
Sennett, Richard 126
sensory engagement 23–6
Sheller, M. 219, 254
'sheltered' accommodation 141
Sheringham, M. 347
Sherman & Waterman 308
shopping malls 23, *123*
Shoreditch 408, 414, 416, 417, 420, 424
Shoreditch beach *405*
Shoreditch canvas *404*
Sinclair, I. 43–4
Smith, R. 31
Smith, Sonia 213
Smithfield Gazette 278
Smithfield Meat Market 263–99, *264*, *265*, *268*, *269*, *270*, *273*
social capital 6, 7
social class 7
    see also class
social field 10
social housing scheme 93–4
    see also Beavers Estate; Brunswick Centre
social identity 13
social rhythms 370–4
social world 13
Soja, E.W. 309
solicitation, active 413–14
'Space' *206*
spaces 218, 253–4, 327, 328, 329
space-time 29
'space–time compression' 105, 106
Spark, Muriel 92
spatial hierarchy 135–44
spectacularisation 420
Spinoza, B.D. de 200
stalling-out 304–5
Stanstead Abbotts *249*
stasis 416, 418
St Mary Abbots 73
stock 314–15
Stonebridge Lock No 16 *236*
'the stones' 171–2, *172*

Lightning Source UK Ltd.
Milton Keynes UK
UKHW020720240719
346685UK00002B/10/P

Stort, river 221
  Roydon, Essex *248*
the street 15, 33–4, 41–2
street art 403–25
  as the ultimate in kitsch *409*
street artists 209
a street art mural 'dogged' by a series of silver and black 'throw-ups' *408*
Stuart-Smith, T. 160
Studdert, D. 310
students, international 110
the subjective 14
suburbs 35–6, 39–41, 178–202
super-gentrification 74
supermarkets 101
Suq: The Bazaar Economy in Sefrou (Geertz, Geertz and Rosen) 266
Surbiton 178, 181, *182*, 183–202
  high street *184*
Sweet Toof street art *206*, 209
Swyndedouw, E. 217–18
symbolic capital 7, 16, 35
synaesthesia 134

Taplin, D. 53
taxi rank 20, 52, 325–6, *327*, 331–8, *331*, *333*, 346, 347–8
Telegraph Hill 7
temporality 33, 416
Terry, Christopher 185
Thames river promenade *183*
theatre, Holland Park 391
thinking 14
Thrift, N. 5–6
Tilley, Christopher 28, 130, 195, 214, 215, 253, 418
time 33, 327, 328, 329, 339–40
'time–space compression' 105, 106
Tokyo 49–50, 51
Tottenham Hale 221
The Tourist Gaze (Urry) 217
tourists 339–40, 396, 397, 398, 420
Tower Hamlets 220, *222*
townhouses 82, 85, 185, *185*, *186*
traders 303–5, 312–17, 319, 321
transient transnational residents 110
Transport for London (TfL) 347–8
trees 161, 162–3, 389–90
trust 320
Tsukiji fish market 49–50, 51

Tsukiji: The Fish Market at the Centre of the World (Bestor) 266
Tudor-style 'Jones' houses *187*

Uber 332, 338, 340, 346, 348–9
  driver *327, 342*
Uber app 332, 341–2, 346
upper class 86, 89
upper-middle class 86, 89
The Urban Experience (Harvey) 4
urbanity 417
Urry, John 29, 212, 214, 215, 217

value 51, 311, 320, 322
Vaughan et al. 178
vegetarianism 287, 288
Victorian working boaters 211
Victoria Park 53, *220*, 221, *222*
Vista building 170
Vote Leave campaign 289

Wacquant, L. 279
walking 26–9, 196, 197, 199, 200, 201
Walking man *358*
Walsh, Kevin 420
Walthamstow Marshes *226*
Walworth Road 21–2
water points 248
waterways, London 204–57
Watson, S. 310
Watt, P. 35
West Ham Stadium, Olympic Park, Stratford *205*
West Market *273*
'Where's Danny?' 'Round ya mum's.' *280*
White Building *206*
whiteness 291–2
'winter garden' concept *120*, 131
women, in Cheniston Gardens 86, 90
woodlands 354, 366, 386, 388–91
Woods, William 186–7
workers' cottages *187*
working class 52, 55, 137, 274, 349
World City Massey) 4–5
Wrights Lane (WL) 67, *70*

youth hostel, Holland Park 372, 394, 396, 397–8

Zafimaniry house, Madagascar 127–8